ITALIAN
POPULAR COMEDY

ITALIAN
POPULAR COMEDY

A STUDY IN THE
COMMEDIA DELL' ARTE, 1560–1620
WITH SPECIAL REFERENCE TO THE
ENGLISH STAGE

By K. M. LEA

VOLUME I

NEW YORK
RUSSELL & RUSSELL · INC
1962

FIRST PUBLISHED IN 1934
REISSUED, 1962, BY RUSSELL & RUSSELL, INC.
L. C. CATALOG CARD NO: 62—10692

PRINTED IN THE UNITED STATES OF AMERICA

'*Tanto ch'io credo che Zanni sia nato
per passatempo, burla, giuoco e festa,
e fare il mondo star lieto e beato.*'

'IL LASCA.'

'*Remember, my dear Will, that good plays can be read;
only the actor's genius makes a bad play bearable.*'

OSCAR WILDE TO SIR WILLIAM ROTHENSTEIN

PREFACE

SCATTERED and undocumented references to the influence of the Commedia dell'arte on Shakespearian drama led to this investigation of the relation between the English and Italian stage during the sixteenth and early seventeenth centuries. Many of the suspicions of these connexions are due to an inaccurate conception of the scope and nature of the Commedia dell'arte and are only based upon a disregard of the other sources of the Italianate influence on Elizabethan drama. The subject has been damaged as much by injudicious exaggeration as by neglect. There are, however, undeniable traces of the Commedia dell'arte to be found in *The Tempest*, *The Comedy of Errors*, and several minor Elizabethan plays. It is impossible to present the connexion between these plays and the Italian scenari satisfactorily without presupposing a common knowledge of the conditions of the Italian popular stage of the period. For English readers this does not exist, nor has the matter been treated in detail by French or Italian critics. The bulk of this study, therefore, attempts to explain the nature and to reconstruct the development of the professional improvised comedy known as the Commedia dell'arte so that the curious part that it played in the history of Elizabethan drama may then be presented in a truer perspective.

Something of what this book owes to the published work of my predecessors may be understood by a glance at its footnotes and bibliography, but how to acknowledge my personal indebtedness to the scholars and institutions by whose advice and hospitality I have continually benefitted I am at a loss to know.

In offering it to Miss Spens and Professor Foligno I am conscious of making but a meagre return for their constant encouragement and the inspiration of their teaching. To the generosity of the founder of the Susette Taylor Fellowship I owe the opportunity of travelling during 1925–7; to the Publications Grant Committee of the University of London, the aid of a grant of £100 towards the expenses of production.

Dr. Sisson, Dr. Greg, Professor Allardyce Nicoll, Dottore Benedetto Croce, and Professore Ferdinando Neri may have forgotten, though I have not, many incidental kindnesses, and it is for me a pleasure to recall the courtesy of Professore Giuseppe Gabrieli of the R. Accademia dei Lincei, of the Librarians of the Biblioteca Casanatense, the Vatican, the Collegio Inglese, of the Biblioteca Vittorio Emmanuele in Naples, in Venice of the Museo Correr, of the Director of the National Museum in Munich, of Archivists in Florence, Mantua, Modena, Perugia and Turin, of the Pepys Librarian at Magdalene College, Cambridge, and above all of the attendants at the Public Record Office and the British Museum. Lastly I would say that of the patience of my family and my friends I am better aware than at times they may have supposed.

K. M. L.

WESTFIELD COLLEGE

9 February 1934

CONTENTS

VOLUME I

Part I

THE NATURE OF THE COMMEDIA DELL'ARTE

x   CONTENTS

Part II

THE DEVELOPMENT OF THE COMMEDIA DELL'ARTE

Chapter IV. ANTECEDENTS AND ORIGINS . *page* 223

Fashions in the theories advanced to account for the appearance of the Commedia dell'arte at the Italian Renaissance. Relation to Asiatic Mimes: to Atellan comedy. Lack of evidence for the continuity of the classical and foreign traditions. Prototypes and tendencies in the dramatic activities of the Renaissance. Consideration of the Venetian stage taken as a type in the years immediately preceding the appearance of the Commedia dell'arte. Contributions of Cherea, Ruzzante, Calmo, and Zan Polo. Development of the private jester into the public entertainer. Extension of the interest in the drama in other cities and to all ranks of society.

Chapter V. PLAYER COMPANIES . . . *page* 255

Predecessors of the regular companies in Padua, Rome, and Naples. The problem of identification. Notices of Italian actors in Bavaria, France, and Spain: *Ganassa* and his companions. Composition and itineraries of the *Gelosi*; *Desiosi*; companies in the patronage of the Duke of Mantua, *Uniti* and first *Confidenti*. Companies of the early seventeenth century: the *Accesi* and *Fedeli*. The second *Confidenti* under the direction of Scala. Lesser and temporary companies. The Players' Economy. Finance: rewards, charges, expenses, taxes. Control: ecclesiastical opposition; civic regulations; system of licensing; private patronage. Production. Co-operation between Comici and Virtuosi: professional adaptation of academic décors. Stage directions in comedies of G. B. Andreini; evidence from plays within plays. Theatrical trick-work. Property lists for comedy, tragicomedy, and pastoral. Decadence in the art of improvisation coincident with the increased facilities for production.

VOLUME II

Part III

THE CONTACTS AND COMPARISONS WITH ELIZABETHAN DRAMA

Chapter VI. THE COMMEDIA DELL'ARTE AND THE ENGLISH STAGE . . . . . . *page* 339

Comparison of the terms of compromise between theatrical and literary values in English and Italian drama. Elizabethan contacts with the Italian stage: traveller's comments; English actors abroad; Italian players in England; itinerant mountebanks; amateur productions by Italians at the English Court; foreign musicians, aliens in the city. Allusions to the Commedia dell'arte in English literature; the masks; experiments in improvisation. Introduction of masks upon the English stage: possible and palpable imitations of the pedant and the braggart: limits of the relationship between the Zanni and the clowns, allowance made for common

CONTENTS   xi

sources and isolation of distinctive 'lazzi' and characteristics. Common farcical 'motifs' in acrobatic displays and Jigs. Importation of Italian plots: devices common to neo-classical drama. Six plays incorporating material peculiar to the Commedia dell'arte and discussion of their relation to the Scenari Collections. The Italian element in Shakespearian drama: elimination of all that may be accounted for by the use of literary or academic contacts: traces of Commedia dell'arte traditions in the *Merry Wives*, the *Comedy of Errors*, the *Tempest*. Service of professional Italian actors in circulating dramatic material and establishing certain comic, romantic, and pastoral conventions.

Appendixes

PLATES

ILLUSTRATIONS of Characters from Frescoes are depicted in plates facing pages 4, 6, 8, 10, 12, and 14; Frontispieces in the Corsini MS. are illustrated in plates facing pages 139 and 334.

PART I
THE NATURE OF THE COMMEDIA DELL'ARTE

CHAPTER I

INTRODUCTION, DESCRIPTION OF A TYPICAL PERFORMANCE

IN the history of the stage the Commedia dell'arte, or 'comedy of the profession'—apparently an Italian invention of the sixteenth century—stands for improvisation, the recurrence of masked characters, professional players, and the appeal to a popular audience. By one or other of these characteristics it is in turn distinguished from the various dramatic activities of the Renaissance; from the Commedia erudita or *sostenuta*, from the *Farse* and rustic plays, and from the amateur theatricals organized by the *Academici*. The lines of distinction do not preclude the interaction of these types and it is rarely that the Commedia dell'arte achieves complete independence. The Commedia dell'arte will not keep still within the bounds of a definition. To stickle for improvisation as the distinguishing feature leads to the exclusion of a group of printed plays which undoubtedly belong to its tradition. To track it by the appearance of the masks causes confusion, for many are to be found straying into the sub-plots of literary drama, or into masquerades and burlesque poems that have no direct connexion with the stage. To describe it as a popular comedy entails an explanation of its resemblance to the neo-classical drama and its cult at the French, Spanish, English, and Bavarian courts. But since these exceptions do not occur simultaneously, the Commedia dell'arte may be said to exist by virtue of a quorum of its characteristics. It presents the drama with no new substance, but with a new flavour, which, once tasted, is as unmistakable as it is hard to define. It is to be studied as a method of playing, evolved as much by accident as by design, which gave to old dramatic material a strange new vitality.

SOURCES OF INFORMATION

There is no lack of material for the study of the development of the Commedia dell'arte. There exist one printed and eight manuscript collections of scenari, or *soggetti*, compiled between 1611 and 1734, and from these and a few separate extant examples we have more than six hundred of the play-plots that were used for improvisation in the sixteenth and seventeenth centuries. Though we can often trace the sources of the scenari, we rarely come upon the names of the authors, and many were the result of collaboration. As stage documents the scenari are circumstantial and businesslike, they make no pretensions towards literary style. This is left to the actors' commonplace books which contain stock scenes, and speeches composed by the players or by their literary friends. They contain prologues, soliloquies, dialogues, tirades, songs, and anecdotes for the buffoons. Taken together with the scenari these miscellanies are as warp to woof. For our further information there are treatises in which the players defend their profession against the criticism of the ecclesiastical and civic authorities, and a few books of instruction in the art of acting extempore which describe the dress and behaviour of the chief masks and local types.

For the history of the rise of actors' companies we are chiefly dependent upon the scanty notices of performances collected from diaries and records of payments made and licences granted by the civic authorities in Paris, Madrid, London, and the cities of Italy and Bavaria. From these fragments it is possible to reconstruct some idea of the make-up, economy, and itineraries of the companies, while from the correspondence between the players and their patrons we know the current scandal about those actors and actresses who were most masterful, attractive, and quarrelsome in their generation.

A secondary source of information is to be found in the work of the rhymsters, comic poets, and minor dramatists of the seventeenth century whose contribution to the repertory of popular buffoonery in the name of the established masks of Zanni, Pantalone, the Doctor, and the Captain helps in tracing the development of the dramatic types.

The iconography of the Commedia dell'arte is as miscellaneous and abundant as the bibliography. A series of frescoes in the castle of Trausnitz in Bavaria, an album of

I

2

1. 20th wall, South. Zanni following a mounted
Pantalone. Zanni bribing the Ruffiana.
2. 15th wall, North. Zanni and Pantaloni fighting.

engravings collected for Louis XIV now in the National
Museum of Stockholm, the exquisite grotesques of Callot's
Balli di Sfessania, a hundred crudely coloured sketches
which serve as the title-pages to the one miscellany of
scenari, a few designs from the manuals of dress and
carnival disguises, and many rough woodcuts found as
illustrations to popular comedies printed in the seventeenth
century give vivid, though not always accurate, evidence of
the costume and setting of this comedy between 1570 and
1700.

It is at once the attraction and the limitation of a history
of the Commedia dell'arte that it must be written from the
green-room. The privilege of familiarity is thrust upon us
at a price. Once behind the scenes, there we remain, free
to turn over plots, commonplace books, masks, and monster-
heads, tantalized by laughter in the auditorium and glimpses
from the wings. We are invited to acquaint ourselves with
all the professional secrets, but we can never have the
chance of testing the magnetic power of the players which
made the Commedia dell'arte possible on the stage. Nothing
but imagination can make good this defect which is inherent
in its nature as improvised comedy.

TROIANO'S PERFORMANCE

Since the first description of a performance of an Italian
improvised comedy is also the most satisfying and self-
contained, it is fitting that it should supersede definition
and preface any attempted reconstruction of the Commedia
dell'arte.

The account occurs as part of the description of the
festivities for the wedding of Duke William of Bavaria with
Renata of Lorraine in the spring of 1568, published in the
same year by Massimo Troiano, a Neapolitan musician at
the Bavarian court.[1]

[1] Discorsi / Delli Tri/omfi, Giostre,
Appa/rati, e delle cose piu notabili fatte
nelle / sontuose Nozze, dell'Illustrissimo
e / Eccellentissimo Signor / Duca
Guglielmo / Primo Genito del Genero-
sissimo / Alberto Quinto, Conte Pala-
tino Del Reno, e Duca della / Baviera
alta e Bassa, nell'Anno 1568, à 22 di
Febraro. / Compartiti in tre libri, Con
uno Dialogo, della antichita del felice
ceppo di Baviera. Alla / Serenissima
Regina Christier/na Danismarchi / Di /
Massimo Troiano da Napoli Musico
dell'Illu/strissimo, / e Eccellentissimo

By the contrivance of a dialogue between two fictitious courtiers, Marinio and Fortunio, Troiano was able to describe his own part in the entertainment. Fortunio whets the curiosity of his companion by referring to the 'Commedia improvisa all'italiana' performed on the evening of Monday, 8 March, in which, although the greater part of the audience was unable to follow the dialogue, the acting of Messer Orlando di Lasso[2] as the Venetian Magnifico with Baptista Scholari as his Zanni was so admirable that all jaws ached with laughing. Marinio is provoked to inquire how it was possible that Orlando, a Fleming, should have played the Venetian, and he is told that this was nothing to the skill of the Zanni who acted as though he had had fifty years' experience of the valleys of Bergamo, and who spoke not only Italian but also French and German as if each had been his mother tongue. Fortunio goes on to

Signor / Duca di Baviera. / In Monaco appresso Adamo Montano. M.D.LVIII, pp. 183-8. A second edition in 1569 was printed in Italian and Spanish at Venice, but Troiano's prefatory letter is dated from Lanzuotto (Landshut) 25 Aprile 1569. The title-page reads: Dialoghi / di Massimo / Troiano: / Ne' quali si narrano le cose piu notabili fatte nelle Nozze dello / Ill: ... Guglielmo VI ... Tradotti nella Lingua Castigliana / da M. Giovanni Miranda; e hora insieme posti in luce, nell'uno e nell'altro Idioma, à benefitio comune. Con le figure dell'imprese, che furono portate nelle Giostre, e due Discorsi / nell'ultimo, co' quali si può imparare à leggere, intendere, / e pronunciare la lingua Spagnuola. Opera molto utile e necessaria à chiunque desidera essere ottimo / possessore della pronuncia Castigliana. Con privilegio. / In Venetia, appresso Bolognino Zaltieri MDLXIX. In this edition Troiano discarded a few colloquialisms: other alterations are noted in the following footnotes. Massimo Trajano [sic] is included in G. B. Tafuri's Istoria degli Scrittori nati nel regno di Napoli (1745), t. iii, pte 2, p. 294, but no details are given to add to the information derived from his title-pages.

[2] Orlando di Lasso was born at Mons in 1530 or 1532. A contemporary biographer, Quickelberg, says that at the age of nine he entered the household of Ferdinando Gonzaga, Viceroy of Sicily, with whom he went later to Milan. When he was eighteen he went to Naples to continue the study of music with Constantin Castriotto. In 1553/4 Orlando was in Rome acting as choir-master at St. John Lateran. After a possible visit to England with Cesare Brancaccio in 1554 he settled down in Antwerp and began to publish his compositions. In 1556 he came to Munich in the service of Albert V, and from 1563 until his death in 1594 he was the chief organist to the Dukes of Bavaria. In 1570 the Emperor Maximilian conferred upon him the patent of nobility. In 1567 and 1574 he travelled into Italy to engage musicians. In 1571 he was favoured at the French court, but three years later he refused the inducements held out by Charles IX and remained at Munich. A. Sandberger, Beiträge zur Geschichte der bayerischen Hofkapelle unter Orlando di Lasso (1894); New Encyclopaedia of Music (1924).

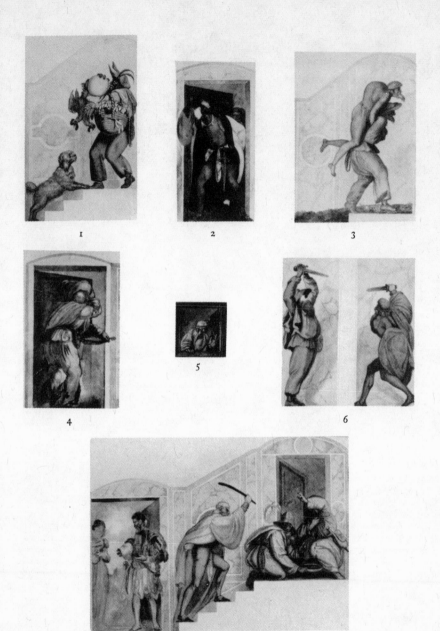

FRESCOES IN THE SCHLOSS TRAUSNITZ

1. 21st wall, East. Zanni delivering love messages disguised as a porter with fowls and fruit. 2. 11th wall, West. Pantalone with Zanni behind (defaced fresco). 3. 29th wall, East. Pantalone pickaback on Zanni. 4. 12th wall, South. Zanni with maccaroni. 5. 15th wall, West. Pantalone wearing spectacles. 6. 21st wall, East, paintings designed for spaces over the door. Zanni and Pantalone fighting. 7. 17th wall, East. Lovers. Pantalone beating two greedy Zanni.

explain that on the morning of Sunday, 7 March, the Duke had a whim to hear a comedy on the following evening, and sending for Orlando his chief musician, he entrusted the matter to his ready wit.

In the ante-chamber Orlando conferred with Troiano who invented the delightful plot, and between them they arranged the words.

In the first act appeared a rustic as it were from Cava[1] so clumsily habited that he seemed the ambassador of laughter.

Marinio. Tell me how many personages there were.

Fortunio. Ten, and the comedy was in three acts.

Marinio. I should like to know the names of the actors.

Fortunio. The excellent Messer Orlando di Lasso was the Magnifico, Messer Pantalone di Bisognosi; Messer Giovanni Battista Scholari da Trento, the Zanni; Massimo played three parts, the prologue of the awkward rustic, the lover Polidoro, and the Spanish desperado, called Don Diego di Mendozza. Don Carlo Livizano was Polidoro's servant, and the Spaniard's man was Georgio Dori from Trento. The Marquis of Malaspina took the part of Camilla the courtesan who was in love with Polidoro. Ercole Terzo was her servant, and there was also a French servant.[2]

To return to the comedy. After the prologue Messer Orlando arranged for a madrigal in five parts to be sung while Massimo who now played the lover, changed his clothes and dressed up in crimson velvet heavily trimmed with gold lace, with a cloak of black velvet lined with the finest sable, came on to the stage with his servant, praising fortune and glorying that he should live so blithe and contented under love's sovereignty.

When behold! his brother's French servant entered as if from the country and delivered him a letter full of bad news. When Polidoro had read this aloud he heaved a great sigh and summoned Camilla

---

1 'Alla Cavaiola.' The 'farse cavaiole' satirizing the doltish peasants of Cava near Naples came to the height of their popularity during the first half of the sixteenth century. See I. Sanesi, *La Commedia* (1904).

2 Ercole Terzo is probably to be identified with the 'Hercules' who is mentioned in the Chapel accounts in 1569 and 1574. Sandberger, op. cit., ii. pp. 42, 75. Trautmann records a payment to 'Hercule Tertio' and 'Agiocohia', a comedian from Mantua who played the

Doctor's part in Munich, 1606. See 'Italienische Schauspieler am bayrischen Hofe', *Jahrbuch für münchener Geschichte* (1887), vol. i, p. 305. A 'Lucio Tertio' occurs in the Chapel accounts in 1573 and there are several payments to a 'Lucio, geiger'. In 1568 'Lucio geigers sonn' received a reward of 20 florins. Possibly this was in connexion with Ercole's performance. Sandberger, ibid., p. 33. Baptista Scholari was a goldsmith. Trautmann, p. 300.

to tell her that he must leave her; he kissed her good-bye and went out.

From the other side of the stage appeared Messer Orlando dressed as a Magnifico in a crimson satin tunic, Venetian hose of scarlet, a long black mantle reaching to the ground and a mask that drew roars of laughter at first sight.

He touched his lute and sang: 'Whoever passes down this street, and sighs not, happy man is he,'[1] and after repeating this twice he left the lute and began to complain of love, saying: 'O poor Pantalone, you cannot go down this street without filling the air with sighs and watering the ground with tears.'

At this whoever had teeth to show bared them in his mirth, so that nothing could be heard above the bursts of laughter, which only increased, my dear Marinio, when a little later Pantalone had a long

---

[1] V. Rossi, *Giornale Storico Italiano,* ix, p. 295, n. 3, quotes: Due canzoni nove bellissime da cantare Con quella tu te parti con mio caro: con la risposta novamente stampata Con una barcelletta de una giovine la qual era inamorata de uno chiamato el Bobo. Et avendolo perso si lamenta e dice

Chi passa per questa strada, che non
   sospira beato se
Beato quel che lo potria fare
Perla reale
Faza chi mo se no chio moro amor
Faza chi mo, &c.

(Misc. Marciana, 2213. 6.)

Among Orlando di Lasso's *Villanelle, moresche, et altre Canzoni, a 4. 5. 6. & 8 Voci,* published in Antwerp, *Per* Pietro Phalesio & Giovanni Bellero, 1582, is a madrigal for Zanni (p. 17ᵛ). In the dedicatory letter to the Duke of Bavaria, dated 20 February 1581 from Munich, he refers to these songs as trifles made in his youth. The words given with the Alto part for the first stanza are as follows:

Zanni dov'estu mo che fast'in cantin'ah
   laro
O rovina de casa mia Vien fuora bestia
O povero pantalon stopalo col naso fio
   d'un asino
Stopalo ben ben caro Zanni che cosa
O forfante mariol mettetelo in bocca
   poltron

Mo stopa presto prest'e vien suso
  Mo perche non postu venir castronazzo
A laro mi crede che ti ze imbriago
  Orsu dorme fio d'un porco
Che vostu adio Zanni adio, adio, adio,
  adio.

Johann Eccard, who studied under Orlando di Lasso and whose name occurs in the Chapel Accounts for 1572 (Sandberger, *Hanns Eckhard,* ii. p. 64), has a song for 'Zanni e Magnifico' in his ' *Newe Lieder / 'mit fünff und vier Stimmen,* Gedruckt zu Königsperg in Preussen bey Georgen Osterbergen, 1589', No. XIV.

He distu, che fastu, che vostu, a bestion, si o d'un laro non tastu ben sfondrao, poltron, poltron che tutt'el di sei stat' a tola, poltron che tutt'el di sei stat' a tola, a tola, tir' in mal hora, trist' a negao.

The words for the second part are:

Desgratiao, O desgratiao, scampao della galia, O laro tene disgratio, O laro tene disgratio, mo fù imbriago, mo fù, mo fù imbriago, non dubitar giotton chastu dah'avere, tio tio tio, tio, tio, tio, tira via, alla malhora, tira via alla malhora, Zanni, O Zanni, me ti racomando, me ti racomando, O Zanni, me ti racomando.

1 2

3

1. 23rd wall, West. Lady dropping a flower.
   22nd wall, North. Pantalone soused by a maid while Zanni accompanies his serenading.
2. 14th wall, North. Ruffiana in a rage.
3. 5th wall, South. Pantalone and a maid-servant. Zanni.

discourse[1] to himself and another with Camilla. Presently there appeared Zanni who had not seen his Pantalone for years, and disregarding him as he walked carelessly along he gave him a great jolt and their ensuing dispute brought about a mutual recognition.

In his delight Zanni put his master on his shoulder and spun round like a mill-wheel, carrying him the whole length of the stage until he was dizzy,[2] and Pantalone did the same with Zanni until they both collapsed on to the floor.

Picking themselves up they had a ridiculous conversation about old times.[3] Zanni asked after his former mistress, Pantalone's wife, and heard that she was dead. At this they began to howl like wolves at the memory of the maccheroni and patties[4] that she used to make in days gone by. They recovered their spirits after this lamentation, and Pantalone instructed Zanni to play the pandar to his beloved Camilla. Zanni promised to speak in his favour and did just the opposite. Pantalone left the stage and very nervously Zanni approached Camilla's door; and Camilla fell in love with Zanni and took him into the house, which is no marvel, since women so often leave the better for the worse.

Then there was music by five viols-da-gamba, and as many voices. Now tell me was not this a ridiculous act? For I swear that of all the comedies I ever saw, I have never seen one so full of mirth.

Marinio. Certainly, what you have told me of it so far is most amusing and delightful, and I am enjoying it extremely: go on, if you please.[5]

Fortunio. In the second act Pantalone came on marvelling that Zanni should delay so long in bringing the reply, and meanwhile Zanni appeared with Camilla's letter which told him that if he would taste the fruits of love he must disguise himself as Zanni should instruct him by word of mouth. Pantalone was delighted and they disappeared to exchange clothes.

Now the Spaniard made his appearance, his heart submerged in the ocean of that frenzy called jealousy. To his servant he recounted his honour, his prowess, and the numbers, reckoned by the hundred, that with his own hand he had dispatched to Charon's barque. But now, a mere woman had stolen his valiant heart, and impelled by love he had come to find his darling Camilla and to implore her to admit him. By flattery Camilla coaxed a necklace from him and promised him entertainment that evening and the Spaniard retired contented.

[1] 'Frappamento', 1568; 'ragionamento', 1569.

[2] 1568, 'quanto piu hebbe cielo di durare giro'; 1569, 'lo posto per tutto il solaro della scena'.

[3] 'In ricordo delle cose antiche', 1569.

[4] In 1569 'raffioli' was substituted for the Bergomask 'sbruffadei' of 1568.

[5] 1569 adds 'passate pure avanti'.

At this point Pantalone and Zanni reappeared dressed in each other's clothes. When some time had been spent in teaching the Magnifico how he should talk (to gain admittance),[1] they both went into Camilla's house.

Here was heard the music of four voices and two lutes, and a plucked instrument and a bass viol-da-gamba.[2]

In the third and last act Polidoro, who maintained Camilla at his expense, returned from the country and found Pantalone in the house in his rough clothes. He was told that it was a porter hired by Monna Camilla to carry a coffer of cloth to Sister Doralice of S. Cataldo. Accepting this excuse Polidoro ordered him to be quick about it, but Pantalone as an old man could not manage to lift it, and after wrangling for a while he was forced to confess that he was a gentleman. Polidoro was annoyed at this and seizing a stick gave him, if I remember rightly, more than he deserved, to the accompaniment of bursts of laughter from the spectators.

When poor Pantalone had escaped, Polidoro, furious with Camilla, went back into the house. Zanni, who had heard the whacks, tied himself up in a sack, and was thrust out on to the stage by Camilla's servant, just as the Spaniard, punctual to the hour of Camilla's appointment, walked up to the house. The servant explained that Polidoro had returned from the country, and the Spaniard, angry at this unlooked-for news, turned to go, casting his eyes heavenwards, and heaving a fiery sigh, ejaculating 'Hai, Margodemi!'[3] he tripped over the sack that contained the wretched Zanni and measured his length on the stage and the servant after him. He picked himself up in a towering rage and undid the sack, pulled out Zanni and dusted his bones with a good beating, and chased him off the stage belaboured by the servant in the rear. After this Polidoro and Camilla appeared attended by their servants. She was told that she must make up her mind to marry, since he, for certain good reasons,[4] could keep her no longer. After a prolonged refusal she decided to obey him and agreed to take the Zanni as her lawful husband. During this discussion Pantalone appeared equipped in unbuckled armour, followed by Zanni who had two muskets on his shoulder, eight daggers in his girdle, a target and a sword in his hand, and a rusty helmet on his head. They were looking for the man who had thrashed them. Presently when they had practised some of the strokes with which they would have you believe that they would dispatch their enemies, Camilla encouraged Polidoro to accost them. As soon as Pantalone caught

---

[1] Added in 1569.
[2] 1569 adds 'un clavicimbalo, un pifaro, et un bass viol d'arco'.
[3] The oath in 1569 is given as 'ahi amargo de mi' and in Castilian 'ay amargo de mi', 'Woe is me!'
[4] 'Perqualche degno respetto', 1568; 'per alcuni degni respetti', 1569.

1

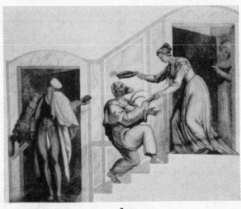

2

1. 26th wall, North. One Zanni unites the lovers, while Pantalone spies ; another Zanni leans from the window.
2. 24th wall, South. Pantalone spies and Zanni peers over his shoulder. Zanni is rewarded for delivering a letter; the maid keeps watch.

sight of him he pointed him out to Zanni, and Zanni who was terrified signalled to his master to strike the first blow. Pantalone insisted that Zanni should have the honour. Then Polidoro realizing that one was as scared as the other shouted, 'Ho! Sir Pantalone', Pantalone replied, 'Oh! Sir Spaniard!' and they drew. Zanni meanwhile could not decide which weapon to use. Their absurd skirmish lasted some time until Pantalone was held back by Camilla and Zanni by the servant. Peace made, Camilla was given to Zanni as his wife and in honour of the marriage they joined in a dance after the Italian fashion, and Massimo, on behalf of Messer Orlando, craved pardon of the princely audience for so unworthy an entertainment and with due reverence wished them good-night, whereat each went to his rest.[1]

ITALIANS AT THE BAVARIAN COURT

The appearances of a Venetian Magnifico and his Italian Zanni during the masquerades and banquets[2] show that there were professional buffoons in attendance for the wedding festivities, but from inception to reminiscence the performance described by Troiano is joyous with the zest of surprise and the vigour of the amateur. The second entry in the Chapel accounts which records a payment to Troiano in 1568 reads:

Dem Maximo Troiano Verehrung wegen ainer gehaltenen Comedj 20 fl.
Simon Gatto gleichfalls Verehrung 17 fl.[3]

The proximity of the names may be due to the fact that both payments were special rewards, 'verehrung', granted by the Duke. But on the other hand it may mean that Simon Gatto, whose name occurs regularly among the musicians between 1568 and 1572, took part in the comedy, though not necessarily the particular performance described in the *Dialoghi*. The coincidence is not to be pressed, but if musicians like Orlando, Troiano, and Ercole Terzo could improvise their parts in a comedy it is not unreasonable to suppose that from among the other singers and instrumentalists whose names occur in the Chapel accounts, some,

[1] A description of the wedding festivities by Hans Wagner records: 'ain lustige und kurzweilige Comedj in Italienischer sprach gehalten worden ist Und darnach hat sich jedermann zu rhue gethan.' Quoted by Trautmann, op. cit., p. 283, n. 94.
[2] *Dialoghi*, Lib. II, dial. ii, p. 126; and Lib. III, dial. i, p. 161.
[3] See A. Sandberger, op. cit., II, p. 35. For payments to Troiano see pp. 36, 43.

at least of the many Italians, may have been called upon
when the Duke indulged his taste for this kind of entertainment.

In 1570 Troiano quarrelled with the violinist Giulio
Romano, killed him in the duel, and fled from the court: by
this the amateurs lost the lover, the Spaniard, and the rustic
at a blow and became the more dependent upon the help of
the travelling comedians. On 29 September 1573 Alexander
Visconti was requested to see that the two tumblers, Bartl
the keeper of the leopard and Baptista the Goldsmith, should
be ready at Landshut not later than Saturday evening,
bringing with them Zanni clothes, masks, fiddles, and the
leopard, and anything else that might be needed for their
performance.[1] There is record of payment to two players
at Landshut in 1572.[2] In 1573 a 'Zanni springer' and a
certain Venturin who had been at Landshut the year before,
received a salary of 120 guilders and food and clothing for
a year.[3] That winter Orlando went into Italy in search of
singers, musicians, and players. Venturino who wished to
remain in the service of the Duke was an amusing travelling
companion, and his wife in Florence kept him in touch
with other professionals.[4] In Bologna they found the tumbler
whom she had recommended, a very smart youth with
many accomplishments such as leaping, walking on stilts,
and playing with various weapons; he was an excellent
dancer and so graceful in every action that Orlando protested
that he had never seen his like and hoped to engage him
for His Excellency.[5] In the same letter Orlando mentions
the 'Magnifico Gerardo' who had made him laugh and weep;
but financial considerations deterred him from engaging
him on the spot, for this actor was a man of 56 with a wife
and family and by himself would have brought up the
numbers of the party to nineteen, most of whom demanded
50 scudi in advance as well as their travelling expenses.[6]
Gerardo himself solved the problem by a disappointing

[1] See Trautmann, op. cit., p. 243.

[2] 'Erstlichen bezalt zwaien SPilleu-
then welliche von Lanndtschuet heer
Erfordert worden verErung . . .' Sandberger, op. cit., II, p. 64.

[3] Trautmann, op. cit., p. 244.

[4] Sandberger, op. cit., pp. 252–4.

[5] 'In fretta di bologna adi 3 del mese
di marzo 1574.' Ibid., p. 257.

[6] 'In primis gerardo Magnifico,
venturino, la moglie, il saltatore, un
suo putto che salta, il basso da camera,

I

2

3

1. 5th wall, East. Zanni and a lady.
   4th wall, South. Jester (?). Young lady dancing.
2. 25th wall, South. Pantalone with a slipper threatens a sick Zanni;
   another Zanni hurls a dish.
3. 25th wall, East. A lover muffled in a cloak is watched by a lady
   and a servant, while Zanni in a winged hat delivers a letter to
   the maid.

performance at Bologna; Orlando heard of another Magnifico in Florence, and meanwhile arranged with 'that Jan Maria who played that little comedy at Landshut with his Flemish wife' to return in a month or two with six companions to give some comedies, acrobatics, and other amusements instead of Venturino who was by now less eager to return, afraid, as Orlando supposed, that his wife was not good enough.

There are records of payments to 'Johann Maria, Silvester, Alexander Barbetta and his boy' in the accounts for 1574.[1] The next year the young Duke found himself faced with a debt of 229,375 guilders. Reluctantly he dismissed fifty-one of his household and among them went Scholari and the comedians.[2] For some years the only Pantaloonery that he enjoyed must have been provided by the genial banter of Orlando's polyglot correspondence. He sends a selection of rhymes in Italian, French, and German, anecdotes and musical rigmaroles, 'cose veramente da far stupir il Sr. Gracian'. The little bundle of letters show that Troiano's appreciation of his quondam companion's wit and versatility was not exaggerated.

In 1576 the Duke afforded himself the consolation of having the walls of the castle of Trausnitz frescoed with Pantaloons and Zanni.[3] The narrow frieze to the ceiling of his bedchamber is alive with buffoons, banqueting, boating, serenading, and 'delivering love-letters;[4] and the spiral

li duoi in roma gia promessj, Il giulio discanto, la sua moglie, 3 figliolj, la sra Jpolita che canta e sona con il suo fr(ate)llo e un servitore, il Lorenzino, Joan baptista con il suo padre, un bon sonator di cornetto; che fanno numero di 20 persone, che oltra esser conduttj a le spese di vra Ex^tia voranno quasi tuttj 50 scudi in primis de presente. . . .' Ibid., p. 257.

[1] Trautmann, op. cit., p. 245; Juan Maria Romano and Silvester Trevisano were at the Imperial Court in 1570. In the Chapel accounts for 1586 is the entry, 'Alexanndern Barbetta Italianern Semel Pro Semper von Anno 85 heer Laut der urkhundt zalt fl. 150'. Sandberger, op. cit., II, p. 159.

[2] Trautmann, op. cit., p. 245.
[3] The painter has not yet been identified. In 1579 Alexander Maler was paid 25 fl. at Landshüt 'für Malwerk im Schnecken und Wartzimmer'. Trautmann conjectures that this may have been Alexander Sieben; Rée favours Alexander Paduano. Ibid., p. 303, note.
[4] I have not been able to find the reproductions mentioned by Trautmann, 'Ornamentale Malereien vom k. Schloss Trausnitz b. Landshut i. Bayern. Aufgenommen und autografiert von Rudolf Gehring. Skizzen i. Massstab ⅛d. Natur, Details i. Naturgrösse, Landshut. Thoman,' and so far it has not been possible to procure

staircase painted with the same figures life-size is known as the Narrentreppe. The stairway has 113 steps, 7 windows, and 6 doors; 26 of the walls are decorated with paintings of ornamental statues or of buffoons. The figures are ingeniously fitted into the awkward spaces left by steps, doors, and windows. Working downwards, the first three walls are bare, on the fourth is a negro page[1] with a white hound, and a lady with a little dog and a basket of flowers. On the next wall is a man dressed in a tunic of large green-and-white checks which give him the appearance of a modern Harlequin; his connexion with the Arlecchino of the sixteenth century is extremely doubtful and he probably does not belong to the Commedia dell'arte any more than the page or the painted statues on the 9th wall.[2] An alcove separates him from the unmistakable Commedia dell'arte personages

reproductions of the frieze. The following description is arranged from my own notes taken on a brief visit to Trausnitz and compared with the catalogue description given by Trautmann, p. 300.

Turning to the right inside the door the sections of the frieze present the following scenes:

1. Two Zanni in a boat belabour Pantalone who is entangled in a net.

2. Two Zanni squat side by side gobbling out of one dish; a hungry dog crouches behind; they look anxiously towards a gallant who approaches with his hand on his sword.

3. Pantalone, knife in hand, stumbles into a net which Zanni is holding out.

4. An astonished Pantalone and a Zanni attack another Zanni.

5. An old man is seated by a basket of provisions, he holds a dish in one hand, over his head is a beehive; in the foreground a Zanni pokes the fire under a tripod, a second Zanni stands behind the old man holding a lantern in his right hand and a bird in his left.

6 and 7 present two positions of a fight; Zanni and Pantalone appear to be wading against the enemy.

8. Zanni offers a tablet to the old man who looks like a schoolmaster, he has spectacles and a staff; in the background three children take part in a reading lesson.

9. A music party of Pantalone and two Zanni.

10. Zanni presents the courtesan with a letter and a chain; Pantalone hovers anxiously in the background.

11. Zanni and Pantalone go serenading.

12. The 'Ruffiana', a leering old hag, delivers a love-letter to a young girl while Zanni holds back Pantalone by the shoulders.

13. Zanni conducts Pantalone to the Courtesan.

14. Pantalone beckons an eager Zanni to join him at a well-spread table.

15. An old man dressed in dark clothes (possibly a Pantalone or a magician) appears to be luring owls, Zanni at the side looks puzzled.

Number 12 is reproduced by Aretin in *Alterthümer und Kunst der Denkmale des bayerischen Herrscher-hauser* (1854), and by Rasi, *Comici Italiani*, ii, p. 1024.

[1] Zahlamtrechnung for November 1573 records payments for clothes for the 'Mohrn unnd die mohrin'. Trautmann, p. 300, note.

[2] See O. Driesen, *Der Ursprung des Harlekin*, p. 232.

1

2

1. 10th wall, North. Zanni with a love-letter and a fowl.
   9th wall, East. A lover beckoning.
2. 6th wall, North. Pantalone and Zanni serenading.

who appear on the same wall with a Zanni leading a young woman along the terrace. She is dressed as a fashionable court lady and wears no mask. Zanni's clothes are of some coarse canvas material, his wide trousers are frayed at the ankle, a double twist of rope ties in his loose blouse and supports a dagger and a pouch, he wears a length of canvas round or over his shoulder like a plaid; his shoes fit like mocassins. The brim of his large felt hat is here turned down all round, on other occasions it is adjusted and trimmed with feathers to suit his mood or disguise. He wears a thick beard, and his mask represents a brown handsome face with a large nose, a wrinkled forehead, and cunning eyes.

On the 6th wall Pantalone is seen playing the guitar. His crimson tights show him as a muscular old man, but the mask gives him a lean face with a huge hook nose, narrow eyes, and a thin white beard. He wears a tight red cap and a voluminous cloak with sleeves. In other positions a knife and a handkerchief can be seen at his belt. When he peers out of a window on the 15th wall he wears horn spectacles.

On the 7th wall there is only a cat on a window-sill; on the 8th the maidservant peers over Pantalone's shoulder as he threatens the Zanni in the opposite doorway. On the 10th the lover appears dressed as a court gallant, beckoning to Zanni and spied on by Pantalone. On the 14th and 20th wall-spaces the 'Ruffiana' appears. Whether scowling or leering she is a hideous hag wearing a coarse skirt and apron, a dark laced bodice, and a mantle over her head. Her sleeves are rolled up to show her skinny arms, she goes barefoot, and carries an open pouch and a bundle of keys. She is first seen charging out of the door with a pot in her right hand and a pitchfork in her left; on the next occasion she is playing the hypocrite and leans on a staff and displays her rosary. The same figure appears in her office of procuress on the frieze of the Duke's bedroom.

These six figures are repeated in various lively groups. There are two good scenes of a fight between Pantalone and Zanni. On the 20th wall Pantalone rides a donkey; on the 22nd he is soused by a maid as he serenades to the accompaniment of Zanni's fiddling. On the 24th wall Zanni is openly rewarded for bringing the lady a letter;

on the 21st he brings 'billets doux' with the poultry and the vegetables, and on the 25th he has arranged wings on his hat to signify his office as Mercury the patron of messengers. At the foot of the staircase he is seen carrying Pantalone pick-a-back.

The artist does not appear to have attempted to represent consecutive scenes from any one comedy. Zanni occurs twenty-four times, Pantalone fifteen, the maid seven, the lover six, his lady five, and the 'Ruffiana' twice. It is the peculiar value of these frescoes that no fancy for the buffoon as a decorative grotesque has distorted the delineation of dress and attitude. They appear as life-like as they are life-size. As Zanni and Pantalone are always masked it is of no consequence that we have excellent portraits of Orlando, but no indication of what Scholari may have been like in the flesh. But there is a remarkable resemblance between the lover and the portrait of Troiano which is prefixed to the second edition of the Dialogue.[1]

Photographs of the Narrentreppe paintings can only be taken from the water-colour drawings in the National Museum of Munich which were made for the Grand Duke by Max Hailer in 1841. Since then the painting of Pantalone on Zanni's back at the foot of the staircase has been obliterated and others have been badly scratched. The colours of the frescoes have faded, but beyond this the drawings are faithful point for point to the original designs. All that are relevant are reproduced here to complete Troiano's introductory description.

[1] Trautmann attributes the engraving to Nicolaus Nellius, 1568.

CHAPTER II
THE MASKS

THE personages of the Commedia dell'arte group themselves as parents, servants, lovers, and minor local
types. All except the lovers wore masks or some correspond-
ingly comic make-up.[1] Given certain broad traits the masks
might be adapted to the taste of the individual actors,
and in one case the mask of Pulcinella is said to have been
cast from the features of a famous impersonator Andrea
Ciuccio.

Masked actors make no attempt to show the development
of individual characteristics but depend for their success
upon their immediate recognition as types. They are not
people but personages. The fixity of expression symbolizes
the self-appointed limitation. As a mask represents a collection of individuals, so the idea of a mask emerges from a
study of individual presentations. The mask of Pantalone
is the abstract of the behaviour of innumerable Pantalones:
anything that a Pantalone did or said is a potential, anything
that he continued to do or say is an actual, formative influence
towards the development of the mask. The character of
a personage in literary drama exists as an actuality: the
character of a personage in masked and improvised drama
as a potentiality. We only want to know what Pantalone
did on a certain occasion in order to enrich our idea of what
he might do in the future. Facts give us his habits, and
habits his tradition. It follows that the quality of evidence
is for once less important than the quantity. We need many
instances to explore the possibilities of masked characters.
The nature of the Commedia dell'arte material favours this
method. The 600 or so scenari give satisfactory evidence
of the function of the chief masks in various types of drama:
and the specimen commonplace books extant yield a sufficient
selection of the speeches and jests that were kept as stock-in-
trade. From time to time the confusion of such a variety of

---

[1] T. Fiorilli, who played Scaramuccia unmasked, is an exception. See
V. de Amicis, *La Commedia dell'arte*
(1882), p. 71.

instances is reduced to order by the description of the masks given in the treatises on the art of improvisation by the professional actors Cecchini, Barbieri, and Riccoboni, and the amateurs Perrucci and D. Placido Adriano of Lucca.

The popular drama of the seventeenth century, in which the favourite masks take their place regularly among the dramatis personae of comedies, tragedies, and pastorals, is particularly interesting as a corroboration of notion of the masks which may be pieced together from the repertories of plots and speeches.

OLD MEN

PANTALONE

The origin of the nickname of the Magnifico, Messer Pantalone de' Bisognosi, is rather a matter of curiosity than of literary importance. Before 1559 'Lasca' writes of Cantinella as the 'Magnifico';[1] in 1565 'Pantaleone' appears in a Roman lawsuit with other actors;[2] by 1568, from Troiano, we have the suggestive surname 'de' Bisognosi'. His 'neediness' may refer to his want of physique, of credit, of domestic consolation, or of authority: perhaps it was by this barb of malice that the name stuck; Zanni's other masters, past and to come, are forgotten names, but two hundred years of the Commedia dell'arte could not wear out Pantalone.[3] It is a name that Gratiano could never catch, he enraged his neighbour by addressing him as Piatlon,[4] Piantalimon, Petulon, Pultrunzon,[5] Pianzamelon,[6] Padelon, Panieron;[7]

[1] A. F. Grazzini, *Canti Carnascialeschi*, XXIX.

[2] 'Per Tarasso vicentino comediante contro Scevola senese idem
Testes *Pantaleone* Comediante,
Georgius de Imola miles,
Soldino Commediante. 12 maggio 1565.' Arch. del Governatore di Roma. See Bertolotti, *Artisti Veneti in Roma nei secoli XV, XVI e XVII* (1884), p. 54. The name is mis-spelt 'Pantalone' in many citations.

[3] In the opinion of some critics, among whom are Del Cerro, and K.

Mantzius, Pantalone is superseded by the end of the seventeenth century by such old men as Prospero and Lattanzio: this is only for a while; he reappears as the chief *vecchio* for Riccoboni and Goldoni.

[4] O. Vecchi, *Anfiparnasso* (1597), I. iii.

[5] P. M. Cecchini, *Frutti delle moderne Comedie* (1628), p. 21.

[6] Fr. Gattici, *La Bizzaria di Pantalone* (1626).

[7] G. B. Andreini, *Le due Commedie in Commedia*.

and the etymologies offered in footnotes only add to these 'spropositi'.[1] But we know this old man by sight long before we learn his name in 1565. The 'senex' of Plautus and Terence derived from the old man of Menandrian comedy, the 'Pappus' of Atellan, and the 'Casnar' of Oscan farces the potent grave and reverend Signiors of the Commed' erudita are his prototypes, and their rakish counterparts Calmo's plays his immediate predecessors. The father ' exists to be wheedled or cheated is indispensable in dom comedy, but it is a dull part: the more active his ch' and servants the more passive the parent's role be The player must fend for himself by making it a c' part or by providing himself with some subordinate The 'Comici' draw upon both these resources. Pa..... comes on to the stage masked as a lean inquisitive old man; in his loose slippers he walks like a hen, one hand is thrust behind to hold back his 'zimarra', and except for this long black gown and for the little cap 'cowched fast to the pate like an oyster', as Gabriel Harvey has it,[2] he is all in red; at his belt there is a knife (*cinquedea* or *pistolese*) for vengeance, a handkerchief for affecting recognition scenes, and often a pouch. Sometimes he peers through spectacles,[3] and by the wag of his finger before his dialect is heard he has established himself as the Venetian. If the caricature was ever a matter of personal satire its significance was soon

---

[1] Possible etymologies are: (1) From S. Pantaleon of Venice. (2) From the phrase 'pianta-leone, plant the lion', satirizing the Venetian colonists (Sand, *Masques et Bouffons* (1860), quotes this as the suggestion of P. de Musset). (3) A. Beijer in the introduction to the *Recueil Fossard*, p. 17, revives an old theory by the suggestion that Pasquati may have learned from some *savant* that the name 'Pantaleone' had already been made famous by a comedian. See Athenaeus, *Deipnosophistai*, 1. i, and Bulengarius, *De Teatro* (1603), f. 104 bis. (4) πᾶς + ἐλεήμων, 'full of the milk of human kindness', Piangiani, *Vocab. etimologico della lingua italiana*. The early spellings, 'Panthaléon' in Grevin's *Les Ébahis* (1561), and 'Pantaleone' in

the lawsuit, favour the first suggestion. Della Porta's 'Capitano Pantaleone' in *La Fantesca* is more probably a compound on the analogy of his other military coinages, 'Dragaleone' and 'Gorgoleone', which figure in *La Chiappinaria*. See p. 47.

[2] G. Harvey, *Foure Letters*, ed. Grosart, vol. i, p. 84. See *infra*, Chapter VI, p. 378.

[3] See the 'Narrentreppe' fresco and *Recueil Fossard*, Plate XX. Cp. 'to them the panteloun and pescode with specktackles' in the plot of the *Deadman's Fortune*, W. W. Greg, *Dramatic Documents from Elizabethan Playhouses*; and *As You Like It*, 'With spectacles on nose and pouch at side'.

lost. Pantalone is like no one Venetian and so he stands for them all.[1]

It is laid down by Cecchini that allowing for a little absurdity in the dialect and dress, the Magnifico's is one of the serious parts. He should rank at least as a citizen and relax his gravity only when he treats of love and feasting with the servants.[2] Given an inch the actor took an ell. Pantalone keeps his place in the plot by dint of consorting more and more with the servants over his love affairs; gradually he loses status. In the scenari that remain to us he is often sentimental and weeps to keep Zanni company,[3] he is sometimes pathetic, but dignified, never.

As a Venetian fugitive in Florence or a victim of the sack of Rome naturalized in Venice, Pantalone is an amiable old man who has lost his wife and one or more of his children. He is an affectionate but an incredibly careless father who is always resorting to moles and birthmarks to identify his children. It is only at a distance that Pantalone appreciates his family: at closer quarters the evil habits of his son provoke the *consigli*, interminable reprimands. He finds a marriageable daughter as perishable a commodity as fish.[4] If he has a wife his time is taken up in escaping her notice as he carries on with a courtesan, for at home he is henpecked, locked out, and his braces are flung from the window after him,[5] he is even birched.[6] As a widower he has first a monologue on his unbearable loneliness and then confides to his servant his passion for a neighbour's daughter, demanding a plan by which he may thwart his own son who is his rival in that direction.[7] He is an incorrigible eavesdropper.[8]

[1] V. Rossi, Lettre di A. Calmo, 1888, pp. lxix, lxiii, quotes Pieri to demolish the double fallacy of the theory still held by C. Levi (*Emporium*, 1920, p. 253) that Ruzzante's Cornelio represents his patron Alvisi Cornaro and is the prototype of Pantalone as the stage Venetian.

[2] *Frutti* (1628).

[3] *Le Astuzie di Zanni*.

[4] F. Gattici, *La Bizzaria di Pantalone* (1626).

[5] *L'Amico Infido*. Villani implies that he always had trouble with his braces. *Ragionamenti dello Academico Aldeano*

Sopra La Poesia Giocosa De' Greci, de' Latini, e de' Toscani, Venetia, 1634, p. 68. Compare Pantalone de' Sbraghetti in *La Bella Negromantessa*, by G. Briccio, and 'Sbraghettai' in *Le Schiave*, by Verucci (1629). The pun probably involves the more vulgar meaning of the word which is used also for a cod-piece.

[6] *Terzo del Tempo*.

[7] *La Ruffiana*.

[8] *Il Thesoro* and *Zanne incredibile con quatro simili*.

Court office and avarice are the only restraints upon his amours. In tragi-comedy Pantalone is the counsellor. He is less brief and more tedious than Polonius and has similar preoccupations. The Duke admires Pantalone's daughter and Pantalone, aware that Isabella, a masterful young woman, is in love with a certain Oratio, shuffles and mumbles that this is too great an honour. It is useless: Isabella refuses the match and there is a scene. Later the Duke notices her absence from the Gallery where he is set to watch a tournament. Pantalone lies, saying that the girl is indisposed, and is horrified when a few minutes later a defeated combatant is ordered to disarm, the helmet is removed, down falls a woman's hair, and there is Isabella.[1] This was Pantalone in difficulty with his daughter; there were also his ducats. The theme of his avarice never palled. He bequeathes his broken shoes to Zanni or sends him to buy a ha'penny egg with a chicken in it so that broth can be made of the bird and an omelette of the egg.[2] Once when Zanni asked for his wages Pantalone produced a pocket book and reckoned that since the morning of Wednesday, 14 August 1606, when Zan Fritella Battocchio da Valpelosa entered his service, his breakages had more than cancelled any arrears of salary.[3] By an old and favourite device Pantalone and Coviello agree to marry each the other's daughter, so that neither need disburse for a dowry. Any charlatan can decoy him with a story of hidden treasure.[4] In his credulity he will shiver all night in his shirt watching for spirits;[5] or go courting in the most absurd and degrading disguises.[6]

Blocked in as a Venetian citizen, father, master, and lover, amorous, avaricious, and gullible, the mask admits of many variations. In battle-pieces Pantalone appears as a superior sentry;[7] in *Orlando Furioso* as an innkeeper; occasionally he is a tutor,[8] and once a doctor of medicine.[9] He is not restricted to Venice as his native city or place of residence.[10]

[1] *La Pazzia di Doralice.*
[2] *Il Vecchio Avaro.*
[3] Verucci, *Li Diversi Linguaggi.*
[4] *Li Finti Turchi; La Feda Infedelta.*
[5] *La Tramutatione;* Verucci, *Pantalone Innamorao* (1619).
[6] *Travestita.*

[7] *La Battagliola.*
[8] *La Fantasma.*
[9] *Elisa Ali Bassa.*
[10] There is a Pantalone in each of the 102 scenari of Locatelli, but the scene is laid in Venice only five times. G. Bricci has a note to *Li Strapazzati*

Outside the Venetian territory even the dialect might be modified to suit the audience or because the actor had it only at second-hand.[1]

Other old men, Tofano and Zanobio,[2] Tartaglia, Coviello,[3] Pincastro,[4] Ubaldo, Pandolfo, Pacifico,[5] Prospero, Lattanzio,[6] and Cassandro take their turns as duped parents and unfortunate lovers in other localities, but the types lapse after a couple of generations and the Venetians, the house of *Bisognosi*, Pantalone himself, has outlasted them all.[7]

PANTALONE AS A SPEAKING PART

Troiano's scenario shows how Orlando di Lasso's tumbling, together with some chop-logic with Zanni, a Venetian serenade, and a wonderful howl helped him to sustain the part. But as professional players came to draw their plots from the Commedia erudita Pantalone became responsible for a considerable share of the dialogue. Besides explaining his adventures he is required to reprove, persuade, command, offer advice, and in a thousand other ways to behave as an able person (*huomo ingegnoso*).[8]

The samples of his speeches given in the second part of Perucci's treatise on the art of representation fall into line with the Pantaloonery that can be salvaged from the plays of Rossi, Verucci, and Briccio who write in the beginning of the seventeenth century. Translation from the dialect dilutes these recitals until they read like the matter of Polonius paraphrased by Euphues. So much depended upon the delivery that even a list of presents received by the *prima donna*,[9] or a catalogue of the cities of Italy with

(1627), 'Si avverta, che il P. non deve esser vecchio, e può andar vestito alla Romana se piacerà'.

[1] B. Rossi in a prefatory letter to *Fiammella*, 1584: 'Del Pantalone per l'obligo dei bestici e versi non auro forse fattolo parlare in la vera lingua di "audao, vegnuo", con tutte che in Venezia a questo modo non si favella.'

[2] See Scala's *Teatro, infra*, iii, p. 6.

[3] Neapolitan scenari. For further details in this and the three notes follow-

ing, see Appendix F.

[4] MS. Barb. Lat. 3895.

[5] MS. Magliabechiano.

[6] Perugian scenari.

[7] Verucci has some variants and in *Li Stroppiati* calls his old Venetian 'Babilonio', and in *Il Dispettoso*, 'Torbolonio Palthanai'. For Stefanello see Appendix E.

[8] P. M. Cecchini, op. cit., p. 25.

[9] Scala, 39.

appropriate local allusions when mouthed in Venetian had a relish.[1]

Asked for counsel, Pandolfo, a Florentine *vecchio*, would tease out the bombast of classical parallels and 'recount the example of the horse of Alexander the Great, that once caparisoned, would allow no other to bestride him'.[2]

In his 'Consiglio' Perucci's Pantalone went round to work:

The ancient Egyptians, most Excellent Prince, wishing to demonstrate the value of good counsel by an Hieroglyphic showed Pluto with a helmet upon his head in the act of snatching away Persephone, meaning to convey by this image that whoever would be master of the event must have his head protected with the helmet of good advice. Whoever will reap fruit from his sowing must consult with the sower of good counsel to find from him the times and seasons. He who would build the mansion of Polity must found it upon Reason, without this the whole structure will topple to the ground. . . .

His store is not nearly exhausted; only signs of our impatience might hasten the recapitulation that closes his period:

Do well therefore Your Excellency, and like Pluto arm yourself with the Helmet of Counsel; like the earth bring forth fruit from the seed of good advice; like the Mansion be founded upon Prudence; in darkness avail yourself of our candle so that you need never go groping; like the galley be steered by the Timon of our accuracy; let the horn of Providence, like the Unicorn, be the antidote to the poison of serpents, and like the horse be managed by the bridle of the wisdom of counsellors.[3]

All the speeches of the Commedia dell'arte are built upon this collapsible principle, they could be protracted or cut short to meet any emergency.[4] Whatever serves to draw out the thread of his verbosity finer than the staple of

---

[1] Compare the speech provided for Barberin (a Pantalone type) in Sir Aston Cokayne's *Trappolin Suppos'd a Prince*, a scenario of the *Creduto Principe* tradition. See Appendix F.

[2] *La Regina d'Inghilterra*. See A. Bartoli, *Scenari Inediti della Commedia dell'arte* (1880), p. 59.

[3] A. Perrucci, *Dell'Arte Rappresentativa* (1699), parte ii; compare Selections

reprinted by E. Petraccone in *La Commedia dell'Arte* (1927), p. 115. For the serious use of this style see the speeches of the six counsellors provided for the *Gesta Grayorum* in 1594 by Francis Bacon; *Works*, ed. Spedding, i, pp. 332–41.

[4] See Prologue on 'homo' written by D. Bruni for a Pantalone, quoted by Rasi, *Comici Italiani*, ii. 232.

his argument will serve Pantalone in his expostulation against his son's evil life. Only the comic effect of the young man's exasperation could carry off such nonsense.[1]

Songs and sonnets parodied in Venetian were part of the stock-in-trade.[2] The Pantalone of *La Fiammella* had collected enough puns to last out a page-long soliloquy at the rate of two a line.[3]

In monologue Pantalone has his own way, but he meets his match in the Doctor. Dattomo's undated play, *La Maga, con Frittellino Mago a Caso*, affords a sample of the conversation that takes place in the favourite scene when the two old men meet to discuss the terms of a marriage settlement between their children.

Pantalone. I am willing . . .
Dottore. Would you rather I used Latin or the vernacular?
Pant. The vernacular, why . . .
Dott. French or Spanish?
Pant. Don't address me in . . .
Dott. Or German, Polish, Russian, Swiss, Dutch, English, Portuguese, or would you prefer Turkish, Greek, Hebrew, or Assyrian?

[1] See 'Consiglio' quoted from Perrucci by Petraccone, op. cit., p. 116.

[2] Sufficient examples are extant:
1. V. Belando, *Lettere Facetie*, contains a letter in Venetian, and a sonnet in three languages, Spanish, Italian, and French, for 'Pantalon a la sua crudel Rizzolina'.
2. G. C. Croce, *La Nobilissima anzi Asinissima Compagnia delli Briganti della Bastina* (1597), contains verses in Venetian, entitled: 'Bizaria del Sig. Zizoletto Coccolini a Madonna Ninetta Teneruzzi.'
3. P. Veraldo, *Mascarate nuove e capricci dilettevoli recitativi in comedie, e da cantarsi in ogni sorte d'Instrumenti operete di molto spasso.* Ristampata, Venetia, 1626.
4. 'Disperation satirica in lingua Venetiana' in Belando's *Gl'Amorosi Inganni*, ed. 1609.
5. *Mattazini e sonetti alla Venetiana Pantalon di Bisognosi* (1590).
6. 'Due Canzonette nuove di un Amte [sic] con la risposta dell'Amata in lingua Venetiana.' See P. A. Tosi, *Maccheronee di Cinque Poeti Italiani del sec. XV*, Appendix (1864).
7. Canzonetta sopra la Guerra Seguia nel Cremonese l'anno 1647 & 48 descritta da Pantalon comigo della Verita sopra l'aria di Bossetto. In Milano, per Lodovico Monza Stampatore alla Piazza de'Mercatori. See Brit. Museum, G. $\frac{5484}{3}$.

[3] Compare *La Fiammella*, Act I. The conceit here illustrated would be more accurately described as a game of chasing the assonance with punning intent. Rasi, i. 458, gives an example of the same kind of equivocation, 'stile in bisticcio', from Bocchini's *Zan Muzzina* rhymes:
Io che passo si spesso, e pur non posso
Se ben batto da Betta un dì far botta
Comporterò s'altrui l'accatta cotta
Ch'ella me sol salassi fin su l'osso, &c.

Pant. Ugh, Sir Latch-Tongue (*Lingua de caenazzi*), speak what the devil you please.

Dott. Good, good! Has it to be verse or prose?

Pant. I'll have it in prose, and end this Rigamarole (*Zirandola*).

Dott. If I talk prose to you, do you wish me to speak by way of demonstration, or deliberation, or judicially?

Pant. But I've told you . . .

Dott. The judicial would not be appropriate, from the deliberative much is lacking, and the demonstrative does not please me. . . . When would you like me to begin?

Pant. Now, at once.

Dott. Once I start I shall have begun.

Pant. Even Brovello knows that much.

Dott. First, allow me to clear my throat.

Pant. As often as you please.

Dott. Could you wait while I spit?

Pant. Still something else? Spit if you must but be quick about it.

Dott. I will address you with such brevity that where another would never end . . .

Pant. But I want to talk to you of my own affairs, not of others.

Dott. For what reasons, for a civil or a criminal procedure?

Pant. No, I want . . .

Dott. By writ or process . . .

A little more of this haggling and Pantalone is frantic enough to take Hortensia without waiting for the dowry.[1]

GRATIANO: THE DOCTOR

Actually on the stage Pantalone had not long to wait for his companion, Dr. Gratiano the Bolognese lawyer. Orlando di Lasso mentioned 'Gracian' in 1574; the mask appears among 'Lasca's' comedians; and for 11 May 1567 Rogna, the Mantuan diarist, has the entry: 'S.E. ha fatto recitare

[1] '*La Maga*, con Fritellino Mago a Caso, Comedia del Signor Antonio Dattomo. In Venetia. Per D. Lovisa à Rialto.' The only copy which I have been able to find, preserved as Misc. in 8vo. 95. in the Biblioteca Casanatense, has no date. The earliest play of Dattomo's to be published was, according to Allacci, the *Sfortunato Pellegrino* for Pisarri of Bologna in 1662: this is important in consideration of the connexion with Domenico Laffi's *Paggio*

Fortunato in which the dialogue between Pantalone and the Doctor is almost identical. The only edition quoted by Allacci is dated 1716, but Sarti (*Il Teatro dialettale Bolognese*, p. 64) records an earlier issue, for Pisarri of Bologna in 1690. A comparison with the scene between the Magnifico and Gratiano in the first of the plays inset in G. B. Andreini's *Le Due Commedie in Commedia* (1623), proves it to be a common type.

Dottore Bacchetone
Gioanelli

Arlecchino. 'Gl'Amori sfortunati
di Pantalone'
Tomadoni

Pantalone Bullo
Gioanelli

oggi una comedia dai Gratiani.' Evidently these players, like other early troops, went by the name of the leading mask; a week later Rogna notes: '18 maggio. Heri si fece nel palazzo del Sig. Cesare Ecc^{mo} una comedia de' Gratiani.'[1]

The illustrated title-page for *Graziano Inamorato* in the Corsini Manuscript presents the Doctor sidling down the street on a wooing expedition; he flourishes a pair of black gloves and wears a black gown heavily padded on the shoulders, and a 'pent-house of a hat'. For his gesture we turn to the procession of comedians silhouetted in Buonarrotti's *La Fiera*: 'Observe that Graziano . . . twirling himself into a fume, look how he swings his arms and shrugs his shoulders; how he moves his lips as he mumbles and pants, betraying his usual absurdity in expounding and arguing.[2] This outline is unmistakable in the clumsiest woodcuts or among the tiniest of Callot's figures. Riccoboni says that the Doctor's dress changed very little: but his design of a modern Gratiano with his tight knee-breeches, ruffled doublet, ample cloak, and the hood worn like a widow's travelling veil, show that the mask of the Doctor was influenced by the shift from the realistic to the picturesque that helps to distinguish between the appearance of the Commedia dell'arte in the sixteenth and the seventeenth centuries.[3] Aldeano in 1634 expected these lawyers of Francolino to have an oily toga, loose hair, and 'habiti alla ciala bardessa'.[4] The only mention of the mask with the wine-stain to which Goldoni refers[5] is in the direction in *Il Cieco finto* for Pulcinella to disguise himself as the Doctor 'con viso tinto'.[6]

As the second father, Perucci considered that the Doctor might be more absurd than Pantalone provided that the part was kept above the level of the second Zanni.[7]

After lamenting the corruption of the Gratiani of his day Cecchini took refuge in the warning that the Doctor's part must be played in a man's own way: 'Poich'io mi rendo

[1] D'Ancona, *Origini del teatro italiano*, ii, p. 445.
[2] *La Fiera* (acted 1618), Giorn. II, Atto III, sc. xi.
[3] Riccoboni, *Hist. du théâtre italien*, Plates 5 and 6.
[4] N. Villani, 'Aldeano', *Sopra la*

Poesia Giocosa (1634), p. 68.
[5] Goldoni, *Memorie*, ed. Moreau, vol. ii, p. 22.
[6] *Il Cieco Finto overo Raguetto Viandante*, Ales. Bombardieri, Roma, 1658.
[7] See Petraccone, op. cit., p. 119.

sicuro, che il fine di colui, che vorrà far da Gratiano sarà di voler far à suo modo.'[1] His own conception of the part was of a scholar who tries to be up to date in spite of his antiquity, one whose learning is just over-ripe, whose Bolognese, spoken as though it were the choicest language in the world, gives the chance for occasional malapropism. Cecchini feared that his censure of debased performances might be too late. It was. The actors had already let the Doctor's learning rot: from all the records that survive it appears that, like Shadwell, he never deviated into sense, and the point of caricature was soon lost by over-emphasis.

According to Perucci the grossest absurdities of the Doctor's part had gone out of fashion by the end of the seventeenth century: his speeches were to be comic not from ignorance but from length. But Riccoboni some twenty-eight years later still recognized two types of Graziani; the one who could support his erudition by authentic quotation, the other who displayed his ignorance in the macaronic jargon of Merlin Coccajo. For the former a man must be learned to avoid a solecism; for the latter even greater talent is needed, for as Riccoboni remarks: 'it is harder to distort a maxim wittily than to deliver it in its proper sense'.

The possibility of these divergent conceptions was inherent in the idea of the caricature of a learned person: the stress was left to the player. The Doctor's ignorance was more popular than his learning. There are but few of the subtler Graziani to counterbalance the wild 'spropositi' and tongue-twisting tirades of the plays and miscellanies. The manner of Bartolomeo Zito described by Cecchini was the gift of fortune:

It was in Naples that I heard two Neapolitans, one playing a Coviello and the other a Doctor Graziano, each, in my opinion, inimitably life-like, . . . the Graziano had so many exquisite parts that I fear to wrong the best by depriving them of the foremost mention, so that I will simply give my impression and leave his merits to take care of themselves. First, he is not one of those who swear by 'Sacra Carlona' when they consult with the king, but in his own words and with conceits appropriate to the subjects, he delivers a

---

[1] *Frutti*, see Petraccone, op. cit., p. 11.

speech that might be written down for print: the salt of his discourse
consists in a manner of working the audience into an ecstatic attention
only to cheat it of the conclusion, which is the memorable part and
nourishes the understanding. His pronunciation might be more
Gratianesque, but still, it would suffice, even in our part of the country,
for one who wished to enrich the wit rather than impoverish the
language. This man is very well read (*studiosissimo d'istorie*) and has
a touch of poesy; what book in the vernacular has not found its way
into his collection is perhaps not worth much: and lest other Neapolitans who play these parts usurp these prerogatives the one (Coviello)
is called A̓mbrosio Buonomo, and the Doctor is Bartolomeo Zito.[1]

As the cold scraps of such a fantastical banquet there are:
*Le cento e Quindici conclusioni in ottava rima, del Plusquam
perfetto Dottor Gratiano Partesano da Francolin, Comico
Geloso, e altre manifatture, a Compositioni nella sua buona
lingua*, published in Bologna 1588.[2] No doubt Lodovico
Bianchi's roundabout and pompous delivery would prepare
for the blank bathos of the conclusions that he propounded:

(3) He who is wrong cannot be right.

[1] *Frutti delle moderne Comedie* (1628).
See E. Petraccone, op. cit., p. 16. On
Zito see Croce, *I Teatri di Napoli*.

[2] I have not been able to examine a
copy of this book from which Rasi
(op. cit., i. 407) gives extracts and
bibliographical details. See also Mic,
La Commedia dell'arte, p. 68, who refers
to a Gratiano miscellany, 'Gratiano
Gratiani Granarense. Scielta di Concetti, etc. per beneficio et commodo
diquelli che desiderano iscriver lettere
famigliari', Venezia, 1619. I have not
been able to examine this and am therefore unable to determine its relationship
to the following burlesques quoted by
O. Guerrini, as the work of G. C. Croce,
in *La Vita e le Opere di G. C. Croce*
(1879).

Item 58. Le cento e dodici Conclusioni / In ottava rima del plusquam
perfetto Dottor Gratiano Partesana da
francolino.

59. Conclusiones / Quinquaginta tres
sustintà in Franculin dal Macilent Sg.
Gratian Godga D. in zò cha vlì vu
Argumintà dal D. Pgnaton cun
'assistenza dal D. Memeo squaquara
E da so Sg. Insulentiss. Tradut unde
versus Materna locutione di G. C. Croce.

115. Indice universale della Libraria
o Studio del celebratiss. Arcidottore
Gratian Furbson da Franculin. Opera
curiosa per i professori delle Sie.
Matematiche e studiosi dell'opere bizare
e capriciose Rac. per M. Aquedoto dalle
Sanguetole riformatori dell'Hosteria
del Chiù di G. C. Croce. 1623.

130. Pronostico perpetuo sopra
l'anno presente calcolato ad Meridiano
della Fiera d'agosto ad instanza del mese
di settembre Alli 25 dell'Estate all'in-
contro dei Salcizzoni da Bologna, si
vende come si trova a due soldi il
Boccale dato di nuovo in luce per un
Dottor Gratiano Pagliarizzo da Bologna
. . . 1624, probably dating from 1607.

139. Lassato over donativo che fa
maesto Martino a Catarinon nella par-
tita sua di Bologna per Fiorenza. Con
la vera canzone di Catarinon fatta da
Gratiano Scatolone da Bologna per far
pace con la sua inamorata. 1621.

247. Stanze dell'Ariosto tramutate
dal Dott. Partesana di Francolino.

259. U̓trom del. Gratiano Partesana.

(4) The ship on the high seas cannot be said to be in port.
(13) A Ferrarese is not a Mantuan.
(22) One who is sleeping cannot be said to be awake.

We have the application of this form of wit in Rossi's *Fiammella* when Graziano proves that a man who is ill cannot be said to be well on the analogy that he who walks cannot be said to stand still. He is determined to 'disseminate science to the fishes' and, with a strange foreshadowing of the Carpenter, assembles those of his new scholars who are fresh, warning them that once they are eaten they will no longer be alive.

The Doctor's miscellany reads like a scrap-book made from an academic waste-paper basket. In Perucci's *Consiglio* the quotations from 'Zizerone, Umer, Menander, Verzil, Terenz, Macrob, Plutarch, Pliny, Senega, Luccan, Marzial, Plautus' are as apposite as they are unnecessary for the support of the platitudes which Graziano has to offer. When the scraps were torn smaller and shuffled again the Doctor entertains slower wits with misappropriated learning. Veraldo has him bequeathing: 'the sighs of Cicero, the plaints of Plato, the rhymed prose of Boccaccio in coloured type on torn paper, Ruzzante's treatise on orthography, together with the statutes of Love by Galileo printed in Turkish and Chaldean.'[1] The Doctor amused himself with fantastic etymologies. Aniello as Spaccastrummolo has a prologue for the city of Bologna in which Jove insists that it commemorates the rape of Europa; as thus, 'Bononia = Bos-non-jam = Bue-non-gia'; it was Jove, not a bull, that carried off Europa. Mars will have it from 'Bonum-onus' for it was there he took up the 'fair burden' of Venus. Pallas says 'Bo = bue = ignoranti', 'non-ha = has not', whence 'Bononia', the city without blockheads. Mercury offers 'Bonus-logos', the city of elegant speech. Spaccastrummolo rejects these and the rest, bows to the audience, and asks, what could 'Bononia' signify but 'Bon-omnia'?[2]

[1] P. Veraldo, *Mascarate e capricci dilettevoli, recitativi in comedie, e da cantarsi in ogni sorte d'Instromenti operete di molto spasso,* Venetia, 1626. See Rasi, i. 214.

[2] For other examples of Gratiano's etymologies see A. Bartoli, op. cit., p. lxxxvi.

As an example of the pedantries that the Doctor here delighted to parody

The Doctor's 'sproposito' was a mongrel form of wit, half pun, half malapropism.[1] Practised Gratiani could sustain long scenes with the untranslatable verbal antics, which we can best understand by analogy as we recall the Mock Turtle's exposition of the different branches of Arithmetic as 'Ambition, Distraction, Uglification, and Derision'.

The Doctor will say 'marinar' for 'maritare', 'in combustion' for his favourite 'in conclusione', and refer to the 'stornemento circa a nostro pan grattado' for the 'istrumento circa questo nostro parentado';[2] 'La Genealogia dei Dei di Boccaccio' becomes 'La Zanolia di Diè de msier Brancaz';[3] 'Africa, Asia, and Europe' figure as 'quest'altr'è l'Asna, e tut el rest' è Groppa'.[4] His most elaborate 'spropositi' were reserved for the scene in which he reads aloud a letter or a dowry list or learns a love-speech line by line. Pantalone or Zanni laughing behind his back make his blunders intelligible to the audience:

Grat. Doi muli crudi di Antinoro moro, colcati un sopra l'altro.

Pant. Mo che volì che fazza de Muli, ne de Aseni? lasseme vardar. Doi milla scudi avanti d'oro in oro contanti uno sopra l'altro. . . .

Grat. Zarlino è morto, e la sua casa è ita a Corneto. . . .

Pant. Zardino, e orto, e la sua casa, cortile e canneto. . . .

Grat. Item, quattro forestieri scoperti da un muto, che è mancino. . . .

Pant. Quattro forzieri coperti de velludo cremesino. . . .

Grat. Diece pazzi de bona razza.

Pant. Diese pezzi di panna de razza.[5]

---

there might be quoted an etymological discussion of 'Bologna' in the travel journal of Nicholas Audebert (1574–8). MS. Lansdowne, 720, f. 104.

[1] The word 'sproposito' is of course current coin in Italian, but it evidently acquired special point from Graziano's mannerism of introducing all irrelevancies with 'a proposito'. See F. Andreini, *Bravure*, Rag. XVII.

Cap. Spavento. Ma à proposito di Bacco, mi sorviene il contrasto, ch'io habbe una volta con la Morte.

Trappolin. Questo vostro dire, mi pare un parler da Gratiano, dicendo voi à proposito di Bacco mi sorvien della Morte.

[2] Verucci, *Pantalone Inamorao*, pr. 1619 (ed. 1663).

[3] Ercole Cimilotti, *I Falsi Dei, Favola Pastorale Piacevolissima Dell' Estuante Academico Inquieto* (1599).

[4] *Gratiana, Favola Boscareccia del Infiamato*, Venetia, 1609, p. 15. A manuscript note in the British Museum copy records a first edition printed in Padua by G. Cantoni in 8o. 1588. The pun is also recorded by Perucci: see Petraccone, p. 120.

[5] G. Bricci, *Pantalone Imbertonao* (1626), iii. 4. For other such scenes see Briccio, *La Dispettosa Moglie*, ii. 3 (1612); P. Veraldo, *L'Anima dell'Intrico*, i. 4 (1621); Veraldo, *Le Tre Mascarate, dei tre amanti scherniti* (1621). In V. Verucci's *Pantalone Innamorao* (1619), a love-speech is

'Lasca' remarked the rage to 'write and talk Zanni' which corresponds to the Elizabethan fashion of 'parleying Euphuism'. Pantalone's love songs and the jargon and 'spropositi' of Gratiano also spread farther than the stage: Bianchi wrote to the Grand Duke of Tuscany 'in lingua Gratianesca' reminding him to send a present of game from Poggio.[1] The imaginary dialogues accumulate into a semi-dramatic literature.[2]

Graziano sometimes shared his stock of maxims and examples with Pantalone and his 'spropositi' with the Second Zanni, but he had the monopoly of the tirade. Except for an occasional Pulcinella no one else cared to master these formidable tongue-twisters.[3] In the prologue 'a la Gratiana' arranged by Bruni, the Doctor is required to enumerate forty-eight virtues, twenty-one vices, and, after a pause for breath, twenty-one appropriate epithets in order.[4]

In the tirade which describes a tournament Gratiano recites the titles of eighteen combatants, among them 'El-mond Milord d'Oxfort' and 'Alvilda Contessa d'Edemburg'; on the next round he allots their horses, to Elmond 'un caval falt chiamato Oltremarin' and to Alvida 'un caval leard rotà chiamato Dolcin'; on the next their dress, the next their arms, the next their emblems and mottoes, and yet again the names go whirring round like hobby-horses at

memorized; in D. Balbi, *Il Secondo Zanne* (1678), a will is mis-read.

[1] Pistoia. Oct. 1589. Bib. Naz. di Firenze. Arch. Med. F^a 809. *c*. 579.

[2] V. Belando (Cataldo), *Lettere facetie, e chiribizzose* (Paris, 1588), has a letter 'in lingua Gratiana' addressed, 'All'Industrio, et molt Incivil Signor, il Signor Sebastian Zamet suo è Zitara.' It begins, 'Molt' Magnifico, et insolent Signor Saladi senza fin', and is signed, 'Dottor Incognito, Accademico balord alias Cataldo'.

Camillo Scaligero della Fratta (Adriano Bianchieri) in *La Nobilissima anzi Asinissima Compagnia delli Briganti della Bastina*, Vicenza, 1597, has an address and stanzas by Dottor Gratiano da Francolino.

P. Veraldo's *Mascarete nuove e*

capricci dilettevole recitative in comedie, e da cantarsi in ogni sorte d'istromenti operete di molto spasso contains: (1) Bando della dottrina del Dottor Gratiano. (2) Procura de trovar la sua scientia bandita, per liberarlo. A Dialogue with Echo. (3) Testamento. I have only been able to find an edition which was 'ristampata in Venetia 1626'. Cp. p. 30, n. 1.

[3] P. Adriano (Bib. Comunale di Perugia MS. A. 20) has a note to the scenario of *L'Innamorata Scaltra*, Act II, that for Pulcinella's tirade against courtesans, Gratiano's eighth Tirata, 'Che cosa sia Donna', is to be given in Neapolitan.

[4] *Fatiche Comiche* (1623), quoted Rasi, op. cit., i, p. 412.

a fair as they are paired off to the tilt.[1] Was this great baby
not yet out of his swaddling clouts that he went on building
on the principle of the nursery tongue-twister: 'Water,
water, quench fire; fire, fire, burn stick; stick, stick, beat
dog; dog, dog, bite pig; pig, pig, get over the stile or
I shan't get home to-night'? Tirades seem to have been
delivered upon the slightest or no dramatic provocation.
La Fortuna non conosciuta is to open with a scene of memory
by the Doctor; the second act of the *Cavalier Innorito da suo
nemico* is to end with a tirade; Gratiano tries to detain the
impatient Cola with a long recital in *L'Amore et honore di
Ramidoro*; and it is put baldly in *Vittoria Cacciatrice*: 'Here
the Doctor delivers a tirade on daring or fear or anything else
after his manner.' In *La Finta Zingara* Sgambetti gives
Gratiano a tirade of the catalogue type that fills three pages,
and Cotta runs to four in *La Pirlonea*.

The Doctor would hover in the background counting
fly's legs[2] waiting for his chance. In reply to the question,
'What was the judgement of Paris?' Adriano's Doctor had
four and a half pages of names, titles, and qualities to draw
on.[3] As a medical man he can go through a list of twenty-
nine patients, their diseases, their cures, and his rewards.[4]
He will rage against your peasant in alphabetical order,[5]
offer advice to one who contemplates matrimony or reproach
a would-be murderer.[6] Occasionally his loquacity is more
effectively timed. In *Il Gratiano Infuriato, overo il Fuggi
l'ozio*, published in 1677 by G. M. Cesarij da Budrio, the
hired cook-bravo calls the Doctor a beast and provokes this
outburst:

'Beast! 'sblood you say "beast" to me? "Beast" to me? Come here
and I'll make the bees buzz in your bonnet. Beast to me! An animal?
that is as much as an ass, as a pig? You will not allow me to be a

---

[1] See Petraccone, op. cit., p. 122.
In the anonymous and undated play,
printed for Lovisa, *L'Invidia in Corte,
overo la Pazzia del Dottor*, p. 12, the
Doctor describes a hunt precisely on
the plan of Perrucci's *Tirata della
Giostra*. The stage direction reads: 'At
each turn Pantalone thrusts in some
pointed comment to provoke laughter;
but these are not given here because

they are devised evening by evening
a capriccio.'
[2] *Pantalone Imbertonao*, II. i.
[3] Bib. Com. di Perugia. MS. A. 20,
Tirata I.
[4] Ibid., Tirata 2.
[5] Ibid., Tirata 4. See Petraccone,
op. cit., p. 261.
[6] Ibid., Tirata 5. 'Un che vuol
uccidere l'uomo.'

rational being so I am an animal! I who have studied, examined, re-examined, and perused all that there is to be studied, examined re-examined, and perused in the world. Beast to me? Beast to me? When I have conned the whole psalter in learning to read, examine, re-examine to make concordances. . . .'

(The Doctor may have known the law, go to, but he was writ down an ass.)

There was a difference of opinion about Gratiano's dialect. 'Some will have him speak Bolognese, some Ferrarese, and some the dialect of Francolino,' said Rossi in the Preface to *La Fiammella*, 'but now the dialects are not used, and it is enough to say everything the wrong way round.'

The Doctors compounded a jargon of macaronic Latin and a debased form of Bolognese that could be modified to good Tuscan for a Neapolitan audience.[1] According to Sarti the dialect of Gratiano 'Bolognese Sensale' in *La Dispettosa Moglie* is more like Venetian than Bolognese. Levi attributes the same dialect to the Doctor in Briccio's *Pantalone Imbertonao*.[2] Verucci in *La Portia* has a Doctor Coviello who mingles Latin with his Neapolitan.

ORIGIN

It is worth while sifting the legends which attempt to account for the origin of the mask of the Doctor before considering his connexion with the Pedant.

The fantastic genealogy given in macaronics in Camillo Scaligero's *Discorso sulla lingua bolognese* presents us with an example in little of the tangle made by four theories.

> Ego Gratianus sum Franculinensis
> Filius quondam d'Mser Tomas;
> Nobilis civis erat Mutinensis
> Oculos habens d'fora dal nas.
> Catlina Mater mea Ferrariensis
> Appellabatur d'casa Bambas;

---

[1] 'appunto come parla la nobilità di quell'inclita città e non la plebe, di cui appena si sente la favella, onde allora ch'ebbi la fortuna d'esservi, al mio compagno sembrava d'esser fra tanti barbari, non intendendo punto quella lingua,' Perrucci; see Petraccone, op. cit., p. 119.

[2] *Emporium* (1920), vol. ii, p. 131.

Gratianus vero addottoratus est
In Bologna, dal trenta, l'ann dal bsest.[1]

Taking the Christian name as the first clue, we come to his compatriot Gratiano of the Decretals, the Canonist lawyer of the twelfth century, under whose name the inventor of the mask may have intended to satirize the profession.[2] Further support for this theory might be claimed from the Doctor's earliest surname, 'delle Cottiche',[3] variously spelt 'Codeghe', 'Godige', or 'Codghe', which may well be a mispronunciation of 'Codici, codexes'.[4]

Taking another thread, and juggling a little with the names of his parents—Mser Tomas of Modena and Catlina of the house of *Bambagioli* of Ferrara—Guerrini finds a prototype in a certain Bongrazia, Graziolo, or Graziano de' Bambagioli, a Dante scholar, whose *Trattato delle virtù morali*, written in the fourteenth century, was falsely attributed to Robert of Naples at its publication in 1642. Guerrini believes in the corresponding antiquity of the mask of the Doctor. Rasi,[5] on the other hand, has a suggestion of stage ancestry to put forward on the evidence of the patronymic 'Bambas', and quotes a letter from Petrarch written to the Rector of Bologna on 10 August 1364 which describes the festivities in Venice after the conquest of Crete, 'and to that end they summoned from Ferrara Tommaso Bambasio . . . who throughout the state of Venice has the reputation that Roscius formerly had in Rome, and is to me as dear a friend as Roscius was to Cicero.'[6] Nothing more is known of this player and Rasi does not attempt to push the coincidence further.

The most substantial theory of the Doctor's origin depends upon his connexion with *Francolino*. Buried in the commentary upon Part LXIX of *Il Predicatore, overo Demetrio Falerio dell'elocutione con le parafrasi, e Commenti*

---

[1] P. A. Bianchieri, *Discorso*; this verse is quoted by O. Guerrini, *La Vita e le opere di G. C. Croce* (1879), p. 123, with the observation that in spite of his alleged parentage Gratiano's dialect betrays his Bolognese origin.

[2] Guerrini, op. cit., p. 123.

[3] See *Il Studio* (1602), by Gio. Gabriele da Modena detto Sivello.

[4] The letter to the Grand Duke (*infra*) is signed: 'Gracian delle Godige.' In 'Codghe' (see *infra*, F. Bartoli) there is probably a double allusion to 'codega', rump.

[5] Op. cit., i. 414.

[6] *Lettere* translated by Fracassetti (1867), vol. iv, p. 231.

e discorsi Ecclesiastici di Monsignor F. Francesco Panigorola, Vescovo D'Asti, published in Venice, 1642, but written before 1594, is the following account of the origin of the Mask of the Doctor:

'It is but a few years ago that Lucio, a famous comedian, and well-nigh the modern Roscius, being in Ferrara, noticed the novel fashions and odd mannerisms (*nuovi costumi e strane maniere*) of an old barber called Messer Gratiano dalle Cotiche, a native of Francolino, and drew upon them for a most ridiculous stage rôle, taken almost entirely from life (*sul freddo*), which was then for a long time excellently played by Lodovico of Bologna, and has since been exploited to such an extent that even off the stage it has occasioned many good compositions both in prose and verse in this manner of burlesque as it is now called.' [1]

If the picturesque quality of this story did not happen to remind us of the legends that account for the origin of Pulcinella and other Masks there would be nothing to prevent us from accepting it with as little misgiving as was felt by Quadrio who first brought it to light. But, however suspiciously well the story fits, it contains fact as well as fiction. Lodovico da Bologna is Ludovico de Bianchi, the author of the *Cento e Quindici Conclusioni*, who belonged to the *Gelosi* at least as early as 1578. The 'famous Lucio' is now hard to identify. The three claimants, Lutio, Lucio Fedele, and Luz Burchiella, may possibly be reduced to two, Fedele and Burchiella. The first 'Lutio' appears in the list of *Comici Uniti* playing in Ferrara in 1584. Here the order 'Gratiano, Lutio' prevents us from recognizing him as the doctor. It seems more likely that he played a lover's part and he is probably to be identified with the *Lucio Fedele Padovano* who belonged to the curiously constituted *Gelosi* in 1590 in company with Bernardino Lombardi, an established Gratiano. Rasi supposes that the second name *Fedele* marks Lutio as a member of the Company of the *Fedeli*, but this is unlikely: this company does not appear until the beginning of the seventeenth century, and it would hardly be appropriate for an actor to describe himself as of a less known company when he was acting with one so famous as the *Gelosi*. It is more likely a surname. Already by 1594

---

[1] p. 366. Note that 'delle Cottiche' is often misquoted as 'delle Cettiche'.

G. C. Capaccio published an imaginary letter to Sig. Lutio Fedele Comico sending him his comedy, 'not so much to thrust it upon the stage as to show his friends what gentle studies are his recreation', and he provides Lutio's response: 'La comedia di V. S. è stata recitata, et è riuscita cosi per eccellenza che non solo si è mostrata degna di comparire nell'humile Teatro di Lutio fedele, ma hà ella havuto bisogno un Cesare . . .'[1] A model answer in every way, but if Fedele had made his name as a Doctor a reply *alla Gratianesca* might have been expected.

The other 'Lutio', surnamed *Burchiella*, exists for us only on the authority of Francesco Bartoli who quotes a letter 'in lingua gratiana elegante' from the *Lettere facetie* of Cesare Rao, and refers to him as the author of a sonnet lamenting the death of Vincenza Armani.[2] I have not been able to examine the first edition (1576) of the *Lettere Facetie* from which Bartoli quotes the signature 'Luz Burchiella Gratian'. In the subsequent editions for 1585, 1596, 1598, 1610, which are advertised as enlarged or corrected, the letter is signed, 'Gracian dalle Codghe sont da Franculin', with no mention of the actor's name.

It was presumably on the strength of Panigorola's account that Mariotti[3] attributed to Burchiella the three letters *alla Gratianesca* which are preserved in the Medici Archives. All three are addressed to the Grand Duke of Tuscany and are dated and signed respectively:

(1) 6 Nov. 1576
Firenze
Graciano delle Godige
Comico Geloso.[4]

---

[1] *Il Secretario* (1594). See *infra*, Chapter IV.

[2] This sonnet is quoted by Rasi, op. cit., i. 534, from the *Oratione / d'Adriano Va/lerini Veronese, / In morte della Divina Signora / Vincenza Armani, Comica / Eccellentissima / Et alcune rime del/l'Istesso, e d'altri auttori, In lode / della medesima. / Con alquante leg/giadre è belle Compositioni di det/ta Signora Vincenza. In Verona, per Bastian dalle Donne, e Giovanni* Fratelli 1570. This is a very rare book which I have not been able to examine. See Rasi, i, p. 204.

[3] F. Marriotti, *Il Teatro in Italia nei secoli XVI, XVII, XVIII. Curiosità e notizie storiche corredate di molti documenti inediti.* Autografo inedito MS. Magliabech, II. iii. 454–6, Firenze, 1874–86.

[4] Arch. di Stato, Firenze. Fª 717, c. 373.

(2) (1578)
Il Dottor Graciano
Comico Geloso.[1]

(3) 6 Sett. 1589
Milano
Il Dottor Gratiano.[2]

A. Bartoli, however, appropriates all three letters for
Lodovico Bianchi, who was certainly 'Comico Geloso' by
1578, but who is not known to have used any surname other
than 'Partesano'. A letter from Venice 11 July 1587 is
signed: 'lodovicho di bianchi da bolognia deto il dotor
graciano di gelosi,'[3] and another from Pistoia, 21 ott. 1589:
'lodovico da Bianchi da Bologna detto il Dottor Gratiano.'[4]
There is no mention of the surname 'Godige' with reference
to a particular actor after 1576, though, like 'de' Bisognosi',
it became common property for the Gratiani of printed
plays.[5] Unless 'delle Godige' was an early nickname
invented for himself by Bianchi, the correct distribution of
these letters is probably the first to Luz Burchiella and the
rest to Bianchi.

It is disappointing that the first three and the last of these
letters are written in what appears to be a formal script and
yield no specimen of the Doctor's autograph. A fourth
(11 July 1587) gives us de Bianchi's hand, but we
have no means of comparing it with that of the possible
Burchiella.   There is, however, a support for belief in the
shadowy 'Luz' in Rossi's *La Fiammella* when Bergamino
recounts his dream of Hell, where, among the crowd of
players he saw:

BARBA PARIANA
Le quel chi mena innanz' e in dre per tut
Domandand Signor LUTI la salcizza?

So by 1584 he was eating his Bologna sausage below: it
takes a ghost from the other world to convince us.

---

[1] Arch. di Stato, Firenze. Fa 717, c.
352. The date is suggested by Marriotti
from internal evidence.
[2] Fa 808, c. 369.

[3] Fa 788, c. 321.
[4] Fa 809, c. 579.
[5] *Il Studio* (1662), and *Pantalone
Imbertonao* (1626).

DOCTORS AND PEDANTS

However futile the attempt to sift fact from fiction in the matter of the Doctor's origin may be, everything points to the development of the mask from a character sketch rather than from a dramatic type. This, as Graziano would say, is 'certificabilitudinitissimamient'.[1] There is nothing to support his derivation from the Dosseno of the Atellan farce, and very little to confirm the theory that he is the popular adaptation of the Pedant of the Commedia erudita. There were pedants as well as doctors in the Commedia dell'arte; functionally they are interchangeable, but the types remain distinct. This is proved by the list of dramatis personae for *La Scola di Terenzio, overo il Dottore Maestro di Scola* which notes: 'Dottor Terenzio pedante, ovvero detta parte si può fare di Dottor Graziano'; and *Gl'Imbrogli di Coviello* which has 'Dottore ò Pedante'. Nor in the plays published by academicians does the Doctor supplant the Pedant; in Gattici's *Le Pazzie Giovenili* (1626) there is Galateo Pedante, as well as Gratiano Sciocco: and in *Travagli d'amore* by M. A. Gattinon (1622), Pomponio Pedante, and Gratiano Dottore di legge. L'Estoile in *Les Comédiens de la Cour* (1603) couples but does not confuse the types:

> Il faut un Gratian, qui fasse le pédant
> Et qu'il ne sache rien au fond de la doctrine.

The Pedant was proper to the Commedia erudita where the satire of his laboured Latin found a fit audience. He strays on to the popular stage over the borderland where the Commedia erudita and the Commedia dell'arte merge, in the plays of Calmo, Della Porta, Verucci, and G. B. Andreini. In *Olimpia* and *Li Due Fratelli Rivali*, before they are reduced to scenari, two clever pedants bandy etymologies in Latin and good Tuscan in the academic tradition; Archibio, Calmo's pedant in *La Travaglia*, talks Bergomask, and in Verucci's *Li Diversi Linguaggi* he is a Sicilian who tries to bribe the waiting-maid with the promise of a Ciceronian oration. Among other masks in the *Lucinda*

---

[1] Ercole Cimilotti, *I Falsi Dei* (1599); cp. Rao, *Lettere Facetie*. Cp. Holofernes' 'Honorificabilitudinitatibus'; this tongue-twister is also used in *The Dutch Courtezan, Lenten Stuff*, and *The Mad Lover*.

of Fr. Solincorte (1633) there is Heraclipostano, and in Righelli's *Serva Astuta* (1632) Diomede, pedants, and another in *Vittoria* by F. Rotondi da Sonnino (1650). Marcone, the 'pedante sciocco' of Bricci's *Tartaruca*, is completely degraded; he hobnobs with Pantalone over the uselessness of Latin. In the second of the improvised comedies which G. B. Andreini introduces in *Le Due Commedie in Commedia* the *Comici Appassionati* present a Pedant and Ceccobimbi, an old Florentine, instead of the masks of Gratiano and Pantalone which have been used already in the rival performance of the *Accademici*. The Pedant hails Ceccobimbi with: 'Maximus vir in oculis vestris' and proposes, 'copulam filiam meam tecum in matrimonio'; the girl is described as, 'lascivula, ha il petto procace, occhi blandienti, e nella rossa fronte, micanti, e ludibondi . . . cum le treccie cumplicate cum cordicelle'. He informs Ceccobimbi, 'lingua vernacula optime intelligo sed non bene loquor'.[1] Another obviously verbose pedant is the Poeta of della Porta's *La Turca*.

It appears that Perrucci was not accurate when he stated in 1699 that Pedants had not been played 'all'improviso'. Cataldo and Claudione are pedants in Scala's *Teatro*; in 1693 M. S. Crivelli played Zabarello, pedante, in *Plauto alla Moderna*. Perucci's notion that the Pedant could be presented by grafting the language of Fidenzio[2] or Merlin Coccajo on to the part of the Doctor had been tried some eighty years before by Briccio in *La Ventura di Zanni e di Pescariello*.

It was the Doctor's most important function to sustain

---

1 Garzoni, *Piazza Universale* (1585), p. 92, gives as an example of Pedantry: 'Dimmi elegante Viatore qual è l'itinere Germano di pervenire alla città di Romalo?' See also a leaflet preserved as 1071. g. 12 (8) in the British Museum, entitled *I Freschi Della Villa* (1634), containing 'Canzonetta alla Pedantesca' (p. 35), in which all the lines end in X. In the same collection (p. 44) are 'Stanzie alla Gratianesca' making play with animal noises.

2 Camillo Scrofa (d. 1576) is appropriately introduced and dismissed in his own epitaph:
Glottochrysio Fidentio eruditissimo
Ludimagistro è in questo gran sarcophago
Camillo crudo più d'un Anthropophago
L'uccise. O caso à i buoni damnosissimo.
'*Aldeano*', *Sopra la Poesia Giocosa*, 1634, recognized a mixture of Latin and Greek with the vernacular as 'lingua Pedantesca' which was to be distinguished from the colloquial use of Latin in Coccajo's *Poesia Maccaronica*.

the part of the second father and old rival lover, but the Pedant of the Commedia erudita, on the contrary, has no family, and little time for diversion: he spends his days tutoring feckless young men and avoiding the parasites and urchins who molest him. It is only on certain rare occasions in the Commedia dell'arte when the Doctor appears as a schoolmaster or as some young nobleman's guardian that the parts may have been confounded.

So far from the Doctor taking over the practice of the Pedant, it is rather that the Pedant on the popular stage is the *locum tenens* for the Doctor, but a remark in *The Compleat Gentleman* (1627) indicates the common practice of the early seventeenth century which led to a pardonable confusion between types originally distinct. 'In Italy,' says Peacham, 'of all professions, that of Pedanteria is held in basest repute; the Schoole-master almost in every Comedy being brought upon the stage to parallel the Zani or Pantaloun.'[1]

THE CAPTAIN

When Captain Spavento told Trappola his servant that he was born from one of the stones that Deucalion threw over his shoulder, and was renewed every century like the Phoenix, he came nearer to the truth than he intended.[2] For a part to tear a cat in the Commedia dell'arte revived the vainglorious captain of the classical comedy. Thrasonian brag delivered in Castilian gave the mask of the Captain a chance to satirize the Spanish adventurers who followed Charles V into Italy and overran the cities of Naples and Milan.[3] Threatening in Italo-Greek, the Captain of Calmo's comedies presents the Greek soldier of fortune, the 'stradiotto', to the Venetians who suffered from the type in real life.[4] Others, speaking Tuscan, are bitten in for us by Garzoni's acid:

If you will name all the vices in a word say, 'modern soldier'. . . . They are effeminate in their persons, devotees of Venus and Bacchus.

---

[1] p. 27.
[2] *Le Bravure del Capitano Spavento*, Rag. LXIV, p. 128, ed. 1624.
[3] For examples of the insolence of the Spaniards see the anecdotes in

'Vincentio Saviolo his Practice'.
[4] Two leaflets printed in 1572 (Brit. Museum, 1071. g. 7 (15 and 19)) are concerned with the buffoon Manoli Blessi, Strathiotto.

. . . And all this has come about because the military profession has become a dunghill of rogues, the scum of the populace, a sink of poltroonery. You will find few who care for the true honour of a soldier, and use in greatness of spirit and nobility of heart to win fame and glory.[1]

There are only too many originals for the mask of the Captain both on and off the stage. Menander's credible Polemon puffs out into the toadlike Pyrgopolinices, Manducus is a military ogre in the Roman farces, the strident voice of Spampana is heard in the *Farsa satyra morale* by Venturino da Pesaro (1521), and Baïf has his bravo Taillebras. There were braggarts in romances and *novelle*,[2] in the streets there were the bullies

who prance like war-horses at the scent of battle and when the quarrel is broached, trumpet like elephants at the noise of the tumult . . . shaking their swords, they flash round like serpents, their hands riveted to their weapons, beating the earth with their feet like so many Baiardos untethered, whirling about their plumes . . . every day, every hour, every instant, every moment they can talk of nothing but of slaughter, the fracture of legs and arms and back-bones. This is the matter of their thoughts, the subject of their profession; this is the intent of their spirits which most certainly are nourished on steel and generated from iron mines. Their study is of nothing but how to kill this one or that, their aim is but to avenge the world's wrongs which they have taken to heart, not to benefit their friends, but to butcher their enemies.[3]

Such a superfluity of material hardly left the Commedia dell'arte scope for invention. It is enough to prick down the grotesque muster-roll of the Captains, they are mostly fantastic names as well on the popular as on the academic stage.[4]

CAPITANO SPAVENTO DEL VALL'INFERNO

From the earliest days of the Commedia dell'arte, with

[1] *Piazza Universale* (1585), pp. 651-2.

[2] F. Novati, *Giorn. Stor.* (1885), pp. 279-82.

[3] Garzoni, op. cit., p. 803. Compare the account of the Venetian bravoes given in Coryat's *Crudities* (ed. cit. i, p. 413): 'There are certaine desperate and resolute villaines in Venice, called Braves, who at some unlawful times do commit great villainy. They wander abroad very late in the night to and fro for their prey, like hungry Lyons, being armed with a privy coate of maile, a gauntlet upon their right hand and a little sharpe dagger called a stiletto.'

[4] See Appendix E, p. 51.

'Lasca's' *Capitani*, the 'Spagnolo delle Comedie' who was summoned in Mantua in 1567,[1] and the Don Diego Mendozza of Troiano's invention, the mask of the braggart captain persisted and flourished like a weed, until, transplanted into the rich soil of Andreini's fantasy, it produced the mask of Capitano Spavento del Vall'Inferno, a great glaring dandelion that seeded itself over the later comedy.

Some active service and a year's slavery in the Turkish galleys taught Andreini something of life. When at last he was settled with the *Gelosi*, something about the mask of the 'arrogant ambitious soldier' attracted him from the parts of the lover, the Sicilian Doctor, and the Magician which he had taken hitherto. He never acted after Isabella's death in 1604, and three years later arranged a collection of all the hyperboles which he was wont to declaim in public and private comedies into the imaginary dialogues between the Captain Spavento and his knowing servant Trappola, and dedicated them to Amedeo di Savoia as the *Bravure del Capitano Spavento*.

This book was translated into French in 1608 and 1638,[2] reissued in Italian in 1609, 1619, and supplemented by nineteen new discourses in 1624. It was the powder magazine for the Captains of the Commedia dell'arte.

Captain Spavento delights to display learning as well as valour. He can mention twenty-two poets in a breath, and call for his shaving water with a fine phrase from Castiglione.[3] He inherits his sword from Xerxes, Cyrus, Darius, Alexander, Romulus, Tarquin, and Caesar.[4] He will write to Isabella on the hide of the dragon of the Hesperides, and seal it with the head of Medusa.[5] He has associated with the *Accademici* and will discuss such abstractions as

---

[1] D'Ancona, op. cit., ii. p. 443.

[2] (a) Les Bravacheries du capitaine Spavente (1608), trans. Jacques de Fonteny Parisien, contrôleur des comédiens étrangers au théâtre de l'Hôtel de Bourgogne. Baschet, p. 174, describes this as rather a redaction than a translation. There is a copy in the Bib. de l'Arsenal which I have not been able to consult. (b) Le Capitan par un com-

median de la trouppe *Jalouse*, Paris, chez Anthoine Robinot, 1638, Baschet, p. 174.

[3] Rag. XXV. He will shave 'prima che l'Aurora scacciando le notturne stelle venga a sparger sopra di noi Rose e viole'; compare the penultimate paragraph of *Il Cortegiano*.

[4] Op. cit., Rag. VI.

[5] Rag. IV.

Friendship,[1] Avarice,[2] Envy,[3] Free Will,[4] or bandy maxims with Trappola:

Cap. The inevitability of death is a bridle upon the pride of man.
Trap. Man fears death because he will not consider life.
Cap. Socrates as he drank the poison, said that then he was beginning to live.
Trap. The birth of a child is the funeral of an old man.
Cap. Man is born weeping, lives laughing, and sighing, dies.
Trap. The bad man is born to die and the good to live.[5]

It is Trappola's duty to lead the Captain by the nose. He tempts him out with questions, goads him to boastings, and peeping between the legs of this Colossus takes his revenge by impertinent asides. The Captain tells how he steered a whale through the straits of Gibraltar, and swallowed up two warriors for the sake of the ransom which they would fetch at Genoa. 'And then as day dawned,' says Trappola, 'you woke up and the dream fled.'[6]

After this fiftieth discourse the servant says wearily that he has heard so many marvels that he does not know which to credit. 'Believe whichever you please, Trappola mine,' says the Captain lost in a world of slain monsters, kneeling tyrants, adoring queens, and cowering Deities. The coursers of the sun take fright at his eyebrow.[7] He has played football with Death and the Devil against Nature, Fortune, and Time.[8] His fantasy numbs all calculation, for he counts in hundreds and thousands. Only America has refused to acknowledge his fame and he goes to subdue it.[9] He slits Time into three, and calls the pieces the Past, the Present, and the Future;[10] sucks up seas,[11] and kicks the moon about Florence.[12] When for a day he played Death's part he was found too destructive, heads rattled over the earth like Neapolitan billiard-balls.[13] He is magnificent in his absurdity, like some glittering, impotent tin dragon.

[1] Rag. XXV, XLIV.
[2] Rag. XXXII.
[3] Rag. XLVI.
[4] Rag. XXXIX.
[5] Rag. XVII.
[6] Rag. L.
[7] Rag. XLI.
[8] Rag. IX.
[9] Rag. XI.
[10] Rag. XXV, XXXIV.
[11] Rag. XII, XV, XVI.
[12] Rag. XLIII.
[13] Rag. XXII.

Now that the martial drum is silent he will tell Trappola
of a warlike idea that flashed across his mind. It is this:

Capt. A few months back I would have you know I had a desire
to assault the glistering stars. It was a memorable day and we should
mark it, not with a white stone as did the Ancients, but with Hieroglyphic columns, with Pyramids and Colossi.

Trap. On such a day it would have been as well to have recalled
the temerity of the fallen Giants, the Sons of Earth and of Titan who
were struck by fulminating Jove and buried under the mighty mountains of Olympus, Pelion, and Ossa for making War upon the glistering
stars.

Capt. So I got me ready [continues the Captain unheeding], and
began to arm strangely, fantastically. I put the Tower of Nimrod on
my back for a cuirass, and Mount Taurus for a morion upon my head;
and when head, breast, arms, and shoulders were furnished I took the
Rainbow as my sling, the Cretan labyrinth for a quiver, and all the
Pyramids of Egypt for bolts and shafts. Then, full of wrath and fury
I went up to the top of Olympus firmly resolved to break and shatter
both the Poles. When I was come to the summit of this great mountain I began to shoot at the Firmament and let fly so many shafts
that it was riddled like a sieve.

Trap. Well, well, this is indeed a tale for women by the fireside
munching hot chestnuts and sipping sweet wine. . . .

Capt. And when I had riddled the sky, the fixed and the lesser stars
suddenly began to fall. At this Father Jove, the Ruler of Heaven,
seeing such ruin and massacre began to shout, 'To arms, to arms, to
arms', and on the instant, in the twinkling of an eye all the Gods
came forth armed with burgonets to make villainous assault on the
madman, as the Divine poet Ariosto hath it.

Trappola interrupts again, but the Captain steams ahead:

And when I beheld the army of the courts of heaven drawn up
to make desperate attack upon me, what did I do? I took aim and
discharged a pyramid into the face of Jove. Jove, seizing that same
pyramid and changing it into a white-hot thunderbolt flung it back
at my head. Taking it with my right I sent it again to the heavens
and made after it with a leap so dexterous that I alighted in the middle
of the heavenly squadrons. Arrived there I drew my sharp and flaming
sword, put the whole army to flight, and taking prisoner the Lord of
the Air I bound him to the axle of the Hemisphere and began to
address him with bitter words.

His threats were interrupted by Venus whose sweet

smiles and sighs displayed 'the rich treasure of her gleaming pearls within the ruby shell of her empurpled mouth'; she addressed him thus:

Valiant Captain Spavento, worthy to reign not in earth only but here among us in the starry spheres, if ever Love's arrows found your heart, if ever Beauty human or divine had power to warm and to inflame your breast, by both of these I beseech you, I pray you, I conjure you to grant me this favour and concede me the Great Father Jove; and when you have done this, according to my hope and trust in your innate nobility, you shall for a reward command the hearts of all the beautiful ladies that the sun discovers on his daily round.

Trap. Adultery would pass for chastity in such language, but what did you reply to these sugared little words of Madam Venus?

Capt. For the moment I was dazzled by the Cyprian loveliness, and overcome by the sweet discourse of Cytherea, I became all gentleness, and releasing Jove on the instant I restored him his realm, and after taking leave of Venus, I leaped toward Mother Earth and landed on the Piazza of Venice at its crowded hour, where I was welcomed and feasted by the illustrious Senators.

Trap. I am not surprised, for it is the custom of that magnificent State to welcome and entertain all strangers.

Capt. Well, Trappola, what do you think of this my noble and warlike conception?

Trap. Splendid, and worthy of your mind. Indeed the world is more delighted with your valour and prowess than Athens was with her philosophers, Babylon with her miracles, and Rome her Emperors. Master, remember that the dinner-hour is almost past, and as the Florentine said, 'It is time'.

Capt. Let us go, for before dinner I want to tell you another military scheme, far greater than the first; it will serve to whet your appetite.

Trap. Master dear, my appetite needs no conversation as a sauce, and it does not matter about telling me other ideas this morning, let us go. It is quite enough for me to know that you are one at whose voice Thunder and Earthquakes are afraid, and at whose eye lightnings and bolts are kindled, and that when your mighty hand is raised to shake the bright steel the Earth is depopulated and the Kingdom of the Underworld enlarged.

Capt. Certainly this is so: then let us go remove the rust from the teeth, beginning with a good broth of iron filings sprinkled with gunpowder cheese, seasoned with arsenic and sweetened somewhat with rhubarb.

Trap. You can swallow this good broth yourself, I will abstain, and if there is nothing else it seems I must make up my mind to a fast although there is no vigil ordained. Come along.[1]

On another occasion the Captain looks forward to 'something tasty in the way of the marrow of lions, serpent's tongues, and a basilisk's brain'.[2] Neptune once sent him a barrel of salted Syrens.[3] When he dined with the Devil they eat some Lutheran roast or the hash of a Calvinist.[4] If this is the meat on which he feeds no wonder he is grown so great. This is no mere caricature, no satire, it is an ogre flown with the essence of fermented vainglory. Captains of Callot's etching with their wild, sharp features, their swords thrust through ragged scabbards, rakish feathers, swinging cloaks, and extravagant attitudes of courtliness or threat are the only fit illustrations of Andreini's freakish fantasy.

In the *Bravure* the Captain casts his slough. In an age that has lost the taste for the windy war of words that exhilarated at the Renaissance, it seems almost incredible that an audience would endure nightly such vociferations. Their popularity is evident. There are Captains in all but eleven of Scala's plays, in forty-six of the Locatelli scenari, twenty-one of Venetian, four of the Florentine, twenty-two in the Neapolitan, six in the Perugian, and at least eight in the later Casanatense collections. Whether it is for soliloquy or dialogue he enters 'facendo sue bravure', or has a 'scena squarcionesca cirimoniosa'.[5]

There is some intimate connexion between Spavento and the Captains of Della Porta's creation, Dante, Gorgoleone, and Montebellonio, who has tossed up Mount Mauritania like a balloon and on Tuesdays diets upon a salad of cannon-balls and bullets that turn to steel inside, and only forbears his earthquaking head out of consideration for Pluto and Proserpina who have already sent a letter of complaint.[6]

CARDONE AND OTHERS

Andreini was the greatest but not the first of the captains of the Commedia dell'arte. Playing *La Pazzia d'Isabella*

---

[1] Rag. II.
[2] Rag. III.
[3] Rag. XVIII.
[4] Rag. XVII.
[5] Perugian Misc. A. 20, f. 297.
[6] *Li due Fratelli rivali*, iii.

at the wedding of Ferdinando Medici with Christina of Lorraine on 13 May 1589 Andreini, 'si mise poi ad imitare li linguaggi di tutti i suoi comici, come del Pantalone, del Gratiano, del Zanni, del Pedrolino, del Francatrippe, del Burattino del *Capitan Cardone*, e della Franceschina'.[1] Cardone is the captain type chosen by Orazio Vecchi for *L'Anfiparnasso*, 1597, and by Boccalini in his *Parnasso*, 1613. 'Aldeano' mentions him with Mattamoros for his Spanish-Italian dialect. In Buonarrotti's *La Fiera* he stands apart twirling his black moustaches fiercely, his hand on his sword ready to meet mountains, penetrate to the Earth's centre, to cut Pluto's horns, take him by the tail, and having soused him in the Stygian marsh to eat him alive and raw, while he is actually a bigger coward than an officer of the watch. He is set down by Callot, but there is no record of the name of the original actor.

In 1607 Jacques Gaultier dedicated to M. Vieillart a little volume of *Rodomuntadas Castellanas, recopiladas de los commentarios de los muy aspantosos, terribles et invincibles Capitanes, Metamoros, Crocodillo y Raja broqueles* with a parallel French translation. It is to this collection that Vincenzo Belando refers in his preface to *Gl'Amorosi Inganni*, 1609, when to clear himself from suspicion of plagiarism he calls his friends to witness that his comedy was begun in jest, and finished in 1593.[2]

To believe in Belando's originality in this instance is only to prove that the actors drew upon a common stock of hyperbolic conceits. Basilisco, Belando's boaster, has hardened himself upon a mattress that is made from the beards of Captains, and the mustachios of Ensigns, and against cushions stuffed with Amazon's hair.[3] An amplification of this notion reappears without his consent in the fifteenth Rodomontade; but the economy had been practised before when Tempesta in Secchi's *La Beffa* confides that: 'There

---

[1] Quoted by Rasi, ii, p. 243, from the *Diario* of Pavoni, 1589, which I have not been able to consult.

[2] 'Che la mia comedia è principiata l'anno del 93 da Scherzo, e finita da vero.' The admitted imitation of the *Seignior Cocodrile* (or *Crocodile*, p. 145)

in J. Eliot's *Ortho-Epia* (1593) confirms this suspicion of common material. I am indebted to Professor Nicoll for drawing attention to this palpably Commedia dell'arte brag (*Masks, Mimes and Miracles*, pp. 250, 309).

[3] Act II, sc. i, p. 61.

was a time when the Captain and I never wiped our shoes but on the beards torn from other assassins, our mattresses and cushions were never made of anything else',[1] Parabosco had given such boasts to Spavento in *Il Pellegrino* (1552). There are echoes of Fiorillo in Rodomontades 8 and 43. Mastica's salutation to Mattamoros as 'Re de Paladin, fior della cavaglieria di Rodomonti, d'Orlandi, di Rinaldi' is merely translated.[2] Mattamoros's tale of how two teeth were knocked out by a cannon-ball which he took out of his mouth and hurled back at the enemy,[3] is improved by the addition of fifty-five casualties: but what are fifty-five to a Captain who reckons in hundreds? There is Andreini's vein in Rodomontades 38 and 45 when the Captain dices with Destiny and kills Hercules, Love, and Death in a shooting match.

By virtue of Andreini's fine style the *Bravure*, published a year later, overtook the pirate. Belando read the book from end to end, and although he maintains his independence, shows his respect of Captain Spavento's reputation. The duodecimo volumes of Rodomontades were reissued, revised, augmented, translated into Italian and English,[4]

---

1 Rasi, op. cit., i. 76, *La Beffa*. I have not been able to see this play, but Allacci quotes a single edition for 1584.

2 *Angelica* (ed. 1584), I. 4, p. 12.

3 *Angelica*, I. 4, p. 14, and Rod. XLIII.

4 1. Reprinted at Lyon, 1619.

2. The edition 'Rouen chez Claude le Villain 1626' prints only the French version and adds nine new Rodomontades.

3. In 1627 Sarzina of Venice added an Italian translation prepared by Lorenzo Franciosini da Castelfiorentino to the Spanish and French of the 1607 edition.

4. In 1627 'chez Jacques Cailloüé Rouen', the augmented edition, was issued in French and Spanish.

5. The original forty-seven are printed with an English translation by I. W., as 'Miles Gloriosus, The Spanish Braggadocio, or, the humours of the Spaniard'. London, Printed by T. H.

for I. E. 1630.' A friend of I. W. assures us that 'There's wisdom under this frivolity'.

6. B. Croce, 'Ricerche Ispano-Italiane', p. 24, quotes an edition by Gio. Pietro Cardi, Milano, 1643.

7. A careless and defective reprint of the first twenty-nine Rodomontades in French and Spanish was published in 1644.

8. An enlarged edition amounting to fifty-two, with the addition of 'Fanfaron, after Rojobroqueles', came from Cailloüé, Rouen, 1650.

9. A rough English translation and transposition of forty-nine Rodomontades was published in 1672, as 'Al-Man-Sol / or, Rhodomontado / of the / Most Horrible Terrible and / Invincible Captain / Sr Frederick Fright-all. / London, / Printed by Peter Lillicrap, for Philip Brigg / living in Mermaid Court at the lower end of Pater-noster-row.'

but they do not rank with the handsome quarto of the *Bravure* that fixed the type of the Captain for the first period of the Commedia dell'arte.

FUNCTION

In a plot the Captain is like Leviathan on a fish-hook. As an elder brother in Locatelli's comedies he can behave quite normally; he is better suited as a jealous rival or an irascible stranger whose luggage the innkeeper gives to the lost twin-brother by mistake.[1]

His cowardice makes a good scene; the challenge is no sooner accepted than he remembers a pressing engagement elsewhere, and in *Li Diversi Linguaggi* he refuses to fight lest the soft blood of the Bolognese should destroy the temper of his weapon; in a Venetian scenario he makes himself wounds of red wax.[2] Sometimes he goes mad for love and flinging down cap, sword, and cloak goes off to drown himself. Pantalone and Zanni find his belongings and try to piece them together in the dark, pretending they are the fragments of some wild beast. The Captain who has thought better of his resolution at the sight of the cold Tiber comes back and is taken for a ghost.[3] In *La Nave* he appears on board ship invoking the aid of Jupiter against the Magician who keeps a Queen in his tower. On another occasion he is not so heroic. Franceschina undertakes to admit him to her mistress if he will consent to be tied up in a sack like a pig. She makes the same bargain with Franzese, and then fetches the pork-butcher and sells him the pigs in the pokes. The butcher flourishes his knife and makes suitable noises until the Captain can bear it no longer and struggles out of the sack and makes off.[4]

SPANISH TYPES

The Captain was only played as a Spaniard at the actor's discretion. There were reasons for and against. Cecchini believes that 'this hyperbolic part sounded better in Spanish 'than in Italian, as in a language more fitted for extravagance'.

---

[1] *Li due simili di Plauto.*   [3] *L'Amante Ingrato.*
[2] *Il Fido Amico.*   [4] *Li Porci.*

The part was beyond reform, but he makes an interesting comparison with the Captains of real life:

In Paris I have listened over the table to some fantastical (or should I say bestial) humour who had served in the fiercest wars in Europe: 'With so many horses, in so many days, he would undertake to seize the Castle of Milan, and pass on through Italy, routing, destroying, doing this, saying that, and so forth.' And when a cooler companion said that was impossible, he would leap over the table and shout in a fury, 'You shall see,' and rush out at such a rate that had they not assured me that he had gone to bed I would have asked him to spare the house property that I have in Ferrara. Come now, let a man like this be presented on the stage and leave those who jump up into the Empyrean to sup with Jove, to the mad-houses.[1]

The dialect, for Spanish was hardly a foreign language to an Italian of the Seicento, was tempting for the opportunities that it afforded for the Zanni for 'lazzi' and equivocations.[2] But it was dangerous; Perrucci remarks that the Spaniard cannot bear to be derided, he may laugh at the bravura but he will not stand the presentation of a soldier as a coward. One wretched actor in Pesaro was beaten to death by Spanish officials for his caricature.[3]

When it was injudicious to hint at the Spaniard, the Captain might have a Calabrian salutation, a Venetian a Neapolitan or a Sicilian dialogue.[4]

Senigaglia[5] and Croce[6] distinguish nicely between the stage representations of the Spaniard and the Captain in the Commedia erudita during the sixteenth century. The degenerate Italian Captains and later the French soldiery came in for the first dash of satiric representation. In Commedia erudita the Spaniard is not necessarily a soldier. But the braggart of the stage and the braggart of the street soon coalesce. The inexact chronology of our notices of the Commedia dell'arte makes it impossible to say whether the

[1] *Frutti della moderna Commedia* (1628).
[2] *La Trappolaria.* For the 'lazzo' of 'hermano non vi conosco', see Bartoli. See also Hondedei to Camillo Oliveri, 11 November 1615. Bib. Oliveriano di Pesaro, Fa 448, c. 18, quoted by Saviotti in *Giorn. Stor.*, xli, p. 63.
[3] Croce, *Saggi*, p. 242, quoted Del

Cerro, *Nel Regno delle Maschere*, p. 116. See also Croce, *Teatri di Napoli*, p. 696, and *Pulcinella*, p. 42, for an anecdote of a Pulcinella who was beaten for satirizing Spaniards.
[4] Rasi, i. 78; 71.
[5] *Captain Spavento.*
[6] *Ricerche Ispano-Italiane* (1898), ii.

distinction was observed on the popular stage, so far as we know the Captain is not always a Spaniard but a Spaniard is always a Captain.[1]

THE BRAVO

Watching the swashbucklers in the piazza, Garzoni distinguishes between the regular soldiery and the free-lances, Bulli, Bravazzi, Spadacini, Taglianti,[2] or Sherri (*Sgherri*, swaggerers) of the piazza: the Commedia dell'arte shows the same division between Captains and 'bravi'.

In *Il Fromento* the Captain hires a bravo to kill Lelio. In one of Scala's scenari Pantalone sends for Nicoletto his bravo to defend him against Capitano Spavento who demands the hand of Isabella: there is nothing to choose between the two spitfires for swagger and cowardice, but the Captain ranks as a gentleman, the bravo as a hireling.[3] A few down-at-heel Captains degrade themselves to the status of the mercenary adventurers,[4] desperately named Malacarne,[5] Affranio, Tarantiello,[6] Momoletto.[7] The bravo is a plot-agent, not a character; in comparison with the reach

[1] Hondedei observes that for the *Confidenti* who played in Bologna in November 1615 'il Capitano fa molte volte il Capitano italiano e così tutti fanno all'occasione parti doppie'.

[2] See G. C. Croce, *La Tremenda e Spaventevole compagnia de Tagliacantoni overo Scapigliati* (1621); *Della compagnia nobilissima de' Tagliacantoni, descrittione universale di Buoso Tomani, Cittadino lucchese* (1602); 'Vanto che fa Trematerra Arcibravo alla presenza della sua Signora'. 'Vanto ridicoloso che fa l'arcibravazzo Smedolla alla sua Signora chiamata Madonna Ninetta Teneruzzi di M. Durindello Rastellanti della valle Bergamina' (1619). See *Miscuglio delle rime Zannesche di Zan Muzzina al Trionfo di Scappino*, by B. Bocchini, for the 'Smargiassata d'un Bravo' (p. 160).

See O. Guerrini, *Vita e le Opere di G. C. Croce* (1879), for 'Bravate, razzate, et arcibulate dell'Arcibravo Smedola rossi sfonna piatti, sbrana Leoni, sbudella Tigre et ancidatore de gli

Huomini muorti. Chillo che frange li monti e spacco lo Monno per lo mezzo e insomma l'arcibravura, terrore e tremore della Tierra e dell'Inferno. Con la capricciosa e ben compita Livrea del detto Smedola rossi' (1612 and 1628); with this compare a leaflet in the British Museum, 1071. g. 71, *La sontuosissima, e capriciosissima ben compita Livrea dell'Arcibravazzo Smedolla Vossi* (1624), and the copy (1071. g. 51), 1596, of the *Brave tremende del capitano Belerofonte Scarabombardone da Rocca di Ferro. Tratenimento piacevole in dialogo*, only quoted by Guerrini for 1629.

[3] Scala, xxxiii.

[4] See Scala, xv, and Capitano Tagliavento bravo in P. Lunardi's *Il Servo Astuto* (1586).

[5] M. A. Gattinon, *Travagli d'amore* (1622).

[6] Gattici, *Le Disgratie di Burattino* (licensed 1619, pr. 1626).

[7] Gioanelli, *Pantalone Bullo* (1693).

of a Capitano, he has only a pawn's move. Uncloak ten
bravi and nine will be Zanni disguised. In *Il Pozzo* Pantalone and the Doctor, between whom there is an old feud,
hire each a bravo, Zanni and Scapino. The supposed
assassins meet and instead of fighting discover that they are
old acquaintances and embrace each other to the disgust of
their employers. To reverse the situation Burattino and
Zanne of Verucci's comedy, *Il Servo Astuto*, quarrel over
Nespola the serving-maid; Burattino engages Pascarello as
a bravo to do away with Zanne, but Pascarello thinks he will
get better terms by encouraging Zanne to bid for his
services against Burattino; he loses his chance of 100 scudi
and is beaten down to a few 'quatrini', while the enemies
forget their quarrel in the excitement of the bargaining and
go off arm in arm.

If the tenth bravo is a lover he may take possession of
the plot. In the first version of the *Basilisco of Barnagasso*
[*sic*] offered in the Neapolitan collection, Flaminia is lodged
with Pollicinella, a spendthrift merchant, as his maid Spinetta,
for the sake of her lover Lelio who is disguised as a bravo
Basilisco. When the Captain threatens destruction if he
cannot have Spinetta, Pollicinella hires Basilisco as a pro-
tector. The bravo is only too efficient, he batters the
Captain until Policinella has to beseech him to desist, and
still he refuses all rewards. At last a donation is arranged,
and after a prolonged refusal Basilisco suddenly accepts all
offers, seizes the merchant's goods, turns him and Spinetta
out of doors and answers all their entreaties with a parcel
of paper spiders. As they turn mournfully away Spinetta
remembers the trick of the soporific flower;[1] they leave it
near Basilisco and get back into the house while he sleeps.
When he wakes it is towards the end of the third act, and
then nothing remains but to explain that he is Lelio and
that this was a plot to cure Pollicinella of prodigality and
Spinetta of suspicion; their marriage restores good feeling,
and the next scenario presents a variant as the *Basilisco di
Berganasso* and the *Dragon di Moscovie*. It was a popular
play with Parisian audiences.

---

[1] The trick of the enchanted flower is also used in *L'Amante Tradito*.

THE SERVANTS

ETYMOLOGY OF 'ZANNI'

The vigour of a crossbreed which works in all the characters of the Commedia dell'arte is most potent in the Zanni. Studied in the scenari the Plautine strain comes out strongest; Zanni performs every function and has every characteristic of the plotting slave, while Zanni of the rhymes, 'lazzi', and anecdotes of the miscellanies, and the dialogue of the printed plays, is to the life the Bergomask porter of the sixteenth century. His mongrel nature might be symbolized in the etymological controversy over his name. For critics who like to contemplate the likeness between the Commedia dell'arte and the Roman popular stage the coincidence of 'Zanni' with the non-classical 'τζάννος'[1] and Latin 'sannio', a buffoon,[2] has stood in the way of the scientific derivation of 'Zanni' as the dialectal pronunciation of 'Gianni' the diminutive of 'Giovanni', for which there is overwhelming evidence.[3]

In many plays the forms 'Zanne', 'Giovanni', and 'Zuanne' are distributed according to the dialect of the speaker.[4] Bartolommeo Bocchini refers to himself as 'Giovanni Bocchini detto Zan Muzzina' and uses 'Zan Gurgolo' for the commoner form 'Giangurgolo'.[5] The name is variously spelt 'Zan, Zane, Zani, Zanni, Zanne, Zagni', but there are instances of each form referring unmistakably to the word as the generic term for actors and buffoons.[6]

[1] Ménage, *Origini della lingua Italiana*.

[2] Riccoboni refers to Cicero, *De Oratore*, Lib. II, 61. Quadrio mentions, and De Amicis persists, in this etymology.

[3] See Croce, *Saggi sulla letteratura Italiana del seicento* (1911), p. 220; V. Rossi, *Giorn. Stor.* ix, p. 285; L. Rasi, op. cit., i. 462; A. Mortier, *Ruzzante*, Chap. IX; D. Merlini, *Saggio di ricerche sulla satira contro il villano* (1894), p. 120.

[4] *Il Servo Astuto* (1610), Verucci. Fritel, given among the dramatis personae as 'Zanne', is hailed by Pantalone as 'Zuanne', I. i, and by Lelio as 'Giovanni', II. ii. In Briccio's *Pantalone*

Imbertonao (1617), 'Zanni' in the dramatis personae is 'Zuane' in II. i. An anonymous leaflet (Brit. Mus. 1071. g. 10 (21)) entitled: *Vita, Gesti e Costumi Di Gian Diluvio da Trippaldo Arcingordissimo Mangiatore, e Diluviatore del Mondo*, uses 'Zan Diluvio' in the rhymes.

[5] *Il Trionfo di Scappino* (1655). Complimentary verses by Zan Trippone.

[6] Zan Ganassa; Zane in '*Il Studio*, per Gio. Gabrielli da Modona detto il Sivello' (1602); Zani in *Vanto del Zani*, see *infra*. 'Zanni' in Loccatelli's MS.; 'Zanne' in Verucci's plays. In *Il Trionfo di Scappino* Bocchini explains

The 'Zan' of 'Zan Polo' and 'Ser Maphio del Re detto Zannin' may represent the Northern pronunciation of the Christian name 'Giovanni' proper to each actor and cannot safely be used as evidence for the appearance of 'Zanni' as a stage mask. In 1513 Macchiavelli writes to Francesco Vettori that Michele sent a message to Filippo by 'un Zanni'.[1]

Rao refers to Zan Ganassa as Giovanni Ganassa when the actor's private name was Alberto Naseli.[2] Locatelli still uses 'Zanni' alone as a proper name in 1622, although the majority of players had adopted distinctive nicknames and kept 'Zan' as a prefix, Zan Ganassa, Giangurgolo, Zan farina, Gianfrone, Zan Coccolino, Zan Fritada; and 'Zanni' as a general term for the stage servants and even for the whole company of improvising players. Carlo Dati explains to Ménage: 'Because this part of the Zanni is perhaps the most important among the comedians they take over the name, and speak of going to the Zanni, and to the comedy of the Zanni, that is of the comedians.'[3]

THE BERGOMASK PORTER AS THE PROTOTYPE OF ZANNI

The prototypes of the Zanni were the Bergomask 'facchini' who swarmed in Venice and were to be found scraping together a miserable livelihood in the other cities of Northern Italy. Garzoni described them as:

Coarse fellows, simple and good-natured enough who come down from the mountains of Bergamo to fetch and carry for the rest of mankind. They serve at the Arsenal or the Dogana, or hawk food and wines about the city, the poorest are basket-weavers and others carry coals: as they ply for errands in the square the sacks slung over their shoulders have got them the nickname of 'Canons of the piazza'.

Is there a touch of irony in Garzoni's defence of the 'facchini' as the most courteous of men?

As they come through the Merceria with a load they will cry 'Way, way' for fear of jostling you with their burden. When

---

that the spelling 'Zagn' and 'Zagni' is his whim.

[1] Lettere familiare, cxliv, pp. 338–9, ed. E. Alvisi, 1883.

[2] I. Sanesi, La Commedia, vol. ii, cap. vi, p. 5.

[3] Ménage, op. cit., p. 498 (1685), quotes an interesting letter in which Dati contends for the derivation of Zanni from 'Giovanni' with many convincing instances.

you arrive at the Piazza, the gate, or the customs with something
to unload or to take away, before you can call or so much as beckon
they swarm up as though they were going to a wedding, and in a
moment they seize on your wallets, your drum, your purse, and
pack them all on to a barrow. Nimble as cats they jump into the
boat, throw out your cases, parcels, packages, and bundles and carry
them off[1] on their shoulders to the other end of the city. They are
sturdier than mules, and when all is done give them a bowl of soup,
a rind of cheese, and a few ha'pence[2] and it is a joy to watch them
go off singing and jesting.

In the markets half a dozen will offer their baskets of fish, poultry,
or vegetables most obsequiously, and will go for you to Calcutta at
a moment's notice, or for a few 'soldi' bring your purchases to your
doorstep before you can get home yourself.[3] If you want wine they
will taste, judge, and procure it for they know all the cellarage of the
city. They will take a message through all obstacles and with cracked
crowns bring back the answer with the solemn loyalty of excessive
stupid courtesy. As panders they are only too accomplished; you will
hardly find one who is not a 'ruffiano'. Their only gleam of worldly
wisdom is their willingness to do odd jobs about the house and gossip
with the ladies to do their errands with their particular sweethearts . . .

As a mountain race the 'facchini' are tough as timber, but not
bulky, the sturdiest people you ever saw, and except for a few who have
become lean with hardship, they are as round as the bottom of a
barrel and as fat as the broth of maccaroni. . . . Their dress is utterly
uncivilized, and you can smell their sacking miles away. Their
speech is so grotesque that the Zanni who are like magpies to mimic
a pronunciation or any other characteristics have adopted it in their
comedies to entertain the crowd.

Garzoni wrote in 1585 when the Commedia dell'arte was
well established, but Aretino described the inimitable performance of Cimador as a Bergomask 'facchino' before the
half-century,[4] and there is record of a 'comedia alla berga-
mascha' in 1530 in Venice.[5]

---

[1] For the translation of the phrase
'peso di nove anni' I am indebted to Mr.
Gantillon whose ingenuity has solved
a little problem which baffled experts.

[2] '2 muraiole o 3 gazette.' Florio
(1611) glosses 'muraiúola, a kind of small
coine'. A gazetta is reckoned by Coryat,
Crudities (i, p. 422), as nearly a penny.

[3] See Coryat, ibid., i, p. 396. 'I have
observed a thing amongst the Venetians

that I have not a little wondered at, that
their Gentlemen and greatest Senators,
a man worth perhaps two millions of
duckats, will come into the market, and
buy their flesh, fish, fruites, and such
other things as are necessary for the
maintenance of their family.'

[4] Ragionamenti (pr. 1584), pte
prima, p. 58. See *infra*, p. 246.

[5] Sanudo, Diarii, LII, c. 372.

Porcacchi records that Simone da Bologna, the Zanni of the *Gelosi*, studied the part from the life: among the *Gelosi* 'essendovi Simon Bolognese rarissimo in rappresentar la persona d'un facchino Bergamasco, ma piu raro nell'argutie, e nell'inventioni spiritose, che si dilettano et insegnano'.[1]

Without these plain statements we could have recognized the model at sight. In the Trausnitz frescoes Zanni's wide trousers and loose blouse with its pouched hood are made of the notorious sacking. His wooden sword is not a survival of the Greek comedian's 'parazonio',[2] but a travesty of the 'facchino's' weapon. Garzoni describes a court buffoon 'acting the Bergomask with a drawn sword as though he were the first man of the valleys',[3] and in some illustrations Zanni is still given a steel instead of a wooden blade.[4]

It is easier to suppose that the first Burattino who played in a black mask had observed the Bergomask colliers ('who will smutch themselves for your sake', as Garzoni remarks) than that he was continuing the tradition of the soot-stained comedian who had appeared, 'fuligine tinto', on the Roman popular stage.

In spite of all the other duties that stage necessity thrust upon the Zanni, his staple occupation is always to carry heavy weights, to run errands, to spy, pander, jest, and sing. He may be thick-headed; he must be thick-skinned, but in spite of every disillusionment he remains very much as Garzoni summed him up, 'a coarse fellow simple and good-natured enough', naively proud of his Bergomask origin.

From a few little leaflets ill-printed and generally undated his fantastic pedigree might be traced. Zan Capella announced that he is sprung of Trojan seed, from

> quel valorus
> E terribel fier porchet

the father of Zampet, for

> De Zampet nasi Frittada
> De Frittada ol Codeghi

[1] I. Porcacchi, *Le Attioni d'Arrigo Terzo di Francia ... descritte in dialogo* (1574), f. 27 v.

[2] De Amicis, op. cit., p. 69.

[3] Op. cit., p. 830.

[4] P. Bertelli, *Diversarum Nationum Habitus* (1594), Plate 67; cp. F. Bertelli, *Il Carnovale Italiano Mascherato* (1642), Plate 26.

Codeghi fe la Stagnada
La Stagnada ol Pentoli . . .

and the rest of his seventy odd ancestors are named at random
from his garments, his food, his pots and pans.[1] There are
dreams of Cuccagna and accounts of sumptuous meals.
The Zanni who is thankful that he had the most capacious
stomach and the most powerful jaws in the world has a
weakness for a calf half-roast and half-boiled. When his
master urges him to follow him to the wars against the
Lutherans 'che si fa in Inghilterra', he is unmoved by the
prospect of glory and retorts,

Mi no conos la plu bella armadura
Che havi ol budel plen, e la panza dura.[2]

Other themes for these rhymsters are the Zanni's adventures
with brigands in the country taverns, or with players and
courtesans in Hell, his descriptions of Venice, his dying
words, his parodying of sonnets, serenades, and romances.[3]
The few leaflets that survive represent a tradition of burlesque
verse associated, but not directly connected, with the stage,
carried on chiefly by G. C. Croce, Adriano Bianchieri, and
Bartolommeo Bocchini.[4] The intimacy with the mysteries
of the Commedia dell'arte shown in the *Corona Macheronica*
and the *Trionfo de Scapino* raised Rasi's suspicions that
Bocchini's writing was based on some stage experience.
From the complimentary verses contributed or faked by
Zan Gurgola, alias Academico Frillato, Zan Capocchia,
Academico Valmonese, Zan Scarpone, Academico Desso-
lado, it seems most likely that his interest in the improvised
comedy was that of the many academicians who followed up
the lead of the professional actors. Zan Muzzina della
Valle Retirada, the hero of his mock-heroic poem, describes
himself as Bolognese and fears that it may not be easy to
distinguish 'el Gratian dal Zagno', but he maintains the
Bergomask traditions by consorting with Scappino, Brighella, and Bagolino. Within the ranks of the profession
Francesco Gabrielli, the original Scappino, amused himself

---

[1] *Genealogia di Zan Capella*, which Rasi (i. 464) dates as *c.* 1600.
[2] *Esordio che fa il patrone al suo servitore Zanni.*
[3] See Appendix A.   [4] Ibid.

by bequeathing his famous instruments to an imaginary group of mourners among whom we recognize his old companions Onorati, Barbieri, and Fiorillo as Mezzettino, Beltram, and Trapolino.[1]

In spite of the corruption of the dialect, and the spread of the Zanni type to the other cities of Lombardy,[2] the trail of Bergamo is still fresh in plays and scenari. Bergamino in *La Fiammella* is homesick for the valleys of 'Voltulina, Val Brombana, Valcamonega . . .'[3] Locatelli's Zanni decides that he will write home before committing suicide,[4] or again to boast of the 'priviligio' granted him after a flogging.[5]

In Gattici's comedy, Betta, an old Bergomask woman, comes seeking her son Burattino and describes him to Nespola:

L'è vestid de canevaz, cai l'ho filad mi bianch, l'ha el mostaz un poch negher, ch'as dis che terra negra fà bon gran, à cà nostra al se nominava Pedrolin.[6]

PIAZZA PERFORMANCES

There are several Zanni among the lively crowd of charlatans that Garzoni in his *Piazza Universale* leaves jostling and shouting in the street:

In one corner you will see our gallant Fortunato spinning yarns with Fritata, entertaining the crowd every evening from 4 till 6[7] with stories, fables, dialogues, mimicking, extempore songs, squabbling, making up, dying with laughter, quarrelling again, throwing themselves against the bench, arguing, and at last handing round the hat to try how many 'gazette' they can raise by their most refined and elegant prattle. In another corner Burattino, yelling as if the executioner were flogging him, with his porter's sack over his shoulders

[1] *Infermità Testamento e Morte di Francesco Gabrielli Detto Scappino . . . in Verona, Padoa, e in Parma* (1638), Bib. Univ. di Bologna, Aula V (ab), N. III, vol. cclxvi, Misc. No. 40, reprinted in *Propugnatore*, anno XIII, Disp. 1, 2, p. 446, Bologna, 1880.

[2] For a discussion of the bastard stage dialects see E. Zerbini, *Notizie storiche sul Dialetto Bergamasco* (1886). By 1699 Perrucci allows the Zanni to use Milanese, Bergomask, Neapolitan, Sicilian, and other dialects. N. Barbieri, who as Beltrame is often associated with Milan, is described as 'Beltrame Bergamasco' by Hondedei in 1615. See *Giorn. Stor.* xli, p. 63.

[3] B. Rossi, 1584, Act V.

[4] *Principe Severo*, Act III.

[5] *Li Tre Schiave*, Act III.

[6] *Le disgratie di Burattino*, Venetia, 1626. Licensed 25 May 1619 (Quadrio, 1623, 1671). Printed as '. . . di Trufaldino*, 1690 (Allacci, 1614, 1628).

[7] 'Dalle vintidue sino alle vintiquattro hore di giorno.' Ibid., p. 760.

and a rogue's cap on his brows shouts to the audience at the top of his voice. The people come nearer, the common folk shoving, the gentlemen making their way to the front, and he has hardly delivered a ridiculous entertaining prologue but he begins some queer story of his master who would break the arms, choke out the breath, and rob the world of as many of the auditors who have made a ring about him. . . .

There is a Gratiano blathering, and a Florentine near by; in another corner Gradella makes a fool of the Milanese lover and leaves him among the jars and boxes on the piazza at the mercy of his enemies. When this adventure is over Gradella sets up a screeching song, or pretends to be a blind man and holding a puppy instead of a theorbo he begins the invention of the 'balle di Macalepo' that lasts two hours, to the disgust of the audience who disperse jeering at the stupid charlatan who stands firm on three whole gazettes and two soldi in small change, protesting to heaven and earth that he would never want to shut up shop except when the audience leaves him without so much as a 'Good Evening'. . . . Cieco da Forli is there with his rhymes and his extempore patter. . . . Nor does Zan della Vigna fail to put in an appearance to divert the mob with all kinds of juggling. Catullo with his lyre, and the Mantuan dressed like a 'Zani', face the crowds and quite quietly put up the bench, adjust the bagpipes, and present themselves in a kitchen comedy in which Zani makes jealousy between Pedrolina and her mistress. . . .

The distinction between the Zanni who accompanied a charlatan and the Zanni who belonged to one of the regular companies is a matter of status.[1] Popular favour and ecclesiastical disapproval classed 'comici' and 'ciarlatani' together.[2] Burattino in the pastoral *Il Capriccio* introduces himself as

> da quei che cazza
> Le carotte a la zente, un Zarattan,

he serves Pantalone a travelling pedlar and Gratiano a quack physician.[3]

[1] See *infra*, chaps. IV and V.

[2] In Milan Don Pedro de Acevedo decided to tax 'comici, ciarlatani, montainbanci' and other such persons for the support of the College of Spanish Virgins, 20 June 1601. See Paglicci-Brozzi, *Gazzetta Musicale di Milano*, 1891, No. 34, p. 551. In 1659 there were still companies described as 'mezzi comici principianti e mezzi ciarlatani', Rasi, op. cit., ii. 752. Cecchini proposed an alternative company to serve the Duke of Mantua instead of the Andreini, and comments that it will be a test 'per vedere se in conseguenza di tanti ciarlatani che sonno riusciti, vi potessero ancor capir questi, quali stano tra il comico et lo ciarlatano'. Quoted Rasi, op. cit., i. 247.

[3] *Il Capriccio del Signor Guidozzo, Dottor e Cavalier da Castel Franco* (1621), Act I. Allacci quotes editions for 1608 and 1610.

Bartoli describes how Giovanni Gabriele would mount a bench in the Piazza 'to tell the crowd his decent, witty tales'. First he would send for his great valise, saying that it contained two vessels (*vasi*), one big, the other small: and he would keep up a varied and delightful discourse as he produced from the valise his elder son Scappino, remarking, 'Here is vessel number one', and as he drew out Polpetta,[1] 'Number two'. Then he would continue pleasantly, 'This first little fellow needs two plates of soup, and this other, only one: therefore, my masters, give me a bolognino each and come, listen to my comedy.'

The crowd would draw up out of curiosity to hear him recite the whole comedy in his own person, presenting one character with, and another without, a mask. He never attempted to disguise himself as a woman but only allowed for her voice to be heard off.[2] For occasions when there was no 'play toward' Ganassa composed his *Lamento . . . sopra la morte di un pidocchio*;[3] and Scappino, Francesco Gabrielli, followed in his father's tradition and wrote his famous *Testamento*. Simone Basilea, a Veronese Jew, was also licensed to conduct mono-comedies in 1612.[4]

IN PLAYS AND SCENARI

The 'facchino' was introduced as a rough type in a few *novelle* and academic comedies at the beginning of the sixteenth century,[5] but made no mark until Calmo saw the possibilities of giving the Bergomask dialect to his intriguing servants, Saltuzza, Brocca, and Scarpeta.

In Calmo's play the Bergomask type serves his apprenticeship to neo-classical comedy. He was found apt and from this time on extreme shrewdness is as much his characteristic as extreme stupidity.

In the scenari of the Locatelli and Correr collections the Zanni manipulates intrigues that would have made Davus

---

[1] Carlo Gabrielli, mentioned only by Quadrio. See Rasi, i. 966.

[2] F. Bartoli, *Fatiche Comiche*. See Rasi, i. 954.

[3] See Stefanel Bottarga. Appendix E.

[4] Rasi, i. 292.

[5] See Merlini, 'Saggio . . . sulla Satira contro il Villano,' 1894, p. 137; Notturno, *Comedia nuova* (1518); G. B. Cini, *Cofanaria*, pr. 1593 (Allacci); Bibiena, *Calandria* (1513).

and Epidicus pale. He is content to run greater risks than the Roman slaves, trusting that the excuse that all was planned for the love of his young master will wring a pardon from Pantalone when he is in a melting mood after a recognition scene. It falls to Zanni to plan the disguise, procure the cloaks, skirts, and turbans, to bribe loiterers to take false messages, and to carry the coffers containing the lovers in and out of the houses. He is in charge of the love affairs of his old as well as of his young master, and as he runs to and fro fetching nurses, apothecaries, sorcerers, and locksmiths he has to invent the circumstantial lies with which one employer is to be played off against the other. What he sacrifices of the art of plotting by crudity of method is compensated for by the energy with which he applies one device after another to squeeze money from Pantalone to buy Lelio's latest fancy in slave girls. The clever Zanni is a monkey to snatch and a lizard to elude: his performance outgoes all probability and we enjoy him as a juggler or an acrobat, mystified by a skill with which we have no concern.

The Zanni proper is not necessarily a servant but will always 'oblige'. Keeping this semblance of independence he takes over the function of another classical type, the 'Leno', and is given monologues in praise of the art of the Pandar,[1] and comments on the list of his clients. But the Zanni who are professional 'Ruffiani' tend to sentimentalize the part. Burattino bursts into tears at the thought of parting with his slaves.[2] All hands are turned against Ballio the disgusting procurer of the *Pseudolus*, but Zanni is not a social outcast; if, after being thoroughly cuckolded, he promises to reform, Isabella is restored to him as his wife.[3]

His appetite, another Bergomask characteristic, qualifies Zanni for the part of the parasite of the Commedia erudita. He sees to it that the gourmand's dreams of groves of Lombardy sausages and turkeys and capons[4] are converted into good 'maccarù e sbrufadei': quantity for quality to be consumed on the premises. He can never resist an immediate meal; Tiburtio who has been forbidden the house

---

[1] *Finti Amici.*
[2] *La Turchetta.*
[3] *Zanni Beccho.*

[4] Leccardo in Della Porta's *Li due Fratelli Rivali*, IV. viii.

in *Pantalon Imbertonao* has only to describe the hospitality of his friends and hire a hawker to pass up and down in front of the window in order to win over Zanni who until then has sided with Pantalone to be sure of his ordinary rations.

THE ZANNI PAIR

The part was so adaptable that by the beginning of the seventeenth century there were virtually two Zanni. Cecchini requires one astute and witty servant to attend to the plot and another to play the awkward booby 'whose pretence of not understanding anything that is said to him gives rise to delightful equivocations, ridiculous mistakes, and other clownish tricks'. The parts are equal in importance, but the second Zanni needs to be kept in hand when by rushing on to announce that the hen is laying an egg or the pot will not boil he robs the serious characters of their well-earned applause or spoils a dénouement for the judicious by delighting the multitude with his tumblings.[1]

Seventy years later Perrucci gives substantially the same definition of the Zanni masks and draws attention to another abuse. The Neapolitan Covielli had confused the types by allowing the first servant who should be so occupied with the plot to take part in the buffoonery and adulterate his own sharp wit with the absurdity of the second Zanni.[2]

Riccoboni has a picturesque legend to account for the two types:

Ruzzante donna le Langage Bergamasque aux Valets et il choisit plûtôt ce Dialecte-là qu'un autre à cause de la riputation du Païs, parce que l'on prétend que le bas peuple de la Ville de Bergame est un composé de sots et de fourbes, qui excellent dans les deux caracteres, et par cette raison, on donna à l'Arlequin Bergamasque le caractere du sot et au Scapin Bergamasque celui du fourbe;[3]

Our faith in the story is a little shaken by finding it transferred to Benevento to account for the shrewd and stupid Pulcinella:[4] but it is no great loss for the idea of a double origin does not fit the facts either practically or historically.

[1] *Frutti*, see Petraccone, op. cit., p. 11.
[2] Ibid., p. 139.
[3] Op. cit. (1727), p. 52.
[4] Op. cit. (1731), ii, pp. 318–19. I have not been able to consult this edition; the passage is quoted by B. Croce, *Saggi sulla lett. Ital.*, p. 231.

The stage career of one 'facchino' type will account for both Zanni. There is hardly a plot where the family arrangements do not demand two servants, and from this dramatic necessity the pair of Zanni in a company soon realized that the sparks of comedy were struck from the flint and steel of opposite natures. The Zanni trained as a Plautine slave undertakes the intrigue, and his fellow with a genius for practical jokes and a vein of droll stupidity manages the intervals with his fooling. There are examples of the collaboration of such extremes among the scenari but the parts are not thus stably related. The fool has flashes of ingenuity, the knave his blind side. In practice the Zanni are to each other as the two parts of an hour-glass; there is just so much wit, or sand, between them, and as time and place shall serve it is variously distributed: the proportions change with each scenario and probably with each pair of comedians. Is the Burattino of Locatelli's *La Gelosia* a witty fool or a foolish wit? In this play Zanni forgets to warn the young man that this affectionate clumsy fellow is not to be trusted with any secret. Burattino is sent to arrange about Clarice's elopement with Leandro: on the way he meets Pantalone and confides that he is looking for that old cuckold of a Pantalone because he has a message to his wife. Pantalone lures this dangerous person into the cellar with the offer of a drink, and turns the key. But Burattino finds the hole in the wall which leads into his master's house—needless to say the reason of all the intrigue; as he emerges he meets Pantalone who has been arranging for his arrest. Pantalone is astounded but Burattino has his wits about him; he gives his name as Menghino, his city as Castraccevo, he has no relations, no master, and knows no one of the name of Burattino. Pantalone cannot understand it and goes down into the cellar. Burattino slips back through the hole and says he comes from Bergamo, has no relations, and knows no one of the name of Menghino. Up comes Pantalone, up comes Menghino, until Pantalone is persuaded that he is seeing the devil and Burattino takes his chance to escape. Meanwhile, the elopement proceeds under the auspices of Zanni. The audience can never be sure of such a character. If he brings off a disguise we laugh at Pantalone, if his beard slips and he is discovered we laugh at Zanni. Such emancipation from all sympathetic concern is the essence of the Commedia dell'arte.

Zanni's original independence as a 'facchino' keeps him free for the sub-plot. The servants of the Commedia erudita never have a chance for more than an impertinent aside or a hasty kiss from the serving-maid, but the Zanni have love affairs, rivalries, and domestic disturbances as complex and pressing as their masters'. They thrust in as rivals to Pantalone with the courtesan: in *Flavio Finto Negromante* Pedrolino will help Cinthio with Flaminia if Cinthio will help him with Franceschina. In *Li sei contenti* Zanni and Burattino forestall Horatio and Pantalone with Lidia and Angelica. All their masters' affairs are calculated in terms of the favour or jealousy of the waiting-maid, who has her own hand to play.

It was not without reason that Elizabethans coupled the words 'apes and zanies'.[1] The Zanni's genius for parody accounts for the popularity of the impostor device when at a moment's notice and with the scantiest disguise he is prepared to pass himself off as Turk,[2] a pilgrim,[3] a rich suitor,[4] a bride,[5] or to impersonate Pantalone, and conduct a mock betrothal scene, convulsing the lovers by mimicking the paternal oath, 'corpo delle sardelle'.[6]

The outline of the main action with its triangle of tricky intriguing lovers is silhouetted so vividly and grotesquely by the two Zanni quarrelling for the waiting-maid who practises all the affectations and subterfuges of her mistress,[7] that the distinction of plot and sub-plot ceases to exist. If Oratio duels with the Captain, Pedrolino must challenge Arlecchino.[8] If Silvio goes to commit suicide, Zanni must make his will too.[9] The bulk of their dialogue in the plays

---

[1] Thou art the Fowler, and doest
     shew us shapes,
     And we are all thy Zanies, thy true
     Apes.
M. Drayton, *Commendatory verses to Coryat's Crudities.*
[2] *Finti Turchi; Li Banditi.*
[3] *Li Banditi.*

[4] *Li due scholari; L'Imbrogliti Intrighi.*   [5] *Horatio Burlato.*
[6] *Le due Simile.*
[7] *Il Finto Tofano; L'Anfitrioni; Sdegni Amorosi.*
[8] *Disgrazie di Flavio.*
[9] *Il Finto Astrologo; La Medaglia; Li Finti Spiritati; La Forza della magia.*

is in burlesque of the ravings, salutations, and protests of their betters.

'BURLE' AND 'LAZZI'

Practical joking is another precious relic of the original independence of the Zanni. When the plot flags it is expected of him that he should contrive a 'burla' to molest his master or his fellow servant, and provide the act with an uproarous ending by jumping out as a ghost or a demon,[1] by banging saucepans, breaking flasks,[2] or being chased off with a cry of 'Stop, thief'.[3]

It is not easy to draw the line between the episodic 'burle' and the more elaborate 'lazzi' which stand to the Zanni instead of the speeches and 'conceits' in the commonplace books of the other masks. The word 'lazzi' must be variously translated as 'antics, gambols, tricks, actions, comic turns' according to the context. Riccobini's derivation from 'lacci, liens', or laces, is sound as far as pronunciation is concerned. Bocchini's Bergomask poem has 'lazzi' for 'lacci' in the description of the hunt:

Inanzi zorno con le rede, e i lazzi,
Pareano (in aspettar Diana allora)
Tanti Atheoni.[4]

There is a unique instance of 'lacci' = 'lazzi' in Briccio's letter to Girolamo Signorelli prefacing the 1614 edition of *La Tartarea*, 'burle, lacci, botte, motti, facetie', which might seem to support Riccoboni's explanation of the 'lazzi' as the 'lacci' or strings of the plot. This theory is upset by the curious form 'azzi' which is used throughout the Locatelli scenari where the contemporary Corsini manuscript has 'lazzi' or 'lazi'. If it were not that 'azzi' occurs in the *Selva di nuove comedie*,[5] and in print in 1728,[6] it

---

[1] *Aquidotto*; *Disprezzare chi s'ama*; *Li Finti Spiritati*.

[2] *La Portia*, Verucci, 1611 (1609), Act II; *Il Falso Indovino*; *I duoi Amanti furiosi*; *Duo Flaminie simile*; *La Donna Serva Nobile*.

[3] *Li Sei Contenti*; *L'Acconcia Serva*; *Il Zanne Beccho*; *Li Due Trappolini*.

[4] *Il Trionfo di Scappino* (1655), pte ii, p. 82;
cp. In questo lazzo Va come un pazzo

Freneticando Et biastemando
where 'lazzo' obviously represents the Bergomask pronunciation of 'laccio'. *Viaggio di Zan Padella*. British Museum 1071, c. 63 (20).

[5] Barb. Lat. 3895. *Forza della Maggia*, 'l'azzo del saluto'; [*Il Volubile in Amore*], 'Gl'azzi delle cerimonie'; *Il Tutore*, 'sui azzi'; [*Celinda*], 'loro azzi' and 'con azzo muto'.

[6] *Pulcinella finto Dottore, overo le*

might have been supposed that the form was a fad of Locatelli's.

'Carletta'[1] explains 'azzi' as a corruption of 'azione' or 'atti', and critics have approved this plausible suggestion.[2] Caprin[3] goes so far as to state that Locatelli's form is 'atti', but it is worth noticing that the manuscript shows 'atti' as well as 'azzi', and the words are distinct. 'Carletta's' theory that 'azzi' became 'lazzi' by the incorporation of the article is damaged by the frequent use of 'azzi' without the article, and by Scala's reference to 'lazzi' as a stage technicality, in the Preface to *Il Finto Marito*, 1619:

altro è distendere una Commedia affetuosa, e sentire un bel distesso con suoi graziosi, e ben formati periodi, che udir dire, dagli lo scaldoletto, i lazzi, in questo, restia (*sic*) e via, all'usanza de Comedianti.

Between the illiteracy of the scenario-writers and the tendency of the early critics of the Commedia dell'arte to adopt puns in place of etymologies, it seems impossible to settle this derivation. So far as we have evidence 'lazzi' and 'azzi' start even; they occasionally interchange but usually co-exist with the words 'lacci' and 'atti' from which they may be derived.[4] 'Lazzi' is adopted in the seventeenth century as the general form.

However it may have originated the word 'lazzo' is invaluable as a technicality to cover all the miscellaneous matter that every play acquires from the actors themselves in the course of production. Del Cerro finds 'lazzi' in Aristophanes.[5] Lytton adjusting his toe, Charlie Chaplin eating bootlaces for spaghetti, and Stanislavsky's comedian who pretended to have a hair in his mouth[6] keep up the tradition. Few comedies would run without some such oiling of the wheels: it only needed the experience of

Nozze Contrastate. Da rappresentare in Roma. Carnevale, 1728. Act I, sc. vi, p. 13, 'Pulcinella con un conto in mano facendo *azzi* e conti con le dita'. Act I, sc. xiii, p. 35, 'Intan(e)to, che Ponsevere dice queste parole in disparte, tornano a far' *azzi* d'affetto com sopra.'

[1] *Nuova Rassegna* (1894), pp. 441, 523.

[2] N. Zingarelli, *Voc. della lingua Italiana*, 1917, suggests 'actio'.

[3] *Rivista Teatrale Italiana* (1905), ix, p. 48.

[4] Piangiani gives no authority for the parallels suggested in the Swedish 'lat, gesture, movement', and the Hebrew, 'latzon, joke, prank; Latin, lax, fraud'.

[5] Op. cit., p. 140.

[6] C. Stanislavsky, *My life in Art*, trans. by Robbins.

improvising comedians to recognize as dramatic technique a process which is carried on surreptitiously whenever the clown does more than is set down in his part.

Riccoboni's definition of the 'lazzi' of the Italian comedians remains the most satisfying that has been propounded:

Nous appellons 'Lazzi' ce que l'Arlequin ou les autres acteurs masqués font au milieu d'une scène qu'ils interrompent par des épouvants ou par des badineries étrangères au sujet de la matière que l'on traite et à laquelle on est pourtant toujours obligé de revenir: or ce sont ces inutilités, qui ne consistent que dans le jeu que l'acteur invente suivant son génie, que les comédiens italiens nomment 'lazzi'.

Beyond Riccoboni's example of Arlequin eating cherries and catching flies, a few instances given by Perrucci, and the explanation of forty-one 'lazzi' in the Perugian Miscellany, we are left to guess the meaning of the tags used in the scenari. Each generation has its slang, and according to Perrucci even the players themselves were baffled now and then. Cryptic to·us are the 'lazzi di Memeo;[1] delle carteglighie e muscoli;[2] cippi-ciappi;[3] del Pasquino e Marfoco [sic];[4] di Bernardone;[5] Ja-Ja, Bella cosa, Vernacchi;[6] del truppa, catruppa e cento zaccagnini'.[7]

Variants of the scenari help us to guess at the less idiomatic formulae: but as indecent jests and obscene gestures were common enough many are perhaps best left in obscurity.

The professional comedians used the term comprehensively. 'Lazzi' of joy,[8] of recognition,[9] of kissing the hand,[10] of hiding,[11] and falling asleep,[12] merely call for appropriate gesture. Others such as the 'lazzi' of nightfall,[13] of the gunshot,[14] of hiding in the corner,[15] demand dumb-show. Some suggest by-play, Pulcinella has a doll in *Il Cavalier Perseguitato*; Fichetto pretends to talk in his sleep;[16] Zanni appears in a bearskin to finish the act.[17] Some stimulate buffoonery:

[1] *Volubiltà di Flaminio.*
[2] *Sdegni Amorosi.*
[3] *L'Oggetto Odiato.*
[4] *Li Tre Turchi.*
[5] *Li due simili d'Andreini.*
[6] *Amanti Volubili.*
[7] *Sorella piccola.*
[8] *La Schiava Padrona*
[9] *La Fantasma.*
[10] *Quattro Finti Spiritati; Mala Lingua;*
Orologio.
[11] *Pensieri Vani.*
[12] *Le glorie de Scanderbech.*
[13] *La Fantesca.*
[14] *Li Scambi; L'Abbattimento di Zanni; Fido Amico.*
[15] *Ausa.*
[16] *Pensieri Vani.*
[17] *La Vittoria Cacciatrice.*

the 'lazzo' of spitting was for Gratiano to delay a speech,[1]
or for Pantalone to get past his shrewish wife,[2] or for Zanni
to be rid of the poison that he had tasted on his way to the
lovers.[3] The 'lazzo della farina' was when Pulcinella threw flour
over his enemy;[4] the 'lazzo' of enlarging the legs is the signal
for Pulcinella to rush out under Tartaglia.[5] In *Dal disordine
il buon ordine ne nasce* Brandino and Ottavio delay the action
with the 'lazzo' of drawing up and down the stage after each
other on chairs in their efforts to provoke or escape a confidence.

Locatelli's phrase 'azzi e parole'—'by-play and banter'—
is telescoped in the less elaborate scenari to 'lazzi' which
are best described as riddles, quibbles, and anecdotes.
Pulcinella delivers a love message darkly with the parable of
the thief and the heart,[6] or asks the lover to choose, 'square
or round', a letter or a ring;[7] he agonizes the lover by
protracting his bad news by sobs,[8] or with an elaborate
pretence of not giving the show away betrays all his master's
secrets.[9] His version of the adventures of the three hunters,
the first without arms who carried the tackle, the second
blind who said, 'I see the hare', and the third without legs
who ran to pick it up, is given as the 'lazzo de' tre cacciatori'.[10]

After the 'lazzi' that delay come those that interrupt the
main action but remain accidental to the plot. They are
episodes in miniature, each involving some dramatic knot
which must be solved before the play can proceed. The
Zanni collected and invented cony-catching tricks. The
'lazzo of the smock' by which Zanni eludes the infuriated
Captain is explained by Locatelli. Zanni begs to be allowed
to undress before his throat is cut so that he need not soil
his smock: after a prolonged struggle with a tight garment
the Captain offers to help and Zanni with another excuse
runs off naked.[11] Pulcinella played a similar trick with a
shoe-lace.[12] The stolen tart,[13] the covered plate that instead

---

[1] See G. B. Andreini, *Le Due Commedie in Commedia*.

[2] *Le Moglie Superbe*.

[3] *Cameriera*.

[4] *D. Pericco Spagnuolo; L'accordie e scordie; L'Insalata*.

[5] *Magior Gloria; Discienzo di Coviello*

[6] *Li Sei Simili*.

[7] *Saccaria*.

[8] *Lo Amante Ingrato*.

[9] *Finto Astrologo*.

[10] Perugian MS. A. 20, Lazzo 32. See Petraccone, p. 270.

[11] *Li Dui Finti Pazzi; Li Dispetti*.

[12] Perugia, lazzo 20, 'della scarpa'.

[13] *Il Banchetto*.

of maccaroni contains a rope,[1] the purse with the false bottom,[2] were favourite hoaxes.

By the 'lazzo' of the architect Coviello pretends to measure the palace and steals Tartaglia's purse;[3] if one thief enthralls Zanni with tales of Cuccagna, where life is one long meal, the other rogue half empties his basket and takes up the story while his companion wolfs the rest.[4] The 'lazzo' of 'mondo nuovo' seems to refer to a peep-show; when her father's head is inside, Celia receives a love-message from Coviello, and they end the act by breaking the cabinet over the Doctor's head.[5]

There were the usual 'lazzi' of justice,[6] of drawing lots,[7] of returning books.[8] The familiar scene in which the servant plays the peace-maker and hurries to and fro across the stage misinterpreting one party to another was announced variously as 'scena, or lazzo in terzo'.[9] The 'lazzi d'amazzarsi' as they are expounded by Locatelli amount to a short scene.

Pantalone is desperate at Flavia's refusal to marry Gratiano; and says to her: 'Listen to me, Flavia, either you take Gratiano or I kill myself.' He unsheathes his knife saying,

I give you three chances and if, at the third time of asking, you do not agree, I kill myself. Speak, Flavia, will you take Gratiano as your husband?

Flavia answers, 'No'. 'That is once,' says Pantalone, and the second offer fares the same. They come to the third and Pantalone says,

I will give you this chance of saying 'Yes', because you would not like me to kill myself; but to please me now, Flavia, this is the third and last occasion, if you say 'No' this time, I kill myself on the spot. Now, Flavia, will you take Gratiano, mind you say 'Yes' or I die.

[1] Nap. i. 41. Compare Donne, Elegy XIV:
Looke how hee look'd that hid his gold (his hope)
And at 's returne found nothing but a Rope.
[2] Il Zanni Beccho.
[3] Nobile Plebeo. Compare Li Due Fratelli.
[4] La Cortegiana Onesta.
[5] Donna Zanni.
[6] Amante Tradito.
[7] La Rivaltà fra Pollicinella e Coviello.
[8] Balia Grande.
[9] Il Banchetto, 'scena in terzo con azzi'. Cp. Li Porci; Zibaldone of P. Adriano, lazzo 30. See Petraccone, op. cit., p. 269.

'No,' says Flavia.

Pantalone. Then if you won't, don't, for I have no mind to kill myself either.

'Not so much fuss,' says Zanni. 'I will soon make her agree.' He borrows the knife from Pantalone saying,

Flavia, if you will not take Gratiano I shall kill myself, and if you refuse this first offer I die. I am certain she will say 'Yes' for she will not want me to die. Speak, Flavia, will you take Gratiano?

'No,' says Flavia. 'Then let him go,' says Zanni, 'no more will I commit suicide.'[1]

INDIVIDUAL ZANNI

The generic use of the word Zanni made it necessary to adopt some further nickname, and 'Zan' became the prefix for such facetious coinages as Zan Bagattino, Zan Battocchio, Zan Biscottino, Zan Bragatto, Zan Burattino, Zan Gurgolo, Zan Gabinetto, Zan Pistone, and Cianfrone.

At least a score of the hundred odd Zanni names were the summer flies of the rhymsters' fancy and are not to be found in plays or lists of companies. Others of unique occurrence such as Mortadella (Bolognese sausage), Pocointesa (little wit), Tombolino (tumbler), Tramezzino (meddler), Coccolino (squatter), Pagnotta (a bun, also 'a squatting down'), Persutto (ham), and Faloppa (the cod of a silk-worm) are palpably invented for the occasion. The compiler of each miscellany of scenari has his favourite group.[2]

Although we can assign many a part to Fichetto, Stopino, Scappino, Mescolino, Gonella, Trivellino, Buffetto, and Coviello from the surviving scenari we cannot be sure of their characters from one plot to the next. Knaves and fools change names and roles. The addition of Zanni names multiplies the moves that a scenario-writer is allowed. To ask for stability of character would despoil the Commedia

---

[1] *Li Intronati.* In the corresponding scenario in the Corsini MS., the scene is summarized as 'lazzi d'amazzarsi'. See also *Li Dubii.*

[2] See Appendix E on Zanni names.

dell'arte of one of its chief resources, the privilege of perpetual renovation.

In the foreground of this crowd of Zanni a few are
unmasked. Beltrame and Panzannini, because we recognize
them as Barbieri, and Gabrieli da Bologna seem real, though
actually we know little of their performance. Simone da
Bologna, the Zanni of the *Gelosi*, and Battista da Rimini of
the *Confidenti*, live by Rossi's praise of their true Bergomask
dialect. Cecchini the critic and theorist in the *Discorsi*, the
'Capo-comico' in his letters, the hen-pecked husband in the
gossip of his acquaintances is real enough for portraiture.
We know something of his comedies. 'Eccovi, O signori,'
he says at the end of *L'Amico Tradito*, 'il ritratto di tutte le
scelleraggini, il compendio di tutte le furbarie, e per dirvi
tutto in una parola: eccovi Fritellino.' In *La Flaminia
Schiava* Lupo identifies him as the swindler, describing him
as of 'middle height, fat, with a chestnut beard, a snub nose,
and a thick hoarse voice'.

Francesco Gabrielli who, as the son of the comedian
'Sivello' knew the world best from the stage, played Scappino
as a musical Zanni and would accompany his own rhymes
on a variety of instruments. From letters that he wrote to
his patron criticizing the behaviour of the *Confidenti*,
privatim et seriatim, we are better acquainted with the man
than the mask. Barbieri has Zecca, remembered longer as
the favourite of the Duke of Savoy for his fine riding and
shooting than as a *Bertolino*. If the Pedrolino of Scala's
scenari represents Giovanni Pellesini, who belonged to many
companies and among them the *Gelosi* during the thirty-six
years of his stage experience, we have the best evidence from
the *Teatro* for the performance of an individual Zanni. He
played the old trusted servant; *La Sposa* opens with his
wedding to Franceschina, the reward of ten years faithful
service, and ends with the discovery that she is his niece,
a convenient way of solving the mutual attraction of Franceschina and Arlecchino which has served for many a plot
of comic jealousy. Pedrolino is always the confidant, sometimes actually the companion of the young men.[1] As an
indefatigable plotter he is found 'troppo sollecito' to contrast

[1] Scala, XVI, XXVII.

with Arlecchino his catspaw, who is 'troppo poltrone'. At his worst he is a sly rogue who will betray his master for a bribe: but tease him and his revenge is swift and comprehensive.[1] Now and then he makes a false move and will ask for his wages just as Pantalone gathers himself into a judicial attitude over a couple of criminals.[2] Occasionally he is outwitted and left on the doorstep doped and talking in his sleep.[3]

ARLECCHINO

Arlecchino and Pulcinella are easily first in the race of the Zanni masks. For us, as we stand by the tape, their lead seems inevitable, but as they toed the line with the rest at the beginning of the seventeenth century there was nothing to guide the backing. Popular favour was more evenly distributed when Cecchini, Onorati, Pelesini, and Gabrielli were alive, but whoever started the race it was when Martinelli took the flag for Arlecchino and Fiorillo for Pulcinella that they got the lead, and applause enspirited the rest of the team. The weaker successors of Onorati and Pedrolino drop before the breath is out of Punch and Harlequin. To allow something for skill and more for chance is the only satisfactory way of accounting for their success. Erudite superstitions of classical origin help little: what's in a name but good or ill luck? But since they are winners we must respect their origins, and make myths of their birth, a saga of their exploits, and relics of their possessions.

The Arlecchino of Driesen's[4] most scholarly study takes as unconscionably long a time in being born as the baby Shandy, but the display of erudition is justified as it supports an etymology for 'Arlecchino' which supersedes the other explanations, plausible or absurd, with which it had to contend.[5]

The derivation given by Ménage deserves a first consideration. He accounts for the form 'Harlequin' as:

Nom de Basteleur. Sous le Regne de Henri III il vint à Paris une

[1] XXIV.   [2] XVIII.   [3] XX.   *Masques et Bouffons*, i. 73.

[4] *Der Ursprung des Harlekin* (1904).   (d) Diminutive of 'harle, herle, a water bird', see Esmangart et Johannean, *Œuvres de Rabelais* (1823), t. iii, p. 492, n. 7.

[5] (a) Charles-Quint; Bartoli, op. cit., clxxiv.

(b) Arlotto, plus Cocchino; ibid., clxxiv.   (e) See Guy, *Essai sur la vie . . . d'Adam de la Halle* (1898), pp. 405, 407.

(c) Achille de Harlay; M. Sand,

troupe de Comediens Italiens, parmy lesquels il y avoit un jeune homme fort dispos qui hantoit fort souvent chez M. de Harlay de Chanvalon; d'où il fut appellé par ses compagnons *Harlequino*, come qui diroit *Petit-Harlay*. Ce nom qui luy demeura tousiours du depuis, a esté pris ensuite par d'autres Basteleurs; si bien qu'apresent ce mot passe par mynous pour celuy de Basteleur. I'ay appris cette origine de M. Guyet, qui m'a dit l'avoir apprise de Harlequin mesme au second voyage qu'il fit en France au commencement du Regne de Loüys XIII et elle m'a esté confirmée par M. Forget Grand-Maistre des Eaux et Forests d'Orleans, qui m'a dit avoir oüy Harlequin sur le Theatre appeller M. de Chanvallon son parrain.[1]

The claim of an unbroken tradition is strong but an actor's word is not oracle. The Harlequin who referred to M. de Chanvallon as his godfather on the stage would be quite capable of inventing a complimentary derivation and upholding the neat fiction behind the scenes. The etymologies offered by the comedians are notoriously fantastic.

Starting from the suspicion that the Italian form 'Arlecchino' is derived from the French 'Harlequin', since the aspirated 'H' could be easily dropped but would hardly be assumed,[2] Driesen traces back the word to its first known literary appearance in the Chronicles of Ordericus Vitalis which recount the experiences of a priest of Saint Aubin de Bonneval who in 1091 claimed to have seen a procession of devils, some armed, some dwarfs, some sooty and scattering fire, conveying the souls of the damned with torture to hell:

Haec sine dubio familia Herlichini est[3]

They are phantoms of Arthur's hunt.[4] They come by night with tumult, warring with themselves; or they crash through Notre Dame like a storm bearing off the soul of a witch.[5] In another fifty years these fierce spirits are milder, Huon de Méry remembers the 'maisniée Hellequin' as he describes Dame Orgeil and her following:[6]

Et pource que plus cointe fust
Ot sonnestes et campenelles

[1] *Les origines de la langue françoise*, 1650, p. 377.

[2] 1606 'que Harlequin'; 1640 'Le Harlequin'; Driesen, op. cit., pp. 14, 15.

[3] 'Coll. des mémoires rélatifs à l'histoire de France' pub. par M. Guizot, *Hist. de Normandie*, t. iii, p. 322.

[4] Driesen, op. cit., p. 64.

[5] H. Guy, op. cit., p. 402.

[6] *Tournoiement Antechrist*, c. 1235, vers 648.

Es armes fresches et novelles,
Qui n'erent pas laides n'oscures,
Qui lotoient d'un baudequin.
De la maisniée Hellequin
Me membra, quant l'oï venir.

Adam de la Halle in *Le Jeu de la Feuillie* (1262) has the
Harlequin rout passing by night with the noise of bells,
leaving on the stage Croquesot, a devil with a shaggy head-
dress (*hurepians*), to conduct the fairy Morgue as a bride to
his master Hellequin 'le gringneur prinche qui soit en
faerie'.[1] In the thirteenth century one of the 'mesnie' is
singled out as the leader, and the plural 'Herlequini' finds
its singular 'Herlequin'.[2]

In the next century the Herlequini take part in the bridal
charivari described by Fauvel. The illustrations of this
manuscript show troops of grotesque figures half-naked or
wearing skins, lions' manes, or ox-horns, some have hoods
and others great felt hats, they carry baskets, drums, or bells.
These are the first of the street Harlequins, human beings
retaining some devilish and bestial features, who incur
ecclesiastical censure for their unlicensed revelling.[3]

It is unquestionable that before the Italian actors came
into France in the sixteenth century there existed for the
Parisians the word 'Herlequin', pronounced 'Harlequin',[4]
denoting a reveller associated with the charivari and the
comic devils of the miracle and mystery plays whose antics
and licence of speech recalled his devilish ancestry and whose
mask and hairy garments his beast development. At what
point and with what result was this personage adopted by
the Commedia dell'arte?

The first mention of Arlecchino among the Zanni is made
in 1584 in Rossi's preface to *La Fiammella* who describes
the part of Bergamino as 'come quella di Pedrolino, di
Buratino, d'Arlechino et altri chi imitano simili personaggi
ridiculosi'. The next year appeared the 'Histoire plaisante
des Faicts et Gestes de Harlequin Commedien Italien Contenant ses songes et visions, sa descente aux enfers pour en

---

[1] *Jeu de la Feuillie*, ed. Langlois,   op. cit., p. 81 seq.
l. 758.   [3] Driesen, op. cit., pp. 104, 245.
[2] *Les Miracles de S. Éloi*, cp. Driesen, [4] Ibid., p. 19 seq.

tirer la mere Cardine, comment et avec quels hazards il en
eschapa apres y avoir trompé le Roy d'Iceluy, Cerberus et
tous les autres Diables. A Paris . . . 1585'.[1] Printed
together with 'La Sallade de Harlequin a luy cenvoiee
par le Capitaine la Roche, appotiquaire Luquoys, pour
la guarison de sa maladie Neapolitaine', and 'Response
di gestes de Arlequin au poëte fils de Madame Cardine, en
langue Arlequine, en facon de prologue, par luy mesme: de
sa Descente aux Enfers et du retour d'iceluy. A Paris,
Pour Monsieur Arlequin 1585.'[2] The Harlequin compositions were probably intended for stage recitation before they
appeared together in 1585. From other satirical pamphlets
it appears that Mère Cardine, a notorious procuress, was
alive in 1570 and dead before 1583. She had had some
dealings with

> Les comedians de l'Hostel de Bourgongne:
> Ils me l'ont dit et si ce n'est mensongne,
> A Saint Cloud et Boulongne
> Tu as mené tant de putaine à pied
> Et de leurs gains tu voulois la moitié,

and her son had offended Harlequin

> Grand fou,
> Je ne suis point bouffon, fils de Cardine,
> Comme l'escrit ton histoire badine.

In an 'amende honorable' this 'poetrillon morfondu' acknowledges that

> Arlequin le Roi commande à l'Acheron,
> Il est duc des esprits de la bande infernale.

It is no wonder that Driesen indulges in some special plead-
ing over this reference to Harlequin as a devil when the
subject of his adventures coincides so nicely with the theory
of his medieval ancestry.[3] Actually it did not need a French
tradition to show an Italian Zanni the way to Hell. Zan Polo
had found it excellent comedy in February 1515.[4] It remained a favourite device for satire and buffoonery throughout the history of the Commedia dell'arte.[5]

[1] Bib. Nat. Inv. Réserve Y², 4151.
[2] Bib. Nat. Inv. Rés. Y², 2524.
[3] Op. cit., p. 167 seq.

[4] Sanudo, *Diarii*, XIX. 443.
[5] See also *La Fiammella* and *La
Tartaruca*; Driesen, op. cit., p. 187.

The Harlequin of the *Faicts plaisants* dresses and be-
haves like any other Zanni tumbler.

> Il le met, il se seint au costé l'escarcelle
> Comme iadis faisoit le facquin Jean Macelle,
> Il masque son visage, e son couteau de bois
> A sa seinture il met, comme il feit autrefois.

He attacks Charon by jumping upon him like a monkey

> [Se l'] ançant plus leger qu'un singe dessus luy,
> Met deux pieds sur le col,

and then entertains him with

> mille gambades
> Mille saults, mille bon[d]s et mille bonnetades,
> En reculant tousiours.

Before Pluto he dances a Bergomask and makes grimaces:

> alors il fait un sault
> [En] arriere courbe de quatre pieds de hault
> [Da]nce en Bargamache, et desployant sa langue
> [Leu]r fait en bouffonnant une gaye harangue.

There are certainly traits of the devil and the beast in the
mask which reminds Cardine of Cerberus himself,[1] but they
are subordinated already to the character of the Italian professional tumbler.

From this time the Zanni personality dominates Arlecchino
and gradually dispossesses him of the medieval characteristics. The Arlecchino of Scala's scenari is commonly used to
wait on Captain Spavento. He carries and drops his luggage,[2]
provokes and endures his Thrasonian brag, helps him to
'una scena ridicolosa'[3] when there is no spying to be done.
In one scenario[4] the part is so shadowy that Arlecchino never
gets beyond the dramatis personae. He has more to do when
he serves Gratiano or Isabella, or plays the Ruffiano on his
own.[5] Beside such regular employment he is everybody's
tool. They send him to find lodgings, to decoy the 'sbirri',
and misdirect undesirable strangers. Pedrolino dresses him

[1]   'le Cerbere chi[en]
Jadis mon espousé, auquel fort tu
    ressemble[s]
Quand tu ioues masqué,' *Faicts*, l. 50.

[2] Scala, III, XXXVI.
[3] Ibid., XII.
[4] Ibid., XX.
[5] Scala, XXXVII.

up as a quack dentist but forgets to secure his beard against Pantalone's tug. For the first two acts of *Il Finto Negromante* he is upset by swallowing the drug intended for the lovers, but by the third act he is ready to be rigged out as a negromancer and even improves on the disguise on his own account by instructing Franceschina to support him as Mercury. Rosalba, the enchantress, spoils him for a time and teaches him magic. Nymphs carry him on to the stage in a chair and he is allowed to illuminate the palace; but when he becomes impertinent, he loses the art and gets burnt. His wit is chiefly physical. In *La Fortuna di Foresta* he is mistaken for an animal and hunted. Elsewhere the magician turns him into a crane so that he may stand on one leg weeping and stretching his neck; his antics as he falls from the ladder enliven many elopements.[1] He has what brains are left over from Pedrolino's composition and an inverse share of the beatings. Franceschina attracts him but she is not always worth an open fight with Pedrolino for it is his nature to be scared and tearful, though his sobs are never allowed to interfere with his appetite. Wit is the exception, stupidity the rule with the Italian Arlecchini until the innovations of Biancolleli in the middle of the seventeenth century. In *Gl'Amori Sfortunati di Pantalone* Arlecchino is told to make the most of his success for his head is usually stuffed with the 'quintessenza dei Pampalughi'.[2]

THE ORIGINAL ARLECCHINO

Who was the model for Scala's Arlecchino? The prefatory letter which Andreini contributed to the *Teatro delle Favole* testifies to the friendship that had grown up after his retirement in Venice with Flaminio Scala, but does not authorize the common assumption that Scala intended his scenari to represent the repertory of the *Gelosi*. The statement that Scala was the director of that company only goes back as far as Francesco Bartoli's *Fatiche Comiche*, 1780. Scala is not mentioned in any of the extant lists of this company, but he was certainly connected with the *Uniti*, the

---

[1] N. Barbieri in *La Supplica*, cap. xliii, mentions the Arlecchini as famous for their *cascate*.

[2] S. Tomadoni, Venetia, undated, Act I, sc. ix.

Accesi, and the second *Confidenti*.[1] When he prepared the scenari for publication in 1611 he was more likely to have drawn on his experience of the star comedians of the several companies that he had known, than to attempt to represent the performance of a company, however famous, with which he had little personal acquaintance. His Arlecchino is typical of the mask at the turn of the sixteenth and seventeenth centuries, but it does not help us to recognize the individual actors, or to determine who the original Arlecchino or who the Harlequin of the *Faicts Plaisants* may have been.

The only objection made by Italian critics to Driesen's account of the origin of Harlequin is on the score of his neglect of the possible prototype for 'Arlecchino' in the Italian member of the 'familia Harlequini', Dante's fiend 'Alichino'.[2] The unusual form of 'Alichino' against the variant spelling of the Commedia dell'arte name[3] might justify Driesen's omission, although it is possible that the Parisian audience may have substituted their own form of 'Herlequin' for a name already adopted in Italy. But since the Italian comedians were almost more familiar with Parisian than with Italian audiences, and since it was in Paris that the word 'Herlequin' had developed its fullest significance in connexion with the stage, until Italian critics produce more examples of Italian 'Hellequini' or find a genuine 'Arlecchino' Zanni before 1570 Driesen's theory holds good and we must proceed to ransack the lists of Italian comedians in Paris before 1585 to give the original Arlecchino his due.

The first mention of Arlecchino is in 1584. The first actor known unquestionably as Arlecchino is Tristano Martinelli. The earliest notice of Martinelli belongs to 1588 when he toured in Spain with his brother Drusiano. Before we put the case for Martinelli as the first as well as the greatest of the seventeenth-century Arlecchini there are the claims of other Zanni who played in Paris between 1571 and 1588 to be considered.

In March 1571 the *Gelosi* played at the Hôtel de Névers.

---

1 See Chapter IV, p. 85.
2 Jaffei, *Rivista d'Italia*, referring to Dante, *Inferno*, XXI, l. 118.
3 Spellings collected by C. Beaumont, *The History of Harlequin*: Harlequinus; Herlequinus; Herlequino; Harlechino; Arlechino; Arlichino; Harlecchino; Arlecchino; Harlechin; Hellequin; Herlequin; Herlekin; Hierliken; Hielekin; Helquin; Arlechin; Arlequin; Harlicken; Harlakeene; Harlequin.

We have no company list for this date, but in 1584 *Simone da Bologna* had earned his reputation as their Zanni. If Simone took the name of Arlecchino it is strange that no reference is made to it by his admirers.[1]

Porcacchi's appreciation of his wit as 'rarissimo in rappresentar la persona d'un facchino Bergamasco, ma piu raro nell'argutie, e nell'inventioni spiritose',[2] suggests that he played the astute Zanni. In Estoile's list of the *Gelosi* as the 'comédiens de la Cour' there is no mention of an Arlecchino, but only of Petrolin and a stupid Zanon. It has been shown that Scala's dramatis personae does not bind us to discover an Arlecchino among the *Gelosi*, but of the two Zanni of that company *Gabriele Panzannini da Bologna, detto Francatrippe*, is perhaps the more likely claimant. This actor played for the *Uniti* in 1593, but in Andreini's list he is associated with the more permanent members of the *Gelosi*. The mask of Francatrippe had become popular enough to be a carnival disguise in 1571.[3] It occurs in one of 'Lasca's' *Capitoli*[4] in the charlatan rhymes,[5] and in an unprinted play,[6] each undated but probably belonging to the sixteenth century. He is mentioned by Pavoni as a mask of the *Gelosi* in 1589.[7]

It is used 1597 in *L'Anfiparnasso* as a typical mask. In *La Fiera* (1618) Francatrippe is a booby servant who leaves the wine cask unstopped to exasperate Pantalone.[8] The

---

[1] D'Ancona offers no authority for describing Simone da Bologna as 'secondo Zanni o Arlecchino', op. cit., ii, p. 468.

[2] *Le Attioni d'Arrigo Terzo Re di Francia, et Quarto di Polonia descritte in dialogo*, Venetia, 1574, p. 27.

[3] 'Ordine, et Dechiaratione di tutta la mascherata, Fatta nella città di Venetia la Domenica di Carnevale. M.D.L.XXI. Per la gloriosa Vittoria contra Turchi. In Venetia, appresso Giorgio Angelieri, 1572.' 'Uno Todesco, et uno Francatrippe vestiti honoratamente con fiaschi d'argento in mano lavorati d'oro pleni di buoni vini.'

[4] Ottave c. III (Lucch. 1513 Pozz.), see A. F. Grazzini, *Rime burlesche*, a cura di C. Verzone.

[5] 'Capitolo in lingua Bergamasca,

qual narra un insonio delettevole, e come il povero Zanni dormendo li pareva esser Alin Ferno, e narra tutti gl'Artigiani che ci sono, corun [sic] lamento bellissimo . . .', among them 'francatripp'. B.M. 1071, C. 63 (27).

[6] Mario Seghi, *Il Nemico*, MS. play in the Vatican Library, Fondo Barb. Lat. II. VII 138. Catalogued as of the sixteenth century, contains 'Francescatrippa parasito servo'.

[7] Rossi, *Diari del Pavoni*, Bologna, 1589, quoted Rasi, op. cit., ii, p. 243; cp. N. Rossi, *Discorsi sulla commedia*, Vicenza, 1589, p. 34, 'Gianni Bergomasco, Francatrippa, Pantalone et simili buffoni'.

[8] *La Fiera*, Giorn. II, Atto III, sc. xi. 'Francatrippe Gli si fa innanzi col zipolo in mano, Che balordo ha lasciato

Bergomask *tripè*, 'tripe', used elsewhere for Zan Tripo and Zan Trippone makes clear the allusion to his greed in the second half of his name.[1] The prefix 'Franca' has not been explained. Its possible connexion with 'Francesco' or 'Francese' is worth considering in view of the curious coupling of Francatrippe and Arlecchino of which there are two undoubted and two probable examples. Nashe couples the names as though they referred to the same person:

> For comming from Venice the last Summer, and taking Bergamo in my waye homeward to England, it was my happe, soiourning there some foure or five days, to light in felowship with that famous Francatrip' Harlicken, who, perceiving me to bee an English man by my habit and speech asked me many particulars of the order and maner of our playes. . . .[2]

The Arlichino in Tomadoni's undated comedy *Gl'Amori sfortunati di Pantalone* answers to the name of 'Sieur Francatrippe'.[3] In the list of Bergomask Zanni given by Scaligero della Fratta in 1597 Francatrip stands next to Arlechi, but as there is a comma, the connexion may be fortuitous.[4] The *Gelosi* lists have a Francatrippe but no Arlecchino, the Scala scenari an Arlecchino but no Francatrippe. If Gabriele da Bologna was the first to earn the nickname from a French audience he made little use of it and preferred to appear as Francatrippe. The illustrations do not support the identification of the two parts. It would be impossible to mistake the Harlequin with his close-fitting tunic and trousers, his black mask and tight cap, for any of the other Zanni, Philipin, Corneto, or Francatrippa, who all wear the wide trousers, loose cape, and reversible slouch hat with a feather, which is also the recognized Zanni costume in the Trausnitz frescoes.[5]

The next Zanni in Paris was Ganassa, who was prevented from playing in September 1571, but returned the following

---

la cannella / Sturata, attinto 'l vino, e bada e indugia; / E goffo scusator dell'error suo / sempre 'l pon piu 'n valigia: mojà, mojà.'

[1] Compare Florio's definition, 'a loggerhead, a greasie scullion-like foolish fellow'.

[2] *An Almond for a Parrot*, dated by McKerrow 1589–90.

[3] Act XII, sc. iii.

[4] *La Nobilissima anzi Asinissima Compagnia delli Briganti della Bastina* (1597). 'Bertol, Zachagna Buratì e Podett, Francatrip, Arlechi, Zórz e Mambrett.'

[5] See P. Bertelli, *Diversarum Nationum Habitus*, No. 69, 1594; *Recueil Fossard*, Plates 9, 29, 37; Callot, *Balli di Sfessania*, 23; Rasi, op. cit., ii, p. 213.

year and made up his arrears of popularity. The claim for Ganassa as an Arlecchino[1] depends upon Pellicer who records his Spanish tour in 1574:

El mismo año de 1574, habia en Madrid una compañia de Comediantes italianos, cuya cabeza y autor era Alberto Ganasa. Rapresentaban comedias italianas, mímicas por la major parte, y bufonescas, de asuntos triviales y populares. Introducían en ellas las personas del Arlequino, del Pantalone, del Dotore.[2]

Pellicer gives no authority for this list of masks, and it is not unreasonable to suppose that the tradition of an Arlecchino in Spain may derive from Martinelli's performance in 1588. The recent discovery that Zan Ganassa is the stage name for Alberto Naseli[3] minimizes the likelihood that Ganassa himself played Arlecchino; 'Zan', of the 'Ganassa' (Jaw), is the distinctive professional name. The punctuation of Barbieri's reference to 'Arlicchino, Ganassa ed altri'[4] supports the theory that they were distinct types of Zanni.

On 11 April 1572 two troupes, the one consisting of nine actors led by a Venetian, Anton Maria, and the other of eleven led by *Soldino*, a Florentine, were paid together for the performance of comedies and acrobatic displays before the king at Blois.[5] These were probably the 'vautors' described by the Earl of Lincoln.[6] The agility of Soldino, who is mentioned by Garzoni[7] as a famous tumbler, is the only fact that suggests a possible Arlecchino among these comedians. Of another company led by Paolo di Padova in 1579 there are no details.

For the identification of Babtista Lazzaro, who had an unsuccessful season at the Hôtel de Bourgogne in 1583, Rasi has two suggestions. He might have been connected either with Battista Vannini da Rimini, Zanni of the *Confidenti* at that date, or with the Battista Lazzarone, who belonged to the company of Diana in 1595 and is mentioned by Martinelli as a safe person to whom his letters might be directed.[8] Some members of the *Confidenti* were evidently in Paris in 1583 and 1584. Fabrizio de Fornaris, who played the

---

[1] Driesen, op. cit., p. 229.

[2] *Tradado Histórico sobre el origen y progresos de la Comedia y del histrionismo en Espagna* (1804), pt. i, p. 53.

[3] I. Sanesi, *La Commedia*, vol. ii, p. 5.

[4] *Supplica*, see Petraccone, op. cit., p. 36.

[5] Baschet, *Les comédiens italiens à la cour de France* (1882), p. 38.

[6] B.M. MSS. Cott. Vesp. F. VI, f. 95.

[7] *Piazza Universale* (1585), p. 463.

[8] Rasi, op. cit., ii, p. 15.

Captain, published *Angelica*. 'Orazio' Rossi refers to Vannini their Zanni as one familiar to his readers.[1] The printing of two plays, and three rhymes, and Battista Lazzaro's poor run suggests that the comedians were making the best of a difficult situation. The Harlequin of the rhymes also refers to the Hôtel de Bourgogne. This is as much as can be said for the theory that Babtista Lazzaro, Battista Vannini, Zanni of the *Confidenti* and Harlequin of the *Faicts plaisants*, are one person. On the other hand it is possible that there were two companies playing in Paris in 1583–4.

After so open an advertisement for the first Arlecchino it is permissible to make a hypothetical case for the actor whose signature in 1599 was Tristano Martinelli detto Arlecchino Comico.[2] It is not impossible, but it is unlikely that other Zanni, his co-equals, should have used the same stage name, and there is nothing to prevent us from supposing that all the references to Arlecchino in the sixteenth century belong to him.

It has been suggested that the Martinelli brothers made the mask of Arlecchino a family concern. Drusiano was probably the elder, in 1572 he was already a 'capo-comico' in Spain and was dead by 1608,[3] and Tristano survived him by twenty-two years, but the only reference to Drusiano as a player rather than a capo-comico is made in 1595 when Tristano's reputation was established.[4] He never seems to have been more than an understudy, and when the Martinelli belonged to the same company the business arrangements seem to have been left to Drusiano and the stage affairs to Tristano. They were not inseparable however. Tristano

[1] Preface to *Fiamella*.

[2] Letter from Martinelli, 8 May 1599. G. Picini 'Jarro', p. 46, *Epistolario d'Arlecchino*, 1896.

[3] Bib. dell'Università di Torino, Codex LXXVII, N. 11. 44. The MS. was lost in the fire in 1912, but the catalogue records, 'Libro di Diversi Pensieri, che tratta della sacra scritura, composto da Drusiano Martinelli Mantovano, fratello di Arlechino comico, et scritto di sua propria mano, et per essere morto, non ha potuto fornirlo, per farlo poi stampare per honor d'Iddio, et per

dedicarlo al Serenissimo Signor Duca di Savoia, che così era il suo desiderio, et per compire al intento suo lo Tristano Martinelli detto Arlechino Comico suo fratello l'ho dedicato alla Serenissima libraria, del Serenissimo Sig. Carlo Emanuel Duca di Savoia Mio Sig. e patron. L'anno 1608.'

[4] Letter from Bellone to Cheppio, 17 June 1595, referring to Arlecchino with the *Uniti*; Tristano at this time was with the *Desiosi*. D'Ancona, op. cit., ii, p. 519. See *infra*, p. 276.

was 'a fair for the maistrye' and could never stand one company for long. The serious vein of his letters is chiefly one of complaint. His companions were equally eager to be rid of him. We do not hear of him until 1588, when he is travelling in Spain with the *Confidenti*. He may very well have belonged to this company in Paris in 1584, playing second Zanni to Vannini. Or, if Babtista Lazzaro led a rival troup, Martinelli's acquaintance with him (as Babtista Lazzarone?) may have dated from that time. This would allow for Martinelli as the Harlequin of the *Faicts plaisants* and help to account for his popularity at the French Court in 1600. The publication of the *Composition en Rhétorique* in this year brings Arlecchino into the open. Simone, Gabrielli, Soldino, Ganassa, and Vannini as Zanni left no distinctive features of name, habit, or dress, but with this M. Don Arlequin there is a recognizable modification of the type.

Martinelli's impudent wit appears as well in the fifty-six blank pages as in the polyglot rhymes which are all the rhetorical compositions that he has to offer. In the remaining fourteen pages there are a jesting letter of dedication, a dream roughly rhymed, a sonnet, an acrostic, and some couplets in a jargon of French and Italian,[1] and six precious

[1] Al Magnanimo

Monsieur, Monsieur HENRY de BOURBON, premier burgeois de Paris, chef de tuts les Messieurs de Lyon, Conte de Mommeillan, Chastellan du fort de Santa Caterina, Gouverneur de la Bressa, Pretentor del Marquisat de Saluces, Armiral de la mer de Marseille, maistre de la moitié du pont d'Avignon et bon amis maistre de l'autre moitié, Conseiller Souverain au conseil de guerra contre les Plamontois, Gratieusissimo courreur de bague, Cappitaine general de France et de Navarre, Despensier liberal de canonades, Terreur de Savoyard, Spavento de Spagnols, Colonel des soldats, qui sont en Savoye, Secretaire Secret du plus secret Cabinet de Madama MARIA DI MEDICI, Reina du Louvre, Grand Thresorier des Comediens Italiens, et Prince plus que tout autre digne d'estre engravé en Medaille tant de moy desiree et plus ultra,

SALUT,

ET

A Madama
Madama sa femme autant.

p. 5. Ha REINE, Colana
Quantunque donné moy,
Autrement m'en iray cert'

ROY Medaglia
per la morbiu
in Itaglia.

(Portrait of the kneeling Harlequin)

Et HARLEQUIN DONNERA A V. M.
Un mezo (C.) Niente,
Con un (O.) Niente entiero,
Accompagnato con un (RE.).

illustrations. One presents Pantalone, another the Captain, and three are of Harlequin: in the first he is striking an

p. 7. LIVRE PREMIER
DE RHETORIQUE
Quantumque la chaine et la Medaglia,
Pour la monstrer à ces Messieurs d'Itaglia.

. . . .

p. 49. LIVRE TERZO

. . . .

p. 51. Above the portrait of the Captain:
Vammo à Paris à fe' da Cavagler
que gannaremo aglia bien da comer,
and below
LEVANTA QUE NO' MATO HOMBRE ENTIERA

p. 57.   Songe.
Je me suis insomniato ce matin,
Qu'un Facquin d'importanza
Mi tiroit par la panza,
et mi disoit, Monsieur Arlequin,
Habebis medagliam colanam.
Je respondis en dormant,
si non me burlat opinio:
Piaccia à Iddio
di farci vedere il maturo parto
di queste pregne speranze.
Per la mia foy en songeant au guadagno
io parlo Toscolagno.

p. 58.   Sonet in
         Ottava rima.
Vient, void e vince, el grand Cesar Roman,
Cosi ha faict HENRY Roy de BOURBON,
Qu'a prins la Bressa, le Fort, e Mommeillan
Plus facilment, que manger maccaron.

A Moy, qui suis Arlequin Savoian
Me semble bien qu'HENRY a grand raisor (*sic*)
De far' que Carlo li tienna parole,
De luy rendre Salux et Carmagnole.

Que venga la verole
A son conseil, qui l'a mal conseillé,
Qu'est causa qu'Arlequin est ruiné.

Ah sacra Majesté,
Fais moy doner tout astheure pour streina
La medaglia, attachee à una grossa chaina.

See L. Rasi, op. cit., ii, pp. 97, 101. Reproduction by P. Duchartre . . . 'Recueil de plusieurs fragments des premières Comédies italiennes qui ont esté representées en France sous le règne de Henri III. Recueil dit de Fossard conservé au Musée National de Stockholm, présenté par Agne Beijer. Suivi de Compositions de Rhétorique De M. Don Arlequin, présentées par P. L. Duchartre, 1928.

attitude with his thumbs in his belt, in the second kneeling with his shoes in his hands, and in the fourth equipped as a sweep with a huge basket and brush, two little Harlequins crouching and begging in the background. The details of his dress are distinct and consistent. He wears a tight-fitting jacket and trousers, sewn over with odd-shaped patches, laced down the front with a thong and caught by a black belt worn very low on the hips. His shoes are flat and black, his cap small, black, and tufted with a rabbit scut: his mask is black, wrinkled, and hairy, with little eyes and a snub-nose: he carries a pouch and a wooden sword. The Harlequin of the *Recueil de M. Fossard* presents exactly the same appearance. If these cuts all belong to the sixteenth century, as M. Duchartre suggests, they go a long way towards confirming the claims of Martinelli as the Parisian Harlequin whom we have been tracking by this slow process of elimination.

In 1620[1] Martinelli informed the Duke of Mantua that he had delivered his messages to the Duke of Savoy, 'half in the manner of Arlecchino, and half as Tristano'. Something of what he was pleased to call the 'Arlecchinesca mia persona'[2] survives in the impudent witty letters written under the mask to his patrons. He addresses them jovially as 'Gossip' and 'Coz'.[3] In 1597 he was 'quasi fratello' to the Grand Duke of Tuscany,[4] Cardinal Gonzaga was 'mio Cari^mo Compadre Tortellino Illmo',[5] and the Duke of Mantua, 'Nostro Comp^e. Car^mo. D. Ferdinando Gonzaga, primo cittadino di Mantova, Signor di Marmirolo, priore della Montada et padrone absoluto del Ponte di Marcheria, in la città dei Bulbari, Trivoli, indivia e luvini, dove sta Monsù Arlechin'.[6] He sends his salutations to 'sua serenissima generacioncina', and signs himself 'Dominus Arlechinus de Martinellis';[7] 'Aff^mo Amico, Tristano Martinelli Alias Arlechino' or[8]

---

[1] 6 Nov. 1620, Turin, quoted by Baschet, op. cit., pp. 277–9.

[2] 14 Aug. 1612, see A. Bartoli, op. cit., cxli.

[3] 'Cosinissimo Cosin et Compadre nostro carissimo', 14 Aug. 1612, to the Duke of Mantua, 'Jarro', op. cit., p. 50.

[4] 28 July 1597, see 'Jarro', op. cit., pp. 11, 46.

[5] 26 Nov. 1612, 'Jarro', op. cit., p. 52.

[6] 26 Aug. 1613, ibid., pp. 54–6. 'Bulbari', a kind of meat used in Mantua (Florio); 'carp' (Hoare): 'trivoli', teazles, thistles: 'luvini', a fruit, see Florio, op. cit., 1611.

[7] 14 Aug. 1612, 'Jarro', p. 51.

[8] 20 Mar. 1597, 'Jarro', p. 44.

'Compadre Stracrestianissimo'.[1] When he pledges Ferdinando de' Medici in 'a beaker of Mantuan Goodwill, wantoning, biting, dancing, sparkling, taken neat in one of those big goblets', and asks him to return the toast in one of his little glasses of aqua vita and water, it is to remind him that he owes him a glass of wine promised on the morning when he gave him that artichoke stalk to eat.[2] In 1613 he writes from Paris to Alessandro Striggi[3] to confide his embarrassment over the christening of the child that his wife was expecting:

His Majesty is to be the God-father, and his sister the Queen of Spain the Godmother, and they want to hold it themselves at the baptism, and if it is a boy the King wants it and if it is a girl the Queen wants it, and my wife wants it herself, so I am in a fix how to content all three of them, and to get over the difficulty I have the idea that I shall have to get my wife with two more and let them have one each like cats, for it looks as if Arlequin's children were to be handed round like kittens. But there, let it be as God wills and it will be best for my child.

He is as shrewd as he is witty. The Duke of Mantua only receives copies of the letters that the Queen of France, 'La nostra Cristianissima Comadre Regina galina', writes to Arlequin.[4] If the Duke of Tuscany does not answer the jesting letter which asks him to renew Arlecchino's security with the brokers in Florence, Martinelli follows it up with a plain letter to Secretary Vinta.[5] He assures Ferdinando Gonzaga that he has gathered from his letter that he loves and will favour him 'and other such delicate little words to be eaten with mustard'. If this is so why does he not send some substantial present?

Love grows from use, and if you had not many a time sent peacocks, capons, cheeses, loins of veal, cakes, and what are much more to the purpose, certain ducats, and other courtesies, if you had not done these things our friendship would not have progressed, for I have no need of gossip and words, they are my merchandise and I sell them cheap, for three hours every evening.

1 3 Feb. 1614, 'Jarro', p. 61.   4 14 Aug. 1612, 'Jarro', op. cit.,
2 20 Mar. 1597.   pp. 50, 51.
3 4 Nov. 1613, D'Ancona, op. cit.,   5 4 Jan. 1612, 'Jarro', op. cit., p. 44.
ii. 530.

Why will his gossip not answer to save him from the fate of Nero's dog who died with gazing at the sausages?[1] He protests to Marie de' Medici that as he can never forget her favours, so neither can he forget the malice of her treasurer 'M. de bonmerchie . . . Malmerchie . . . branmerchie . . . Bufmerchie—devil take him'—who will be the ruin of good comedians and has cheated Arlecchino of a hundred crowns. His son sends his respects to his royal godmother and the father suggests that she would do well if she were to order the most honourable chef of Fontainebleau to make one more plateful of soup for the creature who devotedly awaits a letter which shall say:

' "Good Gossip Arlecchino, bring your little son to us and he will be welcome and we will take him into our household." . . . As soon as I receive such a letter I shall mount post haste on a tortoise with the boy on the crupper and get me to Paris to Your Majesty where I shall be more pleased to see you than a Florentine to eat fish from the Arno, or a Venetian, oysters. . . .'

If Martinelli was the original Harlequin, he was probably the model for Scala. His connexions with 'Pedrolino' Pelesini make this quite possible. On 4 December 1595 he wrote to one in the household of the Duke of Cremona that he could bear Pedrolino's patronizing ways no longer and was leaving his company as soon as he could.[2] The position was reversed in 1612 when Pedrolino at the age of 87 played in Paris under Martinelli's direction.[3]

Although the chief Arlequin documents, the Parisian rhymes and woodcuts, Scala's scenari, and the jesting letters cannot be associated with the person of Martinelli with historical certainty, they cohere sufficiently to convey a clear idea of the conception of the mask in the first period of the Commedia dell'arte.

PULCINELLA

His uncanny faculty for naturalization makes Pulcinella the most elusive of the masks. Croce studies him as the

[1] 26 Oct. 1612, see 'Jarro', op. cit., p. 53.
[2] D'Ancona, op. cit., ii, p. 519.
[3] Martinelli to Duke of Mantua. 26 Nov. 1612, see F. Marriotti, *Il Teatro in Italia nei secoli XVI, XVII, e XVIII.* Curiosità e Notizie storiche corredate di molti documenti inediti. 1874–86. MS. Magliabechiani. II, III, 454–6, Pt. ii, 1, p. 275.

symbol of the Neapolitan populace:[1] but in a companion essay hardly sustains his theory.[2] Magnin insists that in spite of his foreign name, 'Polichinelle me paraît un type entièrement naturel, et une des créations les plus spontanées et les plus vivaces de la fantaisie française'.[3] We are convinced that Pulcinella naturalized to 'Punch' stands for a peculiarly English sense of humour.[4] To England, France, and possibly even to Naples, Pulcinella comes first to spy out the land, and with the detachment of a stranger to satirize his surroundings, but in each case the surroundings get the better of him and he finds himself root-bound. The stranger is converted into a national type to be the mouthpiece of all that is unique and untranslatable in the humour of a race. The change can only be effective in so far as it is unconscious. Dress and manners like the name are modified, but the essence of primitive wit which does not evaporate gives him the savour of antiquity.

ANCESTRY

This mask is the last stand of those who believe in the classical origins of the Commedia dell'arte. Scholars in the seventeenth century were content to associate the contemporary masks with the Atellan buffoons in order to illustrate the nature of the ancient comedy.[5] Riccoboni in 1731 reverses the process and explains Pulcinella as the survivor

1 *Pulcinella* (1899), p. 52 seq.
2 *Il Personnaggio del Napolitano nella Commedia* (1899).
3 Quoted by M. Sand, op. cit., i, p. 142.
4 Note that Pepys recognized 'Punch' as the nickname for 'a large fat person'.
5 G. B. Doni (d. 1647). 'De' Trattati di Musica di G. B. Doni . . . tomo secondo ne' quali si esamina e dimostra la forza e l'ordine della musica antica . . . Raccolti e pubblicati per opera di Anton Francesco Gori . . . aggiuntovi un lessico delle voci musiche, e l'indice generale, per opera e studio del P. Maestro G. B. Martini . . .', Firenze, 1763. Cap. i. 3. 'Del Mimo Antico, delle Favole Atellane, e degl'Intermezzi.' Here the Macci and Morriones are compared to the personages in the modern farces and intermezzi, 'come è *la persona di Tabaria* appresso i Francesi, e in Italia *il Puccinella* [*sic*] introdotto da pochi anni in quà, e come intesi del Sig. Federigo Cesi Principe di Acquasparta (ch'è stato à' dì nostri un miracolo di bontà, gentilezza, ed erudizione) da una Terra del Principato di Salerno, detta *Crifone*, dove gli uominj, per essere il sito palustre, sono panciuti, e pallidi, e parlano fioco, e nel naso: quali forse sono i *Fasiani* (cioè abitatori della Colchide preso al fiume *Fasi*) descritti da Ippocrate nel libro *dell'aria, dell'acqua*, etc.' G. B. Pacichelli, *Schediasma juridico-philologicum. De larvis*, . . . etc. (1693), cap. v, p. 70; Perrucci; see Petraccone, op. cit., p. 145.

of the *mimus albus*. Quadrio,[1] who regarded the mask as a resuscitation of the Maccus of the Roman popular comedy, produced as graphic evidence the cast of a plaster figure of a buffoon excavated in 1727 on the Esquiline Hill and preserved in the Museum of the Marchese Capponi. Somewhat arbitrarily but quite generally this figure is taken for a Maccus, the stupid servant of the Atellan farces.[2] He is presented as bald, with a hook nose and staring eyes, with little tusks at the corners of his mouth, and humps on back and chest; he wears an ill-fitting shirt and goes unsandalled. The theory grows strong by repetition. Ficoroni, Flögel, Galiani, Schlegel, Semmola, and Dalbono continue to compare Pulcinella with Maccus. Caÿlus in 1759 described another Atellan figure 'dont le caractère particulier s'est conservé en Europe, sous le nom de Polichinelle, que les Italiens lui ont donné'.[3] In 1832 Giuseppe Micali attempted to identify a Maccus figure in a painting that was generally supposed to represent a scene from the *Miles Gloriosus*.[4] In 1852 Campana reproduced a plate of an ancient plaster head of a buffoon who is remarkably like the Neapolitan Pulcinella in every feature, but no date or locality is given for the original.[5] The case for the classical Pulcinella is urged by De Amicis[6] on the ground that Pulcinella is a native of Acerra, a little city close to Naples, almost on the site of the old Acerrae. Allowing for the interchange of characteristics among the Atellan masks, he makes up an imaginary prototype for Pulcinella by taking the white garment of the *mimus albus* and the stupidity of Buccus together with the Maccus repertory of disguise parts as it appears in the surviving

[1] *Della Storia e Ragione d'ogni Poesia*, 1739–52, pt. ii, p. 220.

[2] Ficoroni, *De larvis scenicis* (1750), Tav. IX, p. 25: 'haec persona tam a tergo quam dextrorsum gibbosa apparet, capite abraso, naso pando, recurvo, et crasso et sannis argenteis de ore protendentibus, ita ut ipsius vultus a reliquio corpore abnormis, verum monstrum, veramque stultitiae et hebetudinis speciem ostendat, instar fatui illius qui *Pulcinella* dicitur,' following Flögel who depends upon a single quotation from Festus. See Scherillo, *La Com-*

media dell'arte in Italia (1884), p. 54.

[3] *Recueil d'antiquités* (1759), t. iii, p. 275, Plate LXXVI. i.

[4] *Storia degli antichi popoli italiani*, vol. iii, p. 223.

[5] *Antiche Opere in plastica*, Tav. CXV. Scherillo drew attention to this tantalizing illustration, and to the sketch of a buffoon resembling Pulcinella which was scratched on a column at Pompeii and labelled 'ad amphitheatr'.

[6] *La Commedia dell'arte e la commedia popolare latina* (1882).

titles, *Maccus miles*, *Maccus exul*, *Maccus virgo*, *Maccus sequestor*.

Dieterich,[1] upon the evidence of a comedy printed in 1736,[2] and a popular explanation current in the nineteenth century accounting for his cock-like features because Pulcinella 'è gallinaccio', lays stress upon Pulcinella's squeaky voice, and devises an etymological derivation from 'pulcino', chicken, to make out a case for this mask as the survival of the cock-dancers, 'cicirri', of the Greco-Oscan stage depicted in Pompeian frescoes. His argument is prejudiced by a dependence upon the use of feathered hats by buffoons in North Italy and in Bavaria in the sixteenth century, and by the citation of the occurrence of 'Polecino and Polcinella' as family names in the thirteenth and fifteenth centuries. Conscious perhaps of the slightness of his case he incorporates the older theory of the Maccus origin, but here lack of evidence for the Middle Ages drives him to a belief in the periodic revival rather than the continuity of a local mask characterized by a white garment, a baton, a stuffed-out stomach, and a hook-nose. One can hardly take exception to his moderate conclusion that there may well be some local and racial connexion between the 'cicirri', the Macci, and the Pulcinelli, although the complete ethnological sequence cannot be demonstrated.

IMPERSONATORS OF PULCINELLA

Croce's study of Pulcinella shows that in this case the short cut is the historian's safest approach. Pulcinella does not appear among the masks of the Commedia dell'arte until the beginning of the seventeenth century: when Cecchini published his *Frutti delle Moderne comedie et avisi a chi le recita* in 1628 he was afraid that 'to make no mention of Pulcinella might be accounted a sign of malice'. This ultra-doltish part was invented by Silvio Fiorillo, famous as Captain Mattamoros, who

introduced a studied simplicity calculated to banish melancholy altogether or at least to keep it long enough at bay. I say 'studied simplicity' because he spares no pains to outgo Nature in presenting

---

[1] *Pulcinella, Pompejanische Wandbilder und römische Satyrspiele* (1897), Leipzig.

[2] 'Il Prigioniero per amore ovvero Dallo sposo al famiglio con le famose astuzie di Coviello; Opera di Spada e cappa del Signor D. Diego Frisari, patrizio della città di Bisceglia.'

a simpleton who is almost an imbecile, and an imbecile whose dearest
wish is to be thought a wise man.[1]

Cecchini intended the mention of Pulcinella as a compliment
to the Neapolitan actors with whom he had always had
friendly but never professional relations. It is possible that
he had seen Pulcinella when he played in Naples in 1616
and 1618.[2] When Fiorillo's name occurs in a company list
in 1614 it is as Mattamoros and the Zanni of the troup are
Cortelazzo and Trivellino.[3] The first literary appearance
that can be dated is in Cortese's *Viaggio di Parnasso*, 1621,
where Pulecenella introduces a company of players to Apollo.[4]
The first illustration of the dress of the new buffoon in
Callot's *Balli di Sfessania* belongs to 1622. From this time

[1] See Petraccone, op. cit., p. 17.
[2] Croce, *Teatri di Napoli*, pp. 93-4.
[3] Rasi, op. cit., i, p. 359.
[4] *Viaggio di Parnaso*, G. C. Cortese,
Cento Quinto, p. 60. Ed. 1635.

Po quanno lo mesale fo levato
Vennero cierte brave recetante,
che na commeddia haveano se nmezzato,
Da vero, che fo cosa assaie galante,
E da sotta no panno l a npizzato
Uno Polecenella scette nnante,
E pe Prolaco disse, ben trovate,
O state zitto, overo ve ne iate.

Zitto de razia non cracchiate un quanco,
Ca costi mi me vogliove sballare
A la Dovana comica à lommanco
Ducento concettucci da crepare,
E quinci, e quindi con dolor de shianco
De risoio vi faro sparpateiare,
Poscia, che alquante nce fimmo accoc-
chiate,
I cui nomi s'appellan, gli arraggiate.
[E] quantunque siam noi schiuse, e
nasciute
A lo Mercato ed à lo Lavenaro,
Nel Tosco favellar fimmo resciute,
che nosco un Tosco non vale un denaro,
E poscia che nce fimmo resolute,
Disasconder tantosto il Plettro raro,
Vi faremo oltre modo arcar il ciglio,
Hor attendete, io mi vi raquaquiglio;
Rifero tutte quante a schiaccariello
De sto Prolaco fatto a la moderna,
ed ecco scire po no gioveniello

co na spata de chirchio, e na lanterna,
e dire, ove hora sete o mio gioiello
ch'assisa io pur non v'ashio à la taverna,
Ecco l'audace man tozzola l'uscio,
Affacciate, o più dura de camuscio.
chi batte o là, chi tozzola a quest'hora,
Al sicuro farrà quarche cornuto,
(De la fenestra disse la Segnora)
Poiche'l dolce dormir quinci ha rom-
puto;
Respose chillo, ohimè non far ch'io
mora
Parte miglior di me so ashievoluto,
Deh soccurre l'estivo innammorato,
Di cui Cerriglio il core è deventato.

Và via (diss'essa) scria da lloco, hai
visto
Questo melens, commo è presentuso,
S'un mortaio tenesse quinci listo
Un'ernia li farei sopra il caruso,
Più tosto, anzi che far con teco un misto,
Mi cavarei na visola col fuso,
O bel ceffo d'un'alma innammorata,
Fa palillo palillo, e biene a tata.

Disso lo Nnammorato, o di quest'arma
Viva pontella, se t'arrasse caggio,
Ohimè ch'io cado sotto na gran sarma,
Peo, che se fosse un musico di Maggio,
In vasto mar di gioia star tu ncarma,
Io fra cavello, e scigna fo viaggio.
Rise Apollo, e botannose a na Musa,
Bravo disse, per vita de Lanfusa.

Apollo thanks Pulecenella:
'Tu si nmeretarrisse ciento scute.'

on the character becomes common enough in the scenari and printed popular comedies.[1]

Fiorillo seems to have been responsible for the invention of the mask of Pulcinella more as a dramatist than as an actor. In the woodcut which precedes the 1621 edition of *Li tre Capitani* and is used again for *La Lucilla Costante con le ridicolose difide e prodesse di Policinella* (Milan, 1632) he is dressed as the Captain. When the *Affezionati* gave the play of *Il Creduto Principe* in the autumn of 1632 in Venice he may have doubled the parts of Mattamoros and the gaoler 'Puccannello'.[2] According to Cecchini another Neapolitan called Francesco had made the part his own within Fiorillo's lifetime.[3] By the end of the century it had been played by a certain Francesco, or Ciccio, Baldo, and by Matteo Barra, and Michelagnolo Fracanzani, all three pupils of Andrea Calcese called Ciuccio, whose success had so overshadowed Fiorillo's reputation that Perrucci found it necessary to correct a popular misapprehension. Discussing types of the second Zanni he observed:

> In Naples we use the part of Pulcinella, a character invented not by a lawyer called Andrea Ciuccio who performed on the public stage as

[1] Pulcinella appears in: Magliabechiana Collection, 3 times; Casanatense Codex 4186, once; Vatican Scenari, 8 times; Neapolitan Scenari, 163 times; Diarbech 1692 (Bib. Cas.), once; Perugian Scenari, 17 times.
V. Verrucci, *Pulcinella Amante di Colombina*, 1628. Bernardino Todeschini da Vignanello, *La Fida Perregrina*, Bracciano, 1629. Verrucci, *La Schiava*, 1629, Foligno Quadrio cites. Terni, *L'Insolenze di Pascharello Citrolo*, 1635. Carlo Tiberi, *Escharistumerotos, overo I contenti d'amore*, 1639. Fabio Penetti, *Dishonesto Amante*, 1642. N. Barbieri, *La Clotilde*, 1649, Perugia. G. Oranzi, *Rosina*, 1652, Rome. Reviglio Lusai (Virgilio Salvi ?), *Capitano Schernito*, 1653, Macerata. P. P. Todini, *La Violenza Lacrimevole, overo il Traditor Fortunato*, 1654. Ales. Bombardieri, *Il Cieco Finto overo Raguetto Viandante*, 1658, Rome. *L'Onorata povertà di Rinaldo*, 1663, noted by T. Navarra as a free imitation of Lope di Vega's

Pobreza di Rinaldo, the play substitutes Pulcinella for the Trappolino of the scenario Cas: Codex 4186. No. 36. Scola di Pulcinelli, Scherzo Carnevalesco. Ronciglione 1676. Carlo Tiberii, *Li Tre Amanti Burlati*, 1683. B. Lassari, *Gli' Amori Disturbati*, 1687. B. Locatelli, undated, published posthumously after 1656, cited by Quadrio for 1670, *Li Sei Ritrovati*. F. Lachi, *La Finta Spiritata*. The mask referred to as *Citrullo* in 'Scapino' Gabrielli's troop in 1627 was no doubt a Pulcinella, Rasi, i, p. 964.

[2] See 'Sir Aston Cokaine and the Commedia dell'arte', *Mod. Lang. Review*, xxiii, p. 47.

[3] 'Questo [Fiorillo] per far credere che anche la semplicità abbia loco d'albergare fra' napoletani, trovò questo modo d'introdurla, il che ha poi avuto il suo accrescimento dall'immitazione e l'esquisitezza in Francesco, il quale non vuol privar la sua patria di tanto gusto.' *Frutti*, see Petraccone, op. cit., p. 17.

Pacicchelli supposes, but by a player called Silvio Fiorillo who was known as the Captain Mattamoros. Though it is true that it was perfected by the study and natural talent of Andrea Calcese, surnamed Ciuccio, a tailor not a lawyer, who died of the plague in 1561 as every one who remembers him knows well.[1]

As Perrucci conceived the part, 'Pulcinella, which in the Greek idiom means "chicken-stealer", represented the peasants of Acerra, a very ancient city of Terra di Lavoro near to Naples'.

In *La Lucilla Costante*, 1632, Polcinella comes from Ponteselice, but at least since 1639 his birthplace is given as Acerra. In *Escharistumerotos* he is 'Pulcinella Pulcinielli de Civitate Cierra', in *Gli Amori Disturbati* (1687, or according to Allacci 1660) 'Polecenella cetrulo ditto lo bello de la Cerra, manciatore de morzellette'. Galiani's legend of the peasant of Acerra called Puccio d'Aniello who was taken on by a troupe of travelling comedians and created the part which later, by an impossible etymological corruption, was called 'Polecenella', is modified by Scherillo.

Towards the end of the sixteenth century among the many players who filled the piazzas of Italy was one who was either a peasant himself or who wished to present the peasants of Acerra. Perhaps he was a rustic with a comic and satirical vein, to whom clowning came more easily than manual labour, so that he came to the city for a livelihood, depending on the good will of the maids and workmen in the piazza Pendino. He kept the white blouse, or pulled his shirt out over his trousers, as children do who play at soldiers, and fastened his belt and instead of the knife or foil[2] stuck in a dagger, such as we see in Callot's drawing. Then an enterprising comedian, Silvio Fiorillo who was already famous as Captain Mattamoros, took up this popular type and made of it a real creation.[3]

Some such legend is plausible as an interpretation of the facts that in dress, speech, and gross wit Pulcinella belongs

[1] De Dominici, *Vite de' Pittori, Scultori ed Architetti Napoletani*, Napoli, 1742–3, t. iii, p. 87, refuses to accept Perrucci's correction, remarking: 'Andrea Calcese detto Andrea Ciuccio fù Giurisconsulto, benche il Perrucci lo nieghi, che poi si diede à rappresentare ottimamente la parte di Pulcinella, e fù chiamato a Roma di lui vedi nell'Arte Rappresentiva di Andrea Perrucci.'

[2] *Smarazzòla*. 'Smarra' = 'spada lunga', D'Ambra, *Vocab. Napoletano-Tuscano*, compare Florio, *Queen Anna's New World of Words* (1611), where *Marra* is glossed as 'a mattocke, a pickaxe': a MS. note in an Elizabethan hand in the British Museum copy adds 'also a sword wth owt edge to exercise wth, a foile'.

[3] Op. cit., p. 57.

to Acerra just as Zanni to Bergamo. There is nothing to support Riccoboni in making the astute and foolish Pulcinelli citizens of upper and lower Benevento.[1]

DRESS AND DIALECT

All illustrations and descriptions of Pulcinella's appearance agree in the essential features. He has a huge hooknose, a stuffed stomach, peaked hat or cap, and loose white trousers and shirt. Sometimes his mask is black, sometimes he carries a horn, or a wooden sword.[2]

[1] Riccoboni, op. cit., ed. 1731, ii, pp. 318–19, quoted by Croce in *Pulcinella*, p. 33 n.

[2] (1) Callot, *Balli di Sfessania*, IX.

(2) F. Bertelli, *Il Carnevale Italiano Mascherato Ove si Veggono in Figura Varie Inventione di Capritii* (1642). Figure 7 represents a figure with a hump on the right shoulder, a lumpy outline, and huge stomach. The half mask gives a vacant idiotic expression; the nose is large. He wears a high-crowned hat with a dilapidated brim, straight trousers and a loose unbuttoned tunic, shoes with rosettes. Below is the rhyme:

Se una botte vi pur Pulcinella
Vi può ben dar bere anco a Cannella.

In the earlier edition of 1591 by P.

Bertello there is no Pulcinella figure.

(3) Woodcut of six little Pulcinelli as the frontispiece of the Ronciglione *Scola di Pulcinelli, Scherzo Carnevalesco,* 1676. These might illustrate Perrucci's observation that at Carnival Naples was full of Pulcinelli in hempen garments and masks, 'each trying to be witty but proving themselves so good-for-nothing that it would be a charity to supply the galleys with them'. See Petraccone, p. 145.

(4) Riccoboni, op. cit., Plate XV.

(5) Rehfues, *Gemählde von Neapel,* 1808. Pulcinella with a horn, reproduced by Croce, op. cit., in comparison with the description in *La Tabbaccheide,* by F. Zucchi (1636), cap. iv, p. 84:

Vorrei tutto esser Naso à sette cotte;
E che ogniuno imitasse i miei Spagnuoli,
Che son gente nasute, e genti dotte.

Questi, quando piantar vonno i figliuoli,
Cercan di fargli i Nasi lunghi, o almeno
Non di forma minor de li Cetruoli. . . .

p. 85. Ma pure a'dire il ver, trovo più bella
Esser l'invention tra l'altra rara
Del galante buffon PULCINELLA

Questa credo sarà più accetta, e cara
Di tutte l'altre, ch'ora vanno à torno,
E ch'ogniun cercera d'haverla à gara

Potra far questa à tutte l'altre scorno:
Ma qual ti credi (almo Signor, che sia
L'invention che tanto lodo? è un CORNO.

(6) B. Bocchini in *Trionfo di Scappino* (1655), pte. i,

E co i nasi affilai, senza pianelle,

Fin le Zagne parean Pulcinelle.

(7) Perrucci, see Petraccone, op. cit., p. 182, 'cosè un Policinella tutto un

Pacicchelli implies that Ciuccio could imitate the peasant of Acerra without a mask:

Postremus verò Pulcinella, inventum planè ridiculum cujusdam I.C. seu terrae Gesuni, sive Urbe Acerrensis, Causarumque patroni taedio affecti in Magna Curia Neapolitanae Vicariae uomine Andreae Ciuccio, qui ad vultum ex natura accomodum, ventrem straminibus onustum aptavit, plures ad sui imitationem excitans, summamque famam per universam Europam captans.[1]

But according to De Dominici, Ciccio Baldo, who was the pupil of Calcese, presented Michelagnolo Fracanzani with a mask of Pulcinella which was different from the ordinary masks that are seen at a Neapolitan Carnival with their long noses, and was the actual portrait of a rough fellow of Acerra.[2] According to Perrucci the part consists in witty blunders and transformations:

Pulcinella may have in reserve some short comparisons, likening Love to a pig or an ass, for example, or lovers to animals, and such base things as would occur to a natural buffoon. He may play upon words in a gross-witted way or enter with a speech, a salutation, or other drollery so long as it is base and absurd in the manner of the ancient 'planipedes', not raising the style above the level of the ground. . . . Or he may prepare some ridiculous encounter with an innkeeper or a customs-officer, with urchins, doctors, students, or any one else, to raise a laugh by telling his master that instead of the line,

'Sopra un carro di fuoco un garzon crudo',

Petrarch should have written,

'Sopra un carro di fuoco un garzon cotto',

and such other sallies as his own wit and invention or the help of some poet or writer may suggest—although it is indeed hard to find anything that is new as well as witty. . . . Or again the buffoon may betray himself by trying to speak Tuscan and so fall into 'spropositi'.[3]

Perrucci's account and specimen repertory tallies with the fragments that remain in the plays and scenari. The Pulcinella in 1632 made a speciality of animal noises;[4] in

pezzo, sgarbato di persona, con naso adunco e lungo, sordido, melenso e sciocco in tutti i genti . . . con un sacco a guisa di villani'.

[1] Schediasma judidico-philogicum . . . de larvis, de capillamentis, etc. Neapoli (1693), cap. v, p. 70.

[2] De Dominici, op. cit., t. iii, pp. 86–7.

[3] See Petraccone, op. cit., pp. 146, 149, 150.

[4] Il Servo finto (1634), quoted Croce, op. cit., cp. Petraccone, p. 188.

Escharistumerotos (1639) he woos Finetta by comparing her person to the rooms of a house, just as Adriano's Pulcinella compares Pimpinella to a tavern;[1] in *La Fida Perregrina* his *spropositi* are particularly disastrous; and in *Il Finto Servo* he trips up over Tuscan; the Pulcinella of *La Schiava* pretends to be a Florentine. In Naples the dialect seems to have made this stale material attractive; but first Ciuccio in Rome[2] and then Fracanzani in Paris[3] discovered that abroad Pulcinella was more applauded as a blockhead than a wit.

Animals, food, street games, and warfare are the chief sources of the comic imagery with which Pulcinella burlesques the Euphuistic protests of the lovers. He compares a comedy to a wine-cellar where the tears of the lovers, the complexion of the ladies, the boasting of the Captain are the vintages that may be found too heady or too full-bodied for some palates;[4] or in another prologue he offers the audience a salad to which the lovers have contributed their discourses as borrage flowers, the ladies their conceits seasoned a little with vinegar lest they should be too sweet, the wily servant has poured in the oil of intrigue, the old men have prepared these ingredients, Pulcinella has added a pinch of salt, and the maid-servant has stirred it and mixed it with those pretty hands of hers.[5]

Love is like a cannon,[6] a game of mora,[7] or whip-top.

I asked a schoolmaster one day what was this love that tickled the ear like a worm, and he told me that it was an urchin who was always at play. I wondered then what game he would be playing, and I see now that it is nothing else but whip-top. For as the top spins round and round, so the lover is bound to Fortune's wheel; and as the top is fixed on an iron pin, so love pierces the lover more sharply than any arrow. The top is wound up with string, and the lover is tied up in thongs; a top shakes with fear, and the lover trembles for the lady; the top wavers as it runs down, and the faithful lover will not leave the breast of his mistress. Just as tops whirl to and fro and run up against the wall, so I can see the lover striking and beating himself if he is

---

[1] Bib. Naz. Perugia, A. 20, item 19, IX.

[2] See Perrucci; Petraccone, op. cit., p. 146.

[3] De Dominici, op. cit., t. iii, p. 87.

[4] Perugian misc., Prologo Napoli-tano I, *La Cantina.*

[5] Ibid., Prologo III, *L'Insalata.*

[6] Ibid., Prima Uscita Napoletana, 5.

[7] Ibid., *Disperazione Napoletana sopra il gioco della Mora,* p. 57, Intermezzi e Duetti, 7, 9, ff. 343-4.

denied intercourse with the heart of his beloved, he seems to be knocked down, and dashes his head against the wall and tries to leap over it. . . .[1]

The serving-maid may be courted with a sonnet which compares her eyes to jellies or caramels, her hair to sardines and anchovies, and her sharp nose to a purple fly:[2] or reproached because her faithlessness has wasted and soured the wine of grace,

the fish of promises hidden in the grotto of deceit look fresh but they stink; the fruits of love are wormy; the lard of her whiteness looks fresh but will melt. As the paste of maccaroni is discoloured, so within the great pasty of her beauty there are little pasties of fraud, the tarts and wafers of deceit. . . .[3]

From the repertory of speeches, songs, *intermezzi*, and duets provided in the *Arte Rappresentativa* and the Perugian miscellany it is evident that Pulcinella was free to use any of the *spropositi* tirades and animal noises collected for the Doctor, the dialogues with Echo[4] proper to the Arcadian buffoons, and the peculiar type of pun in which Pantalone indulges in *La Fiammella*.[5] A note to the scenario of *L'Innamorata Scaltra* in which Adriana directs Pulcinella to take leave of Rosetta with a tirade against courtesans for which he is to deliver Gratiano's 'Tirata, che cosa sia Donna' in Neapolitan, shows that this was an accepted practice. It appears from Perrucci that Coviello, playing the first Zanni, might also use some comic comparisons, likening love to a worm, or to a flea, misusing classical tags and applying double meanings. For abuse his vocabulary was perhaps even more comprehensive than Pulcinella's, and equally untranslatable.[6]

Perrucci's treatment of Coviello and Pulcinella as the Neapolitan types of the sharp and stupid Zanni is borne out by the scenari, where they take over, with the scenari which they adopt, the offices, *lazzi*, and basic characteristics of the Pedrolino and Arlecchino of Scala, or the Zanni and Burattino of Locatelli.

---

[1] Perrucci; see Petraccone, op. cit., p. 146.

[2] Perugian Misc., Saluti Napoletani in versi III.

[3] Perrucci, *Rimprovero alla serva*; see Petraccone, op. cit., p. 148.

[4] Perugian Misc., f. 60.

[5] Ibid., Saluti Napoletani in versi:
Donna è no' danno, comme disse chillo,
Che fu nemmico dello sesso sasso:
Tu de sto' core mio su lo segillo
E de sta affritta arma lo spisso spasso.

[6] See Petraccone, op. cit., pp. 140–4.

Northern and Southern servants have in common the
same greed and agility, the same habits of eavesdropping
and misdelivering messages, the same pertness in imitating
their masters and slyness in cheating one another. Perrucci's

L'Incauto. N. Barbieri

Scola di Pulcinelli. 1676

observation that it was the common fault of Neapolitan
Covielli to substitute the absurdities of Pulcinella for their
own proper wit,[1] reveals the same tendency to interchange
characteristics which made it impossible to distinguish
rigidly between the two types of Lombard Zanni.

[1] Petraccone, op. cit., p. 139.

Pulcinella differs from Zanni not in kind but in degree. From a type he makes his way up to a personality by preserving his independence. From Pulcinella the stupid servant,[1] Pulcinella the astute and faithful valet,[2] Pulcinella the hired man who can be bribed to run any errand or undertake any disguise,[3] we pass on to a significant phrase 'Policinella da se'. Now that he is 'on his own', he may be a lover, a merchant of pumice-stone,[4] a rich suitor,[5] a travelling painter,[6] a baker,[7] or the guardian of a monastery,[8] his occupation matters very little once he has established his independence. Unlike character, personality resists definition. Even Croce gives up the attempt to hold Proteus and regards Pulcinella as a collection of persons. He is faithful,[9] revengeful,[10] sly,[11] gullible,[12] nervy,[13] audacious,[14] jealous,[15] cowardly,[16] bullying,[17] sentimental, lazy, a scandalmonger, and full of malice in turn,[18] and yet behind all these there is some common quality that we recognize as Pulcinella, just as we are aware of his nose and his accent when he disguises as a bride, a courier,[19] a Spanish grandee,[20] a thief,[21] parrot,[22] astrologer,[23] Cupid,[24] or a simple country-man.[25] He is only to be caught by negatives, for he is uncertain, and immortal. He has queer whims: sometimes he will take part in the most equivocal love-affair and at others he refuses pointblank to play the pandar.[26] Insult him one day and he will cherish his vengeance and return the offence tenfold:[27] let Oratio cuff him on another occasion and he will turn round and thank Oratio.[28] He is given to dangerous silences that

[1] *Le Nozze Interrotte.*
[2] *Patrone e Servo; Pollicinella Pittore; Non può essere; Geloso non amante; La vedova con due mariti,* etc.
[3] *Colonello Indiano; Pozzo Incantato.*
[4] *Disgratie di Pollicinella.*
[5] *Pollicinella pazzo per forza.*
[6] *Pollicinella pittore.*
[7] *Fornaro Geloso.*
[8] *Bastarda Impertinente.*
[9] *Giudicci del Cielo.*
[10] *Gare della gelosia.*
[11] *Inganni.*
[12] *Inganni; Nobile Plebeo.*
[13] *Naufraggio di lieto fine.*
[14] *Grotta di Mescolino.*
[15] *Colonello Indiano; Finto Gioanico.*

[16] *Disgratie di Pollicinella; Bastarda Impertinente.*
[17] *La Forzadella Maggia.*
[18] *Cavaliero Perseguitato.*
[19] *Disprezzare chi s'ama.*
[20] *Cavaliere Errante.*
[21] *Pollicinella Ladro, Spia, Giudice e Boia.*
[22] See *infra,* p. 192.
[23] *Amor per Fama.*
[24] *Arcadia Incantata.*
[25] *Rubberto del Diavolo.*
[26] *Figlia Disubbediente.*
[27] *Pittore Fortunato; Fornaro Geloso; Giostra Amorosa.*
[28] *Pittore Fortunato.*

burst in a yell.[1] In his nervousness he laughs with terror, or escapes between Tartaglia's legs.[2] When he is to be *sciocco* there is no bound to his credulity.[3] In *Il Giardino Metaforico* he pops in and out of a chest to caution us not to disturb the dead, so in the play and out of the play he never dies.

Zanni has usually a sweetheart, but rarely a wife: Pulcinella reverses this position. The scenes of domestic tyranny with Colombina, Rosetta, Fiammetta, Pimpinella, or Puparella lead on to the Punch and Judy *ménage*.[4] As a lover he is affectionate but practical, he caresses Rosetta as his *tortorella* but at the same time catechizes her on the art of cooking:[5] he promises Fiammetta that this is only his week-day face;[6] in *Escharistumerotos* Finetta is taken in part payment of Cloridoro's account at the inn. As a husband, whether stupid or sly, Pulcinella is touchy and full of jealous suspicions that Rosetta has some assignation with Coviello or Tartaglia.[7] He is usually right. As Rosetta smuggles in the lovers on a baker's tray[9] her husband lurks in the doorway to lasso them as they come away,[8] or souses them from the window[9] or beats them in their sacks.[10] If the lovers escape there is always Rosetta to be beaten. As a deserter he is dogged by all the little Pulcinelli who cry 'Pane, Pane!'[11] As matter for the sub-plot the Pulcinella family gives Pantalone and Gratiano a rest; there are comparatively few amorous old men in the Neapolitan scenari.

The substitution of Pulcinella for an earlier Zanni occasionally entails some plot alterations. The dénouement of

---

[1] *Amico Tradito; Gelosia e Fedeltà di Rosalba.*

[2] *Naufraggio con lieto fine; Li Finti Turchi; Padri Ingannati.*

[3] *Medico Volante.*

[4] See the Perugian Miscellany, Intermezzo 5, f. 294. *Pulcinella Corneto* written in twelve scenes for the Doctor, Lisetta, and Pulcinella. The Doctor comes to Lisetta's house as a relation, Pulcinella overhears their plans and tells Lisetta that he has dreamed of what they intended. He tries to murder her but cannot screw himself up to it. He decides to smother her. The Doctor is caught under the clothes and Pulcinella beats them both.

[5] Verucci, *Pulcinella, Amante di Colombina.*

[6] *La Finta Spiritata.*

[7] *Colonello Indiano; Finto Gioanico.*

[8] *Fornaro Geloso;* cp. *La Schiava Padrona* in which Coviello scares Pollicinella by erecting a gallows in his doorway.

[9] *Due Simili d'Andreini;* cp. the reverse trick in *Principe Pollacco* and *La Fortuna non Conosciuta.*

[10] *Finto Gioanico; Fornaro Geloso.*

[11] *Disgratie di Pollicinella* and *Pollicinella Burlato.*

Locatelli's *Finti Turchi* requires the appearance of a Spanish
Captain to confuse Pantalone who has locked up an impostor
Captain in a chest, and eventually leads him to discover the
whereabouts of the other lovers. In the Neapolitan version
the Captain is not needed because Pulcinella with characteristic nervousness hides in the chest himself, and the noises
that he makes inside scare the parents and betray the
concealed lovers. His licence for buffoonery allows for the
intrusion of *lazzi*[1] and sub-plots,[2] and the comic failures
and discoveries that arise from his nervous stupidity increase
the proportion of disguise to a play.[3]

Comparing the repertories of the first, with those of the
second half of the seventeenth century, it is clear that
the popularity of Pulcinella hastened the disintegration of
the Commedia dell'arte by increasing the output of ill-con-
structed farces. Why labour with the complications of a
neo-classical intrigue when the appearance of Pulcinella in
one disguise after another, turning off practical jokes or
quarrelling with Rosetta, is what the audience enjoys? He is
given a free hand, *lazzi a suo gusto*, and thrusts his way into
Spanish tragedy and tragi-comedy on the slightest pretext;
by the end of the seventeenth and at the beginning of the
eighteenth centuries he is the title attraction. As ivy the tree,
so he first kills the Commedia dell'arte and then supports it
when the sap, the *vis comica*, is dried up.

THE LOVERS

The lover is not properly a mask of the Commedia
dell'arte; but a drama of intrigue with its hurrying changes
of fortune encourages the tendency to substitute characteristics for character and sentiment for emotion. Perrucci advised that the lovers should be young, graceful, handsomely
dressed, and well made up; they should study the art of
rhetoric and the pure Tuscan pronunciation. Upon this
neutral ground, the three primary characteristics of fidelity,
jealousy, and fickleness are blent and shaded and alternated
into the Flavios, Oratios, Leandros, Flaminios of the
majority of comedies that depend upon a love intrigue.

[1] *Li Due Simili d'Andreini.*   [2] *Finto Astrologo.*
[3] *La Medaglia; Pozzo Incantato.*

The distribution of names bears no reference to the nature of the lover, though in certain cases it may indicate a memory of a particular actor. At one reckoning there appear to be as many lovers as there are plots, but any dozen plays would serve to show that they are to be regarded not as individuals but as variations of a type. They assume the characteristics that are appropriate to their parts as wooers or deserters, scorned or scornful, in the plots which are ultimately derived from the Commedia erudita. The fluctuations of their moods of generosity and disdain, their relative faithlessness and obedience, are determined by the intrigues for which they are no more than the puppets. The difference between Oratio and Don Alonzo as lovers of the first and second period of the Commedia dell'arte corresponds to the difference between the Italian and Spanish dramatic intrigues to which they belong. Oratio who is usually a student is concerned how to circumvent the avarice of the merchant his father or guardian who denies him the means of freeing the slave or arranges a marriage with a rich stranger; the young man's chief difficulty is lack of money, Zanni is his agent, and the scenes of his intrigue are the piazza, the portico, and the window-sill. Don Alonzo, on the other hand, is not irked by domestic discipline, his obstacle is more likely to be the woman whom he has deserted or some convention of family honour which he violates by following a cloaked lady to her apartment, by escaping from her father through an inner room or over a balcony, or by duelling with her brother. The problem of conduct for Oratio is the conflict between love and friendship;[1] for Alonzo it is love and loyalty, as he has to choose between his mistress and his sovereign.[2] The change in the part reflects a social environment which belongs to a borrowed plot and has nothing to do with the Commedia dell'arte. Ostensibly the lovers make the play, but only in so far as they are the objects of a comedy of intrigue.

To insist that the lover is neither a mask nor person but merely a type is not to imply that the part was easy or insipid.

---

[1] *Cintio Infedele e Flaminia Costante*; *Flavio Tradito*; *L'Amico Infido*; *La Soverchia bontà di Virginio* reverses the theme; Virginio is entrapped by the lady.

[2] *Sapere apporto danno*; *Magior Gloria*.

Cecchini's instruction to those who agree to play the difficult part of the lover is that they should

enrich their minds with a fair stock of elegant discourses covering the variety of topics that can be discussed on the stage. But they must be careful that the words immediately following the delivery of such speeches shall fit uniformly with what was premeditated so that the theft may appear as birthright and not rapine.

'I think it advice not to be despised,' Cecchini continues:

they should be continually reading literature to acquire that habit of pleasing expression which deceives the hearer into supposing that it springs from the natural wit of the speaker. The lover, as well as reading, should learn by heart (which distributes the treasure of premeditated ideas over the wide field of opportunity that comedy offers) so that he may look forward to reap applause rather than the disfavour accorded to those who address a stupid servant or a common wench with forms and sentiments that are only appropriate to men of rank and education.[1]

Barbieri advises histories, tales, verse and prose, and language itself for the lovers' particular study, and declares of the improvising comedians in general:

There is no good book that they have not read, or fine conceit that they have not gathered, or description left unimitated or choice remark unappropriated, for they read wisely and deflower books. Many provide themselves with translated discourses from other languages; others invent, imitate, and amplify, but it is enough that all study, as one can see by their printed work in Rhymes, Discourses, Comedies, play-plots (*soggetti*), prologues, Dialogues, Tragedies, Pastorals, and other such.[2]

Francesco Gabrielli said of Antonazzoni, who used to play the second lover with the *Confidenti*, that being too lazy to study he took to the mask of the Captain.[3]

A fair proportion of this literary output was the work of men and women who at one time or another had qualified themselves to play the lovers' parts. The complimentary and devotional verses of 'Oratio' Valerini, 'Ortenzio' and 'Lavinia' Antonazzoni, 'Flaminio' Fabri, 'Cinthio' Fidenzi, and 'Orazio' Romagnesi, and the dramatic work of 'Flavio' Scala, 'Lelio' Andreini, and later of Pietro Cotta and Marco

---

[1] *Frutti*, see Pettraccone, op. cit., pp. 8–9.   [2] *Supplica* (1634), see Pettraccone, op. cit., p. 33.   [3] See Rasi, op. cit.

Napoleoni are evidence for the literary standards maintained
at the head of the profession.[1] A manuscript in the possession
of Paglicci-Brozzi described by Rasi explains how any such
talent was exploited for the use of the company. 'Fulvio'
Bruni wrote fifty-one 'dialoghi scenici' for various occasions
at the request of his companions 'Flaminia', 'Delia', 'Valeria',
'Lavinia', and 'Celia', the women of the *Confidenti*.[2]

Urging the study of rhetoric to ensure evenness of style
between the premeditated and extempore speeches, Perrucci
has examples of some fifty-two figures of speech which give
grace and vigour to a discourse, with the remark that could
the actor master these he would be able to improvise a conceit
if not a full speech.[3] Perrucci prides himself on the composition of miscellanies of speeches which could be introduced so
aptly that no one would dream that they were not made for
the occasion. As a basis for the lovers' commonplace-book
in which he should collect material under such headings
as 'Love reciprocal, rejected, importuning, disdainful';
'Jealousy, Friendship, Reconciliation, Reward, Leave-
taking' and so forth, he gives *concetti*, soliloquies, dialogues,
and *chiusetti* or rhymed couplets which gave a convenient end
to a speech.

The *concetti* are defined as brief speeches containing some
witty paradox or comparison.

Conceit of Rejection

My heart is the anvil that resists the hammer-stroke of your ob-
stinacy: my breast is marble, nay, agate, to withstand your fire: my
bosom is ice, but ice so hard that your flames cannot melt it, and you
are a fury for my torment in the realm of love.

Of Jealousy

I am jealous because I am in love. O strange mutual revulsion!
The fire of love is so conjoined with congealing jealousy (*gelo della
gelosia*) that they slay me simultaneously, and my passion by reason of
these two torments is a suffering by which I am frozen without while
within a burning fever consumes my vitals.[4]

---

[1] See Rasi, op. cit., *passim*.
[2] Ibid., i, p. 519.
[3] *L'Arte Rappresentativa* (1699), pte

ii, see Petraccone, op. cit., p. 75.
[4] Petraccone, op. cit., p. 77.

It falls to the lady to catch the idea of the conceit and return it in graceful dialogue so that when one speaker compares friendship to a tree which produces the fruit of loving gratitude, the reply will be,

that then of trees it must be the laurel which is esteemed the symbol of immortality because it sheds no leaves in the cold weather, even as friendship loses none of its virtue by change of fortune.[1]

This conversational ball-game is played in a dialogue of un-requited love given in Padre Adriano's miscellany:

He. Behold a lover who offers you his heart.

She. I do not accept the fumes of an incense which does not please me.

He. I am a moth-like lover fluttering round your lovely light, and caring nothing for death.

She. A foolish insect if it courts its destruction, and a stupid heart to seek death in my face.

He. Rather, a noble fly if it prefers a shining tomb above an obscure life, and my heart, rejoicing in your beautiful fire, cares not that it is burnt to ashes.[2]

For his soliloquies the lover is left to amplify such conceits by apostrophe and antithesis as he speculates on the nature, the power, and the torments of love, rails against Fortune and his mistress's cruelty, or marvels over the beauties of a strange city or the joy of returning to his native air. The length and subject of these monologues was left to the judge-ment of the actor with a recommendation to consider the chances of his next speaker: Perucci remembers one young man who substituted the soliloquy of an accepted for that of a diffident lover, and when reproached had replied, 'What matter? I was applauded.'[3]

As the specimen soliloquies from the *Arte Rappresentativa* are now accessible in Petraccone's selections, examples will be taken from the commonplace-book prepared for the lover for a performance of *La Pazzia di Flaminio* in May 1680, a little manuscript belonging to Senatore Croce who gener-ously allowed me to make a transcription.

This repertory allows for some variety: besides soliloquies

[1] Petraccone, op. cit., p. 78.   [2] Bib. Com. Perugia, A. 20, f. 10.
[3] Petraccone, op. cit., p. 88.

on the persecution of fortune, the effects and the pangs of love, and the beauty of his mistress, and entrance speeches for a lover who is tongue-tied, or bold or fearful, there are three speeches on the first arrival in a strange city, and four suitable for night-scenes.

First entrance of a lover, at night

Night, blessed night, happy time for me, if thou wishest to favour my happiness, hide those lights that since the departure of the divinity of [Anchises?] sparkle with everlasting light upon your cloak. Muffle up our hemisphere with the darkest shadows that dwell with thee in Alpine caverns where is thine abode. I know thee for the protectress of thieves, and for one who delights in rapine of others, regarding such things as triumphs of thy greatness; and if thou wilt cover with thy dark bands my lover's robbery, to the eternity of thy name I promise thee for a victim the first sweetness that by thy merit shall be granted me in her bosom who has stolen my heart away.

First arrival in a city

Lo! at last, thanks be to heaven, after the trials of a long and dangerous journey I have arrived at the place which will not only give rest to erring feet, but will bring to a happy end the troubles of the spirit. Truly this city ought to be put above any other; far beyond the delights which it offers to its inhabitants it shines among the abundance of the other cities of Italy as a sun among stars; whence it comes that in walking across its squares, in admiring its magnificence, there creeps over me an indescribable sweetness that makes my heart dance in my breast for joy; and I seem to be made a citizen of Paradise and not the lodger in an earthly city. I account the privations blessed, the troubles welcome, the difficulties sweet, endured in crossing mountains, fording rivers, wandering in forests, now that I have been able to arrive at this place, for all that I have found unpleasant in the journey has been recompensed with the joy that I feel in having come to this city where the sweet conversation of the gentlemen, and the beauty of the ladies, fills me full of happy fancies.

Night, at the ascent of the ladder

Heavens hold back thy lightnings, lest they be awed to behold me attempting to ascend to such giddy heights in so eminent a place, for in climbing this ladder I do not aspire, as perhaps you imagine, like the daring Giants to disturb the repose of the great firmament or to displace Jove from his eternal seat, but to vindicate your offences I seek to subdue the haughtiness of a woman, who scorns the heavens in her beauty and conquers all the divinities of the air in grace and loveliness.

A trifle like a ring, a flower, a ribbon, or a tobacco-pouch, or one of the favourite academic problems such as, 'Who loves the better, man or woman?', 'Which gives more delight, the mouth or the eye?' might afford a suitable occasion for the introduction of premeditated dialogue either plain or ornate. Perrucci implies that the brisker style was more popular than the *stile asiatico* which depended upon conceits and sustained metaphors. The retort of the *stile laconico* was appropriate for scenes of disdain, reproach, and peace-making.

Dialogue of mutual disdain

She. The bonds
He. The chains
She. that bind
He. that fetter
She. this soul
He. my heart
She. crack
He. burst
She. If faith
He. If love
She. constrain you
He. entangle you
She. anger
He. scorn
She. annihilates you
He. disperses you.
She. The prey is relinquished
He. The slave is free
She. Reason
He. Duty
She. has saved it.
He. has freed it.
She. Barbarian
He. Wretch!!
She. What are you saying?
He. What are you muttering?

She. I say I detest you.

He. I say I abhor you.

She. and that I cannot endure the sight of you any more

He. and that I cannot bear to be with you any more.

She. Do you not know, these bonds . . .

He. Do you not know, these shackles

She. which you called gold

He. which you said were of diamond

She. are proved false

He. were only of glass.

She. They were gilded fetters.

He. They were counterfeit stones.

She. Therefore they are burst

He. For this I shattered them.

She. And now I enjoy

He. Now am I freed

She. Liberty.

He. from slavery.

She. I lash at a false impostor

He. I scourge a deceptive alchemist

She. who deluded me.

He. who flouted me.

She. That Gordian knot

He. That twisted thread

She. that you said could not be untied

He. that you boasted was unending

She. has found its Alexander

He. has met its Clotho

She. who has cut it

He. who has shorn it

She. and it was scorn.

He. and it was fury.

She. In your temple

He. Before your image

She. I hang up the chains.

He. I offer the fetters.

She. And thou Cupid

He. And thou Eros

She. Go, throw off your bonds.

He. Go, destroy your ties.

She. So that free

He. So that loosed

She. I am beyond servitude

He. I am beyond disturbance
She. The knot is untied!
He. The bond is burst![1]

The speeches and dialogues in the Perugian miscellany and in the *Arte Rappresentativa* are all in prose, but at one time Perrucci had found verse popular. His miscellanies had such vogue among professional actors as well as the *dilettanti* that we are to understand that at the end of the seventeenth century even in Lombardy an actor would begin a speech on jealousy with his 'Wretch that I am! I burn and freeze at once', or a reflection with 'Leave me, O thoughts'. His compositions had become public property and actors claimed them as their own inventions even to his face.[2]

The last shreds of verse survive in the *chiusette* with which the lover gave a finish to a prose speech either by having on the tip of his tongue some lines of Petrarch or Tasso, or by inventing sententious couplets for various emergencies:

Infelicità

Nel pensare a' miei danni io mi confondo:
più infelice di me non vide il mondo.

Speranza e timore

Di speranza e timore giunto a l'estremo,
fede ho sperando e disperando io temo.

Va a morire

Quest'aure che respiro odio ed abhorro;
se perdei la mia vita, a morte corro.[3]

For the favourite scene of frenzy (*la pazzia*) Perrucci made but slight provision by giving a sonnet in which the raving lover imagines himself a physician, and a short speech jumbling mythology and geography, and referring the actor for further guidance to the works of Doni and Burchiello.[4] The *pazzia* given for Isabella by Scala, the lines for Lavinia's[5] performance as Ariadne deserted by Theseus,[6] and Flaminio's

---

[1] See Petraccone, op. cit., p. 100.
[2] Ibid., p. 106.
[3] Ibid., pp. 109, 111.
[4] Ibid., p. 92.

[5] Rasi, op. cit., i, p. 180.
[6] *La Forsennata Principessa*; see also Bartoli, op. cit., p. xiii, n. 6.

repertory fill the gap. The *Pazzia di Flaminio* gave scope for a discourse in which Flaminio goes mad at the thought of Cintia in the arms of his rival; after pages of frenzied rhetorical questions he loses his wits and tries snatches of song; he imagines he is Atlante and calls on the winds to help to reach Cintia who has gone to the moon: towards the end of the speech, which is left incomplete, he thinks he is on a ship:

Look! the light is out, and thunder and lightning strive with the roaring of the sea. I am lost: let them shoot the volley for succour. Bù! bù! Help, help, already my breast, like a ship, is in danger of wreck, and already the helmsman of discretion and the anchor of hope are lost. Bù, bù, help, help. Succour, succour.

The dialogue with Pollicinella is of the usual elasticity:

Fl. Te, te, Melampo, te, te, Melampo.

Pol. What is this commotion that I hear behind me?

Fl. Up, up, Shepherds, go, waking the sheep with horns; to the chase, it is late, don't you see that already the sun peeps from the golden gates of the East?

Pol. My son you have chased your eyes away, the sun is setting in the west.

Fl. Farewell Master Charon.

Pol. Your servant, Master ——

Fl. I am the soul of a wretched alchemist who in drawing the moon from Mercury and the Sun from Venus, have lost time, money, and wits, and now that I am left with an empty spoon and haven't so much as a miserable farthing to give you, I prithee ferry me to the other side gratis, and when I am in luck we will settle the account.

Pol. You are the soul of an alchemist and I am the body of a resurrected criminal who can do nothing worth while without the sound of the purse.

Fl. Oh! pardon me brother, I mistook you.

Pol. I wanted to tell you that he is not the man you took him for.

Fl. You are not Charon at all.

Pol. Can't you see I'm Pollecinella?

Fl. But do you know who you are?

Pol. Who I am.

Fl. Look at the little Bear.

Pol. The Bear, oh my aunt! where is it?

Fl. Stand still.

Pol. I wish you would talk without beating about; I did not know you were a music master.

Fl. Do you not see that star?

Pol. Indeed you've made me see stars with the knocks you've given me.

Fl. That star that lies behind the tail of the lesser Bear, that is you.

Pol. Then I am not Charon any more, but my lovely features are like the star that lies behind the lesser Bear?

Fl. Biscuits ho! who will buy biscuits.

Pol. Give them to the Turks; are you good at biscuit-making?

Fl. My fine lad, will you play at mora?

Pol. I would sooner play you at unbreeching so that I might cuff you where the midwife first spat on me——

Fl. And play for your life?

Pol. If you double me mind that you really take it.

Fl. What do we want to play for?

Pol. Three *cavalli* at 25, but you, what will you play for?

Fl. I'll play for what I play for.

Pol. Be warned, for whenever men say that it has never rained wine.

Fl. I will play for the state of the grand Cham of Tartary at the first.

Pol. What do you want after that, if I inherit this?

Fl. Now the game begins.

Pol. I wish it were ended. (*They throw*)

Fl. 2

Pol. 5

Fl. Are the poles that sustain the terrestrial frame, the Arctic and the Antarctic poles. 3

Pol. 26

Fl. Are the faculties of the mind, memory, intellect, and wit. 4

Pol. 7

Fl. Are the elements, air, water, fire, ether. 5

Pol. 11

Fl. Are the things to be observed in anatomy, skin, flesh, veins, bone, and nerves. 6

Pol. 15

Fl. Are the Graces and the Furies: Aglaia, Talia, and Eufrosina, Megaera, Tesiphone, and Aletto.

For two more pages they call and interpret numbers; at last Flaminio rises and Pollicenilla sees his back with a relieving curse.

WOMEN'S PARTS

The lover's repertory of speeches was to be shared by the lady, and in return his actions may be best reconstructed by studying the development of her part in the play.

The roles of the lovers in the Commedia dell'arte make little substantial, but an important stylistic contribution to the history of the stage, for it was the tendency of professional comedians, perhaps for economic reasons, to equalize the importance of parts. By the introduction of actresses the dramatic value of the lady was completely changed. From being the passive, she became the active centre of the play and brought the lover with her. For the convenience of academic representation, and in accordance with the convention that honest women were not seen in the street or at the windows, the object of the technique of the Commedia erudita was to conceal the lady. In many plays, though she is continually the subject of discussion, she is never seen, and perhaps never heard. When the practical difficulty of boy-actors taking women's parts was obviated, it became the concern of the popular playwright to invent excuses for letting the actress appear as much as possible. All the scenes that were described by the servants and parents of the Commedia erudita are now to be represented. The beauty that was taken for granted is now put to the test.[1] It is significant that in *La Senese* Florindo thinks first of finding some pandar to take a letter to Clarice and then decides that he will speak for himself. In farce the women are always at the window, or on the doorstep ready with the excuse of a dropped handkerchief,[2] or an escaped hen,[3] to allay the suspicions of parents and servants. In romantic comedy they appear as slaves,[4] pages,[5] pilgrims,[6] soldiers,[7] sometimes they are fugitives inadequately escorted by a brother or a lover,[8] they come to ransom their relations,[9] or claim their lovers.[10] In Pastoral proper they are nymphs; in chivalric pastoral they disguise as shepherds.[11] The adventures of tragicomedy are designed to give them every opportunity for scenes of love-making, lamentation, frenzy, and even of duelling.[12]

[1] *Gli Scambi*; *Li Furti*; *Il Tesoro* with their originals in Commedia erudita. See Appendix F.

[2] *Lo Amante Ingrato.*

[3] *Il Zanne Beccho.*

[4] *La Schiava, Le due Schiave, La Turchetta.*

[5] Scala, VIII, X, XI, XIV, XV, XVI, *Intronati*; *Le due Sorelle Rivale*; *Il Pozzo di Pasquati*; *Inganni di Flaminia.*

[6] *La Pellegrina.*

[7] *La Vedova Costante.*

[8] *La Senese.*

[9] *Li Tre Matti.*

[10] *L'Oggetto Odiato.*

[11] *Li Ritratti.*

[12] *Il Principe d'Altavilla*; *La Guerriera.*

Cecchini writing in 1621 reckons that it had been the fashion for women to act on the public stage for barely fifty years.[1] The few examples that we have of actresses before this date correspond to the scanty notices of the pioneer companies so that the innovation appears to coincide with the development of professional acting. Among the Venetian amateurs inspired by Cherea, Sansovino mentions Zuccato and Polonia his wife.[2] She was evidently playing professionally in Paris in 1572 and is among the comedians seen by Bragato in his dream of hell together with Vicenza (Armani) and Lidia (da Bagnacavallo).[3] The company playing in Rome in 1564 incorporated a certain 'Lucrezia of Siena'.[4] Before 1559 Lasca's Zanni had left 'the women with the Captains and the lovers in the "stanza",[5] and the Flaminia mentioned by De Sommi as young and illustrious in 1556 was probably the actress who rivalled Vicenza Armani at Mantua. For 1 July 1567 Rogna records two comedies:

One in the usual place for the Signora Flaminia and Pantalone, who were accompanied by the Signora Angela, she who leaps so well, and the other, at Purgo (near S. Andrea, in Mantua) in the house of Lanzino for that Signora Vicenza with whom Signor Federigo Gazuolo is in love. Both had good and crowded audiences, but Flaminia drew more nobles and played the tragedy of Dido as a tragicomedy with great success.[6]

As early as 1575 the company who had played with Vittoria Piissimi before Henri III at Venice, went by her name in Florence—'una comedia di Zani della Compagnia della Vittoria'.[7] The players patronized by Cardinal Montalto were known as often as 'the company of Diana' as the *Desiosi*.[8] When Isabella died in 1603 Francesco Andreini retired heart-broken and the *Gelosi* dispersed. Garzoni hardly approved of the brazen comedienne who lead the troup on its advertising parade,[9] but he found the 'divina

[1] 'Brevi discorsi intorno alla commedia', p. 9, quoted by D'Ancona, op. cit., i. 416.

[2] Sansovino, *Venetia città nobilissima et singolare*, 1581. Lib. X, pp. 168–9.

[3] B. Rossi, *Fiammella*, Act III.

[4] *Giorn. Stor.*, lxiii, p. 297.

[5] A. F. Grazzini, *Canti carnascialeschi*, XXIX.

[6] D'Ancona, op. cit., p. 451.

[7] Ercole Cortile to Duke of Ferrara, 3 Dec. 1575.

[8] Sanesi, op. cit., ii, p. 11.

[9] 'Com'entrano questi dentro a una città, subito col tamburo si fa sapere che i signori Comici tali sono arrivati, andando la Signora vestita da uomo con la spada in mano a far la rassegna.' *Piazza Universale* (1585), pp. 753–4.

Vittoria' an 'enchantress ... a Syren ... a perfect comedienne', the learned Vicenza a female Cicero, 'the most excellent actress of our time, the gracious Isabella a name for ever', and in spite of the prodigal superlatives, kept a place for Lidia da Bagnacavallo as 'that gentle Lidia my countrywoman'.[1]

In 1646 Ottonelli observes that a company with no woman had little chance of applause. The early company lists show that the importance of the actress was recognized early. The few exceptions may be mentioned at once. The company of Paduan actors who set out for Rome in 1549 engaged Francesco a smith of Concarolo to play the women's parts. There is no record of actresses with Ganassa in 1572, or in the Neapolitan troop in 1575. The part of Franceschina was played by Baptista Amorevoli in 1584 and by Ottavio Bernardini for the *Uniti* in 1614.[2]

Of all the lists that are to be regarded as at all complete only that of the *Uniti* in 1614 shows no women. The regular provision was for a *prima* and *seconda donna*, and one or two serving-maids.

Thus the company approved of by Francesco Hondedei in Padua in 1612 consisted of 'three women, one of whom, Flaminia, is a delightful and effective actress, three young men, two Zanni, a Pantalone, a Spanish Captain, and a Graziano'.[3] In Bologna in 1615 the company which can be identified as the *Confidenti* had 'four women, one Lavinia the youngest and most beautiful was the best actress of them all, another Valeria, and two more Nespola and Spinetta the wife of Scapino to play the parts of the serving-maids'.[4]

In Barbieri's opinion the introduction of actresses was entirely beneficial.

I should never commend the practice of allowing boys to play the women's parts daily now that I have seen the confusion that they make in certain academies. For they do not know how to put on their own clothes, and they are dressed in the houses of women who may be

[1] Ibid., pp. 753–4.

[2] Amateurs continued to allow men to play the serving-women. Bernardo de Dominici, op. cit., iii, p. 233, records that Francesco Cordini was 'servicciuola astuta, e saputella'. See also D'Ancona, op. cit., 416–17.

[3] Fr. Hondedei, Padova, 21 Sept.

1612. Busta oliv. 981, *Filza delle lettere di Camillo Olivieri*, Bib. Oliveriano di Pesaro. Quoted by Saviotti, *Giorn. Stor.*, xli, p. 51.

[4] Giuseppe Zongo Hondedei to Camillo Oliveri, 11 Nov. 1615, ibid., p. 63.

stray serving-wenches who enjoy playing with these youths, and any one who has not the staidness of age or responsibility may at least slip into vanity. Then, once they are dressed, they parade through the city provoking much comment by their unusual attire; and when they reach the stage they are often touzled, and their friends and instructors must turn round and curl their hair, straighten their collars, and arrange the trinkets at the throat, and sometimes allow them to prink to assure themselves that everything is just so, and flatter them to encourage them to do themselves credit, until, to my thinking, it is enough to destroy the patience of whoever is responsible for them. But the women are more natural and know how to dress themselves, and since they are honest people, so far from encouraging scandal, they rather set a good example. Indeed those who are good-looking and favoured and praised, are so sought after even by persons of regard, and almost besieged with offerings, that they may be considered most honoured among the honourable if they can resist such assaults.[1]

Somewhat discreetly Barbieri only discusses the criticism that the actresses had provoked from the point of view of the audience, though he knew well enough the disturbances that they caused behind the scenes. The stimulating competition with 'Vittoria' in Florence in 1589 provoked an astonishing performance from Isabella, but the rivalry between 'Celia' and 'Lavinia' for the chance of playing the 'Mad scene' for the *Confidenti* in 1618 spoilt the season in Lucca, lost them a licence, and if it had not been for the intervention of D. Giovanni de' Medici, and the tact of Scala, who was wearied out with 'the perpetual turmoil of these cursed women', would have broken up the company. In March 1618 Antonazzoni Francesco, 'Ortenzio', with his wife 'Lavinia' and his sister threaten to leave the company because 'Fulvio' Domenico Bruni has refused to act with Lavinia, and Lavinia's jealousy of Ortenzio and 'Nespola' adds to the complication. Ortenzio writes that he cannot stand this 'continual Inferno'.[2] The stories of these quarrels are only pertinent here to prove the disturbing influence that the actresses exerted within the companies whose livelihood depended upon their unity, or to illustrate the correspondence between the manners and passions of real life and the stage situations for which it is sometimes difficult for us to

[1] *Supplica.* See Petraccone, op. cit., p. 45.   [2] *Arch. di Stato di Firenze.* Fª 5141, c. 389-90.

calculate the values. Thus, Scala's scenario of *Il Ritratto* acquires a new point when it is compared with the letter in which 'Celia' excused her behaviour with the young gentlemen of Lucca. In the play Vittoria, the *prima donna* of a company of comedians playing in Parma, is represented as an adventuress who makes use of the gentlemen who come to visit her as a means of providing herself with valuable properties on permanent loan, and regards her elderly admirers Pantalone and Gratiano as 'pigeons to be plucked'. She contrives to steal from Oratio the miniature of Isabella the wife of Pantalone, and the plot is concerned with the husband's jealous suspicions and the wife's reproaches to her lover. In the third act the comedienne is the cause of a scuffle among the audience, and before she can explain the circumstances to Pantalone and Gratiano who have escaped with her from the interrupted performance, the armed gallants rush out and carry her off. The affair Lucca when 'Lavinia' was hissed off the stage by 'Celia's' faction ended with a similar scuffle. 'Celia's' practice of receiving gentlemen of the city in her lodgings and allowing raffles and gambling was called into question. Her letter to D. Giovanni is delightfully naïve:

Of the rare visits received in my rooms, or the *riffa* conducted there, I have given you an account to show my obedience to you in this, as in all other respects; and as I told you, both here and in other cities I have been visited by the academicians who are well-read and cultured gentlemen, who, I acknowledge, have helped me to educate myself, for I have no other means of putting myself into the way of knowledge and study for I lack all support and assistance. Further I made use of the interest from the *riffa* sometimes when I found myself embarrassed with debt, sometimes because I judged it necessary and convenient to do so.[1]

What the women cost the profession in private life they repaid on the stage by making full use of the dramatic possibilities latent in the scenes between the girl page and her fickle lover, the wilful daughter and the avaricious father, and the situations caused by calumny and jealousy which in farce would end in fisticuffs, in tragedy with death, and in tragicomedy with temporary madness. On the whole they

---

[1] Firenze, 2 Nov. 1618, *Arch. di St. Fª 5141, c.* 225 (quoted also A. Neri, *Scena Illustrata*, 1 Aug. 1886). For an explanation of *riffa* see *infra*, p. 299.

are represented as having more courage and resource than the young men, who will argue with Zanni over the risks of a deception into which the girls will rush without a moment's hesitation. They appoint the lovers' disguises,[1] write their own letters,[2] woo vehemently. Clarice makes love to Lelio as he passes under her window,[3] or with Pantalone as he rides out of the city.[4] Angelica will have Horatio by fraud when open love is hopeless.[5] In the absence of her Captain husband Aurelia tries to intimidate Leandro her slave.[6] If a lover could not be coaxed, he must be tricked into an interview; one Flavia pretends that she has been wronged by Silvio and Pantalone swears he shall be made to marry her;[7] another asks her father to return the gloves that a suitor has thrown in at her window, and by this ruse sends love-letters to and fro.[8] Few take care to be thought 'honesta ma povera', a reputation that Laura claims for her daughter Isabella in *Li Dubbii* with almost immodest insistence. In *Lo Amante Ingrato* Clarice and Livia reach the limit of independence and demand a husband each, indicating the lovers of their choice, and saying that they want them at once. Pantalone promises to satisfy them; the women say that if they are not given them soon they will take them of their own accord. Pantalone implores them to have patience. In a few minutes they come out again to ask if the husbands are ready. Pantalone says he has not got them tied to his braces, but that he will find them soon. Meanwhile the girls make an assignation with the lovers and pester the old man until he is glad to keep out of their way.

In the woman who has inherited money the Shrew develops. Clarice in *Lo Amante Interessato* keeps even the Zanni at arm's length with her 'Lazzi di bravura' and violent temper. When the Magnifico tries to exert his authority she throws him his braces out of the window and locks the door. Oratio's efforts to woo and tame her are ineffectual; it takes Pantalone's discovery of a fault in her aunt's will and an official arrest for bankruptcy to reduce her pride.[9]

[1] *Il Zanni Beccho.*
[2] *Li due Trappolini.*
[3] Ibid.
[4] *Li due Venetiani.*
[5] *L'Abbatim ento di Zanni.*
[6] *Li Tre Schiavi.*
[7] *Le Astuzie di Zanni.*
[8] *La Forestiera; Il Banchetto.*
[9] *La Ricca Superba.*

Popular opinion demanded that such extreme shrewish-
ness should be tamed. There are a few plays in which the
husbands get the better of their curst wives. Virginio has a
clever trick to punish Flaminia in *Il Castigo della Disonesta
Moglie*. In *Le Moglie Superbe* Pantalone coaxes out Flavia
by telling her that a gentleman wishes to speak with her; when
she comes down 'the gentleman' proves to be a great stick.
Coviello beats Hortentia into submission in the same way.

The types range from queens to serving-women and courtesans; except for a few 'Ruffiane' they are all young, and it is
on the grounds of youth that all their passions are to be excused.
When Clarice by her intrigues with the student Leandro obliges
the doddering Pantalone her husband to renounce his claim
she is as much to be congratulated as Delia the daughter of
Coviello who has secretly married the other student.[1]

The conventional marriage which was based on the prospects of a dowry made an excellent motive for comedy.
Thwarted affection is the pivot of almost every intrigue;
'forza d'amore' is the excuse for the crudest infatuations. It
is taken for granted that Cintio will ask Pantalone for
Clarice 'only because he is unable to obtain her by any other
means'.[2] Such circumstances make the inexperienced children of Pantalone and Gratiano, who are threatened with, or
have been forced into marriage with some rich old man,
agents as suitable for an intrigue as the practised courtesans.
Their behaviour was to seem more modest[3] but their passions
and their actions are quite as brazen.[4]

When they are annoyed Isabella and Flaminia go beyond
abuse and scratch and pinch like vixens; first they come to
blows and then 'to hairs'.[5] Livia reduces Lelio to tears with
her cuffing.[6] Elsewhere Isabella relieves her feelings by
smashing dishes.[7] In more romantic circumstances their
passionate natures drive them to stab the men who have
wronged them,[8] or to offer to commit suicide in desperation
over an old lover's desertion.[9]

[1] *La Gelosia.*
[2] *La Tramutatione.*
[3] Perrucci; see Petraccone, op. cit.,
p. 93.
[4] *Le tre gravide.*
[5] *Le due Simile.*

[6] *Lo Amante Ingrato.*
[7] *Li due Capitani Simili.*
[8] *L'Amico Infido; L'Amico Tradito;
Principe d'Altavilla.*
[9] *Il Finto Astrologo.*

The most shameless type in manners and morals is Isabella the wife of Zanni the pandar, who is first hired and then trades herself to all the town;[1] or Delia who allows Leandro to make love to her over her husband's shoulder and is openly twitted by the ironical Zanni as 'an honest woman'.[2] It was regarded as a sufficient sop to morality that when they had got all that they wanted they should promise to reform and to live honestly ever after.[3]

THE SERVING-MAID

Once the academic convention that the lady shall appear as little as possible was abolished, the part of the serving-maid as her substitute to the audience was seriously diminished. In the Commedia erudita the maid is often on the stage, but she is always full of her mistress's affairs and has rarely time for more than a grumble at the incivility of porters, or the unreasonableness of lovers. In the Commedia dell'arte the maid sometimes precedes but usually accompanies her mistress; she is sent to advise her of a lover or a messenger, but she brings the lady herself to the window to conduct her own scene of love, suspicion, or reproach in full view of the audience. There is little left to describe or explain when all interviews are to be represented. In the name of the liberty, equality, and economy of a travelling company this was not enough for the third woman. She must provide for herself in other directions. As occasion offered she took over the parts of the Innkeeper's wife,[4] the nurse,[5] the procuress,[6] the midwife,[7] and the countrywoman,[8] under the names of Franceschina, Filippa, Olivetta, Nespola, or Spinetta. A new part was worked out in which the 'fantesca' became the counterpart of the Zanni in function and the reflection of her mistress in manner and mood. While Isabella planned to elope with Flavio, Franceschina conducted a brisk intrigue with Burattino, or decoyed the Captain[9] or one of the old men as her lover.[10] The love affairs of Franceschina and Filippa

1 *Il Zanni Beccho.*
2 *Li Spiriti.*
3 *Il Carnevale.*
4 *La Mancata Fede; Il Capitano.*
5 *La Finta Pazza; La Balia Grande.*
6 *La Ruffiana.*
7 *La Schiava.*
8 *La Pazzia di Filandro; Il Proteo.*
9 *Li due finti Zingari.*
10 *La Fortunata Isabella.*

with Pedrolino and Zanni in the Scala and Locatelli scenari culminate in the domestic drama of Pulcinella and Rosetta in the later period. According to her standards of refinement in each several plot the maid might choose between Tuscan and the dialects of Naples or Lombardy.[1] No scruples or conventions restrict her wit and resource, so that in practical joking she scores more often than any other intriguer.

MINOR MASKS
PEASANTS

The charlatans from Milan, Forli, Mantua, and Arezzo who meet in Garzoni's Piazza are not regular masks but every now and then they are drawn into the intrigues of a comedy.[2] From here and there among the popular plays and scenari there collects a motley crowd of local types and professions representing the turn for satire and mimicry of forgotten actors who helped to maintain the variety of the popular stage.

The development of the peasant as a stage type is due to the farces of the 'Rozzi' of Siena, Carracciola of Naples, and Alione and Ruzzante in Northern Italy; in the Commedia dell'arte the peasant is only a chance survival. Locatelli has a Contadino in *Li Banditi* and a Villano in *Il Giusto Principe*. A peasant appears as Cavicchio in Troiano's prologue; in Scala's *Teatro* there are two peasants who discourse on the afflictions of the jealous husband and sing in the dialect of Norcia.[3] Three actors, Matteo, Andrea, and Frosia, were paid 30 scudi for playing 'da Norcino' before the Pope in 1551,[4] and 'Norcino' is the name of the butcher in Locatelli's *Li Porci*. In Veraldo's *Mascarate nuove* (1626) and Briccio's *Zingara Sdegnosa* (1634) the Norcino is a type. According to Rossi the dialect was used by the Northern Zanni as an alternative to Bergamask.[5]

In Pasqualigo's pastoral *Gl'Intricati* (1581) the Villano is from the Maremma. In *La Bizzaria di Pantalone* he is Verzone of Bologna. The type lingers chiefly in the pastorals. The Zanni and Nespola who are native to Arcadia in

---

[1] Perrucci; see Petraccone, op. cit.,
p. 152.
[2] Op. cit., p. 745.

[3] VI; L.
[4] E. Re, *Giorn. Stor.*, lxiii, p. 296.
[5] N. Rossi, *Discorsi sulla Commedia.*

Locatelli's scenari have the characteristic thick-headedness of their prototypes in the rustic farces. According to De Dominici, Luizi Ridolfi invented for himself the part of Schitirzi, 'contadino goffo', at the beginning of the seventeenth century.[1] Gelso, Cervino, and Zeffa are the rustics in *La Gratiana* (1609); Gelso, Cervino, and Zippa in *Il Capriccio* (1621); Corbaccio in *Diana Vinta*; Sciaramello a Neapolitan bumpkin in Fiorillo's eclogue *La Ghirlanda* (1652); Cola in *La Zingara Fattachara* (1654), and Pelliccia the goatherd and Scaramuccia an old man in Briccio's comedy *La Rosmira* (1676) keep up the tradition. Pelliccia is described only as 'servo sciocco', but his dress and behaviour show that he was intended to satirize the countryman. He compliments the nymph for being as white as a junket and round as an omelette: when she refuses his suit he begs Scaramuccia to suggest suitable means of suicide. He agrees to be hit on the head with a spade but interrupts the blow to make his lament. Then he decides to poison himself, and Scaramuccia insists on sharing the poison which is served with cheese. Pelliccia feigns death until the success of his rival, Ciufalone, becomes too exasperating, but when he has revived and fought for the nymph he finds his liking for her has evaporated after all.

In comedy, as the Fachino becomes sophisticated, the 'Villano' takes his place as the rough servant.[2] In Briccio's comedy *Li Strapazzati*, Babbiona, 'villano goffo', is merely an ultra-stupid servant, and a note explains that his more astute companion Rampione, who is also a peasant from the mountains of Norcia, should be dressed coarsely, not in skins or with the smock and pouch of a shepherd but in black cloak and cap like a townsman.

TRADESMEN

Notaries, barbers, apothecaries, physicians, couriers, and watchmen (*sbirri*) only appear on the popular stage on business: Jews, money-lenders, and clothes dealers are sometimes distinguished by proper names.[3]

---

[1] Op. cit., pp. 233-4.
[2] S. Martini, *Bragatto* (1596). *L'Innocente in Duplicati Sponsalitii.*
[3] Sciabbadei, Hebreo, in *Est Locanda* (1648). Bedana and Menacai in *Pantalone Bullo* (1693). Cf. *La Fantesca*, Hebreo, regattiere; *Il Fate Voi*, 4 Hebrei; *La Mula*, 4 Hebrei.

In the second improvised play in *Le due Commedie in Commedia* Andreini gives directions for the make-up and dialect of genuine artizans. The sweep is to be from Bergamo, the baker and the cook from Bologna, the confectioner is a Frenchman, and the gardener is from Naples. Locatelli has a baker (*Incanti Amorosi*), and a bricklayer (*La Fabrica*), as well as a French gardener (*Li Dispetti*), but it is comparatively rare for professional types to be introduced without the ulterior motive of disguise. The properties required for cobblers, locksmiths, hawkers, chestnut sellers were usually to accommodate the lovers or their servants in an amorous intrigue. A play such as *La Travestita* in which Flavia dressed up as a gardener, Filippa as a gipsy, the Captain as a porter, Pantalone as a woman, Silvio as a sweep, Zanni as a German, and Coviello as a Jew; when Zanni begs 'alla Franzese, alla Borgognese, alla Spagnuola, et alla Italiana',[1] when he coaches Pantalone how to behave in his various disguises, and the occasion on which Pulcinella as an itinerant painter demands his fee, would give ample scope for satirical mimicry.[2]

LOCAL TYPES AND DIALECTS

Of the local types the *Neapolitan* was the most popular. In the seventeenth century this dialect encroaches upon the Venetian, Bolognese, and Bergamask of the earlier period. Satirical studies of the Neapolitan had been introduced into the Commedia erudita of the sixteenth century, such as Capitano Trinca and Signor Parabolano by Aretino,[3] Messer Ligdonio and Giovancarlo by Piccolomini,[4] Cola Francesco Vacantiello[5] in Cini's *Vedova* (1569), Giovan Tommaso Spanteca in Castelvetro's *Furbo*, Pannuorfo a simpleton in Della Porta's *Il Moro* (1607), and Bell'Humore a servant in Castelletti's *Stravaganze d'Amore* (1597).[6] The tradition was kept up on the popular stage by Cola Silverio a boaster in Veraldo's *L'Anima dell'Intrico* (1621), Col'Ascanio in

[1] *Li Porci.*
[2] *Policinella Pittore.*
[3] *Talanta; La Cortigiana.*
[4] *L'Amor Costante* (1536); *Ortenzio* (1560).
[5] See also T. Boccalini, *De' Rag-*

guagli di Parnasso (pub. 1613), in which Cola Vacantiello is mentioned among the personages of a professional company.
[6] See Croce, *Il Personaggio del Napolitano nella Commedia.*

Verrucci's *Le Schiave*, Pasquarello in *La Spada Fatale*, and the
Neapolitan variously known as Col'amiccio or Pasquarello
who appears in the little woodcuts to Briccio's Comedies
dressed in long black trousers with a black cloak and cap.
Salvator Rosa invented the part of Formica a Neapolitan
servant.

More important than the individual characters is the way
in which the dialect and accepted characteristics, the laziness,
avarice, and extravagant speech, of the Neapolitans are in-
corporated with the chief masks of the Commedia dell'arte.
Tartaglia the stutterer joins Cola and Pasquarello and becomes one of the regular old men in the Neapolitan scenari.
There are Neapolitan doctors in Cola of *La Fortuna* by
Sicinio (1610), Cola Ventrozzo de Babionis in Guglielmi's
Intrighi d'Amore (1666), and Coviello in *Pantalone Imbertonao*
(1617). Among the Neapolitan Captains are Strappaferro,[1]
Ascanio,[2] Giovan Tiburtio,[3] Polimestre,[4] and Fiorillo's
Mattamoros. In popular poetry the Neapolitan Bravo is
distinguished as the 'guappo' or 'Smargiasso'.[5]

Calabrian was also used for the boaster. From Estoile's
poem it appears that among the 'Comédiens de la Cour' in
1603 there was 'Epouvante, un vaillant Calabrois'. Giangurgolo as he appears in the scenari has no dialect assigned to
him, but Riccoboni describes him as Calabrese.[6]

Sicily yields a dialect rather than a type. Fiacavento is a
Sicilian soldier in Cini's *Vedova* (1569), Andreini played a
Doctor, and Verrucci has a Pedant, talking Sicilian.[7] Be-
lando makes it the most important dialect in *Gl'Amorosi
Inganni*. Perrucci allows it as an alternative servant Trava-
glini or Tabbarini of Palermo; Quadrio has Giovanello of
Messina.

The Tuscan pronunciation of the lovers was to be studied
from the manuals of the academies of the Onamastici
and della Crusca,[8] but the plebeian dialect of Tuscany was
used by the masks of Ceccobimbi the fig-merchant of Poggi-

[1] G. Briccio, *Bella Negromantessa*, 1621.
[2] Gattici (1626), *Gli Pensieri Fallaci*.
[3] L. Riccato (1638), *Pazzi Amanti*.
[4] F. Gattici (1626), *Le Pazzie Giovenili*.
[5] Croce, op. cit., quotes G. C. Cortese, *Micco Passaro*.
[6] Op. cit. (1728), Plate XII.
[7] *Diversi Linguaggi*.
[8] Perrucci; see Petraccone, op. cit., p. 74.

bonsi[1] and sometimes by Cassandro another of the extra old men.[2] Lavinia in *Li Diversi Linguaggi* speaks this dialect, and it is possible that Pandolfo, an old Florentine in *La Finta Spiritata*, spoke with a local accent like his namesake in the Magliabechian scenari.

Of the ten dialects used by Verrucci in *Li Diversi Linguaggi* (1609),[3] all except the Matricciana of Franceschina had their turn in the Commedia dell'arte; the babel was increased from time to time by representatives of Rome,[4] Milan,[5] Parma,[6] Genova,[7] Ragusa,[8] Pavia,[9] and later of Piedmont[10] and Apulia.[11]

Italian misused by foreigners was also a source of amusement on the popular stage. Graeco-Italian is peculiar to Calmo, Spanish, both the pure Castilian and pigeon Spanish, was appropriated by the Captain, but the Frenchman with his 'Gallicitalian' manner was a useful variant for the stranger merchant, the second father, the inn-keeper, or the servant. As Claudione, Scala uses the type once as a merchant (XXVI) and again as a preceptor (XXXIV). In VIII he is merely 'Francese'. The Frenchman of the Locatelli scenari acts as a gardener, a schoolmaster, a judge, or a merchant,[12] he is hoaxed by the servants and usually, though not invariably,

[1] *La Fantasma*; *Le due commedie in Commedia*; *L'Incamisciata*. Cf.Aldeano, op. cit. (1634).

[2] Cassandro d'Aretusi in Scala XI, XIII, XIX comes from Siena, in XXVII from Bologna. When he appears in the Locatellian, Corsinian, and Venetian scenari it is not specified where he comes from. In *L'Onorata Fuga di Lucinda* Cassandro is 'Gentiluomo Romano'.

[3] M. Claudio, Franzese; Pantalone, Venetiano; Zanni, Bergamasco; Giorgetto, Romanesco; Pedante, Ceciliano; Silvio, Bolognese; Capitano, Napolitano; Franceschina, Matricciana; Lavinia, Fiorentina; Aurelia, Perugina. With the last compare Guazzetto, servitor Perugino, in *Pantalone Innamorato*, Verrucci (1619).

[4] D. Pasquale mentioned by Perrucci. Perna, serva Romanesca, in *Stravaganze d'amore*, Castelletti, 1597;

Giorgetto ragazzo in *Li Diversi Linguaggi* (1609); Romano in Veraldo's *Mascarate nuove* ... (1626); Argentina Romanesca in *L'amore vince lo Sdegno*, by Fruscadini (1673).

[5] Barbieri appeared as Beltrame da Milano.

[6] Bartoli connects the Desevedo of *La Bellissima* with Dessevedo di Malalbergo mentioned by Quadrio, op. cit., ii, dist. iii, cap. iii, p. 200. The mask is also to be found in the Modenese plot of *La Peregrina*.

[7] Veraldo, op. cit.

[8] Calmo. See Chapter II.

[9] Ceccon, servo Pavanese, *Diana Vinta* (1624).

[10] Gianduja, see M. Sand, op. cit.

[11] Pancrazio il Biscegliese. Ibid., ii. 34.

[12] *Li Dispetti*; *Li Due Trappolini*; *Li Ritratti*; *Trapolino Invisibile*.

speaks Italian with a French lisp. In *La Fantesca* Coviello has 'lazzi' of learning how to speak French, saying 'Io mi Favetta di Francia, Uhi, uhi'. Pantalone suspects him as an impostor; he objects that he had always been told that this French client of his had a short nose, Lelio says that the heat of the journey has lengthened it, and Pantalone is content. Ottavio the changeable lover in *Il Volubile in Amore* hires Pulcinella as an interpreter, but Pulcinella knows no French. Briccio and Verrucci have a variety of names with some suggestive spellings: Gismondo,[1] Ciriaco,[2] Monsu delle Sciapelle,[3] Mestre Sgian,[4] Guglielmo,[5] Braghetto.[6] The French servants are Bubbobo,[7] Coglietto,[8] Quaglietto,[9] Jacobillo,[10] and most commonly Raguetto.[11]

In the Corsican version of *Le Burle di Filandro* a German takes the part of Locatelli's Francese. There were Todeschi among the Carnival disguises in Venice in 1572;[12] Veraldo has a Todesco-Italianato in 1626; Tiberio is a German Captain in Bulgarini's *Li Scambi*; there is a German Inn-keeper in *La Tabernaria*, but otherwise the type is not common. The German is one of the few drunkards in the Commedia dell'arte; in two pastorals and a comedy he lurches across the stage hugging a bottle and shouting to his shipwrecked companions to 'Trinch'.[13]

A study of the resources of the masked actors should correct all crude ideas of what was implied by the improvisation as a condition of the Commedia dell'arte. No simple statement will cover the diversities of practice. In many cases it

---

[1] *Dispettosa Moglie* (1629).

[2] *Servo Astuto* (1610).

[3] *Portia* (1611).

[4] *Vendette Amorose* (1625).

[5] *Pantalone Imbertonao* (1617).

[6] *Le Schiave* (1629).

[7] *Est Locanda* (1648).

[8] *La Lucinda* (1633).

[9] C. Tiberi, *Hoggi, Corre Quest'usanza*, 1641.

[10] F. Righello, *Il Pantalone Impazzito*, (1613).

[11] *La Senese*; *L'Incamisciata*; M. Cellio, *Florinda* (1629); F. Panetii, *Disonesto Amante* (1642); [R. Lusai], *Capitano Schernito* (1653); V. Comi, *La Zitella Cortegiana* (1653); Bombardieri,

Il Ciecofinto, overo Raguetto viandante (1658); Acc. Moschina, *La Pazzia de' due Vecchi Amanti* (1676).

[12] 'Ordine, et Dechiaratione di tutta la mascherata, Fatta nella Città di Venetia la Domenica di Carnevale, M.D.LXXI. Per la gloriosa Vittoria contra Turchi. In Venetia, Appresso Giorgio Angelieri, 1572.'

[13] Infiammeto, *La Gratiana* (1609); G. Guidozzo, *Il Capriccio* (1621); Fr. Guglielmi, Accademico Incognito, *Intrighi d'Amore* (1666, Orvieto). Barbetta the Captain's German servant who only wants to drink: 'Trinche Signore Capitane, io, io. Pone vine, pone vine', p. 12.

seems to have meant little more than horseplay and extempore rhyming in the piazza, encouraging the substitution of 'lazzi' and grimaces for dialogue; in others it amounted to a clumsy shuffling of the stale wit of the miscellanies. Riccoboni exposes the dangers of the use of these 'robbe generiche':

Cette façon de dialoguer ne vaut rien, car il arrive souvent que l'on place des belles maximes si mal-à-propos, qu'elles ne quadrent point à ce que l'Acteur vient de dire, et sont tout-à-fait hors d'œuvre; cet inconvénient en produit un autre: ce Comédien qui ne sçait autre chose que ce qu'il a appris par cœur et qui très-souvent n'entend pas ce qu'il dit, après une Scène, où il aura étalées les plus belles pensées qu'il doit à son Poëte, et non pas à son imagination, et qu'il aura touchés les Spectateurs par du brillant emprunté: ce Comédien, dis-je, en quittant sa Maîtresse ou son Ami est obligé de parler à l'impromptu avec son Valet, dont les Lazzis [*sic*] et le jeu de Théâtre demandent qu'il y réponde à l'impromptu ne pouvant pas alors employer ses lieux communs, il se trouve tellement déconcerté qu'il se fait connaître pour ce qu'il est. . . .[1]

But while Riccoboni remained painfully aware of the failures, he persisted in a belief in the ideal actor who besides appearance, memory, voice, and feeling should have a vivid, fertile imagination, a faculty of self-expression, and an acquaintance with all the delicacies of the language and the manners of the parts in which he intended to improvise. 'Quelle éducation ne faut-il pas pour former un tel acteur! Et ceux qui sont destinés à cette profession ne trouvent-ils pas mille obstacles à une excellente éducation?' The letters of the comedians, however, show a great variety in the standards of culture, and the reputation of the Andreini, the Martinelli, and the Fiorelli suggests that there were a few in each generation who made use of the tradition of improvisation in exercising the sense of an audience which stimulates inspiration in a Latin wit. Such a gift must often have been wasted in isolation; it is Riccoboni's second condition of success in an improvised comedy that the actors should be equally matched, for the dialogue of the best actor is entirely dependent upon the response of his companion.

The practice of improvisation among professional comedians resolves itself into a method for the preservation of

[1] Op. cit., pp. 63-4.

the effect of spontaneity. It is not impossible that such an impression should be produced in the recitation of literary drama, but it is only the greatest who do not betray the artificial conditions of premeditation. The Italian players, from choice and necessity, took the other risk. As Riccoboni remarked, 'Le bon comédien marche au milieu du chemin, et l'excellent comédien va sur le bord du precipice.'

CHAPTER III

THE SCENARI

ALTHOUGH instances of the term 'scenario' for an actor's summary of a play-plot might be quoted from Andreini and Barbieri between 1622 and 1634, Perrucci in 1699 still preferred the older word 'soggetto', and it was not until the eighteenth century that 'scenario' became current.[1] It is by now firmly established, but since it was grafted on to a conventional form it still needs some explanation. The scenari, or skeleton plots, of the Commedia dell'arte are not literary but theatrical documents, and are thus distinct from the 'argomenti' which precede many early Italian plays and are provided for the scenari of Scala, as well as from the authors' plots such as those mentioned in Henslowe's diary.[2] Perrucci describes the conventional form of the scenari for improvised comedy thus:

The 'soggetto' is nothing but the scenic fabric woven from an 'argomento', to which is added the description of an action marked out into acts and scenes, which is to be spoken and presented extempore by the performers. The scenes are begun at the margin with the indication of the entrance of each personage, and are ended with a dotted line signifying exit or exeunt. At the top of each scenario is written the supposed locality of the play, such as Rome, Naples, Genoa, Leghorn, &c. . . . An asterisk in the margin, known as the 'osservatoria', warns the actor to enter unobserved to watch what is happening on the stage. The phrase 'in questo' denotes that the player remains on the stage after the exit of the other characters. . . . Marginal notes such as 'Night, Day, Dawn', instruct the actor to introduce some appropriate remark, and if necessary to enter with a light. The stage directions, 'City, Wood, Chamber,' are for a scene-shifter or the manager of the play (*concertatore*).[3]

Perrucci takes for granted the list of the dramatis personae which is usually numbered or ruled off into families; later he refers to the list of properties given at the beginning or end

---

[1] G. B. Andreini, *Le Due Commedie in Commedia* (1622); Barbieri, *La Supplica* (1633), xxxvi, 'quei suggetti, o siano scenarij di comedie'; Perrucci, *L'Arte Rappresentativa, passim*; L. Riccoboni, *Histoire du théâtre italien* (1728), p. 31.

[2] Ed. W. W. Greg, i, pp. 70, 82; ii, p. 289.

[3] See Petraccone, op. cit., pp. 190-2.

of each plot. A glance at the scenari printed in Appendix G will illustrate this bare description. It is important that these scenari should not be confused with the theatre plots consisting of abstracts of entrances, exits, and properties which were hung in the wings for the convenience of the prompter. The five plots preserved among the Henslowe papers are chance survivors of these necessary, but artistically negligible, documents. We have it on the authority of Riccoboni and Gozzi that all Italian actors made use of them;[1] a specimen printed by Lazaro Agostino Cotta at the end of his dialect comedy *La Pirlonea* is, for our confusion, also described as a scenario.[2] The idea of a scenario as a plot-scheme misled Collier into supposing that there was a connexion between the Elizabethan 'platts' and the scenari of the Commedia dell'arte; had he had an opportunity of examining the Italian documents he would have seen the essential difference at once. The Henslowe 'platts' were evidently drawn up for the prompter and merely tantalize the reader who has no further means of acquainting himself with the play. The scenari, composed for or by the Italian *capocomico* describe every turn of the plot as it is to be presented in action. Perrucci explains that some of the scenari were drawn up from old or modern plays that had already been printed in full, whilst others were specially composed to be played 'all'improviso' in order to avoid the inconvenience and disappointment so often occasioned by the tedious preparation of premeditated drama. Ideally, the scenari should indicate the subject matter or style of conversation, the grouping, and the gestures which mark the critical moments of the plot's evolution; actually, they give, with varying adequacy, a scene by scene résumé of the play.

L'Arte Rappresentativa contains instructions for the use of a scenario. Before the company assembles the leader[3] should

---

[1] Riccoboni, op. cit., p. 39 describes Scala's scenari as 'Canevas qui ne sont pas si concis que ceux dont nous nous servons et que nous exposons accrochés aux murs du théâtre par derrière les coulisses, mais qui ne sont pas plus si prolixes que l'on puisse tirer la moindre idée de Dialogue'. Gozzi, *Opere*, iv, p. 35, *I Contratti Rotti*. Leone de Somi

also recommended such charts for the use of the prompter. See Rasi, op. cit., i. 115.

[2] See Appendix B for a discussion as to the date of this play.

[3] In Perrucci's academic terminology, 'Corago, guida, maestro o più pratico della conversatione': in the Company lists, 'Capo-comico.'

work over (*concertare*) the scenario to assure himself of the action, the occasions for speeches, and the opportunities for fresh comic business. It is his duty to expound the plot to the actors, to describe the personages, the place and conduct of the action, to assign the stage houses, arrange the 'lazzi' and collect the properties. Let him be warned to put no trust in the actor who says that he has played in this particular scenario before, he must be drilled in the details of the performance along with the rest until he is perfect in his knowledge of the time and place of the story, the names and roles of his fellow actors, the laws of exit and entrance, and has been instructed in the 'lazzi', metaphors, irony, or hyperbole judged appropriate to each occasion, and further, has been cautioned to avoid any impropriety, 'or at least, as far as possible'. After this general exposition the actors may disperse to run over the play for themselves, rehearsing 'lazzi' and dialogues, and selecting conceits and soliloquies from the miscellanies, incorporating new material at the discretion of the leader to whose care the proportions of the play are commended.[1]

Some seven hundred Italian scenari which I have been able to examine fall into three groups; printed collections, manuscript collections, and single scenari saved either in manuscript or print. I will describe these in approximately chronological order within this classification, leaving the question of their acting dates for later discussion.

Apart from the scenario published in Troiano's *Dialoghi* in 1568, which has been dealt with already, the first and last printed collection is: '*Il Teatro delle Favole rappresentative overo la Ricreatione Comica, Boscareccia e Tragica,* / Divisa in cinquanta Giornate; / Composte da *Flamineo Scala* detto / *Flavio Comico* / del Sereniss. Sig. Duca di Mantova / All' M. Sig. Conte Ferdinando Riario Marchese di Castiglione di Vald'Oreia et Senatore in Bologna / In Venetia, apresso Gio. Battista Pulciani / M.D.CXI.' The courteous readers are given to understand that but for the pressure of his friends these plays would never have been offered to the public except on the stage, but for those who like them a second part will follow. The best known of the seven well-wishers who

[1] See Petraccone, op. cit., pp. 193–6.

contribute complimentary verses is Francesco Andreini, Capitano Spavento dell' Vall' Inferno, who gives also a prose note on the author:

This same Signor Flavio both could and would have expanded his compositions and written them out word for word according to the accepted custom, were it not that now-a-days regular printed comedies have become so common that he devised this new notion of setting out his comedies as scenari leaving it to those excellent wits (born to the elegance of language) to clothe them with words.

Scala had a sense of what was becoming in print and studied our convenience. Each plot is preceded by its 'favola' explaining previous adventures of his characters which have brought about the dramatic situation which he proceeds to develop with a nicer regard for the unities of time and place than for the unity of action. Each play is divided into three acts but not into numbered scenes: the names of personages about to enter are given in the margin, and heralded by the only stage technicality which Scala permits himself, the phrase 'in quello' (in later collections 'in questo'), which may be variously translated as 'to them' or 'at this'.

Of the 48 plays contained in Scala's *Teatro*, the first 39 are comedies in which the slave and love intrigues negotiated by wily servants for unscrupulous young men and shameless young women outdo Plautus; these are brought up to date by the racy buffoonery of the masked and dialect speaking characters Pantalone, Arlecchino, Gratiano, and Captain Spavento. Number 40, *Il Giusto Castigo*, takes a step towards tragi-comedy and has a villain condemned to a solitary life. The only tragedy, *La Forsennata Principessa*, is followed by a curious entertainment *Gl'Avvenimenti* well labelled *Opera Mista* which consists of three one-act plays, a comedy, a pastoral, and a tragedy, brief and bloody: each has a cast of ten or eleven speaking parts with a few mutes extra for the tragedy, and with a change of garments and style the parts were probably trebled for each actor.[1]

Scala has only one pastoral proper, *L'Arbore Incantato*, but

---

[1] The mixture was evidently a success, 'for Giovan Battista Andreini, son of Captain Spavento, published a similar 'dramatic monster' in his *Centaura* (1622). On composite plays see W. J. Lawrence, *The Elizabethan Playhouse*, 2nd series.

the pastoral elements are used freely in the other fantastic plays which are classed as 'Opere heroiche, regie, or reale', wild fairy-tale creations, one of them, *L'Orseida*, with matter enough for three days.

Scala's invention makes his *Teatro* unique: it is the only collection which appears to be completely independent of written drama. For one scenario, *Il Marito*, it is true we have a correspondent in printed comedy, but this is Scala's own publication of *Il Finto Marito*,[1] in which he expands the earlier scenario. With pardonable exaggeration, the *Comico* who appears in the Prologue as the exponent of the author's theory of comedy informs the *Forestiero*, who is a little dubious as to the merits of this 'players' play' that Scala is an experienced dramatist and in his time has composed 'mille suggetti' which have pleased wherever they have been presented. Francesco Bartoli in *Le Fatiche Comiche* (1780) believes in Scala's originality. This, however, is not to say that no motifs in his plays are to be traced to the 'novelle', or to Latin comedy, nor does it take into account the co-operation of the actors belonging to the companies for whom the plots were designed.[2]

LOCATELLI'S MISCELLANY

The first dated, and probably the earliest manuscript collection, is that of Basilio Locatelli,[3] whose two small, thick volumes in the Casanatense Library are dated 1618 and 1622 respectively. They were discovered in 1890 by *Carletta*, alias A. Valeri, who waited four years gathering up notices of the Commedia dell'arte in preparation for an edition of the scenari, but in 1894 contented himself with two articles in the *Nuova Rassegna*.[4] But for his find we should still be tantalized peering through the key-hole of the following note in F. Bartoli's *Notizie Istoriche de' Comici Italiani*, 1782:

Locatelli the comedian flourished in 1650 and provided the stage

---

[1] Printed in Venice, 1619.

[2] Riccoboni, op. cit., supposes that Scala's scenari represent traditional pieces going back at least a century. It has often been stated that Scala was the director of the *Gelosi*, but this is on the authority of Maurice Sand whose wish was often father to the thought. See *infra*, Chapter V.

[3] As T. Beltrame points out in *Giorn. Stor.*, xcvii, Jan.–Mar. 1931, 'Loccatello' is the spelling in the manuscript, but the use of one 'c' which has been adopted by 'Carletta' and become familiar might be supported by the title-page of his comedy.

[4] *Gli scenari di Basilio Locatelli*, pp. 441, 523.

with a manuscript work entitled 'La Scena' divided into two parts. It contains a number of plots for comic, tragic, heroic, tragi-comic, and pastoral plays to be played extempore. The original until 1654 was in the possession of Vincenzo Buzzi, a professor of medicine in Rome.[1]

Adolfo Bartoli in 1880 had found the list of Locatelli's titles in Allacci's *Drammaturgia* (1666) and gave in a footnote the titles of other plays and scenari which might be connected with them. Meanwhile from parish registers Valeri gleaned some information about the Locatelli family and gave the bare facts for what they are worth. Basilio was the younger brother of an advocate Cesare Locatelli with whom he lived in the parish of S. Stefano del Cacco near the quarter of Sa Marta in Rome. After their mother's death in 1624 Cesare married, and nothing further is heard of Basilio until 1629, when he comes to live with his sister-in-law Giovanna in the Borgo Nuovo. Giovanna died that year, leaving Basilio a legacy of 15 scudi per annum on condition that he showed due reverence to his brother. He evidently behaved circumspectly, for in 1632 he inherited all Cesare's possessions and five years later saw to the publication of his *Breviarium sive Compendiarium lucubratis quaestiones iudiciariae.*

Bartoli says that he flourished about 1650, but if his manuscript was in Buzzi's possession by 1654, its author must have been already dead. His only expanded comedy, *Li Sei Ritrovati*, was published in a little undated duodecimo by Francesco Leone.[2] Valeri erred in hailing it as wholly new. Locatelli had used the plot twice before in *Il Servo Ritornato*, i. 6, and *Il Servo Scacciato*, ii. 35. For this shell of information we are duly grateful now that in the two stout little volumes we have the kernel of the matter. There are here 103 scenari.

Locatelli wrote in a firm delicate cursive hand on thin paper folded small ($7 \cdot 25'' \times 4 \cdot 88''$). He inscribed the title of

[1] Compare *Biographie degli artisti* (1852), p. 572, where Abate Filippo Boni asserts that many copies of Locatelli's manuscript were distributed among the players who profited greatly thereby. For a possible relation of this Dr. Buzzi see the note in Appendix F on *Il Finto Servo.*

[2] Li Sei / Ritrovati / Comedia nuova, e / ridicolosa Di / Basilio Locatelli / Dedicata / al molto Illustre Signor / Cataldo Belloni: [ornament] In Roma, / Nella Stamparia di Francesco Tizzoni. / Con licenza de' Superiori. / Si vendono in piazza Madama all'inse/gna del Leone. Undated but licensed by Rev. P. Mag. Sac. Pal. Ap. 1 de Aug. Archiep. Urbin. Vicesg. Fr. Raimundus Capisuccus, Sac. Pal. / Ap. Mag. Example in Bib. Vittorio Emanuele.

each scenario in capitals on the recto of a sheet with its classification 'Commedia, tragicommedia, pescatoria'; gave on the
verso a numbered list of dramatis personae, assigned the
imaginary locality, 'Si finge Roma . . . Napoli . . . Arcadia',
made a list of properties, and began the plot on a new sheet
using capitals for Act headings and the names of persons
about to enter. Only in the case of *Orlando Furioso* does he
vary this order and gives the property list which fills several
pages at the end of the plot. In four scenari the locality is
omitted.[1] The alphabetical indexes which Locatelli prepared
refer to the numbers of the scenari: the pagination is modern,
the first volume containing 335, and the second 421,
sheets.

To each volume there is a preliminary discourse and a note
to the reader, and to the first a sonnet by way of *Propositione
dell'Opera*. The discourses may be summarized at the loss of
only a parade of quotations from Aristotle, Cicero, Ambrogio
Calepino, Seneca, Plutarch, Horace, and Giovanni Pontano.
In the first, 'Per il quale si mostra esser necessario le facetie
a la vita humana, et faceto chiamarsi il comico', he defends
such jesting as respects time, place, and occasion, and considers stage recreation permissible so long as the comedian
avoids unnecessary buffoonery and contrives to mingle
pleasure and profit. In his second, 'Per il quale si mostra il
comico essere l'Academico virtuoso, le representationi et
comedie del quale si possono ascoltare et permettere, et non
quelle dell'Histrioni infame', he makes sharp distinction
between comedies represented 'per lor gusto e piacere' by
the lettered academicians, and the farces of the public players
whose mercenary habits have persistently debased the stage.
Modern professionals 'mentre essi dichiariti per infami dalle
leggi' are no better than their notorious predecessors who
were condemned by the Fathers and moralists.

If any one wishes to have further discussion on this matter, let
him read my objections made to the discourses concerning comedy,
comedians, and spectators by a certain Sier Maria Cecchino of Ferrara,
of the Company of the Accesi and as he is pleased to call himself 'Fritellino' a common player (*publico Histrione*): there I have advanced these
and other teachings and arguments in opposition to what he would

---

[1] *Il Veneno, Le Grandezze di Zanni, La Nave, Serpe Fatale.*

have simple youths believe. But for the meanwhile enough of this matter.[1]

Locatelli's first address to the reader is more pithy and whimsical and deserves translation:

Many times, (gentle reader), have I pondered in my own mind the foregoing arguments and by practice I am convinced it is perfectly true that jesting is necessary to this mortal life and that your jester is called the comedian. Thus as a recreation after my work I set myself to write the first part of my theatre of comic themes, and such pleasure have they afforded me as almost to have made up for the labour of restoring them to their present condition, for in the beginning they were so ill-arranged that hardly the sense or the first words were intelligible so sadly had they been patched up and misused. They were despoiled of any ornament or dignity and in fact were so lost and abandoned that it seemed impossible to restore them to perfection. But at last I have clothed and adorned them, if not richly, at least decently so that they may appear on the stage in any company without shame. If they have not garments enriched with gold and embroidery, and far less with enamelled ornaments, with jewels or precious stones, at least they will not appear naked, ill-clad or ill-appointed, when we bear in mind that this is no Golden but an Iron Age in which all things are shrinking and declining so that humility and moderation befit the comic Muse. And if in these themes I have not observed all the desirable precepts of poetic art, remember that they are intended for extempore representation and so depend upon the actor's skill, for the player's function is one thing and the poet's another.

I hope, God willing, to compose a second part before long; and let no one condemn me for flippancy for I am sure that I cannot be accused of such a fault if the saying of Aristotle be borne in mind: 'requies, et iocus in vita esse necessaria videntur'.

In the second part Locatelli takes fright at his own discourse and his address to the reader reads like a retraction. He is nervous that Argus eyes may spy out the many errors in 'this faulty stuff that I keep by me to solace my own mind'; he would burn it all, or at least,

I pray God that of his mercy he will pour into me such gifts of knowledge and understanding that I may make some restitution for the

---

[1] This seems to refer to an early work of Cecchini's: 'Discorsi intorno alle comedie, comedianti, e spettatori di Piermaria Cecchini Ferrarese. Dove si comprende quali rappresentationi si possino ascoltare, et permettere.' Vincenza, 1614. I have been unable to examine a copy of this pamphlet.

many days wasted in such occupations. And I beseech you, kind
reader, if you have any wisdom, that if by chance (for it could be by no
other means) you should happen on this second part of my themes or
other of my works, leave them aside if in the beginning they do not
please you, else will you deserve greater punishment for wasting time
in reading than I in composing them, for you will have had a warning
at outset which I have not had until the end.

Eighty of Locatelli's scenari are for Comedies, and of
these, twenty would be better described as farces[1] and in a few
others the balance between buffoonery and intrigue is so even
that their classification calls for later discussion.[2] Twelve
tragi-comedies, eight pastorals, one heroic play *Orlando
Furioso* and two tragedies, or rather two versions of the same
tragic theme make up the tale of 103: from which, however,
seven scenari[3] may be put aside as variants, for he made good
use of the stage licence of re-working old material.

Locatelli has less claim than Scala to be regarded as the
inventor of scenari: he is confessedly a collector and reno-
vator. It seems most likely that the scraps which he describes
as 'talmente malcondotti che intendere in alcun modo non si
potevano' were some old theatre plots or actors' notes. Precisely what fragments he may have had we do not know, but
in the course of reconstruction he referred freely to printed
drama and narrative. In the scenario of *Orlando Furioso* he
gives as many details of the action as appeal to him at the time
and says frankly that all this may be read in such and such
a canto of *Orlando Furioso*. Boccaccio is the ultimate if not
the immediate source for *L'Innocenta Rivenuta*, and *Le
Grandezze di Zanni*. Terence accounts for one and Plautus
for four comedies.[4] And the debt of 20 more scenari to
printed Italian plays which I am able to prove only increases

---

[1] Farces, vol. i, nos. 1, 2, 12, 15, 16,
20, 35, 40, 42, 49; vol. ii, nos. 11, 12, 20,
23, 25, 27, 29, 34, 35, 43.

[2] Tragi-comedies, i. 3, 4, 5, 6, 7, 8, 9,
10; ii. 39, 40, 41, 42. Pastorals, i. 41;
ii. 4, 13, 21, 26, 28, 50, 51. Tragedies,
ii. 52, 53.

[3] Variants. *Li Ritratti*, pastorale, i. 3;
cf. *Ritratti*, pescatoria, ii. 51. *La Pazzia
di Doralice*, i. 9; cf. *La Giostra*, ii. 41.
Il Servo Ritornato, i. 15; cf. *Il Servo

Scacciato, ii. 35. *La Gelosia*, i. 47; cf. *La
Lite*, ii. 48. *La Pazzia di Filandro*, ii.
45; cf. *La Pazzia di Dorindo*, ii. 5. *Il
Serpe Fatale*, ii. 39; cf. *La Cometa*, ii. 40.
Il Principe Severo, ii. 52; cf. *Il Giusto
Principe*, ii. 53.

[4] *Il Fromento*, i. 39; cf. *Adelphi*. *La
Fantasma*, i. 19; cf. *Mostellaria*. *Li due
simili*, i. 26; cf. *Menaechmi*. *Li Prigioni*,
ii. 31; cf. *Captivi*. *La Tramutatione*, ii.
36; cf. *Amphitryon*.

suspicion of the originality of many others whose titular correspondents I have been unable to examine.[1]

It is important to realize that whatever polish Locatelli supplied from his literary models the plays had evidently been already adapted to the stage by professional comedians. If we make allowances for Locatelli's style which lends itself somewhat to detail and diffuseness we have another trustworthy collection of the plots used for improvisation at the turn of the sixteenth century when the Commedia dell'arte was in its prime.

CORSINI MISCELLANY

Very different from the Locatelli manuscript are the two volumes of scenari, preserved as Codices 45 G. 5, 6 in the Biblioteca della R. Accademia dei Lincei in the Palazzo Corsini. This manuscript is the work of two transcribers, one (A) who wrote a thick, clear, ugly, sloping hand was responsible for eighty-eight scenari, and the other (B) copied the remaining twelve in his small, wriggly, unformed writing. They used the same paper folded into sheets $11 \cdot 5 \times 8 \cdot 5$ inches and were evidently working in collaboration, for the numbers endorsed on the last two sheets of each scenario fit

---

[1] The relationship between scenari and printed plays will be analysed later in this chapter; the list is sufficient in this connexion: *L'Innocentia Rivenuta*, i. 4; cf. V. Verucci, *Il Dispettoso Marito* (1612). *L'Abbatimento di Zanni*, i. 11; cf. N. Secchi, *L'Interesse* (1581). *La Fantesca*, i. 17; *Horatio Burlato*, i. 21; cf. Della Porta, *La Fantesca* (Allacci, 1592). *Li due schiave*, i. 28; cf. L. Groto, *Emilia* (1579). *Il Finto Schiavo*, i. 30; cf. Della Porta, *Olimpia*: cf. F. Fornaris, *Angelica* (1584). *Il Finto Marito*, i. 32; cf. F. Scala, *Il Finto Marito* (pr. 1619) (pr. as a scenario 1611). *Il Finto Servo*, i. 36; cf. Ariosto, *Gli Suppositi* (pr. 1524). *Li Porci*, i. 42; cf. Verucci, *La Moglie Superba*. Allacci gives an edition for 1621 which I have not been able to examine. This post-dates Locatelli scenario 1618, but see later discussion of the relationship be-

tween these two dramatists. *Il Granchio*, i. 46; cf. L. Salviati, *Granchio* (1566). *L'Intronati*, i. 50; cf. degl'Intronati di Siena, *Il Sacrifizio* (1531). *La Trappolaria*, ii. 14; cf. Della Porta, *La Trappolaria* (Allacci, 1596). *La Zinghera*, ii. 19; cf. Bibbiena, *La Calandria* (Allacci, pr. 1523). *L'Amor Costante*, ii. 24; cf. A. Piccolomini, *L'Amor Costante* (1536). *Li Scambi*, ii. 30; cf. G. Razzi, *La Balia* (1560). *Li Furti*, ii. 32; cf. Fr. d'Ambra, *Il Furto* (1566). *Il Serpe Fatale*, ii. 39, and *La Cometa*, ii. 40; cf. V. Verucci, *La Spada Fatale* (Allacci, 1618). *Il Tesoro*, ii. 49; cf. L. Groto, *Il Thesoro* (Allacci, 1583). *La Forestiere*, ii. 17, is a version of Bargagli's *Pellegrina*. *La Turchetta*, ii. 15, gives a popularized version of the slave-intrigue which had already been used by Dolce in *Fabritia*. See *Giorn. Stor.* xcvii, p. 16.

FRONTISPIECE IN THE CORSINI MS.

into a scheme for 102 scenari in which sequence we now lack numbers 45 and 50.[1]

Each scenario constitutes a separate gathering, though they vary in size from four to ten sheets; occasionally end leaves are missing. The indexes and title-page which read:

Raccolta / di / scenari / piu scelti / D'Istrioni / Divisi in Due Volumi

are written on new paper by some librarian and inserted after a covering sheet of old paper which has some irrelevant and partly illegible scrawl of accounts. Volume i contains 242, and volume ii 203, sheets.

In one respect this manuscript is unique: it is illustrated. Each title-page has a crude coloured drawing of some scene or group of personages from its scenario. Here, if the nice delineation of faces and the calves of legs was beyond their skill, the artists did their best to indicate dress and properties. The laws of perspective meant nothing to them: they expressed themselves as naïvely as children, and once we come to understand their notation these drawings can tell us more about the stage of the Commedia dell'arte than the decorative grotesques of Callot.

RELATIONSHIP OF THE LOCATELLI AND CORSINI MSS.

Attention was first called to this collection by A. Zenatti who noticed that the titles of forty-four scenari corresponded to the Locatelli titles recorded by Allacci.[2]

In 1891 F. de Simone Broüwer printed two scenari whose titles *Li due Fratelli Rivali* and *La Trappolaria* had misled him to suspect their connexion with Della Porta's comedies.[3] He brooded over the Locatelli titles and noted two more probable correspondents. Meanwhile Valeri had known for a year of the existence of the Casanatense scenari and waited until 1894 to produce them as a triumphant proof that the Corsini manuscript was nothing more than a redaction of the Locatelli collection, 'a patching together in telegraphic style

[1] B copied. i. 30 (70); i. 44 (68); ii. 3 (98); ii. 11 (59); ii. 12 (72); ii. 19 (74); ii. 20 (58); ii. 22 (101); ii. 24 (57); ii. 27 (69); ii. 31 (71); ii. 37 (75).

[2] *Rivista critica della letteratura italiana*, ii, p. 156.

[3] *Giorn. Stor.* xv, p. 277.

of what may be considered as the most interesting body of scenari yet known'. Valeri finds 'nearly 70' correspondents between the two collections, prints a specimen *L'Acconcia Serva* in its dual form, annotates the list of Locatelli's titles referring to their Corsini counterparts, and thrusts aside the latter collection arguing that since they cannot have been the fragments 'talmente malcondotti' on which Locatelli worked, they must be later than the Casanatense scenari and so of inferior interest. Since then the Corsini manuscript has been discredited, and scholars have not troubled to consult it. But Valeri's collation is not adequately stated and his conclusion is unreasonable, as I wish to show by a more minute statement of the comparison between the two manuscripts in order to establish the independence and suggest the limits of a possible acting date for this lively repertory of the Commedia dell'arte.

One point in Valeri's argument that the Corsini manuscript is derived from the Casanatense is that the crest of a cardinal's hat and tassels stamped on the red leather covers belonged to Maurice of Savoy only during his Cardinalate 1621–42. So much for the covers, but not for their contents which, judging by their crumpled edges and the disturbed sequence of numbers, represent a rearrangement of old material.[1]

Stating a relationship between the two collections Valeri prints Locatelli's title-list and forgets to mention the thirty odd scenari from the Corsini manuscript for which he can find no correspondents. These alone should receive due attention, but they are not all. Among the seventy scenari common to both manuscripts the degrees of correspondence are so variable that they must be divided into eight classes. Sixteen scenari in group A correspond entrance for entrance;

[1] Since last examining this manuscript Tina Beltrame (*Giorn. Stor.* cxvii, Jan.–Mar. 1931) remarks that on the title-pages of *Gli Scambi*, i. 7, and *La Schiava*, i. 2, it is possible to make out a signature: *L'Occulto*. Acco Humsta. It is pointed out that the academy connected with the house of Maurice of Savoy was not the *Humoristi* but the *Desiosi* and it is possible we have here a couple of borrowed scenari. This may be a clue to the likeness to the Casanatense collection, since it has suggested that Locatelli belonged to the 'Accademia Humorista' on the grounds that its meeting-place was next door to his house and that one of its members was the Dottor Buzzi in whose possession his MS. was found in 1654.

here and there a name is altered, often the Corsini draft is so condensed that coincidence cannot be gauged detail for detail, but within a given outline the scenari may be said to be identical.[1]

Seventeen in group B correspond at all critical points but show independence in the rearrangement of entrances, the explanation of the dénouement, and in occasionally varying or adding to the 'lazzi' required. The Corsini version of many of these scenari is so scanty that one could hardly suppose them to be copied from Locatelli's manuscript, for if he was copying why should the transcriber trouble to change names, entrances, and 'lazzi' and make these changes consistent?[2]

[1] Cors. i. 1.   *Gran Pazzia d'Orlando*   = Locatelli, ii. 1.
　　 i. 8.   *Il Furbo*   =   *La Fantesca*, i. 17.
　　 i. 26. *La Pellegrina*   =   *La Forestiera*, ii. 17.
　　 i. 32. *Li due Trappolini*   =   i. 13.
　　 i. 36. *Consigli di Pantalone*   =   i. 40.
　　 i. 39. *Due Fratelli simili con la pazzia*
　　　　　　　d'amore   =   ii. 8.
　　 i. 40. *Sardinello Invisibile*   =   *Trappolino Invisibile*, i. 14.
　　 i. 41. *La Battagliola*   =   ii. 42.
　　 i. 43. *La Pazzia di Doralice*   =   i. 9.
　　 i. 44. *Horatio Burlato*   =   i. 21.
　　 ii. 4. *Elisa Alii Bassa*   =   i. 38.
　　 ii. 27. *Li Finti Mariti*   =   *Finti Morti*, i. 35.
　　 ii. 36. *Li Dispetti*   =   i. 7.
　　 ii. 39. *Gl' Adelfi di Terenzio*   =   *Il Fromento*, i. 39.
　　 ii. 40. *Il Veleno*   =   *Il Veneno* [*sic*], i. 5.
　　 ii. 51. *L'Acconcia Serva*   =   i. 16.

[2] Cors. i. 11. *Li due Simili*   =   Loc. i. 26.
　　 i. 18. *Li Tre Turchi*   =   *Finti Turchi*, i. 31.
　　 i. 27. *Li Stroppiati*   =   *Travestita*, ii. 37.
　　 i. 29. *Il Giardino*   =   ii. 46.
　　 i. 33. *La Nave*   =   ii. 26.
　　 i. 34. *Commedia in Commedia*   =   i. 43.
　　 i. 45. *Il Proteo*   =   i. 41.
　　 ii. 2. *I Sei contenti*   =   i. 2.
　　 ii. 12. *L'Innocentia Rivenuta*   =   i. 4.
　　 ii. 15. *L'Intronati*   =   i. 50.
　　 ii. 19. *L'Anfitrioni*   =   *Tramutatione*, i. 36.
　　 ii. 21. *La Fabrica*   =   ii. 45.
　　 ii. 31. *Finti Amici*   =   i. 34.
　　 ii. 32. *Prencipe d'Altavilla*   =   i. 6.
　　 ii. 38. *Ragazzo per le lettere*   =   *Finti Amici*, i. 34, see *supra*.
　　 ii. 48. *Le Teste Incantate*   =   i. 8.
　　 ii. 49. *La Schiavetta*   =   *La Turchetta*, ii. 15.

In the next group (C) the modifications increase. Several scenes or 'lazzi' are changed;[1] minor comic parts are developed;[2] a final flourish or an extra explanatory excuse is added[3] or omitted;[4] the method of dénouement is changed;[5] an extra personage, such as D. Agna wife of Pantalone causes new complications and retributions in *Claudione Fallito*.

There are 18 scenari in this group and another 13 in group D in which modifications of the same nature occur more frequently.[6] Thus *La Zingara* substitutes Olivetta for Zanni in the sub-plot, adds 'lazzi' and details for love-scenes

[1] Cors. ii. 16, 20. *Pantaloncino* = Loc. ii. 50.
    i. 17.   *Ritratti*   = i. 3 and ii. 51.
[2] Cors. ii. 28. *Fonte Incantato* = Loc. i. 44.
[3] Cors. ii. 30. *Il Granchio* = Loc. i. 46.
    i. 14. *La Sepoltura* = i. 20.
[4] Cors. ii. 45. *Li Tre Schiavi* = Loc. i. 29.
[5] Cors. i. 23. *Arme Mutate* = Loc. i. 48.
[6] Group C.
Cors. i. 14. *La Sepoltura* = Loc. i. 20.
    i. 17. *Li Ritratti* = i. 3, ii. 51.
    i. 23. *Arme Mutate* = i. 48.
    i. 24. *Il Giusto Principe* = ii. 53.
    i. 25. *Il Pazzo* = ii. 47.
    i. 30. *Claudione Fallito* = ii. 25.
    i. 31. *Le Moglie Superbe* = ii. 29.
    i. 47. *I Sei Simili* = ii. 11.
    ii. 5. *La Nobiltà di Bertolino* = *Grandezzi di Zanni*, i. 10.
    ii. 10. *Astuzie di Zanni* = ii. 12.
    ii. 20. *Pantaloncino* = ii. 50.
    ii. 22. *Il Tesoro* = ii. 49.
    ii. 24. *Il Serpe Incantato* = ii. 39.
    ii. 28. *Il Fonte Incantato* = i. 44.
    ii. 30. *Il Granchio* = i. 46.
    ii. 33. *Li Tre Matti* = ii. 2.
    ii. 41. *Graziano Innamorato* = i. 27.

Group D.
Cors. i. 2. *La Schiava* = i. 28, *Le due Schiave*.
    i. 3. *Il Tradito* = i. 22.
    i. 5. *Il Gran Mago* = ii. 21.
    i. 9. *Li Tre Satiri* = ii. 28.
    i. 12. *Gl'Amorosi Incanti* = ii. 20.
    i. 16. *Le Due Schiave* = *Li due sorelle schiave*.
    i. 21. *La Zingara* = *Finto Astrologo*.
    i. 22. *L'Amante Ingrato* = i. 23.
    i. 38. *Le Burle di Fedele* = ii. 13.
    ii. 1. *La Cieca* = *Zanni Beccho*, i. 12.
    ii. 11. *L'Amor Costante* = ii. 24.
    ii. 34. *Li Porci* = i. 42.
    ii. 46. *La Spada Mortale* = ii. 39.

and has a more effective opening. The difference between *Le Burle di Fedele*, and *Le Burle di Filandro* and the two *Amante Ingrato* scenari is mainly due to the drastic shortening of the Corsini version. If the transcriber had access to the Locatelli scenari he managed to miss their spice and skill with remarkable obtuseness. In the cases of *Il Tradito* and *La Schiava* the change might easily be due to the rearrangement of a producer who was accommodating the talent at his disposal. This implies that there is at least an acting version between the two manuscripts, and is probably to be explained by the fact that each is derived independently from a common source of popular professional scenari.[1]

In the fifth group (E) of seven scenari additions to the cast and changes of 'lazzi' necessitate a rearrangement of the third act, and in some cases disturb the entrances throughout. New opening scenes are supplied.[2]

In group F the contrasts outweigh the connexions. Beyond an obviously common theme the scenari are not related to each other.[3]

In two plays (of group G) there is only a generic resemblance between the plots.[4] While two others, *Li due Scholari* and *Il Torneo*, which correspond in the dramatis personae and the opening situation, for the rest of the play have no connexion whatever. Eleven comedies, six farces, two pastorals, a tragedy, and a tragi-comedy are entirely new.

[1] T. Beltrame (*Giorn. Stor.* xcvii) points out that both collections are admittedly *rifacimenti* and belong to the *virtuosi* who imitate the professional players. See *infra*, p. 146 seq.

[2] Group E.

Cors.	i. 6.	*Li Spiriti*	= Loc. i. 18.
	i. 7.	*Li Scambi*	= ii. 30.
	i. 15.	*Li due Fratelli* =	ii. 10.
	ii. 3.	*La Senese*	= ii. 16.
	ii. 16.	*Pantaloncino*	= ii. 50.
	ii. 18.	*Li Dubbi*	= ii. 34.
	ii. 35.	*La Nobiltà*	= i. 10, see *supra*.

[3] Group F.

Cors.	ii. 13.	*Il Falso Indovino*	= Loc. i. 37.
	ii. 23.	*Il Vecchio Avaro*	= i. 45.
	ii. 25.	*Il Tradito*	= i. 22.
	ii. 29.	*Il Figlio Prodigo*	= *Li Porci*, i. 42.

[4] Group G.

Cors.	i. 4.	*Li due Pantaloni*	= Loc. ii. 6.
	ii. 9.	*Sentenzia in Favore*	= *Giuoco di Primiera*, i. 1.

The object of this tedious comparison is to uphold the independence of the Corsini miscellany. I have come by no external evidence for its date, but it seems unjustifiable to regard it as certainly later than 1622 when its claims for priority balance so evenly with Locatelli's collection. Locatelli found the originals of his scenari in a wretched condition, which decay implies an early acting date. It is just as likely that the Corsini scenari were written up from the same plays and scraps adapted to the needs of a different company as that they were copied from the Casanatense manuscript. The fact that where scenari in later collections correspond to scenari common to the Casanatense and Corsini collections, they tend to follow the Corsini version[1] suggests that this collection is probably in the direct theatrical tradition and Locatelli's in an academic side-track. At least it is certain, as we shall see by detailed collation, that every now and then the Corsini manuscript can throw light on Casanatense scenari by recording a detail of performance which Locatelli took for granted.

MISCELLANY IN THE MUSEO CORRER, VENICE

In 1896 V. Rossi, describing the collection of 51 scenari found in Codex 1040 of the Museo Correr, assigned them tentatively to the first half of the seventeenth century on the score of the handwriting and of the connexions between two of the plots and Della Porta's printed comedies, *L'Astrologo* and *La Trappolaria*. The scenario from Ariosto's *Li Suppositi* Rossi had already printed without comment: some resemblances to the title-lists of the Scala, Locatelli, and Corsini collections were pointed out.[2]

S^a Tina Beltrame in a valuable article recently printed in the *Giornale Storico*[3] has managed to confirm Rossi's impression by interpreting a note in the catalogue of manuscripts in the Biblioteca Marciana in which this codex, originally belonging to Soranzo, is described as containing, 'Commedie 51 a soggetto, o siano abbozzi e ossature per commedie divise

---

[1] See p. 22. Cf. Cors. *La Schiava*, i. 2 and Nap. *Emilia*, i. 15. Cors. *Granchio*, ii. 30 and Nap. *Granchio*, i. 12.

[2] *Rendiconti del R. Ist. Lombardo*

(1896), Serie II, vol. xxix, p. 883, and *Per nozze*, Flamini-Fanelli, 1895.

[3] Loc. cit., vol. xcvii, ff. 1–2, Jan.–Mar. 1931.

cadauna in tre atti li titoli delle quali sono . . . ma siccome sono di pochissimo pregio e fatte per il teatro S. Casiano cosi non ne diremo di più.'

The reference to the theatre S. Cassiano is a valuable clue. The first theatre of that name appears to have been situated in the Corte Michiel near to the Campanile, and to have been only for the performance of comedies; it was extinct by 1630. Sᵃ Beltrame might have observed that this miscellany is peculiar in containing only scenari of comedies. The second theatre is said to have belonged to the Troni of S. Benedetto; it was rebuilt after a fire in 1629 and after 1637 seems to have been used chiefly for musical performances. It is perhaps worth noting that the Troni were the owners of the *stanze* with whom Scala negotiated on behalf of the *Confidenti* in 1619.[1]

The scenari have been copied into a manuscript book of 137 pages preceded only by an index of titles. The spellings are said to indicate a dialect mixture of Northern and Central Italy. The usual conventions in setting out a plot are observed: the text of letters for reading aloud is sometimes supplied at the end of the scenario. Nothing is wasted on headings or fresh sheets.

In spite of the uniform label of *Commedia*, three plays, *L'Amico Infido*, *Isole*, and *Li Due Fratelli Avelenati*, border on tragi-comedy, and in many farce runs riot. The jealous misunderstandings brought about by the misdelivery of letters and by eavesdropping lovers are persistent to the point of monotony: it would be interesting to know whether they represent the taste of a company or a collector.

One scenario, *Il Pozzo* described as 'del Pasquati', led Rossi to suppose the authorship of Giulio Pasquati, Pantalone of the *Gelosi*. This seems plausible, though oddly enough title hints are usually untrustworthy: the puzzle of *Il Mostro di Terentio*, which suggests a Latin original, is cleared up by Sᵃ Beltrame's emended reading, *Il Mastro (maestro)*, which is confirmed by the correspondence with the Neapolitan *La Scuola di Terentio*, where Terentio is not the dramatist but the proverbial Pedant of Renaissance satire.[2]

---

[1] See *infra*, Chapter V, p. 76.

[2] This description of Correr MS. was written some time before Sᵃ Beltrame's article appeared: I have, I hope, acknowledged all that I have taken from it.

So far I have been unable to find a play or title which will explain the ascription *Il Finto Servo del Cicognini*. To Rossi's three source plays, however, we may add *Li Due Amanti furiosi* which is taken from Della Porta's *La Furiosa* (1609, Allacci); *Li Due Sorelle Rivale* from Eusebio Luchetti's play (1609); *Oratio Inavertito* from Barbieri's comedy (1629). Sᵃ Beltrame points out that *I duo Simili con le lettere mutate* resembles Andreini's *I Duo Lelii simili* (1622) and *Isole* his *La Turca*, and that *La Finta Sorella* owes something to Della Porta's *La Sorella* and, at the dénouement, to the popular *Emilia* of Luigi Groto. Three scenari go back to Scala, three to Locatelli, and nine will reappear in the Neapolitan miscellany.[1]

SECOND CASANATENSE MISCELLANY. CODEX 4186

A note to the first scenario 'recitato per la prima volta in Firenze Venerdi a di 17 ottobre 1642' makes 1643 the earliest possible date for the compilation of the collection of 48 scenari in Codex 4186 of the *Biblioteca Casanatense* to which F. de Simone Broüwer[2] drew attention in 1901. This manuscript consists of one unnumbered and 234 numbered sheets (292 × 203 mm.). Substantially it is the work of one scribe, but a few additions and corrections are made by another hand.[3] Each scenario is folded to itself and, when unsewn, may have been in actual use by the comedians.

On the vellum binding is scrawled: 'Ciro Monarca / Dell' opere Regie', and within: 'Comedie manoscritte' with an old collocation C. 210. On the recto of the first sheet: 'de Cencinis H. Florent.' A further heading to the first scenario 'Opera Tratta dallo Spagnuolo' gives the key to this miscellany. In thirty-eight of these scenari the comic masks are completely in abeyance to the complicated excitements of plays which bring on to the Italian stage the names, scenes, manners, ideals, and dramatic conventions of seventeenth

---

1 Ven. 3, *Li Quattro Finti Spiritati*; cp. Scala 33. Ven. 12, *L'Amico Tradito*; cp. Scala 5. Ven. 22, *Fido Amico*; cp. Scala 29. Ven. 9, *Mala Lingua*; cp. Loc. i. 22, *Tradito*. Ven. 50, *Amante Tradito*; cp. Loc. i. 22, *Tradito*. Ven. 51, *L'Intronati*; cp. Loc. i. 51. For Neapolitan variants see *infra*, p. 48.

2 *Rendiconti della R. Acc. de' Lincei*, Serie V, vol. x, p. 391. Broüwer prints sc. 5, *L'Ateista Fulminato*, and discusses the literary origins of *Il Convitato di Pietra*, sc. 24.

3 See 8, 10 verso, 11 verso, 21.

century Spain. Fourteen of these plots can be referred to
their literary sources. When in some cases the borrowing
seems indirect we may suspect a lost Italian translation or
adaptation between the scenario and its ultimate Spanish
source.[1]

With the exception of seven farcical plays which are probably of Commedia dell'arte composition, two pastorals and
one morality which belong to the Seicento of Italy, the remaining twenty-four—tragedies, tragi-comedies, romances,
historical melodramas, and melodramatic moralities—show
the influence of Spanish drama so strongly that we cannot but
suspect that they derive from plays which are no longer
accessible to us.

By ransacking Allacci's 'Dramaturgia' and catalogues of
Spanish drama I have been able to add a little to the list of
similar titles begun by Broüwer: these waifs which are relegated to the appendix support my belief in the literary origins
of this miscellany. The demand for 'scene premeditate'
points the same way. Extravagance in intrigue and apparatus
is characteristic of these scenari. The elaborate scenes of
palaces, woods, sea-shores, bedchambers, and fortresses are
shifted freely. Ghosts and apparitions, spectacles of battles,
executions, conflagrations, and panoramas of heaven and
hell evidently presented no difficulty. Once we are told 'Il
Mago trova l'inventione di far parlare gl'alberi con la solita
cosa del cannone sotto terra'.[2] There is a considerable use
of music for entertainment and prophecy.

Some of the lists of dramatis personae in this manuscript

---

[1] (1) *Il Medico di suo honore*; cp.
Calderon, *El Medicò de su honra*. (2) *La
Regina statista Regnante*; cp. N. Biancolleli (1668). (6) *Il Crispo*; cp. printed
scenario of a tragedy by D. Ansaldo
Grimaldi played in 1628, preserved in
Bib. Casanatense Misc. 4° 668 (4).
(14) *Marescial di Biron*; cp. Perez de
Montalban; see W. Smith, *Mod. Phil.*
xx. 3. (16) *Baldovino e Carlotto*; cp.
*Marquès de Mantua o, Baldovino y Car-
lotta*, Lope di Vega. (24) *Il Convitato di
Pietra*; cp. G. A. Cicognini, undated.
(28) *Lo Schiavo del Demonio*; cp. Miro
de Mescua through Cicognini (1664).

(29) *Belisario*; cp. G. A. Cicognini,
adapted from the *Belisario* of Lope
di Vega. (31) *La Ruota di Fortuna*;
cp. Mira de Mescua. (36) *L'Onorata
povertà di Rinaldo, con i tradimenti di
Florante, e codardia di Gano Maganeze*;
cp. G. A. Cicognini, or a prose version
by L. Raimondi, pub. 1679. (39) *Don
Bernardo di Cabrera*; cp. Lope di Vega.
(40) *La forza l'Astimosa*; cp. Lope di
Vega. (48) *Gl' honesti amori della Regina
d'Inghilterra con la morte di Conte di
Sessa*.

[2] *Vittoria Cacciatrice*, sc. 9.

are particularly interesting. Alongside the characters proper
to the play are written the stage names of their impersonators,
so that for seven scenari we can reconstruct the cast of speaking parts.[1] I have arranged the list to show the possible
changes in the make-up of this company. Reckoning name
by name we have thirteen men, ten women, and two boys,
which is an unprecedented number: by observing the occasions and groupings of their appearance we can make a
plausible reduction to eight men, five women, and two boys.

	A	B	C
Lovers.			
	Aurelio (5)		
	Mario	Virginio (5)	
	Capitano Ortenzio (5)		
Old Men.			
	Pantalone (5)		
	Dottore (5)		
	Beltrame (5)		
Servants.			
	Bertolino	Capellino (5)	Pollicinella (13)
	Buffetto	Trivellino (5)	Coviello (13)
Pages.			
	Checco (5)		
	Momolo (5)		
Women.			
	Leonora	Vittoria (5)	
	Angiola	Lucetta (5)	
	Maria	Flavia (5)	
	Fioretta	Spinetta (5)	
	Olivetta	Diamantina (5)	

The characters in column B appear only in scenario 5; those
in column C only in scenario 13; their correspondents in A
do not appear in these scenari but take their places in scenari
8, 23, 32, and 47. The parallel names, therefore, may

---

[1] (5) *La Casta e Constante Ipsicratea con
i Trionfi di Pompeo nel Regno di Ponto nella
Farsaglia.* (8) *La Semiramide.* (11) *Il
Famoso Triumvato con lo spartimento del
Mondo tra Ottaviano, Lepido, e Marc'
Antonio.* (13) *L'Arcadia travagliata per*
l'ira di Diana contro Enea. (23) *Il
Cavaliero da i tre Gigli d'oro.* (32) *Il
Fratricida crudele, le finte caccie con Ber-
tolino Impiccato.* (47) *Avocato Criminale,
cioè il Rosildo.*

represent a variety of stage names for the same actors, or a change in the personnel of the company. Too little is known of the composition of the companies from year to year to allow for a certain interpretation, but the majority of the masks can be identified with individual actors and a tentative grouping suggested. The cast of scenario 5 most nearly fits the Company of the *Confidenti* under the patronage of Don Giovanni de' Medici and the direction of Flaminio Scala. *Beltrame* is unmistakably Nicolò Barbieri. *Capitano Ortenzio* might be Francesco Antonazzoni who played the soldier and the lover under this name; *Aurelio* was the stage name of Marcello de' Secchi. Domenico Bruni, generally *Fulvio*, would take the Doctor's part when necessary; Marc' Antonio Romagnesi was their Pantalone. *Spinetta* is easily recognized as the wife of Gabrielli. The other women's parts are not recorded in the lists for this company but they may have been allotted to younger actresses whose services were in request for one of the frequent temporary amalgamations. Vittoria Amorevoli, *detta Isabella*, Virginio Costante and Aurelio de Secchi acted together as *Comici Costanti*. The wife of Girolamo Garavini played *Flavia* normally for the *Fedeli*. *Lucetta* cannot be traced, but *Diamantina* was probably Beatrice the wife of G. B. Fiorillo who was associated with the *Confidenti* in 1638. The coincidence of parts is broken by the Zanni. Instead of the famous *Scapino* and *Mezzettino* of the *Confidenti*, *Capellino* and *Trivellino* are the masks recommended. The former is, so far, not to be associated with any actor. Domenico Locatelli (1613–71) had hardly made his name as *Trivellino* until the second half of the century, possibly the reference here is to his predecessor Andrea Frajacomi who took the part for the *Uniti* in 1614. It is hardly to be expected that the names of the pages, Checco and Momolo, should offer any clue.

The remaining masks connect the other scenari with companies of the second half of the seventeenth century. *Angiola* is most likely to be Angela d'Orso, a remark in whose letter to her patron in 1672 brings to light a possible *Mario*.[1] *Buffetto* is almost certainly Carlo Cantù. For *Bertolino* there is a choice between Nicolo Zecca (fl. 1635–70) and

[1] See Rasi, i, p. 793. For other *amorosi* of this name see the list in Appendix.

his successor A. Broglia. In 1627 Leonora Castiglione was acting with the *Confidenti*, and until June when she was dismissed as unsatisfactory *Olivetta* was a member of this company. *Maria* is not distinctive, and the only recorded *Fioretta*, Vittoria Piissimi, belongs to an earlier generation: these names, however, are not uncommon and might easily have been adopted for the occasion by less well-known actresses.

MAGLIABECHIAN MS. FLORENCE

Modern studies of the Commedia dell'arte begin with the twenty-two scenari published with a critical introduction by A. Bartoli in 1880. By a curious slip Bartoli[1] refers to the Magliabechian Codex (II. 1. 80) as 'di carattere del secolo XVIII', actually it is described as containing: 'Commedie XXII all'improviso, o spartiti per le medesime cod. Chart. in fol. Saec. XVII. exeuntis pagg. Scriptt. 113 in quo huiusmodi exstant comoediarum argumenta.' A duplicate copy preserved in the Laurentian Library as Codex F. Riccardiana 2800 also belongs to the seventeenth century.[2] The style of the scenari justifies an earlier mention. Whoever compiled this miscellany made a somewhat unsuccessful attempt to give the authors their due. *Le Tre Gravide* is attributed to Fr. Riccolini, *La Spada Fatale* to G. Bricci. I can find no trace of the first play, but the second has surely been confused with *La Spada Mortale* by Verucci which Locatelli used in two scenari. *L'Intrighi d'Amore overo la fenestra incantata* is cryptically described in the Riccardi MS. as 'Com: di Pandº C'; *L'Incauto*, Barbieri's comedy and *Il Medico Volante* are described as 'de comici' or 'fata da i comedianti'. Anon, or N.N., who claims nine more scenari leads us to suspect individual rather than collaborate authorship. In the cases of *Il Finto Principe* and *Dottore Bacchettone* it is impossible to say whether the scenario or the undated printed plays, *Il Finto Principe* by C. Ambrosi, and *Il Dottore Bacchetone* by Gioanelli, have precedence.

Except for *La Regina d'Inghilterra* which, like its counterpart in the Casanatense collection, is probably derived from

1 Scenari Inediti, p. clxxxii.
2 See G. Caprin, *Rivista Teatrale Italiana* (1905), vol. ix, p. 53.

N. Biancolelli's tragedy, the scenari of this miscellany are innocent of literary polish or Spanish influence. To six comedies, one tragedy, and one tragi-comedy there are eleven farces, and everywhere buffoonery is unbridled as it has not been since Scala's *Teatro* and the hey-day of the sixteenth century.

VATICAN MISCELLANY

A miscellany which has hitherto received no attention beyond a notice from Valeri is preserved in the Vatican Library. This Codex—Barb. Lat. 3895—contains five complete plays, three *intermedi* and the fragment of a drama: as item 6 occupying sheets 127–83 is a *Selva di nuove comedie*, consisting of nine scenari. They are written upon large sheets of a uniform size (279·8 × 184·4 mm.) in a variety of hands, all, however, characteristic of the seventeenth century.[1]

The last six of the scenari are numbered by an eleventh hand IX to XIV respectively. Possibly we have here only part of a larger collection.

We are left to reconstruct the property lists for all but No. 3, and the dramatis personae, usually given at the end, for Nos. 2 and 9. Only three have regular titles, *Forza della Maggia* (1), a pastoral, and *Il Tutore* (4) and *L'Amor supra l'Odio e la Ragione* (8); these are Spanish tragi-comedies relieved by a lively Pulcinella. So far I have not been able to discover the plays which I suspect lie behind these last two scenari and their counterpart which has been suitably dubbed by Valeri, *La Gelosia e fedeltà di Rosalba* (No. 2).

There is a Spanish tinge to the names in No. 3, but its farcical intrigue was dear to the Commedia dell'arte and its title should evidently be taken from the closing words *Il Volubile in Amore*. No. 5 (*Celinda, o La Dama di Brusselles*) is a re-working of the old story in which a woman disguised as a man follows a fickle lover and by some sharp practice wins him back.

For the farce of undesirable lovers in No. 6 Valeri suggests

---

[1] Hand A, scen. 1, 2, 3. Hand B, scen. 4. Hand C, scen. 5. Hand D, scen. 6. Hand E writes *Mi Bargiazzi*, f. 164 verso; and list of *personaggi*, f. 163. Hand F contributes to list of *personaggi*, f. 163, and writes *sette personaggi* for scen. 8 on f. 170 verso. Hand G writes scen. 7 to Act III. sc. viii. Hand H finishes scen. 7. Hand I writes scen. 8. Hand J writes scen. 9.

a title from the central character *Monsieur Enrico*, a French suitor cheated of the hand of Rosalba. An alternative version in No. 7 may have been called *Mi Bargiazzi*: these words are scrawled above its list of dramatis personae on the back of f. 164.

The setting of the last scenario in Seville gives Spanish colouring to the old comic situation of lovers wooing in the disguise of visiting masters. Either Valeri's *Li Finti Maestri* or the last words 'La donna in questi casi vuol far a suo modo' might serve as a title.

In spite of the variety of hands, and inconsistencies of numbering, these scenari take the standing of a collection from the system of names and from the remarkable use of the form 'azzi' or 'azi' for 'lazzi' throughout.

Pulcinella is ubiquitous: when he needs a companion it is always Coviello. Discounting the pastoral, Cintio is always the chief lover, Rosalba six times is the prima donna, four times the serving maid is Rosetta; Pincastro as the father is only once supplanted by a Pandolfo.

I am indebted to Professor Allardyce Nicoll for a reference to the description of another collection of scenari in the Vatican Library. Codex Vaticanus Latinus 10244 is described by Vattasso and Carusi as of 'Saec. XVII et XVIII', and containing twelve three-act scenari.[1] I have not had the opportunity of examining the manuscript but from the typical masks of Pulcinella, Cola, Ponsevere, Rosetta, Cintio, Odoardo, and Isabella, and such hints of the intrigue as can be gathered from the titles it seems that they are closely akin to the other late Roman miscellanies in style and substance. Seven of the titles may be assimilated into the general lists as variants of plots found in the other collections.[2] Another Codex 10206 preserves, upon two inserted leaves, the fragments of a scenario showing Flaminia, a Captain, and a Doctor.

---

[1] M. Vattasso and E. Carusi, *Codices Vaticani Latini. Codices* 9852–10300, Rome, 1914, p. 578.

[2] *La Donna demonio. *Il Cavaliere pazzo o sia il giuoco di fortuna. La Finta Madrigna. Il Servo Sciocco. *Pulcinella disammogliato. *Cintio giuocatore. L'A-mante volubile. L'Amante astuto. La forza dell'amicizia. Il basilisco. La maggior gloria d'un grande è il vincere se stesso. *La principessa tiranna.

(* for those which are not found elsewhere.)

MISCELLANY IN NAPLES

The most substantial collection contains 183 scenari. Through the generosity of Senatore Croce this is now Codex XI. AA. 40, 41 of the *Biblioteca Nazionale di Napoli*.[1] The first volume contains ninety scenari and is in a good state of preservation. Volume ii has been injured by fire and in spite of careful repair two scenari are defective and seven more difficult to decipher.[2]

The title-page of the first volume reads: Gibaldone Comico di Varii Suggetti di Comedie / ed Opere Bellissime / Copiate da me Antonio Passanti detto / Oratio il Calabrese / Per commando / Dell' / Ecc^{me} Sig^r Conte di Casamarciano 1700. Of the second volume: Gibaldone de Soggetti / Da recitarsi all'impronto / Alcuni proprii, e gl'altri da diversi / Raccolti / di / D. Anibale Sersale, Conte di Casa Marciano.'

This is followed by a misplaced page numbered '23' which belongs to scenari 5, *La Schiava di Messina.* Volume i contains 281, and volume ii 476, sheets.

The tables of contents are arranged alphabetically and against the majority of the scenari there are markings of one perpendicular or one, two, three, or four horizontal dashes, the significance of which I have not been able to discover.[3]

There were four copyists. The first who wrote a clear undistinguished hand and was addicted to a superfluity of 'H's' was responsible for the first eighty-six scenari. The second, very fine and careful of detail, finished volume i. The third, who numbered his scenes and gave the names of the personages in the centre of the page, wrote scenari 1–77, and 93, 94 of the second volume; and the fourth, scenari 78–92.

As the title-page hints here is old and new material. Forty scenari are variants of plays that we have met with in earlier

[1] *Giorn. Stor.*, xxix, p. 211; see also Levi, *Rivista Teatrale Italiana*, A.X, vol. 18, pp. 14, 257, and a. xi, vol. 16, pp. 1, 257.

[2] Scen. 79, 80. Scen. 61, 81, 82, 83, 85, 86, 92.

[3] Unmarked. Vol. i. 28, 47, 55, 58, 63, 64, 65, 67, 68, 71, 72, 73, 74, 75, 77, 79, 85, 86, 88; vol. ii. 8, 9, 15, 16, 17, 29, 38, 50, 51, 52, 66, 71, 90, 93 = 33. Marked 'I'. Vol. i. 3, 27; vol. ii. 78, 82, 89, 92 = 6. Marked '—'. Normal. 136 in all. Marked '═'. i. 54; ii. 58. Marked '≡'. i. 17, 82. Marked '≣'. i. 42; ii. 70.

collections, six more reappear in the Perugian miscellany,[1] and *La Maggior Gloria* was acted in the seventeenth century in Modena.

I have been able to trace sixteen to their sources in Spanish drama, and nine more derive from Italian printed plays.[2] *Le*

[1] (*a*) Corresponding to *Scala* collection: Nap. i. 38, *Finto Cieco* = Scala, 34. Nap. ii. 65, *Il Marito* = Scala, 9.

(*b*) Corresponding to Scenari in Locatelli and Corsini Collections: Nap. i. 3, *Arme Mutate*, Loc. i. 48; Cors. i. 23. Nap. i. 12, *Il Granchio*, Loc. i. 46; Cors. ii. 30. Nap. i. 15, *Emilia*, Loc. i. 28, *Le due schiave*; Cors. i. 2, *La Schiava*. Nap. i. 21, *Giardino Metaforico*, Loc. ii. 46; Cors. i. 29. Nap. i. 25, *Grotta di Mescolino*, Loc. *Gelosia*, i. 47; Cors. *Le due Scolari*, ii. 7. Nap. i. 26, *Balia Grande*, Loc. *Gli Scambi*, ii. 30; Cors. i. 7. Nap. i. 37, *Giostra Amorosa*, Loc. *Finti Morti*, i. 35; Cors. ii. 17. Nap. i. 63, *Figlio Prodigo*, Loc. *Porci*, i. 42. Nap. i. 79, *Avaritia*, Loc. *Vecchio Avaro*, i. 45; Cors. ii. 23. Nap. i. 81, *Figlio del morte*, Loc. ii. 39, 40; Cors. ii. 46. Nap. ii. 3, *Innocente Rivenduta*, Loc. i. 4; Cors. ii. 12. Nap. ii. 10, *Pellegrina*, Cors. i. 26. Nap. ii. 20, *Le Trapole*, Loc. *Trappolaria*, ii. 14; see Della Porta. Nap. ii. 21, *Il Tradito*, Loc. i. 22; Cors. i. 3, ii. 25. Nap. ii. 25, *Finti Turchi*, Loc. i. 31; Cors. i. 18. Nap. ii. 37, *Ragazzo per le lettere*, Loc. i. 34; Cors. ii. 38. Nap. ii. 44, *L'Amante Ingrato*, Loc. i. 23; Cors. i. 22. Nap. ii. 46, *Le Fabriche*, Loc. ii. 25; Cors. ii. 21. Nap. ii. 60, *Trappolaria*, Loc. ii. 14; see Della Porta.

(*c*) Corresponding to Venetian collection: Nap. i. 9, *La Sorella picciola*; cp. Ven. 8, *La Finta Sorella*. Nap. i. 6, *Prigioniero Vendicativo*; cp. Ven. 18. Nap. i. 30, *Sdegni Amorosi*; cp. Ven. 42. Nap. i. 36, *Isole*; cp. Ven. 4. Nap. i. 48, *Due Simili d'Andreini*; cp. Ven. 29, *. . . con le lettere mutate*. Nap. i. 60, *Fratelli avelenati*; cp. Ven. 43. Nap. i. 61, *I Quattro Policinelli Simili*; cp. Ven. 45. Nap. ii. 75, *Baron Tedesco*; cp. Ven. 48. Nap. ii. 14, *La Scuola di Terenzio*; cp. Ven. 31, *Il Mastro di Terenzio*.

(*d*) Corresponding to Casanatense

Codex 4186: Nap. i. 28, *Renegato per Amore*; cp. 4186, sc. 25; 46, *Lo Spechio overo la Turca Costante*. Nap. i. 47, *Convitato di Pietra*; cp. Cas. 24. Nap. i. 67, *Ricco Epulone*; cp. Cas. 33.

(*e*) Corresponding to Magliabechiana Codex: Nap. i. 56, *Soldato per vendetta*; cp. *Vedova Costante*, Mag. 1. Nap. i. 59, *Medico volante*; cp. Mag. 8. Nap. ii. 13, *Tappetti Alessandrini*; cp. Mag. 21. Nap. ii. 26, *Amante Inavertito*; cp. *L'Incauto*, Mag. 7, and see Barbieri. Nap. ii. 66, *Li Tre Principi di Salerno*; cp. Mag. 14. Nap. ii. 72, *Il Dottore Bacchettone*; cp. Mag. 22.

[2] i. 10, *Casa con Due Porte*; cp. Calderon. i. 14, *D. Giovanni d'Alvarado*; cp. Scarron, *Jodelet maître valet*. i. 33, *Non può essere*; cp. Moreto, *Non puede ser*. i. 46, *Finto Astrologo*; cp. Calderon. i. 47, *Convitato di Pietra*; cp. Adaptation by Cicognini, see Broüwer. i. 57, *Le Sette Infante del'Ara*; cp. Lope di Vega. i. 65, *D. Gile Schiavo del Diavolo*; cp. Mira de Mescua. i. 66, *Diavolo Predicatore*; cp. Lope de Vega. i. 69, *Giudicci del Cielo*; cp. Perez de Montaluan, *Lo que son juyzios del cielo*. i. 70, *Guardia di se stesso*; cp. Calderon. i. 72, *Belisario*; cp. Lope de Vega. i. 74, *Bernardo del Carpio*; cp. Lope de Vega. i. 86, *Samsone*; of Spanish origin on the authority of Riccoboni. ii. 55, *Demonie sono le donne*; cp. Lope de Vega, *Los Milagros de el Desprecio*. ii. 71, *La Donzella di Lavoro*; cp. Perez de Montaloan. ii. 79, *Huomo da bene*; cp. Lope de Vega. i. 12, *Il Granchio*, pr. 1556; cp. L. Salviati. i. 15, *Emilia*, 1579; cp. L. Groto. i. 26, *Balia Grande*, 1560; cp. G. Razzi. i. 64, *Conte di Sex*; cp. N. Biancolleli. i. 81, *Figlio del morte ovvero Cardelino cornuto volontario*; cp. Verrucci, *La Spada Mortale*. ii. 65, *Il Marito*, 1619; cp. Scala. ii. 92, *Il Moro*, 1607; cp. Della Porta. I am indebted to T. Beltrame (*Giorn.*

Disgrazie di Pulcinella was to be expanded and published in 1824. I have the titles only by dramas which may be connected with ten more scenari, and these, together with the style of another fifteen, suggest further literary origins which await identification until certain rare plays can be found.

As for the rest of these scenari, they are credibly the result of collaboration among professional comedians working up old favourite situations borrowed remotely from the Commedia erudita, or letting 'burle' and 'lazzi' accumulate into new farces.

MISCELLANY OF D. PLACIDO ADRIANO IN PERUGIA

The *Selva overo Zibaldone di concetti comici*, which is Codex A. 20 of the *Biblioteca Communale of Perugia*, contains twenty-two scenari.[1] This miscellany, which was composed by D. Placido Adriano Priest of Lucca in 1734, is the tool-box of the Commedia dell'arte equipped with plots, lazzi, *chiusette*, songs, sonnets, echo conceits, prologues, salutations, soliloquies, tirades, dialogues, riddles, and musical or comic intermezzi. The manuscript is a stout volume of 800 pages with an index to guide the reader through the picturesque jumble of material.

Adriano's calling apparently did not interfere with his hobby, amateur acting. Another manuscript (D. 46) in the Perugian library contains four of his plays, *La Scola Cavaiolo —scherzo comico*, and *Lo Schirichio* (1735) are mainly in the Neapolitan dialect; and two others *L'Ommo propone, Lo Cielo dispone, ovvero Le Nozze nella Vecchia*, and *La Commedia in Commedia* are conveyed from the Spanish. This last was prepared in 1736 and in introducing himself to the reader of his miscellany he confides other plans and achievements:

Volevo fare *L'homo al punto d'Onore, d'Amore, e d'Amicizia* e dopo haverne ritrovata l'Istoria in Tito Livio fù concluso recitarsi all'improviso e così l'anno 1737, venne da Napoli con il Sig. Cristoforo Rossi, bravo ingegniere e Pittore, e eccellentissimo in rappresentare la

Stor. xcvii) for pointing out the correspondence between *I dui simili d'Andreini* and G. B. Andreini's *I duo Lelii simili* and *Isole* to *La Turca* by the same actor-dramatist.

[1] Croce, *Giorn. Stor.* (1898), xxxi, p. 458.

parte di Pulcinella con un bravo Coviello, e altri Recitanti in musica per gl'intermezzi. Avevo ancora mentre fui in Castrovillari di Calabria concertata l'opera intitolata *S. Francesco di Paolo* quale riuscì assai bene, e ciò fu l'anno 1719. In Perugia gl'anni 1730, e 1731 si recitò all' impronto. In Assisi poi il 1732 comandata da una dama composi una comedia intitolata *La Pietra Incantata* ove recitorno i Figli di detta dama, e gliela concertai.

His heart was in improvised acting:

I have made this miscellany because I have proved by my own experience that even the finest extempore actors having 15 or 20 different parts on hand may lack suitable words, and for the most part will merely repeat themselves; or again because those who take the parts of the lovers or ladies are not always ready for their dialogues of love or disdain and so forth. Therefore I have collected altogether all kinds, so that each may have cloth for his coat.

His particular study of the Neapolitan dialect made during his fifteen years' residence in Naples was turned to good account in the miscellany: all eight prologues, a generous half of the scenes, and songs are in this dialect. In the *Metamorfosi di Pulcinella* Adriano played Pulcinella himself in S. Pietro di Perugia 1730. Some of the scenari are dated. The earliest represented was *La Trappolaria* in Albaneta 1711. This was repeated in 1730. January festivities in Albaneta called for *Li due Simili*, *La Sorella*, and *La Tabernaria* in 1736, and the following year *L'Insalata*, *Il Basilisco di Bernagasso* and *Li due Pulcinelli*. These titles betray the fact that Adriano and his friends did not despise old material. Nine of the scenari we have met with before in the Naples collection.[1] *La Tabernaria* derives from Della Porta's comedy. *Le Furbarie di Coviello* is said to be by 'Sig. D. Plicado Daniria di Velac', Placido Adriano de Lucca anagrammatized; a process which he evidently applied to the scenario, for it is merely *La Trappolaria* decked out with a few fresh 'lazzi'. The invention of his friends Annibale Caro and Christofero Rossi accounts for *Gli Straccioni* and *Il Vecchio*

---

[1] (2) *Il Servo Padrone*; cp. *D. Giovanni d'Alverardo*, Nap. i. 14. (3) *Non piu essere overo la Donna può cio, che vuole*; cp. Nap. i. 33. (4) *L'Insalata*; cp. Nap. ii. 45. (6) *Arcadia Incantata*; cp. Nap. i. 1. (7) *Pulcinella Marchese* da *Chio-chiava*; cp. *D. Pericco Spagnuolo*, Nap. ii. 27. (12) *La Cameriera*; cp. Nap. i. 7. (14) *Il Basilico*; cp. Nap. ii. 23. (16) *Pulcinella Finto Prencipe*; cp. Nap. ii. 48. (17) *La Trappolaria*; cp. ii. 60. See Della Porta.

Avaro, comedies of complex intrigue. If Adriano did not trouble himself to invent he was full of ideas. He spins good farces in the *Descienzo di Coviello*, and *Medico Paneralio*, *Pulcinella Medico per Forza*,[1] and shows an unparalleled head for intrigue in *Gl'Imbrogli di Coviello* and *L'Innamorata scaltra*. His is the success of the enthusiast, for he can still wring fresh comedy from the old theme of mistaken doubles in *Li due simili* and *Li due Pulcinelli*, from Boccaccio's joke of supposed invisibility in *La Pietra Incantata*, from the situation of Razzi's *Balia* in *La Sorella*.

For stage-craft these are the most instructive scenari that we have. The lazzi are numbered and explained as a special item of the miscellany; it is suggested what riddles and salutations are to be used; when the Captain in *L'Innamorata Scaltra* is to talk at cross-purposes with his son the ticklish passage is provided verbatim. In the *Arcadia Incantata* we are told that Silvio may easily double the part of the Magician, and he is warned of the best moment to retire to change his make-up.

SMALLER COLLECTIONS: MODENA

The handful of Modenese scenari to which Emilio Re called attention[2] can hardly be called a collection, but may be taken together as a group regardless of the chronological order of the single scenari which I am presently to enumerate. Two of these, *La Schiava*, a comedy, and an untitled Opera Regia are contained in a Miscellany I. 740 (a s. 8. 14) of the Biblioteca Estense and probably belong to the sixteenth century. Another dozen are to be found copied on to fragile unbound sheets in a pile of theatrical documents (*Busta V*) in the *Archivio di Stato di Modena*. Four of these are connected with scenari in the Neapolitan collection;[3] a comedy dated 1643, *Le bizarre d'Argentina cavaliere e gentildonna*—

---

[1] There is also a similar theme and farcical device in *Pulc. Finto Dottore ovvero le Nozze Contrastate* (1728).

[2] *Giorn. Stor.* (1910), lv, p. 325. *La Schiava* is reprinted, and the Opera Regia summarized in this article.

[3] *Spirito folletto*, 3 redactions dated 1675, 1682, 1683; cp. Nap. ii. 68. *La*

Maggior gloria d'un grande è vincer se stesso, con Rastellino spia muta, buffone attaccato alla corda; cp. Nap. i. 34. *Il Villano creduto Principe*; cp. Nap. *Il Finto Principe*, i. 11. *Truffaldino ballordo, flagello alle fortune del suo padrone* (1680); cp. *Servo Sciocco*. See *Rivista Teatrale Italiana* (1910).

Ippolito e Boffetto creduti Turchi con Zaccagnino amante disperato, is printed by Dr. Paglicci Brozzi.[1]

Two comedies, *La Peregrina* and *L'Inocente inganata coi duplicati sponsalizi*, and an untitled scenario are marked with the Estense eagle and written in an early seventeenth century hand. Re attributes an 'opera regia' to the end of the same century. I will give here some account of *Gl'Inganni dell' inimicizia con le multiplicate stravaganze de matrimoni* which seems to have escaped his notice.

The leaf is headed 'Comiche' and undated. The plot is given in narrative not yet disposed into acts and scenes.

The daughter of Pantalone, Podestà of Padua, who is betrothed to a stranger, Oratio, elopes with the secretary. Spolverino the servant gains time for the lovers by telling Pantalone that they have only gone to Murano for an airing. Pantalone meanwhile gives his attention to his son who has fallen in love with the daughter of Dr. Gratiano. Their betrothal is just about to take place when Giangurgolo, a rich merchant on his way to the East, calls on the Podestà and discloses his intention of murdering the Doctor, whose son had killed his son years ago in Bologna. Nothing that Pantalone can say will patch up this feud, and when Giangurgolo assaults the Doctor in the street, his daughter throws herself at his feet and implores him to take her life instead. Giangurgolo falls in love with the daughter and agrees to Pantalone's hasty proposal that they should marry and forget the feud. The Doctor is obliged to consent, but plans to smuggle his daughter away that night with Pantalone's son, her lover. In the confusion of this escape the wrong couple are caught, and when the enraged Podestà finds what has been going on between the secretary and his daughter, he swears he will kill the girl himself and have the secretary publicly executed.

At the gallows Giangurgolo recognizes the young man as his long-lost son. He is pardoned and no more is said of the elopement. In this happy hour Pantalone's son appears with the Doctor's daughter. Giangurgolo cedes his claim as the Doctor reveals that after all the intended bride is a boy petticoated for safety. He obligingly produced 'another daughter' for Pantalone's son.

1 *Rivista Teatrale Italiana* (1908), Anno VIII, vol. 13, fasc. 2.

Representing the eighteenth century are *Il Matrimonio Egale*, an old-fashioned farce, and '*Il Pandolfo* Comedia Per Musica, Rappresentata da Comici Riuniti L'anno 1748'.

SCENARI IN THE REPERTORY OF BIANCOLELLI

A manuscript in the Bibliothèque de l'Opéra and a transcript in the Bibliothèque Nationale, 'Traduction du scenario di J. D. Biancolelli et avis au lecteur contenant les noms, les rosles, les naissances, les débuts, les mots et les faits principaux qui concernent les comediens italiens, qui ont paru en Italie et en France depuis 1577, jusqu'a la presente année 1750 et les années qui suivront . . . par M. Gueullette', contain memoranda for the performance of Biancolelli, Arlequin between 1661 and 1668 in seventy-three plays. The original Italian notes are lost. In many cases the main action is indicated sufficiently to establish the connexion of these plots with earlier Italian scenari and with the titles of Italo-French comedies by Riccoboni and Parfaict.[1]

MISCELLANY OF SCENARI IN LENINGRAD

There exists in the Bibliothèque de l'Académie des Sciences, Leningrad, a unique printed copy of a Russian translation of thirty-nine scenari (thirty comedies, one tragedy, and eight *intermedii*), made in 1733–5 probably by V. Trédiakovsky. By the kindness of Professor Allardyce Nicoll I have been able to consult the edition of the Russian text prepared by V. Peretz in 1917, which is quoted in the third edition of Miclachevsky's *Commedia dell' arte*, p. 26, but I rely upon the description given in Masks, Mimes, and Miracles.

SINGLE SCENARI

The earliest of the single scenari, *L'Anfiparnasso* by Orazio Vecchi, 1597, is brought forward by A. Solerti as a real Commedia dell'arte with madrigal music.[2]

Judging by Soldano's prologue, which is dated 1610, the scenario of *Flaminio Desperato* published by Martucci is next in time;[3] followed by *Li Sdegni Amorosi*, burleta di commedia

---

[1] See Appendix F, *passim*.
[2] *Albori della melodramma*, p. 17.
[3] Codex 1641 Fondo Sant'Andrea

della valle Bib. Vittorio Emanuele Roma; see *Nuova Antologia* (1885), vol. iii.

all'improviso per S. Frandaglia da Val di Sturla; 25 Nov. 1615[1] in Rouen.

A letter from Bernardino Bernardini, dated 1632,[2] requests a friend to expand the scenario of *Gl' Amici Infidi*, which is enclosed; it was published by Bartoli in *Li Scenari inediti*.

Uniquely elegant is the *Scenario della Tragicomedia Del Principe Sidonio* Consecrato alla Regia Magnanimita del Prencipe / Di Pelestrina—de Urbino Giorgi 15 Agosto 1654.[3] It is exquisitely written out with a fresh vellum sheet to each scene. The names of Herbosco and Gripa, the comic gardener and his wife, and the form 'atti ridicoli' for the usual 'azzi' or 'lazzi' hardly suggest a popular origin. If it were not that the main incidents of the plot recur in one of the Neapolitan scenari, *L' Amore tra Nemici*, one would hardly be justified in claiming this dainty thing for the Commedia dell'arte. The Neapolitan title is misleading, for the play has no connexion with Cicognini's *Amore tra Nemici*, though there is a trace of the same situation in his *Il Principe Giardinero*. It is possible that a common source explains these inconsistencies, but so far I have not been able to find it.

Maddalena, who reprinted from a Viennese manuscript *Un pazzo guarisce l'altro*,[4] argues that it was derived from Girolamo Gigli's play printed in Venice 1704 and represented four times at the court of Vienna in 1723.[5] Two printed copies of an earlier version, however, are extant in Rome as scenari di *D. Chisciotti della Mancia*.[6] 'Commedia da recitarsi nel Seminario Romano nelle Corrante Vacanze del Carnevale 1692, da Sig. Convittori delle Camere Mezzane.'

Among the plots for Jesuit plays which have nothing to do with the Commedia dell'arte the same Casanatense miscellanies of printed scenari yield two indubitable specimens of popular comedy in *Diarbech*, 1692,[7] and *Plauto alla moderna*, 1693.[8] Stylistically these comedies of slave intrigues and

[1] Fondo Coquebert de Montbret di Rouen; see Mazzatinti, *Biblioteche di Francia*, iii. 179.

[2] Codex Magliabechiano, II. i. 90; see A. Bartoli, op. cit., p. lix, n. 4.

[3] Vatican Library Codex Barb. Lat. 3737.

[4] Bib. Palatina di Vienna. 10124 (Rec. 1491). See *Sitzungsberichte der K.*

Akademie der Wissenschaften, Philosoph.-hist. Classe (1900), vol. cxliii.

[5] Allacci, op. cit., quotes an edition published in Siena, per il Bonetti, 1704, in 12° dell'Economico Accademico Intronato.

[6] Bib. Casanatense, Misc. fol. 152,172.

[7] Misc. fol. 152 (2); 172 (1).

[8] Misc. fol. 172 (3) two copies.

agnitions might belong to the sixteenth century but for the masks of Pullicinella and Tartaglia.

La Trappolaria is probably the best known of all the scenari since its publication by A. Perucci in 1699, and it was in demand on the stage ever since Della Porta stole it from *Pseudolus*.

A seventeenth-century codex (976) of the Corsini Library contains two untitled scenari. The first is written on the outer half of the folded page and occupies six sheets (196·8 × 282·5 mm.): the second is written across the page in the same fine clear hand and occupies sheets 204–10. The first, a tragedy after the Spanish manner, might be called *La Vendetta ritardata*. A dishonoured husband pretends to pardon his wife and her lover, only that he may revenge himself on the man at a sinister banquet, and on the woman after a brutal scene of reproach in her bedchamber. The comic relief afforded by the Servants Brandello, Fichetto, and Lisetta does not go beyond the scope of the typical 'Graciosi'. The other scenario should evidently be entitled *Dal disordine il buon ordine ne nasce*, Brighella's summing-up of the action. A slight love-plot is combined with the favourite farcical theme of a stupid Prince who is being taught to govern, and the confusions caused by his blunders in the art of war and the administration of justice take up the lion's share of the plot.

Another untitled scenario, evidently belonging to the seventeenth century, was published by Stoppato from a manuscript in the *Museo Correr*.[1] This is a play of court intrigue ingeniously thwarted by an eavesdropping servant, Brighella, and his master, a young prince Alfonzo, who baffles his would-be murderers by feigning madness. Pantalone, a time-serving counsellor, is played off against a Spanish captain who goes mad temporarily by swallowing a love potion.

Scenari belonging to the eighteenth century are: *Cristoforo Colombo*, played at Genoa in 1708;[2] *I Contratti Rotti*, Paris, 1716;[3] *Giovanna d'Arco*.[4]

---

[1] Cod. Misc. 998–2546 (Racc. Cicogna). C. 592–5. See *La Commedia popolare in Italia* (1887).

[2] See P. Corboni, Milano, 1892.

[3] See C. Gozzi, *Opere*, iv, p. 35.

[4] Bib. dell'Arsenale Paris. Cod. 6099. See Mazzatinti, op. cit., iii. 153.

TITLES AND REFERENCES TO NON-EXTANT SCENARI

Notices of new or kindred scenari whose titles only survive help us now and then to trace the career of comic themes. This information is drawn chiefly from the repertory of Biancolelli as it is preserved in the manuscripts of Gueullette and in the rare *Histoire de l'ancien théâtre Italien* of the brothers Parfaict; from Riccoboni's lists in the *Histoire de la théâtre Italien*, 1727; from *Dictionnaire des théâtres de Paris*, and the *Mercure de France*. Titles of seventeen scenari played in Modena were taken from a manuscript catalogue in the Biblioteca Estense by Emilio Re. Rasi has notice of *Li Tre Gobbi*, played by the *Gelosi* before the Gonzaga in 1582, and Allacci catalogues 'scenario de gl'accidenti del *Vittorio Goffredo*', 1648.

We may mention by way of dismissal two ghost collections. Goldoni[1] declared that he had once handled a good parchment manuscript of the fifteenth century containing one hundred and twenty scenari: a statement which Bartoli can only accept by supposing that Goldoni wrote 'decima quinto secolo' for 'millecinquecento'. This plausible correction carries us but little farther, for, as Valeri remarks, if Goldoni was referring to the Locatelli volumes (actually of the early seventeenth century), he also miswrote 120 for 102 (and Valeri 102 for 103!).

The error of Stoppato's announcement that M. V. Cian[2] had found in the memoirs of Alessandro Piccolomini a mention of three hundred scenari as part of his unpublished work arises from consulting only the list of 'opere inedite' given by Fabiani in *Memorie per servire alla vita di M. A. Piccolomini*. The entry runs: 'Trecento scenari, o siano Parti di diversi caratteri di Personaggi a uso di Teatro'. In another connexion (p. 36) Fabiani compares these scenari to the characters of Theophrastus and refers to a letter written by Piccolomini in 1564 to Antonio Cocco and prefixed to the *Sfera del Mondo*. Piccolomini replies to his friend's inquiry, saying that he has no more comedies on hand.

Ma che io haveva ben gittato il modello d'un disegno, e dato prin-

---

[1] *Memorie*, ii. 24. 'J'ai un manuscrit du quinzième siècle très bien conservé, et relié en parchemin, contenant cent vingt sujets en canevas de pièces italiennes, que l'on appelle comédies de l'art.'

[2] Op. cit., p. 83; cp. *Novelle Letterarie* (1759), xx, p. 698.

cipio ad una impresa, la qual riuscendomi, haria potuto reccar qualche
aiuto à i Comici de i nostri tempi.[1]

His plan is to assemble the various types of persons suitable
to the comic stage in all their variety of rank, relationship,
occupation, fortune, or disposition, and to compose for each
soliloquies and dialogues which may be easily adapted to any
plot. He projected about six hundred of such scenes, but the
book containing the rough drafts of the first three hundred
was stolen, and the reflection that his work would be destroyed,
mutilated, or pirated, discouraged him.

While this letter rules out the prospect of discovering
a collection of scenari belonging to the sixteenth century, it
reveals something of the economy of dramatic composition
practised by the 'academici' of the Cinquecento.[2]

There are extant in Italian over seven hundred scenari at a
gross reckoning, but by discounting variants this bulk reduces

[1] 'La sfera del Mondo / Di nuovo da
lui ripolita, accresciuta, e fino à sei Libri,
di Quattro che erano ampliata, e quasi
per ogni parte rinovata, e riformata',
Vinegia, 1573.

[2] Dramatic fragments which might
be loosely described as scenari but which
have not I think any real connexion with
the Commedia dell'arte are:

(1) MS. Vat. Ott. Lat. 2418. A
scribbled plan for a Greek tragedy on the
story of *Athamante*, cp. F. Neri, *La
Tragedia* (1904), p. 160, n. 1.

(2) MS. Vat. Ott. Lat. 2418, pt. ii,
c. 597 (XVIth c.). A narrative synopsis
of a five-act comedy *Le Gemelle*; and the
prologue and *argomento* of a comedy *La
Forza d'Amore*, attributed to 'un gentile
e gratioso cavalliero di Napoli . . . Sr
Costante'. On stylistic evidence these
are academic productions.

(3) *La Galatea*, by A. Lollio. Rejected by Solerti and Neri from the
repertory of popular pastorals.

(4) The skeleton plots in G. Barto-
lomei's *Didascalia cioè Dottrina comica*
(1658) are regarded by Bartoli as experiments never intended for representation.

(5) Reference has already been made
to the separate printed scenari preserved
in the dramatic miscellanies of the seventeenth century in the Biblioteca Casanatense. I have examined fifty such scenari,
seven of which were duplicates for reproduction on different occasions. The
form of these scenari suggests that they
were printed to be distributed among
the audience as programmes. The names
of the amateur actors are given and in
some cases even the names of those taking
part in the *intermezzi*. The plot is explained scene by scene, but the entrances
have no marginal marking. There is
one scenario of a Nativity Play (Misc.
4°. 658), one ballet, *L'Acquisto di Durin-
dana* (1638), and one pageant. Seven
are 'per musica', and three of these, together with the majority of the tragedies,
are concerned with the lives of saints,
martyrs, or Scriptural heroes; they were
to be presented by the members of the
Collegio Romano or the Collegio Inglese
and belong more properly to the history
of Jesuit Drama between 1622 and 1695.
Two, however, should be mentioned
here: *Ne Meno Amore si libera da amore*
(1682) corresponds to Calderon's *Ni
Amor si libra de amor*; and *Il Crispo*,
Tragedia Latina da D. Anselmo Grimaldi (1628), has its popular counterpart
in the Casanatense MS. 4186, no. 6.

itself by some two hundred. Of these thirty-six have been reprinted. The network of these variants and the details of dates
and whereabouts may now be left to the list in Appendix F.

MEANS OF DATING THE SCENARI

The date of a miscellany in which a scenario appears gives
us only a date *ad quem*. Variants prove that scenari collected
in 1700 were in acting currency a hundred years earlier,
while others in the same collection can only have been derived
from plays printed in the second half of the seventeenth
century. The only satisfactory way of determining the limits
of the acting dates of a given scenario or group of scenari is
by tracing the theme back to the earliest-known variant in
another miscellany or to its source in a published play. Such
a process is not always possible, but it can be carried out
often enough to establish certain principles of style which
enable us to give an approximate acting date for the majority
of the scenari. These principles will appear as we examine
the scenari group by group as tragedy, tragi-comedy, comedy,
romance, pastoral, and farce, comparing each type with the
contemporary printed drama. The object of this analysis is
to investigate the connexion between the Commedia dell'arte
and the Commedia erudita, of which, so far as I know, there
is no accurate statement, in order to estimate the real contribution of the Commedia dell'arte to the European stage.
The way is pointed by Belloni:

> sarà necessaria sottoporre a un paziente e conscienzioso esame tutti
> gli scenari pervenutici e indagare attentamente quali relazioni essi pos-
> sono avere con le commedie scritte ch' hanno lo stesso soggetto, se si
> vorrà formarsi un' idea precisa di ciò che dovete essere una commedia
> dell'arte.[1]

The interest of such an inquiry is twofold: as we calculate
what the Commedia erudita did for the Commedia dell'arte
we see what the improvising comedians did for Italian drama.
Riccoboni, its first historian, recognized two periods in the
development of the Commedia dell'arte, and suggested 1620,
when the imitation of Spanish plays set in, as the turning
point. The miscellaneous character of the scenario collections
makes it impossible to observe this division, since the tangle

[1] *Il Seicento,* ed. 1900, p. 301.

of the plots is all on one thread. We must now return to the
artificial limits of this study by dealing first with the Spanish
scenari which may be classed apart as belonging to the second
period. These are chiefly tragedies taken from Roman
history, from the heroic legends of Spain, and the comedies
of 'capa y spada' intrigue. The intricate plots worked out by
Lope de Vega, Mira de Mescua, and Calderon did not allow
the improvising players much scope for deviation: the path
is too dangerous and exciting to attempt short cuts or ex-
cursions. For the nineteen Spanish plays extant in the repertories of the Commedia dell'arte the scenari generally present
faithful précis.[1] Now and then Policinella and Coviello take
a little more than the comic servant's licence in courting and
noisy jesting; extra appearances of the devil were not to be
resisted;[2] the dignity of a Spanish father is a little unsteadied
when an amorous old Tartaglia takes the part.[3] But this is all.

With Perez de Montaluan the comedian took greater
liberties. According to the play *Lo que son juyzios del Cielo*,
Alessandro, returning unexpectedly, catches his rival Ruberto
making love to Rosaura his betrothed and innocent lady. He
stabs Ruberto who dies blaspheming and bites out his tongue.
Alessandro questions the use of providing masses for the
damned soul and decides that he will do nothing that might
incur suspicion. But when the ghost of Ruberto appears to
explain that his bitten tongue was a token of his repentance,
Alesandro goes post haste to Rome to pray for his victim.

In the scenario *Li Giudicii del Cielo* the king erects a temple
and a statue to the victim and sets a price upon the head of
his murderer. Alessandro goes to the temple and is told by
the statue to await the judgement of heaven at the scene of the
crime. He obeys the supernatural command in spite of
Policinella's warning that the king is on the track of the
criminal, and is addressed again by the statue who explains the
meaning of the bitten tongue. Alessandro repents, and when
the king's officers arrest him the statue pleads for his release.

[1] In the case of *D. Bernardo di Cabrera*, which is curiously different from Lope de Vega's play, I suspect that a lost version by Mira de Mescua might account for the scenario. 39 in Codex 4186.

[2] (1) *Don Gile, Schiavo del Diavolo*, Nap. i. 65; cp. Mira de Mescua, *Comedia famosa del esclavo de Demonio*. (2) Lope de Vega, *Diavolo Predicatore*, and Nap. i. 66, *Diavolo Predicatore*.

[3] *Casa con due porte*.

Here one may suspect the influence of *Il Convitato di Pietra* in which the speaking statue proved an effect too popular to be wasted by using a mere ghost. It is plain that these changes, great and small, were made to accommodate the popular stage, they are always and only for theatrical effect.

If we cannot yet trace the exact sources of other groups of scenari, the titles, names, and codes of manners and morality make their Spanish origin unmistakable. The heroes are called Don Garzia or Don Roderigo; we are taken to the courts of Aragon and Seville to witness the daring of a jealously guarded daughter who plays with the love of the Infante, and elopes with a poor cavalier under the very nose of the royal rival, so skilfully on one occasion that at the dénouement 'Infante si tace'.[1] Repressed by Spanish etiquette the old poison of jealous misunderstanding works itself out into tortuous intrigue.[2] The Spanish drama brought grist to the mill of the professional players by demonstrating the possibilities of embarrassment when lovers cannot discover each other's identity;[3] teaching them how to smuggle away the lovers from the clandestine meetings which are interrupted by a suspicious relation;[4] by introducing the problems of conflicting love and loyalty,[5] love and honour,[6] love and friendship,[7] hospitality and revenge,[8] family honour against love and royal favour,[9] loyalty to a master and love of a mistress,[10] old dramatic knots that are pulled tight by the rigidity of Spanish etiquette. In religious tragedies they released ghosts, apparitions, ghastly miracles,[11] and sensational repentances like that of Casimira *La Ninfa di cielo* who in her day ordered massacres and now crawls on all fours, clad in sackcloth and skins to be tempted by the devil and rescued by Mercury.[12]

With so much melodrama even the comic relief curdles. In

---

[1] *Vengame qui si voglia, ovvero il fischietto.*

[2] *Amore et honore di Ramidoro.*

[3] *Huomo da bene*; *Dama creduta spirito folletto.*

[4] *Vengame qui si voglia*; *La Donzella di Lavoro*; *Casa con due Porte*; *Non puo essere*; *Ladro Amoroso*; in *Pittor Fortunato* the scene takes place in Tartaglia's room.

[5] *Huomo da bene*; *Magior Gloria.*

[6] *Ladro Amoroso.*

[7] *Sapere porta danno.*

[8] *Il Cavaliero Innorito dal suo nemico obbligato con aggravio.*

[9] *Prodezze di Roderigo.*

[10] *L'Ermaphrodito.*

[11] *Donna Caterina d'Aragona.*

[12] *La Ninfa del Cielo tradita nel honore, con la forza del pentimento.*

La Giustitia Catalana Berlingerio is imprisoned for murdering his brother, and the Magnifico as a counsellor is entrusted to plead his cause before his father the count. His speech is so tedious that the Count falls asleep; the Magnifico 'non vuol sturbarlo' and with grim justice the Count only wakes in time to sign the death sentence. Berlingerio's head is to be displayed alongside the corpse of his victim.

CLASSIFICATION

COMEDY

In the first period, 'Commedia', the commonest of all classifications, is an unmanageably wide term. The subdivision which I propose is into comedies classical, comedies Italian, and farces.

Scenari derived from Latin comedy.

Classical comedy is a courtesy title for the scenari which exploit Plautine and Terentian themes derived either directly from the Latin or through Renaissance versions.

It has often been lamented that Italians never left the apron-strings of Roman dramatists. Playwrights were not enterprising and a dare-devil spirit of experiment soon shivered for the comfort of a covering authority. They valued the imaginary approval of Plautus and Terence and had uneasy consciences when out of bounds. It is characteristic of the influence of this cult that classical comedy is the basis of popular as well as of academic drama. Locatelli provided seven Latin comedies whole and others in fragments for his *Teatro de soggetti comici.*[1] Elsewhere we take up the crumbs.

The treatment of these borrowed plots gives us the clearest example of the interdependence of popular and erudite drama. Improvisation was the relish that made this stale fare delicious.

To his scenario of *Il Fromento* which he acknowledges is

---

[1] *La Fantasma,* i. 19; cp. *Mostellaria. Li due simili di Plauto,* i. 26; cp. *Menaechmi. Li due schiave,* i. 28; cp. *Epidicus. Il Fromento,* i. 39; cp. *Adelphi. La Trappolaria,* ii. 14; cp. *Pseudolus. Li Prigioni di Plauto,* ii. 31; cp. *Captivi. La Tramu-* tatione, ii. 36; cp. *Amphitrion.*

Riccoboni notes that the scenario of *La Schiava perduta e riperduta* acted in Paris 24 June 1716, was from the *Mercator. Dict. Théâtres de Paris,* ii. 458.

'cavata dal *Adelphi* di Terentia' [*sic*] Locatelli adds the sub-plot by which the play is renamed. Pantalone, who corresponds to Terence's strict father Demea, is allowed to exaggerate the part by extreme avarice: this tempts Zanni to dress up Burattino as a Merchant who tries to sell Pantalone his own grain at bargain prices. Zanni whispers to his master that this is not an offer to be missed: and Pantalone hastens off to raise the money. Zanni meanwhile labels Pantalone's house 'For Sale' and entertains the lovers within: when Pantalone returns they are sitting on the window-sill feasting, drinking toasts, and singing catches. He hovers about anxiously all through the next act and brings this incidental comedy to a climax by discovering from his agent that he has bought his own goods twice. Beside himself with disgust he offers 100 scudi for the acquaintance of the ingenious rascals —Zanni and Burattino are tempted out with this bait, and as soon as they declare themselves Pantalone chases them off, knife in the air. But avarice was the unforgivable sin in the Commedia dell'arte code, and Zanni has the last word. Pantalone is driven to reform by the jeers and scoldings of every acquaintance, and is only readmitted to their society by deciding that for ever after he will be 'Splendido'. 'Viva la liberalità' they cry and the audience rises.

With *Li Prigioni* it is the inevitable love-interest that gives a farcical turn to Plautus's *Captivi*. Hegio, Plautus's 'senex', becomes a flippant old Pantalone much more interested in the favour of a courtesan than in discovering of his lost child. When the master changes clothes with his slave and goes for his own ransom he never thinks to tell Flavia of the exchange. She cannot understand the servant's coldness, and this is matter for new scenes of embarrassment.

There are no Gods in *Anfitrioni* and its counterpart *La Tramutatione*, but the lovers Lelio and Burattino emulate Jove and Mercury in *Amphitryon*. By means of a necromancer they are changed into the very being of their rivals Cintio and Zanni and like their prototypes they have their own way in love and argument.

Epidicus and *Pseudolus*, two of the most popular Plautine comedies, come to the Commedia dell'arte by way of the adaptions of Groto and Della Porta. The connexion between

the scenari, the play, and the Plautine original of *La Trap-*
polaria has been analysed by two Italian critics whose opinion
it is that though the scenario coincides at all points with the
play it is more likely that the version for improvisation was
drawn up from Della Porta's comedy by the professional
actors than that the comedy was expanded for publication
after Della Porta's own experiments in improvising on a
scenario.[1] As *La Trappolaria* is the most accessible of all the
scenari it may be passed over here in favour of the *Epidicus*
theme which became part of the Commedia dell'arte repertory
through Groto's *Emilia* (1579). In Locatelli's version, *Le*
due Schiave, Pantalone explains to Zanni that he has sent his
son Leandro to Antwerp in search of his mother Laura and
her daughter Clarice. Zanni explains to the audience that
Leandro has commissioned him to procure from Gratiano,
against his return, the slave Cintia with whom he is in love.
More of a rogue than Groto's servant, Zanni tries to drive
a bargain with Gratiano but cannot get off under the price
of 200 scudi cash down for the slave. He gets the money out
of Pantalone by a breathless tale that Clarice is in the hands
of pirates and must be ransomed. The next scene with
Gratiano, which takes the place of a conversation on the
extravagances of a woman's toilet between the servant and
the Ruffiano of Groto's play, is a typical production of the
Commedia dell'arte. For once we are not fobbed off with the
enigmatic 'lazzi': the details are all before us. Cintia comes
from the house habited as a slave and learns that she has been
sold to Zanni, she laments asking Gratiano: 'Who will pet
you now, and make you tasty soups and scratch your chin?'
'Come then,' says Gratiano to Zanni, 'You can take back your
money.' Zanni argues that since the slave does nothing but
eat and drink, it would be better to have the money. Gratiano
takes back the purse. Again Cintia pleads and complains at
his lack of affection. Gratiano begins to cry himself and
restores the purse. After repeating this trick two or three
times Gratiano reckons up the expense as against the use of
a slave, hardens his heart, takes the money, and hands her
over to Zanni, saying, 'Be patient now, I don't want you in

[1] Scherillo, 'La Commedia dell'arte',   *R. Ist. Lombardo* (1896), Serie II, vol.
Studi e profili. V. Rossi, *Rendiconti del*   xxix, p. 883.

the house again, I'm sick of your carryings-on.' Cintia is left weeping with Zanni who says this will soon pass off and asks her if she is in love. Cintia reviles Leandro as a deserter, and Zanni after giving her play explains that it is to be with Leandro that she is to be presented to Pantalone as his long-lost daughter. Then instead of a dull passage in the play in which she is told baldly what to say when she meets her supposed father, Zanni seizes this opportunity for the favourite scene of coaching the fake. He poses as Pantalone and puts Cintia through her paces, squeezing the last drop of comedy from her mistakes. When he thinks she is perfect he introduces her to Pantalone and goes through agonies trying to prompt her when all the wrong questions are asked. Between them they manage the hoax.

As Zanni struts about the piazza he meets a sulky Leandro who has fallen out of love and in again on his journey. Zanni is told that he may get rid of Cintia as best he can, but at all costs he is to procure the new flame who is waiting to be sold at the harbour. Zanni pulls himself together for the second plot and coaxes more money from Pantalone by advising him to buy up this slave himself in order to keep Leandro out of temptation. He hands over the money to Leandro and passes off a stray courtesan as the slave on Pantalone.

A Zanni it seems could work harder than the astute servant of the academic comedy, for Locatelli whips him to yet another intrigue by introducing a ferocious Captain who comes to borrow 200 scudi from his friend Leandro. Zanni is told to provide. He trumps up a story of ransoming Leandro from imaginary bandits and Pantalone disburses for the third time. With this money the Captain forestalls Leandro in buying the slave at the harbour and their friendship is only saved by the discovering that she is Leandro's lost sister.

It only remains for Laura to turn up to inform her husband Pantalone that he has been cheated into supposing that the slave Cintia is his daughter; for Zanni to confess all his intrigues; and for Gratiano to discover in Cintia his own lost child. Leandro returns to his first love and gives the Captain his sister Clarice.

The Corsini version of *La Schiava* is on the whole slighter and more farcical though at one point it is closer to the play.

By the end of the second act Pantalone gets wind of Zanni's double-dealing from the Captain who, with his own ready money, comes to buy back the harbour-slave from Pantalone. He discovers the fraud of the courtesan and denounces Zanni. This gives the Commedia dell'arte the chance of a night-scene. Zanni raises money behind Pantalone's back from a dealer, a Jew, and Coviello by privately giving each a key for Pantalone's warehouse, and leaves them to encounter by lantern-light and settle the bargain between themselves ending the act with a row. This scene was incorporated with the Commedia dell'arte tradition: it occurs again in the Neapolitan *Emilia*, and more significantly in the play of *Le Schiave* by Virgilio Verucci, 1629.

The 'Menaechmi' theme.

In the scale of Plautine comedies that the actors of Renaissance Italy were never tired of playing the *Menaechmi* was the dominant note. Translated by Ercole d'Este it was given in Ferrara in 1486; in Florence by Paolo Comparini with the choristers of S. Lorenzo in 1488; in 1511 in Rome; the adaptations of Trissino, Firenzuola, and Cecchi make free with the theme.[1] The most faithful version for the popular stage is Locatelli's *Li due simili di Plauto*. Even here action is increased and relation minimized. Menaechmus' thin little theft of his wife's cloak is expanded by Zanni's contrivance of wheedling Flavia into lending her garments to some fictitious comedians. By introducing an Innkeeper the final recognition scene is worked up to a climax by the alternation of the twins Silvio and the Captain in a grand quarrel over some deposited luggage. Comic jerkiness of action is made more effective by sending the father-in-law, Pantalone, in search of the erring husband and so risking extra contradictory encounters with the brothers. In the *Menaechmi* situation Plautus sets up an electric battery. The comedians could not resist playing with it and the vibrations tickled their audiences for long enough. They took on the twins at sight and worked them hard. Sometimes they are young lovers, sons of Panta-

---

[1] Trissino, *I Simillimi* (1548); Firenzuola, *I Lucidi* (1549); Cecchini, *La Moglie* (1550).

lone. In *Li due Simili*[1] Lelio is told that he is to make a match
with a rich young lady from Bologna: privately he is pledged
to Flaminia, daughter of Coviello. Oratio, his lost twin, arrives
from Constantinople. Flaminia, leaning out of the window,
mistakes him for Lelio and reproaches him for a certain coldness; she believes he even prefers Aurelia the courtesan.
Horatio does. He enjoys his visit and promises to come
again. Pantalone now becomes the hub of confusion. He
meets Oratio and tries to persuade him, as Lelio, to agree to
the wife from Bologna. Oratio plays him a little and then
goes into the inn. Pantalone rages and threatens to disinherit
him. Horatio in a spirit of adventure pretends to consent to
the marriage. He goes into the house and Zanni is left on
guard. Then Lelio and Horatio pop in and out of the window
alternately sending Zanni on contradictory errands, and so
bring about a recognition. Leavening this old material is
a sub-plot with excellent fooling at the expense of Pantalone
and Coviello as rivals for Aurelia. They steal in uncomfort-
ably armed with iron morions and spears to crouch at opposite
sides of the stage like Tweedledum and Tweedledee, and in
come two desperate gamesters; absorbed in their argument
they sit down on the warriors and batter them with their
swords in the excitement of the dispute, until the seats rise
up with a yell and rush off the stage.

Sometimes we have twin Pantalones, or twin Captains;[2]
when it is twin girls the element of disguise is superseded.
Le due Flaminie has one Flaminia masquerading as Lelio to
conceal her love-affair with Oratio, to be confused with her
sister who comes in search of Oratio muffled in a cap and
cloak, and is thus mistaken for Flaminia-Lelio even by those
who are in the secret of the latter's disguise. When real twins
could not be had they were faked. What happens when
a girl imitates her lost brother we know from Viola and
Sebastian. The Commedia dell'arte gave another turn to the
screw when Delia disguised as Lelio and redisguised as
a woman is confused with her sister Aurelia. The labyrin-
thine plots of faked doubles are in indirect descent from the
Menaechmi theme; I only touch upon them here to note that
they present the same situation and so increase the vogue

[1] Loc. i. 25.   [2] *Li due Venetiani*; *Li due Capitani Simili*.

of scenes of confusion. To be a servant twin was hard for it entailed all the evils that befell the Dromios.[1]

A sixteenth-century audience had a stronger head for intrigue than a twentieth-century reader. Having mastered the art of addition we must learn to multiply. Locatelli evidently enjoyed the giddy pace of a plot which doubled and even trebled the twin confusion. In *Li Sei Simili*, besides one pair of genuine twins, we have Fabritio disguised as Lidia the adopted daughter of Pantalone to gain access to her friend Clarice daughter of Gratiano, and Trastullo coached to ape Gratiano to raise a misdelivered dowry quarrel in the interests of Oratio. Surviving this we are not surprised to come upon a scenario in the Venetian miscellany with two pairs of genuine twins in the cast.[2]

Here the double twin confusion is harnessed to the usual love-intrigues with a girl whose rival lovers come disguised at night, and a courtesan whose comic wager shows up the infatuated old men. According to the dramatis personae the Zanni brothers are independent, but they are hired so easily and worked so hard that we have virtually twin-masters and twin-men. This is actually the arrangement in *I Quattro Simili di Plauto* when the two Pulcinelli serve the two Orati. From the score or so of scenari that in main or sub-plots make use of the *Menaechmi* theme we can collect the most popular situations. The courtesan wheedles the stranger into her house and sends him on an errand: his twin in the meanwhile stirs up trouble and the stranger is reviled on his return.[3]

A lady mistakes a stranger for her lover and reproaches him for his intercourse with the courtesan which she has observed from the window: this will give rise to as many scenes of jealousy as are desired.[4]

Pantalone is usurped by his double in his own house; he is locked out by the servant and gainsaid until he hardly knows his own identity.[5]

The host gives the stranger's luggage to the wrong servant and is breathless from arguing with the twins who enter alternately to threaten or placate him.[6]

[1] *Li due Trappolini.* See *infra*, Chapter VI.
[2] *Il Zanne Incredibile, e li quattro simili.*
[3] *Li due Simili di Plauto* (Loc. i. 26).
[4] *Li due Simili* (Loc. i. 25).
[5] *Li due Venètiani.*
[6] *Li due Capitani Simili.*

Money or messages entrusted to the wrong servant twin involve lovers or parents in incessant contradiction and misunderstanding.[1]

The attraction of the slave plays depends upon the astute servants to whom the invariable problems of how to pay for the slave, and how to house her, are committed. We have no sentimental satisfaction in the solution which invariably entails agnitions; our interest is concentrated into curiosity to see how a hoax can be neatly contrived. We need not demand new devices. The intercepted dowry,[2] the impostor with a forged security,[3] the emergency ransom,[4] the feigned or deliberate theft[5] are used to pay for the slave who is then accommodated in a friend's house,[6] or smuggled in as Pantalone's daughter[7] or his mistress, or left in his charge by a faked merchant.[8] All we ask is that the old material should be neatly dovetailed. The art of construction was the most valuable lesson acquired by the Commedia dell'arte in imitating Latin comedy. As an example of this I print Locatelli's scenario of *Le due sorelle schiave*—an excellent piece of plotting for which I have not been able to find any source.

Scenari derived from Neo-classical Renaissance Comedy.

In the Commedia erudita the comedy of Plautus and Terence is brought up to date. The revival of classical drama at the Renaissance had proceeded to translation, translation to adaptation, and adaptation to imitation with the servility that was the mark of honourable slavery in that brilliant age. The piazza was the fixed scene, love was the theme, intrigue not character was the interest, servants were the agents. As a dramatic convention it would be difficult to find anything better. Unfortunately Italian dramatists were content with their security. No genius stirred to break the mould so that

[1] *Li due Trappolini.*
[2] *Giuoco di Primiera.*
[3] *Arme Mutate;* cp. *Asinaria; Li Scambi.* This is an excellent trick because it is amusing at any stage. We are delighted to see Pantalone hoaxed, or the trick may be inverted and Pantalone discover the hoax, or Pantalone may be warned and double the trick by suspecting the first arrival who is genuine

as in *Sorella Piccola.*
[4] *Le due Schiave,* Loc. i. 28. *Il Thesoro.*
[5] *La Schiava,* Cors. i. 2. *La Turchetta.*
[6] *Adelphi; Arme Mutate,* Loc. i. 48.
[7] *Le due Schiave,* Loc. i. 28; *Il Finto Schiavo,* Loc. i. 30; cp. Della Porta, *Olimpia.*
[8] *Turchetta.*

the roots of originality curled up and withered. The academic comedies were the production of great talent. Some were preserved by sound and ingenious construction, others by the salt of wit. As we pass the personages of these plays in review the piazza dances. Hypocritical old gossips tell their beads with one eye on the elegant lovers who betray themselves through every disguise: that slim page over there is surely a girl, and so is her neighbour breeched and muffled in a cloak, we follow them eagerly. Here Pedants lumber with their yelping Parasites, lurking over there are bravoes and swashbucklers, the most picturesque swearers that ever ran away from cold steel; rogues in livery and rogues in rags, customs officers, factors, astrologers, monks, and street-urchins move in and out of the arcades, where lawyers, merchants, and physicians confide to each other the cares of wives, marriageable children, and argosies. It is a fascinating crowd and yet there is not a soul among it for whom we have a pulse of sympathy or affection. At the hands of the professional comedians this drama met the fate that it deserved. It had never been the comedy for poetry, and its prose was staled by repetition: the Commedia dell'arte rendered it in dialect and slang. With an unerring instinct for what was theatrically effective they presented their versions of Ariosto, Della Porta, Groto, Piccolomini, Secchi, and D'Ambra at the risk of vulgarity and melodrama. The academic comedy was treated joyfully, irreverently, and whisked into a new lease of life. To take an instance as a symbol: there is a dull verse soliloquy in Groto's *Il Thesoro* rendered by the 'lazzo' of the dropped coin.[1] Zanni wants to bring a message to the Ruffiana, he wheedles her out of doors to help him look for an imaginary piece of gold and as they jostle each other in the dust contrives to whisper his plans. There is always a place for a Captain to be thrust in; there is always time for a love-expedition by Pantalone or Gratiano or by both; the servants can be trusted to contrive some practical joke when the plot flags. According to the conventions of the Commedia erudita young women appear very seldom: their affairs and affections are described by the Nurses or their maids; it is not uncommon for the girl about whom the plot revolves to have no

[1] *Il Thesoro,* Loc. ii. 49.

speaking part at all. Professional actresses soon broke this convention. A few Nurses survive as pimps, or help the pert Franceschina with the errands, but Isabella and Lidia see to it that they have their share of the stage, or the window-sills. In future all proposals, quarrels, and refusals are publicly represented. The Commedia dell'arte had a way of taking as much liberty as it pleased with the Commedia erudita. At one end of the scale we have scenari from Della Porta's comedies faithful to a detail, and at the other the introduction of a single theme from Secchi's *Interesse* in combination with entirely new farcical material in *L'Abbatimento di Zanni*, or the use of an old joke from *La Calandria* as a sub-plot to *La Zinghera*.

The scenario and the play of *L'Amor Costante* may be compared as typical of the effect of the popular methods, before considering the bulk of what the Commedia erudita bequeathed to the Commedia dell'arte.

The elaborate background of Piccolomini's play is in accordance with the convention of the sustained comedy and accounts for the elaboration explanatory prologue. There were in Castile two brothers Pedrantonio and Consalvo; for political reasons Pedrantonio was forced to fly the country, and his daughter Ginevra was left in Consalvo's charge while Joandoro his son went to try his fortunes in Rome. For many years Pedrantonio lived safely in Pisa under the assumed name of Guglielmo. Meanwhile Genevra fell in love with Ferrante, a young man belonging to an opposite faction in Castile. Consalvo opposed the match and the lovers eloped, only to be captured at sea by the Moors. Ginevra was rescued and sold again until she came into Guglielmo's possession as the slave Lucrezia. After many years of slavery in Tunis, Ferrante at last escaped, and coming to Pisa recognized Ginevra, and, to be near her, entered the service of Guglielmo disguised as a slave Lorenzino. Joandro, now known as Gianino, was also by chance in Pisa languishing for love of Lucrezia. In spite of the advice of his servant Virgilio, he refuses to consider the proposals of Margharita, the daughter of a physician Guicciardo, who is desperately in love with him.

The play opens when Squazza the parasite is sent by

Gianino to ask Guglielmo for the slave. Guglielmo refuses because he has promised Lucrezia that she need never be troubled to marry. Gianino then goes round to work and makes Lorenzino his go-between. But Lorenzino takes this opportunity of planning to elope with Ginevra, killing Guglielmo if necessary. A maid overhears their plot and warns Guglielmo, who decides to poison them both. In spite of all the representations Gianino refuses to believe that Lucrezia has played him false; he decides to raid the house, to kill Lorenzino and Guglielmo, and free the slaves. Again a spying servant warns Guglielmo, who prepares to defend himself. The street-fighting between the two parties is rearranged by the Spanish Captain as a formal duel which is interrupted by the arrival of Consalvo, who recognizes his brother and begs forgiveness for his children. We have all the luxury of a death-bed scene when Fra Cherubino relates how pitifully the lovers drank their poison. Lucrezia wishes to speak to Guglielmo before her death, and as she finishes her story she is recognized as Ginevra. They send in haste for the Doctor, who assures them that he took the precaution of sending only a sleeping draught. Both victims revive, and Gianino consents to marry Margharita.

Actually we witness very little of the main action which is retailed to us by the parasite, the fop, the confessor, servants, confidants, and errand-boys, who fill in the moments when there is no scandal to relate by comic intrigues of their own. None of these minor characters reappears in the scenario version: the sub-plots are remodelled by the Zanni, and as much narration as possible is converted into action. The modifications of the main theme are still more significant. The parts of the three old men are divided between Pantalone and Gratiano. Gratiano has the two lost children, a daughter Lidia whom all unwittingly he has brought back as a slave called Delia, and a son Fabritio who has returned to Genoa after the wars; ignorant of the relationship they are in love. Pantalone takes the role of the banished Consalvo and combines with this the part of the second father. His daughter Clarice corresponds to Margherita and is in love with Fabritio. The two families are more closely knit together by making Leandro Clarice's old lover into Pantalone's lost son.

As a tragi-comic father who is not needed until the dénouement Pantalone would be wasted. Therefore for his chief concern he has a casket of jewels to guard. He decides that they are not safe under the stairs and takes them elsewhere, but his anxiety is so palpable that Burattino soon smells it out and conveys the casket to another hiding-place. Zanni has a drubbing to pay off on his fellow servant: he waits until Burattino has gone to fetch his sweetheart Filippa to tell her of the trove, and then takes the money, leaving in its place a piece of string. Filippa's disappointment as she opens the casket is only less than Burattino's, who tries to kill himself with despair. When they have played their antics there is still Pantalone to discover his loss. As he runs up and down the stage shouting that he has been robbed, Gratiano comes out of his house lamenting and saying, 'I have just found them, I have just found them.' Pantalone thinking he refers to the jewels cries out, 'They are mine, they are mine; I have just lost them.' At length after many quibbles and antics Gratiano explains that he has found Lidia and the servant together and intends to punish them. Pantalone suggests poison. Gratiano agrees and leaves Pantalone bewailing his misfortune. At this Leandro comes out of the house in great cheer saying, 'I have found my treasure, my jewel, my wealth.' Pantalone thinking of the casket shouts, 'Restore them, they are mine.' At last after many quibbles and antics Leandro says that it is his wife that he has found. Pantalone is left despairing. It is by such equivocal conversations—'scena in metafora' is the term—that the tragi-comedy is concealed as by an overgrowth of buffoonery. The 'burla' with Pantalone is not merely a sub-plot: it affects the main action. He is given the ducats to provide comic relief and he does so most successfully at the price of his dignity, and the omission of the poison-scene. He is a caricature of the father, and he belongs to the *bourgeoisie*: the society of the play descends to his level. In the scenario the piazza seems smaller: the girls are not sent to convents in the father's absence, they lean out of the windows and conduct their own love affairs; duels become beatings; the dependants have been pensioned off until only the two essential Zanni are left and the lovers do their own eavesdropping.

The corresponding liberties taken in the remodelling of *L'Amor Costante* are typical of the Commedia dell'arte. The first change is quantitative. The chances of buffoonery are multiplied: instead of comic speeches from a parasite we have practical jokes, and instead of incidental flirtations a regular love-plot between Zanni, Burattino, and Filippa in imitation of their betters. Meanwhile farce encroaches more subtly in another direction by handing over a share of the main plot to Pantalone and Gratiano. However air-tight the plot, a bubble of laughter is let in with them: dignity flees before the breath of parody. The values alter as soon as these influences work.

Plainly the process of modification varied in degree with each scenario, and it was probably further affected by change of cast and audience. We cannot measure the pace of every performance, but it seems fair to say that comedy broke into a trot which quickened every now and then into a galloping farce.

Borrowed themes and devices.

When we come to examine the material from which the scenari are composed we must consider another aspect of the intercourse between the Commedia dell'arte and the Commedia erudita. The debt of the popular stage is greater than the list of borrowed scenari suggests, for plots in the possession of the Commedia dell'arte were used and adapted like properties. Perhaps the best way of describing this method is by tracing a few of the principal themes, motifs, and situations which are so commonly used in the Commedia dell'arte that it is only an effort that we recall their academic origin.

It is profitless to distinguish between the immediate and ultimate sources of these borrowings: trade was brisk among academicians before the professionals captured the market.

Girls as boys.

What struck Lord Herbert of Cherbury about the Parisian performance of the Italian comedians in 1608 was that the 'women play boys'.[1] He had evidently seen one of the plays which helped to make the theme of *Twelfth Night* into a

---

[1] Satira Secunda—Of Travellers—From Paris (1608). See *Poems*, ed. Moore-Smith, p. 16.

dramatic convention. The situation of a girl disguised as a page in the service of her careless lover, who is ordered to woo against her interests and whose identity is discovered by the confusion caused by the appearance of her twin brother, is plainly a shoot off the *Menaechmi* theme. The first graft was made by Cardinal Bibbiena in *La Calandria*, where the twins are girl and boy. Santilla has been saved from the Turks and, dressed as a boy after the fashion of her lost brother Lidio, serves Perillo; when the play opens she is embarrassed by her master's wish to marry her to one of his daughters.

Lidio comes in search of his lost sister and by the way falls in love with Fulvia, wife of the foolish Calandro; he arranges to come to visit her in disguise as a girl, while Calandro goes courting Santilla whose sex he has guessed. The love-interest gave vigorous life to the new slip in doubling the chances for scenes of confusion and dramatic irony.

The next branching off is in 1531, when the Intronati of Siena presented their comedy of *Gl'Ingannati*. Here Lelio follows her lover Flaminio as his page and is sent to further his suit to a new mistress, Isabella. The poignant irony of the page's protests is new, and so too is the scene in which Isabella falls in love with the girl-page and kisses her while Flaminio's attendants listen in the porch.

When the resources of the girl's disguise were nearly exhausted Della Porta evolves yet another plot of double deception in *La Cintia* (1601). In order to deceive her father, who wanted a son, Cintia has been brought up as a boy. This secret is kept so well that when the play opens Lidia is already in love with the supposed boy and Cintia has lost her heart to a schoolfellow, Erasto. Erasto is in love with a certain Amasia, who is really a young Ghibelline disguised as a woman for political reasons: and Cintia has often impersonated Amasia to be with Erasto. The supposed Amasia is in love with Lidia, and tries to persuade her to love an unknown young man—'his very double'—that is, himself.

These three plays may be taken as prototypes of the chief girl-page situations commonly used in the Commedia erudita.[1] They soon found their way onto the popular stage.

---

[1] *La Zinghera*; cp. *La Calandria*. *L'Intronati*; cp. *Gl'Ingannati*. The girl kept as a boy by her parents appears in *Carnovale*.

For the convenience of scenario-writers there were many motives by which such a situation might be hammered out in scenes of comic confusion or tuned up to the pitch of tragi-comedy through the modulations of dramatic irony. Once established this was a device which could be exploited according to the talents of individual actresses.

Isabella is kept in breeches by a nervous father, or by a jealous husband,[1] or because of a bet,[2] and she feels the freer for a love intrigue. She appoints to meet her lover disguised as a page, and before she arrives he has eloped with her twin brother by mistake.[3] When she is poor or shipwrecked she passes as a boy for safety:[4] when she is restless she assumes the disguise to follow a banished lover;[5] or one whom she has driven away by her petulance;[6] or one who has forsaken her.[7] She rights herself by interrupting the marriage;[8] or by forestalling her rival at the trysting-place and tricking the man by a substitution plot which she carries through on her own initiative.[9] On one occasion she runs away to escape marrying Oratio a stranger, and brings false news of her own death. Oratio's grief is so sincere that the page is led on to describe the dead Isabella by comparing her features to her own; in gratitude Oratio embraces her and she finds herself in love with him after all.[10] Again she enlists under the Captain who has forsaken her and wins him back by fainting in his arms;[11] more resolute as the 'Constant Widow' she tracks down her husband's murderer and would fight him in the wood but that the husband whose wound was not fatal hears of her enterprise in time to prevent it.[12] Lastly there is one tragic case where she is tricked of her lover whom she has followed and kills herself.[13]

The trick becomes so common that Pantalone has it on the brain. In *Li due Fratelli Rivali*, he is in love with widow Cintia. Leandro, brother of Cintia, comes to look for her.

[1] *La Gelosia.*
[2] *L'Abbatim ento di Zanni*, deriving from *L'Interesse* of Secchi.
[3] *La Sepoltura.*
[4] *Finto Astrologo*; *Isole.*
[5] *Il Pozzo del Pasquati.*
[6] *Ersilia.*
[7] *Torti Amorosi*; *Discordia d'Amore.*
[8] *Carnovale.*
[9] *Inganni di Flaminia*; cp. *Inganni* by Secchi, and *La Ruffiana.*
[10] *La Mancata Fede*, Scala 27.
[11] Scala.
[12] *La Vedova Costante.*
[13] *La Casta e Constante Ipsicratea con i Trionfi di Pompeo nel Regno di Ponto nella Farsaglia.*

Pantalone sees him passing in the street and takes him for Cintia, merely wondering that she should have adopted man's clothes so suddenly, and from this imagined disguise springs the whole confusion plot.

It would be as dangerous to uphold the originality as it would be useless to seek the immediate source for any of these plots. Their origin is best seen from this group: their profusion is from the stock of the academic drama.

Supposed poison.

Another device for which the Commedia erudita provides the type is the poison-draught which is only a soporific. All the apothecaries of the Commedia dell'arte had the prescription and kept it on tap. This mixture does not deceive us, but it is most effective with villains and lovers in tragi-comedy, with parents and servants in farce.[1]

Stock-in-trade for modern comedies.

Beyond these two devices, plots which make use of disguise, madness, and supposed death, substitutions, and lovers concealed in coffers, were by no means new to the popular stage. Almost all the material of the Commedia dell'arte might be reviewed in terms of its debt to the Commedia erudita, but such an inventory would be out of date. Possession is nine-tenths of the law, and the professional comedians made this second-hand material their own by wearing it out. Turning over the miscellanies we can have some idea of the stores which they collected to furnish their comic intrigues. By way of an opening situation two pairs of lovers will be indispensable, and their affections must be unevenly divided. Two students will be in love with the wives of old citizens, and we are evidently meant to sympathize with the young people who get the best of it by fair means and foul. Rivalry runs in a vicious circle: Angiola loves Cintio, who loves Celia, who loves Oratio, who loves

---

[1] Il Veleno; Li due Fratelli avelenati; Li Tragici Successi; Le due sorelle rivale: Figlia disubbediente; L'Inimicizia; La Creduta Morta; Cameriera; Tre Orbi. In Figlia disubbediente the harmlessness of the poison is so taken for granted that no explanation is offered. See also La Pirlonea, by L. A. Cotta.

Angiola.[1] A lady who has been faithful to an absent lover for ten years is at last persuaded to entertain another suitor; on that very day her lover returns incognito from the wars or slavery. Lovers wait on their ladies disguised as servants to save them from the rich old men forced upon them by avaricious fathers. A lover consigns the lady with whom he has eloped to a friend's charge; the friend is torn between love and loyalty. Faithful servants withstand the wooings of their mistresses and suffer for their loyalty in their master's absence. When there is no initial difficulty the lovers themselves are changeable or deceitful; they misunderstand each other on the slightest provocation and jealousy delays the dénouement.

It is the servant or the 'ruffiana' who is called in to deal with all these problems. They beseech them to interrupt the marriage—'sturbar le nozze'—or more vaguely 'dar aiuto'. Through them appointments are made, serenades provided, disguises and ladders procured, impostors hired, dressed, coached and presented, and dowries intercepted. As there are always two or more pairs of lovers the arrangements clash. In the dark the lovers elope in the wrong pairs,[2] the women hand out the jewels to their own parents,[3] the lovers are arrested, or the impostors forestalled. When the Zanni is single-handed he is bidden to try again and the plot takes its second-wind. When there are several servants, as in the Venetian scenari, the catastrophe may be averted by the undercurrent of spying, bargaining, tale-telling, and revenge which keeps the plot moving. In nine cases out of ten the dénouement is managed by agnition. Towards the end of the second act a stranger will appear; he comments on the beauties of the city, looks about for a lodging, and explains to us that he is in search of his child who was lost, stolen, or strayed, maybe yesterday, maybe ten years ago. He is drawn into the plot by some frenzied intriguer and solves impossible rivalries by discovering that one pair of lovers are brother and sister, or by assuring Pantalone of the noble birth of some sudden son-in-law: whereupon Pantalone's eyes are opened and he finds among the lovers a son or daughter of his own to be wept and rejoiced over.

---

[1] *Sensale di Matrimonii; Finte Morte.*   [3] *Equivoci d'una notte; L'Imbrogliti*
[2] *Mascherata Nova.*   *Intrighi; Pensieri Vani.*

When there are to be no surprise relationships it appears that the dénouement is thought of when 'Time' is called. If the lovers can hold out until the end of the third act they are sure of an amnesty. They prove that the marriages which they have violated were invalid before; they send Zanni to unravel his mischief-making which was all for the sake of his master; or they run out themselves and, kneeling before Pantalone, confess that love was the cause of all their mis-behaviour. He melts, for at all costs there must be marriages and the partners for life are paired off as lightly as partners for a dance. If the first act of one comedy could be regarded as the result of the third act of its predecessor we would not wonder at unsatisfactory marriages.

Every now and then we come upon a streak of romance. In the *Figlia disubbediente* Florindo is a wastrel, and in spite of all the appeals of his wife Flaminia he squanders her sub-stance on a courtesan. Silvio, an old lover, finds out Flaminia's unhappiness and offers to defend her: before she can reply, Florindo, who was spying, leaps out upon them. After this Silvio risks a letter offering to help Flaminia to run away. By the stupidity of Policinella this falls into Florindo's hands. Flaminia is told to choose between the dagger and the poison-cup. She drinks and Policinella after her, whereupon Florindo with some hasty directions to Coviello to bury the bodies hurries away to marry the courtesan. Meanwhile the victims, who have only drunken a soporific, wake up in the tomb; their moans are overheard and they are taken into Cintia's house. Here Silvio asks to see Flaminia and explains about the letter. She thanks him but begs him to go away for ever because she still cannot help loving Florindo. The husband was luckily spying again and her fidelity converts him. Silvio marries the courtesan. For Flaminia and for a few of the lovers who come back as pilgrims our numbed sympathy begins to tingle: it would depend upon the powers of the actors whether it could be brought to life and made to throb. Coney-catching tricks of innumerable sharpers, the gulling of some stupid Zanni, or the horse-play of a servant's love-plot interlard this intrigue with horse-play so that it is not always easy to distinguish between comedy and farce, for the dramatis personae are constant and the material is common to both grades of entertainment. The type of interest evoked may be taken as a touchstone. When a play interests us because of the fortunes of certain characters it appeals to our affections and may be called romantic comedy. When it interests to see how a given end is to be achieved, how a wager is to be lost or won, how a slave is to be smuggled in, its appeal is intellectual and belongs to the comedy of intrigue; when we care for neither character nor motives, but are content to be amused by whatever absurdity may be trumped up, it is farce. We do not care about Pantalone and his mistress: we do not mind if Colombina and Pulcinella quarrel for ever; nor do we ask for probability in the ways that they obtain or cheat each other; all that we want is to see them doing it again; to watch them fight on the merest excuse, to run into their own booby traps. We want a palpable gross play. On such licence the Commedia dell'arte throve.

FARCE

Farce is comedy reduced to commercialism. The best farce is what gives the maximum of amusement for the minimum of intellectual effort. The few go to the theatre to consider, to cry, to conjecture; the many go to be amused. Farce is as universal and perennial as the need for laughter. The burden falls on the inventor: for this we may take the word of Nahum Tate: 'There are no rules to be prescribed for that sort of wit, no patterns to copy, 'tis altogether the Creature of Imagination.'[1]

This strain is felt as soon as farce emerges from the primitive stage of ale-house buffoonery. The village clown has his office thrust upon him: his 'funny face' comes by nature. As soon as his unconscious drolleries are imitated professionalism begins. Farce goes to the piazza and takes turns with the quack who is crying his wares. Mountebanks collaborate and their jokes are pre-arranged: they are engaged to entertain between the courses of banquet and the acts of a comedy.

Horse-play and extempore wit have made their way thus far in all popular drama. It remained for Italian drama to allow such an apprenticeship as should enable farce to support itself upon the popular stage.

[1] Preface on Farce to a *A Duke and No Duke* (1693).

The analysis of Plautine adaptations showed the gradual intrusion of buffoonery. First, Zanni's 'lazzi' increase in number and elaboration until they blur the outline of the main action: next, comic interludes combine into sub-plots which presently are felt to be the more attractive parts of the plays which they entitle; another step and the love-interest falls into the hands of Pantalone and all is burlesque, until at last pretence is put aside and the love-affairs concern Pulcinella himself and the matter in hand is frankly a practical joke.

Burle.

This practical joke is the unit of farce construction. A 'burla', to use the technical term, is something between a 'lazzo', or comic turn, and a regular sub-plot, and should involve an action which ties a knot that must be cut or undone before the play can proceed. In all plays that keep above farce the 'burla' is subordinate. It is usually concocted by servants or thieves to end the act, prolong the main action, or delay the dénouement. The coney-catching trick is its simplest form. The sharper offers to teach Zanni how to play chess on a piece of marchpane and takes care that he wins the chess-board. This is known familiarly as the 'chess' or 'tart burla'.[1] Zanni the countryman is taken in by the thief who can make dead birds fly by whistling: he teaches Zanni the whistle and the birds fly away under the rascal's arm.[2]

The 'burla' of the false arm is expounded by Locatelli:[3]

The thief comes down the street pretending that he wants to buy Zanni's cloak and remarking aside that he will play him a trick. Zanni points out the beauties of the cloak, but refuses to let him handle it until the thief gives him the false arm to hold while he examines the garment and inquires the price. After talking a little the thief makes off, leaving Zanni with the false arm in the middle of his antics of admiring the cloak. Presently he realizes the hoax and goes in pursuit.

The 'burla' of the false arm is inverted in the scenario of *Rosalba Bizzarra*. Rosalba is a shrew of the most violent

---

[1] *Sei Contenti*, and *Acconcia Serva*.   [3] *La Fantasma; Finto Schiavo*.
[2] *Li Banditi*.

type, she tricks, beats and beards her relations, her suitors, and her servants until the 'burla' of the wooden man is suggested. The Magnifico stands in the piazza like a stock, Rosalba hits it hard, it hits her harder and she is so taken aback that her spirit is broken and she becomes an exemplary woman.

Thieves in the Roman miscellany, and demons in the Neapolitan, provide the commonest 'burle'. Pimpinella jumps out on Policinella in a devil mask;[1] Policinella as a ghost scares Coviello;[2] or Stoppino frightens Pantalone with the apparition of a death-mask in the doorway.[3] It may be to clear the coast for the lovers, it may be to cudgel their rivals, it may be sheer exuberance. The properties were there, why not use them? That the act should end with a noise and a devil scare was no doubt cheaper than the dish-breaking and the *fiasco* tricks which are sometimes recommended.[4] The 'burla' of the country of Cuccagna has been often quoted from Scala's *Teatro*; the trick of the prize dream expounded by Locatelli was quite as popular.[5]

At this stage the terms 'lazzo' and 'burla' are often interchanged. By the usual standard it is a 'burla' when Coviello brings a ring to Celia and gives it her by playing the 'lazzo' of the new world on the Doctor. From the context the 'new world' was evidently a peep-show in a cabinet which was to be broken on the chaperon's head when he emerged.[6]

The tricks that end the act with an uproar establish themselves as comic intermedii, and the term is used in several Neapolitan scenari.[7] Coviello, Tartaglia, Pulcinella, and the Doctor are busy counting out money when the thief creeps up and steals it all with the 'intermedio del zitto'; in another instance they are directed to play the usual 'intermezzo' of drawing straws. As 'intermezzo' suggests these 'burle' are still episodic. What Zanni loses at the end of Act I, he

---

[1] *Il Vecchio Ingannato*; *Demonie sono le Donne.*

[2] *Aquidotto*; *Giostra Amorosa*; *Bastarda Impertinente.*

[3] *La Costanza di Flaminia con le Furbarie di Stoppino.*

[4] *Il Falso Indovino*; *Li Duo Amanti Furiosi.*

[5] *Li Ritratti.* See Appendix G.

[6] *Donna Zanni.*

[7] *La Rivaltà fra Policinella e Coviello*; *Inganni.* Nap., *La Rivaltà fra Pollicinella e Covello*; *Il Capitano Burlato.* The *fiasco* trick is used in *Giostra Amorosa* and *Li Due Amanti Furiosi.*

recovers at the beginning of Act II. However brutal the 'burla' it is to be taken as a practical joke; if it is successful it justifies itself; and if it fails the plotters plead 'burla', they may be liable to a beating from their masters or to a revenge 'burla' from their fellow servants, but from the dramatist's point of view there need be no such consequences. It is a tidy way of padding out a plot or manœuvring a side-issue. As the hatchet may be buried, so it may be sharpened at a moment's notice. The desire to play practical jokes is innate in every Zanni; he hardly needs the cue of a love-affair. Many a flagging plot was picked up by Zanni saying to Burattino, 'Let's do the old man', and when the trick was over by Burattino saying to Zanni 'Let's do him again'.

As the 'burla' is elaborated it becomes structurally part of the play. If a page's pick-pocketing is left unexplained the grievance develops into a plot-factor.[1] Revenge 'burle' combine to make a sub-plot. In the scenario of *Fate voi* Horatio and Leandro have been disinherited and have no money to enjoy the courtesan: they decide to play a 'burla' on some Jews. They waylay Zanni as he loiters to school and tell him that they are strangers looking for an honest man who will be handsomely rewarded for his service. They dress up Zanni in cap and cloak with a huge paper collar as the Prince of Cucovia and rehearse his walk. He is to reply, 'See to it yourself'—*Fate voi*—to all questions. When the Jews arrive they are told that this is a great Prince who will commission them to furnish his palace. They are delighted with Zanni's magnificent 'See to it yourself' until it comes to the bill. By this the young men have sidled away and the Jews call in Coviello the justice and his clerk. Still Zanni has only one reply, and they decide that he will do best in the mad-house and send for the keeper. The lunatics are brought in procession and Zanni mimics their antics imagining it is all some princely ceremony in his honour; but when the keeper tries to bind him his mother-wit returns; he struggles away, beats them all round and escapes. For the *Fate voi* 'burla' Zanni gets his own back on the young men by visiting their

---

[1] As in *Zanni Barbiero*, or *Veste*, where a borrowed garment is made the excuse, or *Policinella Pittore* where the itinerant painter sketches the likeness of the wrong lady.

mistresses with Tartaglia, first as beggars, in which disguise they are discovered, and then as gentlemen in their masters' clothes.

The 'burla' that involves disguise needs forethought and incorporates itself with the plot. The object is to kill two birds with one stone.

In the scenario of *Zanni Beccho* Pantalone and Gratiano and Silvio are rivals for Isabella, Zanni's wife: and Zanni the Captain is in love with her neighbour Clarice. By the third act many minor 'burle' have been played out and Zanni decides to sweep all the lovers into his net. Each old man is told that if he will come to the piazza in a sack he will find Zanni in another sack and Isabella in the middle. She will call 'Kiss me my love', and whoever gets there first shall have her. Silvio, on the other hand, is told that in half an hour he will find two sacks in the piazza, Zanni will be in one and Isabella in the other. He is to call out 'Kiss me my love', and Zanni will reply so that Silvio will know in which sack to find Isabella, and if he can race Zanni he shall have her. The rogue waits grinning while the sacks settle themselves and Silvio calls. There is a kissing scuffle and then a beating and they discover the hoax. But Zanni has still a trump-card. The Captain has been told to visit Clarice as a porter. He appears just as Zanni's victims are blind with fury; the clothes deceive them and they beat him as Zanni, bundle him in a sack, and would have him in the river before he can persuade them of their mistake. Zanni and Isabella enjoy the scene from the window. The servants became very skilful at planning disguises which should serve a double turn. Pantalone and his wife embrace in public and revile each other in asides, with the result that the wife flirts with the neighbour and Pantalone with the neighbour's daughter:[1] hen-pecked husbands engage to tame each other's wives.[2] The Doctor gives his pupil lessons in the art of love which the pupil (who has evidently read Strapparola) practises on the Doctor's wife.[3] All the ladies reject their suitors for love of the servant;[4] two old men plan to marry each other's

[1] *La Sepultura.*
[2] *Le Moglie Superbe.*
[3] *Scola di Terenzio*; cp. Strapparola,
Tredici piacevoli notti (1569), i. 129.
[4] *Zanni finto Morto.*

daughters to cancel the dowries.[1] Father and his son are rivals for a neighbour's daughter.[2]

It is the treatment rather than the theme that distinguishes farce. In comedy our interest is focused upon the young people: in farce their affections are so light that the plotter can offer alternative banns[3] and if the wrong couples are married because Pulcinella had too much in hand they agree to stay as they are.[4] Their mischief slips by like froth off the grosser fool's play of the old men and the servants. When Zanni was idle he could not resist practising for his own amusement the tricks that he borrowed or invented when his master's affairs had made intrigue a necessity.[5] When the 'burla' is played for its own sake farce is upon us.

Parody: supposed death.

If we consider the fate of the two common dramatic devices, supposed death, and disguise, we shall see how soon parody makes its way. Zanni's brisk treatment of supposed death made excellent fooling. The victim is stretched on the stage and told not to talk: occasionally it is allowed the decency of a coffin, always candles are provided. A crowd soon collects. When Pantalone hears that his wife is dead he is glad to be saved the necessity of poisoning her and runs off so quickly that he does not see the corpse making merry with Silvio the lover.[6] Or a miser is lying low to discover the hypocrisy of his relations.[7] For those who are trying to evade their enemies, their creditors, or the law there is a spice of danger. There is a good scene in Lachi's *Inimicizia tra i due Vecchi con il finto Indovino*, a play written up from a traditional scenario.[8] Pandolfo feigns death to avoid the wrath of the Captain who has been hired as his enemy's bravo. The notaries hold an inquest and suspect poison. Pandolfo endures their personal remarks until some one says, 'Take this knife, George, and open him up.' Exit Pandolfo.

---

[1] Notably in *Trappolino Invisibile*; *Giardino*.

[2] Notably in *Giuoco di Primiero*; *Finti Amici*; *Falso Indovino*; *Fate Voi*.

[3] *Bastarda Impertinente*.

[4] *Sensale di Matrimonii*.

[5] *Finti Turchi* contains five 'burle'.

[6] *Le Finte Morte*.

[7] *Il Vecchio Avaro*.

[8] I have only seen an edition published in Bologna 1684; Quadrio cites one for 1667. The play corresponds mainly to *L'Inimicizia*, Loc. i. 49.

On another occasion the ladies can find no better way of evading their parents than by pretending to be dead on the doorstep. When inspection is invited they rise up as spirits and frighten away the crowd.[1] The Commedia dell'arte saw to it that ghost scenes might be manœuvred simply on the report of death. They were invaluable for clearing the stage with 'lazzi' of fear, for conveying lovers from one haunted house to another; and they were equally appropriate in tragi-comedy, comedy, and farce.[2]

Disguises.

The network of assumed disguises gives the Commedia dell'arte the appearance of a charade. As the seventeenth century grows old Policinella and Coviello hardly ever enter in their own characters. They are for ever cheating somebody, or scaring each other as necromancers, Indian colonels, widows, lame doctors, brides, noble Romans, or foreign princes. The servants change clothes with the masters; Coviello appears as the Judge at his own trial.[3] The Zanni turns his peaked hat back to front,[4] ties on another beard, muffles in a cloak, and passes for a stranger; he turns down the brim and puts a patch over one eye and begs from his master; he wraps his head in a towel and walks like a duck[5] [sic] and his accomplice presents him as the bride elect to cozen the rich stranger; he puts Mercury-feathers in his cap and plays the pandar. A black mask makes a Turk, a rod and turban a Magician. For the rest he goes invisible in make-believe.

As for the disguises that Zanni provided for his master, the more ridiculous they were, the better. The Doctor hawked soap or wooden shoes, Pantalone borrowed Franceschina's petticoat, the Captain went as a lunatic with straws

---

1 *Finte Morte.*

2 See Scala, 3, 7, 14, 22, 24, 30. *Lo Amante Ingrato*; *Il Veleno*; *Teste Incantate*; *Aquidotto*; *Giostra Amorosa*; *Fratelli Avvelenati*; *La Pazzia di Cintio*; *Li Incanti Amorosi*; *Gratiano Fallito*. This list is by no means exhaustive nor is it reckoning for the prophetic and avenging ghosts of tragedy.

3 *Naufraggio di lieto fine.*

4 For comment on the adaptability of Zanni's hat after performance in Strassburg, 1567, see Trautmann, op. cit., pp. 226, 227.

5 *Horatio Burlato*; cp. *Li Finti Amici* in which Zanni instructs the page 'come deve caminare pian, piano, et strenga le gambe, che non facci tanto il culo in fuori'.

in his hair. Smuggling plots were still more exciting. If the lover was concealed in a chest Zanni would pretend to throw it into the river;[1] if he was waiting in the tomb the necromancer sent some one else to fetch a deadman's tooth for a charm;[2] if he was in a sack Franceschina would sell him to the pork-butcher;[3] hidden under the washing he is nearly tipped into the boiler;[4] Coviello comes to tame the baker's wife on a covered trestle as bread.[5] Della Porta had a lover brought in as a bear buttoned into a skin.[6] Truffaldino capped this by appearing as an Indian parrot; and he held his own until the tail feathers came out.[7] What wonder if the old disguises of lovers as tutors, merchants, and locksmiths were a little threadbare? The magnet of all this farcical material has been the love-affair; the only alternative theme of any importance is the reversal of fortune.

Plays with a moral.

If laughter had not choked all moral consideration out of them we might have expected to find in the scenari of the Prodigal[8] son, Dives and Lazarus,[9] the hypocrite,[10] the miser,[11] and the proud rich woman,[12] some survival of the didactic intention of the morality plays and satirical farces of the early Renaissance. If Cecchi and Barbieri as moralists convinced themselves of the educative value of these fables they knew very little of the powers of suggestion. The pigs which gave the opportunity for a 'sack burla' with the Captain, were more attractive than the Prodigal. There is still some satiric gall in the farces of the hypocrite doctor, the oily pedant,[13] and the miser whose fawning relations recoil at his death, but there is little matter save mirth when an overbearing woman is tamed, or a clown suddenly raised to great rank. This last theme had a long run. For us its first appearance is in Locatelli's *Le Grandezze di Zanni*, a scenario which has

[1] *Il Giardino.*
[2] *Bastarda Impertinente.*
[3] *Li Porci.*
[4] *Li Tre Becchi.*
[5] *Fornaro Geloso.*
[6] *La Chiappinaria.*
[7] *Trufaldin finto paagalo* (sic) *per amore Filosofo per conversatione nell'assemblea de Matti.* N. Monaseni. s.a. Venetia;

cp. Della Porta, *Il Moro*; cp. Parabosco, *Il Marinaio* (1560).
[8] *Li Porci*; *Figliuol Prodigo.*
[9] *Il Ricco Epulone.*
[10] *Il Dottor Bacchetone.*
[11] *Il Vecchio Avaro.*
[12] *La Ricca Superba.*
[13] *Il Pedante.*

two brief counterparts in the Corsini collection. A Prince falls in love with Flaminia, the daughter of Zanni, a peasant, he marries her and puts her through trials which show that he was brought up on the story of Griselda. Zanni, now 'Don Elmo, Conte di Alta Polvere, Marchese di Terebin-ni-bi-binto', is brought to Court and given *carte blanche* with the menu. He orders a calf half roast and half boiled, two sucking pigs, and four Parmesan cheeses, and his other ideas are to scale. The two counsellors who had insulted him in the first act are degraded to the most menial offices. This sub-plot lasts out the second act while Flaminia is still in favour, but it was evidently important enough to usurp the title in place of the tragi-comic plot.

The Peasant-Prince.

In the plays of the 'Supposed Prince' this farcical theme has more scope. All the five versions extant belong to the second half of the seventeenth century, but the scenario was evidently well established by 1632, when Sir Aston Cokayne saw it played twice in Venice by the *Affezionati* and wrote it up in English as *Trappolin Suppos'd a Prince*.[1]

According to this tradition the buffoon, who may be surnamed Zanni, has a charming wife Fiammetta, who is coveted by two old counsellors, Pantalone and the Doctor. The play opens when the Prince, absent on some pretext of war, wooing, or jousting, has left in their charge the kingdom, the Princess, and a noble slave Brunetto. The counsellors at once turn their attention to Fiammetta, and when Zanni protests after a mock trial he is banished. In the woods he meets with a Magician, who has an old grudge against the absent Prince, and the usual foreknowledge of everything that has happened at the court. His devils fit Zanni up with a hat and cloak, which transform him into the likeness of the Prince, and the Magician provides him with a mandrake root which will turn the real Prince into a Zanni. Meanwhile at court the Princess and the slave, who is a noble suitor in disguise, have been spied upon by the Captain and imprisoned by the Counsellors. The second act is filled with the welcome of the Supposed Prince, who has a triumphal ride pick-a-back on Pantalone

[1] First printed 1658.

and the Doctor, orders immense meals, releases his old friend
Brunetto, teases his wife, and imprisons the counsellors. The
real Prince returns and all this is reversed; and the two
countermand each other's orders until the clamour of contradictions reaches a climax. The real Prince meets Zanni, who
defends himself with the magic root, and has his rival arrested
and brought to the foot of the gallows. Here the Supposed
Prince offers to play the executioner, but this last morsel of
revenge is snatched from him by the Magician, who appears
to explain the transformations and settle the marriage of
Brunetto and the Princess.

This theme was written up as a comic opera,[1] and again as
a play by Carlo Ambrosi,[2] and persisted on the English stage
until the beginning of the nineteenth century.[3] For the
Zanni who had a trial scene, an encounter with a Magician,
a scene of administering justice and an execution to fill with
his 'lazzi', it must have been a benefit performance. A taste
of Gueulette's translation of Biancolelli's memoranda will
show how coarse, harmless, and highly-flavoured this farce
was wont to be.

Construction of farces.

Examining the structure of the farces of the Commedia
dell'arte I find that for the crudest three 'burle' strung together will serve;[4] while in the finest the management of
absurd motives is as neat as in any comedy of intrigue. The
travelling comedians could not afford 'supers'. As plot-
agents the masks are of equal value and each has its interest
to exploit; any two might give rise to a side-issue which
enriches the play but is not managed without considerable
skill. Locatelli's deftness in manipulating plots, counter-
plots, sub-plots, end-of-act 'burle', and incidental 'lazzi'
amounts to style.

The most interesting contribution to the art of farce construction made by the Commedia dell'arte was the device of
deliberate repetition. When something happens three times

---

[1] *Il Girello*, Ronciglione, 1668; 1674.
[2] *Il Finto Principe*, Bologna s.a. Allacci cites an edition from Venice, 1729.
[3] See *Mod. Lang. Review*, xxiii,
p. 49. The comedy of the stupid ad-

ministrator is used again in *Del disordine
il buon ordine ne nasce*.

[4] *Quattro medici, quattro astrologi,
quattro vammene*; cp. *Aquidotto*.

in succession we laugh whether it is a joke or not.[1] Why? The professional comedians did not linger over the problem but made use of the fact.

Duplication of their scenes of protestation, jealousy, and despair shows up the comic extravagance of the lovers; by parody servants[2] make capital out of the dullest masters; it is used for climax and for dramatic irony. It excites the audience to anticipate the result when a stupid Zanni is taken in by the same trick twice, or when his clever counterpart turns the tables on his master.[3] He gives the slow-witted time to catch up round the corners of an intrigue.[4] By this artificial symmetry of balanced parts we are prepared for the artificiality of the farce material.

Farce-plotting generally breaks down at the dénouement. We do not insist on a high standard of probability but we do expect it to observe the rules of its own game. It is recognized in improvised farce that all letters are common property, that every one is an eavesdropper, that jealous lovers poison each other, servants beat each other, and the ladies scratch and 'come to hairs' (*vengono ai capelli*). All old men are misers, and believe in necromancy, their young wives are fair game for young lovers. Such is the code of manners in this primitive society: if we accept it the plotting is rational enough: an action is rarely left unmotived although the motives may be crude. The weakness is at the end when the knots are cut and not untied. A magician is called in as lightly as an apothecary, his magic water revives the dead, cures the lunatic, acts as a love potion, or transforms the lovers into the likeness of Tartaglia to please the ladies.[5] A lost wife and six little Policinelli turn up to bar Policinella's claim to Isabella.[6] The initial difficulty of a blood-feud is withdrawn by declaring that after all only a bandit was killed.[7]

---

[1] The simplest form is the 'burla' of the cuff. When Aurelia and Flaminia are tired of arguing in the street, Flaminia gives Aurelia a blow and goes into the house, leaving Aurelia's blow to fall on Pantalone, who comes up the street at that moment; Aurelia disappears and Pantalone hits Coviello, Coviello's blow falls on Lelio, Lelio's on Franceschina, and Franceschina's on Zanni, who is the last arrival. *Li due simili*, Loc. i. 25.

[2] As in *Sdegni Amorosi*; *Amico Infido*.

[3] *Trappolaria*.

[4] *Finti Amici*.

[5] *Il Pozzo*; *La Pazzia di Cintio*; *Incanti Amorosi*; *Zanni Finto Morto*; *Donna Zanni*.

[6] *Disgratie di Policinella*; *Policinella burlato*.

[7] *La Volubiltà di Flaminia*.

A doctor is bribed to prescribe the society of the lovers as the cure for the ladies' feigned diseases. When the ladies will not go round, Pantalone can always send into the house for a spare child. Lovers wrongly coupled agree to stay as they are with the primitive complacency of rustic farce.[1] Now and again the plot descends to kidnapping, might becomes right, and we have no further interest.[2] This is shoddy workmanship. Perhaps it is as foolish to look for artistry as it would be to demand morality. These Zanies whose every action indicates their descent into the puppet world are, *par excellence*, a-moral. We have enough to do to avoid the glaring indecencies without imputing obscenity where none was meant: laughter is the best disinfectant. If we reject these, we reject the whole of the Commedia dell'arte; farce was its element, farce kept fresh only by the continual absorption of alien dramatic material. The action of the farcical spirit upon these acquisitions constitutes the history of improvised comedy. The new wine bursts the old skins. The Commedia dell'arte begins with Zanni and virtually it ends with Pulcinella. Farce it is and to farce it must return. We hunt out its development astride the horse of a merry-go-round that is predestined to a circular career. The drama is not advanced, but it has had a glorious pennyworth on the way round.

TRAGEDY AND TRAGI-COMEDY

Tragedy as it was understood by the Greeks or by the Elizabethans cannot be reproduced by improvisation; melodrama, however, is found to be an effective substitute. According to the standards of the Italian drama it was for comedy to end with weddings and tragedy with deaths until the Commedia dell'arte popularized the economy by which the funeral baked meats were made to furnish forth marriage tables even before they had gone cold. Experimenting with tragic themes on the popular stage the professional comedians stumbled upon tragi-comedy, a new form in which magic was to combine sensationalism, pathos, and comic relief into a happy ending. Death was the pivot of tragedy: supposed death of tragi-comedy; beyond this there is no essential

[1] *Sensale di Matrimonii.*   [2] *Chi la fà, l'aspetti.*

difference between them. Buffoonery finds its way into the one as surely as horror into the other. Pantalone's jests sound grimly in the tragic presentation of the *Measure for Measure* theme when his daughter is the victim:[1] the Magician excites us by a show of heads in a charger, although the lovers are actually safe and sound in the tragi-comedy of *Le Teste Incantate*. The types were easily modified; Flaminia is reported to have played the tragedy of *Dido* 'mutata in tragi-comedia' in 1567.[2] The players were for the law of the writ as well as of the liberty, and it is not always possible to tell whether the 'tragedia' referred to in the records of performances at court was a premeditated or an improvised affair. There is a curious anomaly in the scenario of *Adrasto*, which is cap-à-pie of the Senecan fashion armed with *intermezzi* presenting the myth of Jason. Its occurrence without any remodelling in the Corsini repertory suggests that players would draw on the Academic tragedy when their own small reserve of adaptations was exhausted.

When tragedy was presented the properties were not stinted. In Scala's *Forsennata Principessa* the scene was to be prepared so that the actors might speak as from dry land or from the sea. According to the illustrations of the Corsini manuscript the prospects of palace and forest that were required alternately were combined into a single scene. This may be due to the economy of a frontispiece, but it is worth noticing that Locatelli has none of the directions for changes that occur in the later Casanatense collection. There, the note, 'qui si voltano li baluardi e la prospettiva di palazzo o salone addobbato si muta in fortezza'[3] and the Venetian reference to a 'prospettiva che si leva' imply the use of a back-cloth.[4] From the first, however, spectacles of naval battles, assaults, sieges, and tournaments were not spared, to entertain such Princes as would pay for the apparatus.

Tragi-comedy, like erudite tragedy, was fed from the reservoirs of the 'novelle' and the romantic poems. The grand-children of Griselda and Angelica appeal to this generation from the stage.[5] The details of their adventures are rearranged

---

[1] *Principe Severo.*
[2] Rogna, 1 July 1567; D'Ancona, op. cit., ii. 449.
[3] *La Semiramide.*

[4] *Il Cavalier Discreto.*
[5] *Li Dispetti; Orlando Furioso; L'Innocente venduta e rivenduta; Principe Severo.*

to suit dramatic presentation, but the old situations and motives hold good. Plot-hunters did not respect the integrity of stories but collected their material theme by theme. Such shuffling is typical of the Commedia dell'arte.

Dreams, wagers, portents, and oracles were freely used. A Prince offers half his realm to be rid of an ominous sign,[1] or proves his wife through poverty, slander, and temptation.[2] Lovers who were separated, abused, or tormented by calumny or misunderstanding lose their wits; Orlando's disease had been most infectious.[3] A Prince whose demand for Pantalone's daughter is modestly refused in favour of a humbler suitor orders the execution of the lovers.[4] To remedy these and other crises there is a magician. He will satisfy the Prince with the show of an execution;[4] he will resuscitate a corpse in the wood, and send back the victim to recover his fortune priming him with a secret of the oracle or the miraculous cure.[5] On another occasion the Goddess of Peace herself interrupts a fatal tournament.[6]

Once, by extreme ingenuity, the *deus ex machina* is avoided.[7] Doralice has been defamed by Fabritio, who stole a ring from her as she slept and showed it to her husband on his return. Burattino is told to decoy her into the wood and kill her there. Doralice pleads with him to spare her life and deceive his master with an animal's blood. As she lurks in the wood she changes clothes with a Turkish sailor who in gratitude confides a sovereign remedy for gout. This happens to be the Duchess's ailment, and Doralice, who is captured and sold as a Turkish slave, cures her and claims the reward. She makes use of the privilege by dressing as a judge and examining her own case, proving the villainy of her detractor, she forgives him, and reinstates herself with a repentant husband.

Tragi-comedy is the benefit night of the *prima donna*. Suffering or militant, the heroine makes the play, whether she is the Isabella who is poisoned in the first act, who sends protestations of her innocence to the Duke her lover, faints as she bids him farewell, and is revived to be his bride

---

[1] *La Cometa.*
[2] *Dispetti.*
[3] *Pazzia di Doralice; La Nuova Pazzia; Le Grandezze di Zanni.*
[4] *Le Teste Incantate.*
[5] *La Cometa.*
[6] *Il Principe d'Altavilla.*
[7] *L'Innocente venduta e rivenduta.*

by the end of the play,[1] or that other Isabella who tries to stab, and later jousts with her rival for the possession of Cintio.[2]

Valerini says that Vittoria Piissimi's figure was so fine that in page's clothes she deceived every one; Flaminia made moving laments out of Ariosto; Vicenza was famous for her voice; Isabella's turn for 'la Pazzia' propagated endless mad scenes. It is evident that the composer of scenari was to consider such things and arrange accordingly.

By ignoring the rigid academical distinction between comedy and tragedy the 'players' were able to temper their appeal to the emotions of pity and horror with comic relief. Instead of perfecting tragi-comedy as a new type they preferred to use the mixture of melodrama and buffoonery in combination with other dramatic forms. It was introduced into a pastoral setting,[3] or made the framework for the stereotyped love plots of disguise and elopement which came in from the comedy of intrigue. In the *L'Hospite Amorose* we have just such a display of farce against a tragi-comic background as Shakespeare favoured in the *Comedy of Errors*. Warned by an evil dream, Pantalone the Governor has prohibited the use of arms, and ordered the welcome of strangers. Lelio is in love with Flaminia, the daughter of Coviello, the secretary; he follows her from Naples accompanied by Coviello's son Oratio. Franceschina favours the lovers and advises them to return disguised. In the second act Pantalone receives the lovers as Polish nobles and lodges them in his palace. They are to be brought to Flaminia when Pantalone has gone hunting. Unhappily Pantalone is superstitious and at another omen he turns back: the lovers are caught and bound. Lelio is in despair, and hearing a rumour of Flaminia's death he loses his wits: his mad scenes involve the arrest of Oratio. Zanni is sent to Flaminia with a bleeding heart; believing that it is Lelio's she swoons. At this Coviello begs an audience and says that he can interpret the first dream by discovering in Lelio Pantalone's lost son. He heals him with a magic water, which also restores Flaminia, they are embraced, forgiven, and married.

[1] *Il Veleno.*   [2] *Principe d'Altavilla.*   [3] *Li Ritratti.*

ROMANCE

Every now and then the Commedia dell'arte is swept out on the receding wave of a fairy tale: the problems of tragedy, the intrigues of comedy, all the bases of drama are out of reach and the 'Opere heroiche, regie, reale, miste' are left to sink or swim. Scala ventures farthest and tries all the currents and whirlpools of romance. We are made free of the courts of Egypt and Scotland, Persia and Muscovy with a glorious disregard for geography: royal children are suckled by wild beasts, ladies cherished by hermits; young Bradamantes are revealed as they remove their helmets, melancholy princesses shut themselves into their towers; love at first sight is no venture in comparison with love by report. How Sidney would have laughed at these Princes who have only three acts for all their adventures. Swift action and the lightness of improvisation must have saved the delightful indefensible conglomerations. Clinging to the raft of magic and trusting to Arlecchino's buoyant humour Scala keeps them afloat. No one had quite the same gallantry of invention. Locatelli followed Orlando more stiffly; knights errant ride into his Arcadia but they are sooner harnessed to the plot.[1] The current comes stronger in the second Casanatense miscellany when Arcadia is afflicted by Diana's wrath against Aeneas,[2] and when the Cavalier of the three Golden Lilies wins the Infanta at a joust, conveys her to the sea-shore, leaves her as he pursues the eagle which has stolen his ring, comes to the Persian court and interprets a dream and is made General of the Sultan's army by his wife's friend Enrico.[3]

Fantasy is smothered by magic in the Neapolitan presentation of the fable of Pietro Bailardo which required, among other things:

A machine of clouds to hold Angiolina in mid-air; a subterranean cavern; dragon on the ground to fly away with Dario; balcony to carry off Isabella; apparatus to transform Dario into a fountain and back again; apparatus for hanging which will enable Policinellia to fly through the air and leave a dog hanging in his place.

This was evidently a benefit night for the property men.

[1] Li Ritratti.
[2] L'Arcadia travagliata per l'ira di

Diana contro Enea.
[3] Il Cavaliero da i tre gigli d'oro.

PASTORAL

The three sources of dramatic interest in the pastorals of the Commedia dell'arte are the love-affairs of the natives of Arcadia, the power of the Magician, and the horse-play of shipwrecked buffoons. From this common chord I may be excused for playing over the air with one finger as a prelude to the variations which abound in the miscellanies.

The scene is laid on the coast of Arcadia[1] or in a lost island[2] inhabited by nymphs and shepherds who have wholly forgotten their sheep in the unhappiness of their love-affairs. The Magician who broods apart is averse to these wooings and practises enchantment to avert the marriages which portend the end of his dominion:[1] he conjures up his familiar spirits, devils,[1] satyrs,[3] or demons dressed as nymphs,[1] and orders them to hang up the magic garlands which cause unexpected love or loathing towards the wearer.[4]

Occasionally the buffoons come to Arcadia to trade with the peasants who work the land for the lovesick swains:[5] more often they are shipwrecked.[2] When the tempest is raised by the Magician we witness its horrors;[2] when it is accidental we hear of them from Pantalone who comes in hallooing for his lost companions who make their sensational entrances, Burattino is belched up by a whale, Zanni emerges from a stone.[6] When they have recognized each other 'with "lazzi" of touching and of fear'[7] they begin to quarrel and depart in search of food. After some lewd adventures with the islanders and the satellites of the Magician who snatch away the food that has been magically provided,[8] they either dress up as the Gods to live on the temple sacrifices,[9] or make common cause with the shepherds to kill the Magician and steal his book.[10] The latter plot is thwarted by the Magician's foreknowledge,[3] and when he has had his revenge by transforming the intruders into beasts he decides to relent.[1] The spells are undone, the lovers are sorted out as the lost children

---

[1] *Gran Mago.*
[2] *La Nave.*
[3] *Le Tre Satiri.*
[4] *La Nave* and *Mago.*
[5] *Proteo.*

[6] *Li Tre Satiri; La Maga.*
[7] *Arcadia Incantata.*
[8] *Gran Mago; Li Tre Satiri.*
[9] *Il Mago.*
[10] *Li Tre Satiri; Arcadia Incantata.*

Scaramuccia   Pelliccia   Mago

Mago   Mertillo   Ciufalone   Pelliccia

Ciufalone   Rosmira   Tamarici

'Pelliccia, Servo Sciocco, overo   G. Briccio (1676)
La Rosmira'

of Pantalone and Gratiano,[1] and sometimes of the Magician himself,[2] who declares that his empire is at an end, renounces his art, breaks his rod,[3] and not infrequently agrees to go back to Venice with the travellers.[4]

This norm of the popular pastoral tradition is drawn up from ten pastorals in the Locatelli collection, eight in the Corsini manuscript and the single Neapolitan example *L'Arcadia Incantata* with its Perugian variant. Five of these scenari are accessible in Professor Neri's *Scenari delle Maschere in Arcadia*, the rest are reprinted, collated, or translated in the Appendix.[5]

Discounting the draft of *La Galatea* which belongs to the academic tradition,[6] the earliest pastoral scenario is Scala's *L'Albore Incantato*. Carino, father of the frenzied Sireno, on his way to seek the aid of his brother Sabino the magician meets Ergasto who has lost Fillide the sweetheart of Sireno. They make common cause. Fillide meanwhile disguised as a shepherd Liseo is roaming Arcadia grieving for her lover: worn out by her adventures she tastes the enchanted apples that cure the mad and madden the sane, and as Sireno recovers his wits she loses hers until the Magician is persuaded to withdraw the spell.

As a shepherd plot Selvaggio loves Clori, Clori Corinto, Corinto Timbri, and Timbri Selvaggio, this vicious circle is only broken by the wild man's assault upon Clori. To escape him she changes into a tree from which she can only be released by the blood of Arcadia's most constant nymph. This, conveniently, is Timbri, who with the old ruse stabs herself and falls from the cliff: when Selvaggio's heart is turned towards her, she is restored.

---

[1] *Pazzia di Filandro*; *La Nave*.

[2] *Proteo*; *Pantaloncino*.

[3] *Pantaloncino*; *Gran Mago*.

[4] *Gran Mago*. Cors. version.

[5] *La Pazzia di Filandro*, Loc. ii. 4; printed F. Neri. *La Pazzia di Dorindo*, Loc. ii. 5; collated F. Neri. *Il Gran Mago*, ii. 21; printed F. Neri. Repr. from Cors. i. 5, App. G. *La Nave*, Loc. ii. 26; printed F. Neri. See Cors. i. 33. *Li Tre Satiri*, Loc. ii. 28; printed F. Neri. See Cors. i. 9. *Li Ritratti*, Loc. i. 3; Tragi-commedia pastorale. See Cors. i. 17. *Li Ritratti*, Loc. ii. 51; piscatory tragicomedy. *Il Proteo*, Loc. i. 41. See Cors. i. 45. *Il Pantaloncino*, Loc. ii. 50. See Cors. ii. 16. *Il Pantaloncino in cinque atti*, Loc. ii. 20. *Il Mago*, Cors. i. 3. *La Maga*, Cors. ii. 8.

[6] See Carducci, *Opere*, xv, p. 438. Solerti, *Propugnatore di Bologna* (1891), N.S. vol. iv, p. 199. F. Neri, op. cit., pp. 18, 21.

For comic relief Arlecchino, a rustic, and Pedrolino, Carino's man, court the nymphs, and venturing into the grotto are scared by the thunder and flame that herald the arrival of the Magician. Pedrolino is sworn to silence; Arlecchino, for abusing the gods, is turned into a crane, and left to finish the second act with his antics of weeping and stretching his neck.

The Magician as master of the situation teases, punishes, threatens, and rewards, and is not least important for his spectacular art. At the end of the first act spirits are summoned from Averno to bring pitchers of sweet-smelling fire, the wild man sprinkles the water of forgetfulness, there is a great rumbling, the prospect divides, and immediately there arises a sea-cliff on the one side and a tree of enchanted apples on the other. The wild man is warned against the fruit, and he offers to pick it, he hears the noise of musical instruments, two spirits dance in and taking him by the hand disappear with him into the grotto.

This is Scala's only sample of the pastoral proper, but the elements creep in elsewhere. *Gl'Avvenimenti* has a one-act pastoral between its comedy and its tragedy. Magic and 'pelle da pastori' come into *L'Alvida*, and *Rosalba Incantatrice*. In another plot, 'Arcadia del Peloponesso' is infested by a bear, it carries off Dorinda, daughter of the Priest of Pan, and Sileno Prince of Cyprus goes in mad pursuit. Eurilla, a royal shepherdess, tries to console him. Sileno thanks her 'dicendo voler che il ventre dell'Orso sia sepoltura commune con quella della sua ninfa et infuriato si parte'. Eurilla says she will prevent him and share that tomb. But Dorinda is not killed, she marries the bear, and the heroics of their progeny in Arcadia and Amatunta are made matter for two days more of *L'Orseida*.

In *La Forza della Maggia* among the Vatican scenari, Zoroaster 'da agnitione esser Mago e che per castigo di quella villa, quale ha profanato il tempio di Diana, e rove le leggi comuni è stato destinato per flagello di quella gente'; he invokes his familiar spirit Crolo to wake Pulcinella and promises them that he shall be the happiest man in Antiniana. Pulcinella is then worshipped as a god by the nymphs and shepherds and teases the unhappy lovers with magic garlands until Zoroaster, sufficiently revenged, ends his pranks, settles the love-affairs, and takes Pulcinella into his grotto to learn magic arts.

In the second Casanatense collection pastoral portents, oracles, deities, and satyrs appear in *L'Arcadia travagliata per l'ira di Diana contro Enea*; and for *Vittoria Cacciatrice* were needed 'bears, lions, and tigers, a mountain range opening to show the temple, Amazonian tunics for the nymphs, and "da vestire Zaccagnino da Apollo, ma bene"'.

Although there are no scenari of pastoral plays extant for the sixteenth century we have seen that the miscellanies give us merely a date *ad quem*: while a handful of printed plays closely connected with the Commedia dell'arte of the sixteenth century justifies our use of the later scenari as evidence of the elements for a popular pastoral tradition of the sixteenth and early seventeenth centuries.

We have an example of the fully developed pastoral of the Commedia dell'arte in '*La Fiammella* / Pastorale / di Bartolomeo / Rossi, da Verona / Comico. In Parigi . . . 1584'. The dedication to 'Signor mio Padrone Colendissimo il Signor Duca di Gioiosa' is signed *Oratio*, Rossi's stage name.

Fiammella, Montano, Ardelia, and Titero make a circle of lovers who woo, refuse, and lament to each other, or to an Echo, or to the apparitions of Time, Patience, and Hope sent by the Magician to lead the shepherds to his cave, where, by changing their identities, they are able to deceive and win their nymphs. The lewd spirits of the comic plot are far more entertaining. In a soliloquy that has two puns in every line Pantalone explains that his companions have been lost at sea: he is famished and concludes from the Echo that the place is enchanted. He stands aside as the Magician enters announcing his power over all Inferno and the virtue of his rod which he prefers before all devils and charms. Pantalone addresses him in a stanza asking for news of his servant and the Doctor:

> Se vu podesse far senza sconzuri
> Senza Diavoli, spirti, e ste zente,
> O me fasse a piaser; perche con loro
> Non ghe ho amicitia de sorte niguna.

But the Magician raises the Furies who bring in Bergamino and Gratiano. When they are left alone we hear their adventures. The first thing that happened to Gratiano as he fell into the sea was that he got wet. Pantalone says he can hardly believe it, and he and Bergamino burst themselves with laughter over the Doctor's *spropositi* as he describes his efforts to educate the benighted fishes. They quarrel over his stupidity and go off in search of food.

In Act II Gratiano comes upon Fiammella who from his strange behaviour takes him for some god. He soon disillusions her:

> Son Gratian Dottor da Francolin,
> A ve vorria un po vituperar
> Per semenar la scientia quà in Arcadia.

She escapes. Then Bergamino enters parodying Pantalone's rural ditty:

> O che piaser a star in ste collinè

with,

> O che plasi a star a una taverna
> Dov che ghe sia cogo, che governa
> E non chilò che'l corpo ne deventà una lanterna
> Che se la dura trop canterò requiem eterna.

They meet Ardelia, and woo her in alternate stanzas of competitive indecency: she leaves them to the parasite Famelico whose gastronomical descriptions put them to exquisite agony. In the next act the buffoons play the favourite scene of recounting their experiences in Hell. Bergamino's most interesting list of the players he had met below is interrupted by Salvatico the wild man who captures the clowns for his dinner. Two at least are philosophers:

> Se'l me manza costù non son piu viu

says Gratiano, and Bergamino:

> Parecchemos pur d'esser magnadi.

Evidently they escape, for in the next act they carry on an alphabetical dialogue with Echo until Pantalone, who has been hiding in a shepherd's hut, organizes a hunt for provisions.

In the last act they fall in with Jove, Pluto, and Neptune, who force the Magician to confess his crimes. As a punishment he is to be tantalized by retaining only the memory of his powers, and Ignorance, in whom Gratiano recognizes a schoolmaster, carries him off. The Doctor and Bergamino in a rickety ship are entrusted to Neptune. Pantalone, on the plea of telling his adventures at home, is dispatched by Jove to Venice, he leaves them shouting 'A dio'.

In plays written up by professional comedians the skeleton plot is fleshed and we are almost enabled to witness a full dress Commedia dell'arte performance. Rossi no doubt was only superficially the author: *Fiammella* is obviously the product of actors' collaboration. The idiosyncrasies of the masks are to be found in any actor's miscellany; 'Oratio' collected and recorded but need not have invented them. What currency the play had before Rossi chose to print it we have no evidence, but the idea of introducing dialect-speaking characters into Arcadia for comic effect goes back at least as far as the four *Eclogues* of Calmo published in 1553.

In the second Eclogue Alpheo, a satyr, springs out upon Cornisiol, an amorous old Bergomask shepherd, and speaking Slavonic tells him that steeped and softened he will make excellent eating. Tegola the Torcellan sits up a tree chuckling, but Alpheo catches him in spite of his attempt to pass himself off as a grasshopper. The nymph Candida rashly unties their bonds and is only rescued from their fawning by the hermit who conducts them to the sacrifice before the Oracle. 'In manus tuas me metto io Paralitico', says Tegola helplessly.

In Calmo's pastoral we have the masks *incogniti*, they have come to spy out the land. In five other printed pastorals they show themselves openly. Alvise Pasqualigo introduces three dialect-speaking buffoons, Calibaza, a Spaniard, Graciano da Budri di Francolin, a Bolognese Doctor, and a Villano from Maremma to make havoc among his four couples of wailing lovers who give the appropriate title of *Gl'Intricati* to the pastoral comedy which he published in 1581.

Towards the end of the sixteenth, and at the beginning of the seventeenth century, academic dramatists who professed to despise the Zanni drama experimented with their pastoral comedy. Ercole Cimilotti, or as he preferred to style himself, Estuante, Accademico Inquieto, was unable to resist the pressure of friends beyond 1599, and in that year printed *I Falsi Dei*, a youthful composition, he assures us, and one which he hopes will not prejudice his reputation as a serious student. The plot is simple and the speeches more than usually tedious. Pantalone and Gratiano, with their servants Zanni and Burattino, are shipwrecked in Arcadia and take refuge in a temple. As they crouch behind the altar, Fileno, a love-lorn shepherd, comes to implore the gods to soften the heart of his Galatea. Hunger has sharpened the strangers' wits—Gratiano had had the best hunting with a catch of four flies—and Pantalone assumes the god and advises the shepherd to return with an offering. After a counsel of war in which Gratiano displays his hopeless ignorance, Pantalone allots the parts: he will pose as the Genius of the place, Zanni is to be Pan, Burattino Cupid, and Gratiano Priapus. Love has made the Arcadians very blind, only Montano who is fancy-free is sharp enough to suspect the behaviour of these hungry deities. While the shepherds weave them garlands, the supposed gods keep up the comic action by spying upon each other in order to intercept the provisions, until at last as they settle to their banquet they are scattered screaming by a satyr who makes off with all their food. It takes some time for them to reunite and the entertainment is prolonged by ingenious scenes with an Echo which deceives them into thinking that there is a tavern near by. When this last hope has gone they throw caution to the winds and the dénouement is imminent. Zanni gets beaten for thieving a lamb; Pantalone is smeared with stolen honey; Gratiano is caught stealing milk, and Burattino is dragged out from under a nymph's couch. Bound back to back they are left to the wolves and bears, and are only rescued by the kindness of the herdsman Selvaggio, who entrusts Pantalone with the secret that Fileno and Urania who have apparently poisoned themselves in agonies of unrequited affection have, in reality, only swallowed sleeping draughts. Pantalone makes a pretence of restoring them to their repentent lovers and is himself forgiven.

    In 'Il Capriccio, Favola Boscareccia, del Signor Giacomo Giudozzo, Dottor Cavalier da Castel Franco, Nuovamente data in luce da Ludovico Riccato da Castel Franco, . . . Venetia 1621',[1] the strangers Pantalone, Gratiano, Burattino,

---

[1] Allacci cites editions for 1608 and 1610, which I have not been able to examine.

and a German servant are charlatans: Burattino introduces
himself to Gelso:

> de quei che cazza
> le carotte a la zente, un zarattan,

and Gratiano impresses Cervino with his quack remedies.
They are tantalized by a banquet which rises from the ground
and is snatched away as suddenly by spirits. Burattino and
the German who defiles the steps of the temple are trans-
formed the one into a stone and the other to a pine. The
Magnifico sits on Burattino and tries to cut a stick from the
tree. Gratiano, who is changed into a bear for insulting Lippa
the country woman, refuses Pantalone's offer to flay him, and
prefers to wait until the Oracle grants his release.

Another German drunkard, Guglielmo Tedesco, carries
his bottle to and fro among the familiar masks in 'Gratiana.
Favola Boscareccia, del Infiamato. Venezia 1609'. 'Diana
Vinta, overo la Pazzia di Florindo, Traggi Satiri Comica,
Del Confuso Accademico Ordito', was not printed until 1624:
it came to Alexandro Ingegneri among the papers of his
uncle Angelo Ingegneri whose theories on the art of representation were published in 1598. This play is confessedly
an academic exercise, 'fu fatta a gara della Roselmina con il
Signor G.B. Leoni amico, e compagno carissimo dell'Autore'.
It never trod the stage but was perfect in all its parts of
nymphs, shepherds, angry goddesses, magician-priests,
rustics, satyrs, and strangers who seek lost children and, more
urgently, a meal.

I Forestieri, by Oratio Sorio,[1] the next play in this tradition,
is so rare that it may be well to describe it with more detail.
The play is advertised as showing the true and feigned loves
of nymphs, shepherds, and buffoons. Readers are assured
that all pagan mythology is to be taken in a Christian spirit.
Pantalone, through greed for treasure, is shipwrecked into
Arcadia. He is succeeded on the stage by his servant Bragato
who enters with a Bergomask song and curses his master's
ambition. At the appearance of the shepherd lovers Bragato
retreats into the temple, and posing as Cupid answers their
invocation; he will deign to accept an offering and instructs

---

[1] In Verona, 1611. There is a copy in the Biblioteca Communale di Verona.

the shepherds to leave the food on the temple steps. Left alone the hungry Cupid gloats over his meal:

> Quest' è polenta, e questo
> E formaggio salò,
> Che no vorrave sempre star chiatò
> Con polenta, e formaggio, ò che magnare,
> O che gusto, ò che pasto da Sagnore
> Da Prencipe, da Rè, da Imperadore.

His gobblings and whistlings are interrupted by the return of Pantalone who falls to on Bragato's leavings. He plans to disguise himself as a nymph to enjoy Coviello's bounty. With this he retires and Bragato appears to his worshippers, assuring them that his godhead is harmless for he has taken on a human shape:

> ho muò la mia pelle, à son fatt'homo.

He collects the gifts and promises success in love at a further price.

In Act III Pantalone as a nymph regards himself in the fountain and decides that but for his beard he is a very Venus. Presently he comes upon Bragato sleeping beside the unconscious Amarilli and lies down beside them. The nymph wakes in time and leaves Diana's curse upon them: the buffoons fondle each other and then in the excitement of recognition forget the hoax. Before Bragato can explain his odd appearance,

> Caro Bragato fio, così taiao
> Ti pare un Babuin dal cul pelao,

they begin to quarrel and cuff each other. As they continue to molest the inhabitants Bragato gets tipped into the fountain, and Pantalone is blindfolded and led to embrace a tree, until at length spirits conjured up by Licida, priest of Diana, 'con l'arte mia, arte di Mago', carry them off and rid Arcadia of the pest of the strangers.

Virgilio Verucci found yet another adaptation for Locatelli's comic pastoral material in *La Vendetta Amorosa*.[1] There is a slight love plot in which Selvaggio begs the Magician to

---

[1] Allacci catalogues an edition for 1624. Viterbo. The earliest that I have been able to find is for Viterbo 1625. (Bib. Vitt. Em. in Rome.)

free Dorotea from the stone into which she has been pent as a punishment for her hardness of heart. After some misunderstanding caused by a jealous nymph Ricciolina, which sends Selvaggio out of his mind, they are restored and wedded. The main action is carried on by the shipwrecked buffoons who cheat Zanni the innkeeper so riotously that the Magician is convinced that all the ills of Arcàdia are due to their excesses. He sends his spirits to lead them to his grotto, and torments them with devils who drive out Coviello as a dog, Gratiano as a bull, Franzese as a pig, and Burattino wearing an ass-head.

In the grouping, motifs, and conduct of the shepherd love-affairs the Commedia dell'arte is palpably dependent upon the literary pastoral. The device of suicide by which Tasso's Silvia breaks down the ruthless Aminta, the circle of lovers best known to us from *Il Pastor Fido*, are vulgarized by the children of Pantalone. The girl-page and the frenzied lover, knights-errant, and love by report[1] from 'novelle' and romance, were all transmuted by 'lo stile pastorale' for which Vicenza Armani and Isabella Andreini were famous. Italian 'literati' made a pleasure-ground of Arcadia: Pantalone, the Zanni, and the Doctor invaded it like a picnic party. In *Il Proteo* Burattino in spite of a warning dares to pick flowers, 'he has no dealings with the gods, they will not know him', he says. But at this devils rush from the wings, beat them all round and vanish. Their lewd flesh knew no refinement, and they leave unchastened after wrecking all dignity and repose. In the scenari they appear not merely for comic relief but in burlesque of the main action. They are subordinate in *Li Ritratti*, but gaining ground in *Proteo* with the episode of the birth of Zannolino, in *Pantaloncino* they usurp the title and the lion's share of the interest. As by their wenching propensities they encroach upon the love-plot, so their hunger thrusts them upon the Magician. First they are his victims; in *Il Mago* and *Arcadia Incantata* they grow bolder and inhabit the temple; in *Li Tre Satiri* and *Il Mago* they steal his book and play with his mysteries; in the Neapolitan scenario Policinella is made a mock king of Arcadia for the Magician's amusement. This intrusion of buffoonery

---

[1] *Li Ritratti.*

upon literary pastoral which constitutes a new dramatic type
was one of the most fruitful of the comic ideas fertilized by
the Commedia dell'arte.

PRINTED PLAYS OF THE COMMEDIA DELL'ARTE

In view of the interest of the scenari in relation to Shakespearian drama the popular pastorals have been treated in
what might otherwise seem disproportionate detail.   The
evidence from the scenari has been supplemented from
the plays whose partial connexion with the popular comedy
needs some further explanation.   The plays expanded and
published by Rossi, Barbieri, Cecchini, Fiorillo, Andreini,
and Scala and other professionals are as much a part of the
Commedia dell'arte as anything in the miscellanies, and are
invaluable as illustrations of the way in which the plots and
speeches were put together, and as links in tracing the development of certain masks and thematic traditions.   But
that printed plays composed by gentleman amateurs in which
the dialogue is fully expanded should be used as documents
of the professional improvised comedy, demands as an explanation some account of the interaction between the
Commedia erudita and the Commedia dell'arte during the
seventeenth century.

Relationship of Comici and Virtuosi.

The boundary between *Virtuoso* and *Comico* is never discarded but it is frequently crossed from either side.   The
actors covet literary honours and justify their academic titles
by formal compositions of the stiffest and most unstage-
worthy description.   Isabella Andreini qualified for the
wreath with which she is adorned on her medallion by her
verse pastoral, *La Myrtilla*; her son redeemed his popular
plays and kept up his literary reputation by designing classical and religious tragedies.   The four mask plays of Silvio
Fiorillo were preceded by a couple of regular verse eclogues.
Nicolo Biancolelli, Marco Napolioni, Domenico Antonio
Parrino, Zanotti-Cavazzoni, Cotta, Angelita Scaramuccia,
and Orsola Biancolelli devoted themselves chiefly to the
Spanish drama.   Their taste in melodrama and intrigue

comedy probably accounts for the Spanish element in the Neapolitan and second Casanatense miscellanies. Apart from this link their productions in this line belong to the Commedia dell'arte only in so far as they provide one of the many exceptions to the rule of distinctions between the popular and academic drama.

The amateurs, on the other hand, adopt the masks and rival the professionals in their zeal for improvised comedy. The practice of playing extempore was one of the recognized diversions of the members of Academies in the seventeenth century. Tinghi records several occasions when Pisan youths played 'all'improviso' after the manner of the Zanni before the Grand Duke of Tuscany. Cicognini's company of amateurs the *Inconstanti* made Scala jealous for the reputation of his *Confidenti* in Florence. It is to Padre Adriano of Lucca and his companions that we owe the substantial miscellany in Perugia as a case in point. When as a young man in Rome Salvator Rosa found that his obscurity was growing irksome he made a hobby of acting extempore a means of self-advertisement. He began by masquerading as a charlatan all through the Carnival of 1639 playing a Coviello called Formica, and was so successful that in the summer he went on to give comedies just outside the Piazzo del Popolo: later, in Florence, he joined the academy which had pledged itself to a season of public performances of comedies 'all'improviso' in the palazzo. Baldinucci, a contemporary, describes their plays as 'soggetti nobili e gravi, senza l'aggiunta di parti ridicoli', but among the masks that he notes were Viviani's Pasquella, Rosa's Pascariello, and the Dottore Gratiano of Francesco Maria Agli, an old merchant of sixty, who for years would come especially from Bologna to Florence, leaving his business for months on end for the pleasure of acting with Salvator, with whom he would make scenes over which the laughter was so violent that it was pronounced physically dangerous. Rosa's masks were evidently modifications of the stage Neapolitan. He borrowed from the Commedia dell'arte to enrich it by variation. The development of Pulcinella was due to a like contamination.

In the plays of Giovanni Bricci, another artist who diverted

Prologo

Coviello   Gratiano   Zanni   Pantalone

Gratiano Pantalone Lover   Tiburteo   Zanni

Zanni   Pasquarello   Hawker   Zanni   Lover

Pantalone Imbertonao
G. Briccio. 1617

himself with extempore acting, we have more tangible results of the dilettante imitation of the Commedia dell'arte. Bricci, who was the son of a Roman mattress-maker, by his own profession a painter, styled himself on his title-pages 'Il Circonspetto nella Congrega de'Taciturni'. Nine of his plays, six pamphlets, and two miscellaneous works were published during his lifetime, and Allacci gives the titles of ten plays left in manuscript at his death in 1646. Two were published by his son, Basilio, thirty years later, and a popular romance, *La Flavia*, appears in several undated chap-books. Bricci had a real flair for popular comedy and imparts a vivacity to the stalest material. There are sparks of originality in the controlling ideas of the *Difettosi* and the *Tartaruca*, in his pastoral and his eclogue, which substantiate the hope expressed in the prologue to the *Tartarea* that his plays may be found a little out of the ordinary run. Bricci's invention distinguishes his plays from the typical pastorals and comedies with which we are familiar from the miscellanies, but his reputation among those interested in improvised comedy is proved by the misattribution, either by fraud or ignorance, of a couple of scenari in the Florentine collection.[1] The attribution of *La Spada Mortale* to Bricci, when it is palpably derived from *La Spada Fatale* by Verucci, leads up to the puzzle of the relationship between Verucci and Locatelli, which is a clinching example of the traffic in plots.

Verucci's title-pages are the only source of information at present available. He describes himself as 'Gentil'huomo Romano, Dottor di Legge detto l'Universale nell'Academia dell'Intrigati di Roma'. In 1624, dedicating *La Vendetta Amorosa* to Olgiati, he describes it as his tenth comedy and hopes that it may enjoy the same applause as the others which have been reprinted eight and ten times in various cities of Italy. Verucci's plays correspond in every way to the actors' plays. There is hardly a theme, a situation, a device that might not be paralleled from the miscellanies. The action depends upon the regular masks who deliver themselves of just such tirades, counsels, puns, verses, and salutations as are appropriated for their use in the commonplace books. For dialects Verucci was polyglot. He normally

---

[1] *Supra*, p. 40.

Ortenzio   Zanni

Aurelia   Ortenzio   Silvia

Colamicco   Pantalone   Marcone   Pantalone

La Tartaruca   G. Briccio (1677)

used Venetian, Bergomask, Bolognese, and Neapolitan, but in *Li Diversi Linguaggi* he added French, Romanesque, Sicilian, Matriccian, Perugian, and Florentine to the babel.

Five of Verucci's plays correspond point for point with scenari in Locatelli's collection. The wide range of acting currency for the scenari and the possibility of the disappearance of earlier editions of the plays makes it impossible to decide satisfactorily to whom the credit of invention is due. We are at a loss to know whether Verucci was the inventor and Locatelli the collector, whether they collaborated, or again whether they worked independently from common material. The remarkable coincidence in the matter of detail between *Li Diversi Linguaggi* and *Il Tradito* makes the theory of common material insufficient. There must have been some closer connexion. Even Zanni's complaint against his master whose meanness would make him cut off the rim of the basin so that it should hold less soup appears in both.

As the matter stands it seems that the honours were evenly divided. In three cases the scenario has precedence. The play of *La Moglie Superba*, of which the earliest extant edition belongs to 1621, corresponds to the scenario of *Li Porci*; *Pulcinella, amante di Colombina*, anonymous in the 1628 edition but attributed to Verucci in the *Apes Urbanae* (1633), is preceded by Locatelli's *Fantasma*; and Verucci's *La Schiava* (1629) by the scenario of *Le Due Schiave*.

Against these there is the undisputed priority of Verucci with *Il Dispettoso Marito* (1612) in comparison with *L'Innocente Rivenuta* in Locatelli's first volume, and the problem of *La Spada Fatale*. There are two scenari in Locatelli's second volume matching this play, one, *La Cometa*, is a plain tragicomedy, and the other, *Il Serpe Fatale*, has a pastoral setting. The earliest edition of the play which I have been able to examine is for 1627, but Allacci quotes two earlier issues, 1618 and 1620, both for Discepolo of Viterbo. The prologue printed in 1627 refers to the play as the author's eighth 'operetta comica', and observes that it is more than ten years since he began to publish. Counting back from 1627 this is meaningless; Verucci's first comedy appeared in 1609, the prologue was evidently for one of the earlier editions. If

either should turn up Verucci's claim would be established
since the corresponding scenari belong to the 1622 volume.
Numerically the odds are still with Locatelli, but other considerations adjust the balance. For two out of the three plots
in which the play came out later than the scenario the alternative theory of a common source might be revived. So that
when the prologue to an undated issue of *La Schiava* (of
which the first known edition is 1629) declares that the
author had drawn upon the Latin play which afforded *Emilia*
—that is upon the *Epidicus* from which Groto had taken his
plot—we are bound to give him the benefit of the doubt
before we insist that he built up his play from the scenario.
So with *Pulcinella, amante di Colombina* (1628), and Locatelli's
Fantasma, ultimately both depend upon the *Mostellaria*. The
possibilities of explaining the two pairs of tragi-comedies by
the theory of a common origin is less satisfactory. The story
of *Il Dispettoso Marito* and *L'Innocente Rivenduta* can be
traced to the Decameron, II. ix: we are told in the prologue
that the tragic theme of the *Spada Fatale* is drawn from the
'Avvenimenti d'Erasto' and other romances. Such books
were also at Locatelli's disposal, but the theory of independent dramatization entails a double coincidence only less
remarkable than the birth of the four twins of Syracuse. We
cannot get far if we insist on deciding between Locatelli and
Verucci in the matter of invention. Once again in the prologue
to *La Spada Fatale* there is a clue. Here it is admitted that
beyond the sources in the romances 'perhaps there may be as
well some part of the comic business—("qualche burla, o di
parte di essa")—that will have appeared in the improvised
comedy, since nowadays there is nothing that some one or
other has not said already'. The defence continues, 'if this
author has borrowed, he has also lent during the ten years
since he began to publish'. From this we gather that Verucci
would not have claimed exclusive originality. A more tenable
theory would be that he and Locatelli shared the responsibility and worked together as companion dilettanti and fellow
academicians. In the prologue to *Li Stroppiati* Verucci
remarks that the comedies were written as a pastime while
he diverted himself in various compositions among other
young *virtuosi* in the Accademia degl'Intrigati which he had

himself founded in 1606. It is not known to what academy
Locatelli may have belonged. Valeri suggested the *Umoristi*,
because of his friendship with one of its members, Buzzi.[1]
In view of the connexion with Verucci the Intrigati might be
preferred. In the one case they would be perhaps rivals, in
the other, companions in the art of acting 'all'improviso'.

The chance of being able to demonstrate the relationship
between this group of plays and scenari puts Verucci in a
conspicuous position, but his work does not stand alone: it
is rather to be considered as representative of a number of
plays which were long ago set apart by Quadrio as of mongrel
strain, half popular and half academic. Notices of the majority
of them are included in Allacci's *Drammaturgia* (1755), but
they have hardly found a place in the histories of literature
and have escaped the notice of historians of the stage until
attention was drawn to a few in the recent criticism of
Bartoli, Neri, and Croce.

Knowledge of the intercourse between *comici* and *virtuosi*
and a little preliminary discrimination enables us to use this
body of drama as supplementary evidence of the nature of
the Commedia dell'arte. Some are more important than
others, and while it is impossible to make a precise, it is
essential to attempt an approximate, classification. Verucci's
production is typical of the plays which correspond in every
way to the actors' publications. Presented as anonymous
comedies they might be taken for expanded scenari. Bricci's
comedies are popular at one remove and stand at the head of
the second division in which the popular element is in abeyance to an attempt at originality. On the outskirts are plays
in which the masks are permitted in the sub-plot only;
Pulcinella and Arlecchino intrude as servants, Pantalone and
Gratiano as counsellors. None of the plays in the third and
few in the second group can be considered to belong properly
to the Commedia dell'arte: they are not of its substance but
its reflection, and are mentioned here only as further evidence
of the interaction of the popular and erudite drama, the
neglect of which has so often led to a miscalculation of the
importance of the improvised comedy.

Looking back on the traffic in plots, it seems that beyond

[1] See *supra*, p. 134, note.

some ingenious buffoonery, the Commedia dell'arte had little to add to the common stock of dramatic material. More important than the tangible results in the form of printed plays or miscellanies of scenari was the method of the professional comedians. They took Italian drama over Europe at the double, propagating all its favourite themes and situations by playing them over and over again with an impudence that just avoids parody and is the essence of farce, keeping them in circulation until Molière, Goldoni, and Gozzi should pass by.

PART II

THE DEVELOPMENT OF THE COMMEDIA DELL'ARTE

CHAPTER IV

THE ORIGINS

IT has seemed better to postpone a discussion of the ancestry until some acquaintance with the nature of the Commedia dell'arte should be established. We may now return to trace its evolution by studying the development of improvisation on the popular and academic stages.

The origin of the Commedia dell'arte has been the subject of much fascinating but barren speculation. From the middle of the seventeenth century scholars have felt it their duty and pleasure to find an ancestry for it in European mime or Roman popular comedy. Critics of another persuasion have fostered the legends that describe it as the invention of one particular actor or dramatist, claiming now 'Cherea', now Angelo Beolco, known as 'Ruzzante', now Andrea Calmo, as the 'father of improvised comedy'. It is the tendency of modern criticism to reject both theories as lacking in satisfactory evidence and to turn instead to a general comparative study of the drama, leaving the actors to speak for themselves unencumbered by suppositions. This method is sound, but cautious to the point of being inconclusive. There is a value as well as an interest in following up both old theories, for, when all is said and done, the possibility of a classical origin cannot be denied, it is in abeyance only as it bides the proof, and the claims of the several 'fathers' lead us to investigate the dramatic activities of the period. While it was not in the mind or in the power of any individual to invent the Commedia dell'arte, which can exist only by the practice of a group, it seems that during the period just before the rise of the regular companies single actors and dramatists make their contributions. They work unconsciously and we deal with tendencies. In the second half of the sixteenth century with the development of professional acting the Commedia dell'arte becomes a fact in the history of the stage, and is to be studied first by tracing the rise of the professional troups and next by observing their effect upon the practice of amateurs.

Broadly speaking, what the actors took from the academicians in substance they paid in terms of form: they took old plots and taught a new method of lively presentation. Most of the misapprehensions as to the nature of the improvised comedy are due to a neglect of this relationship. The Commedia dell'arte would never have subsisted without the Commedia erudita, and conversely, the tradition of neo-classical drama would have perished sooner but for the popularity of the professional comedians. It will have been realized from the preceding chapters that the continual give and take is too complex a matter to be reduced to a simple definition. The Commedia dell'arte does not exist as an independent body of drama. The practice of improvisation is not absolute, but varies in quality and degree according to the skill of the actors for whose convenience it was gradually evolved.

RELATIONSHIP TO ASIATIC AND EASTERN EUROPEAN MIMES

From the altitude of German erudition in Herman Reich's *Der Mimus* the Commedia dell'arte is considered in relation to the mimes of Asia and Europe. In the Turkish puppet Karagöz, Reich finds such a likeness to Pulcinella that he cannot but conclude that they were the twin products of the Byzantine mime 'which in its turn is derived from the mime of Greece'. He suggests that after the fall of Constantinople in 1453 the Byzantine mime had its third migration into Italy by way of Venice, and combining with whatever the Middle Ages had preserved of the Roman mime generated the Commedia dell'arte.[1] It is only when he tries to make a precise connexion between Karagöz and Pulcinella that it becomes impossible to give unconditional assent to his theory. It could not but be fascinating to brood over the accumulated information of *Der Mimus*, but as Croce has shown Reich's evidence is inconclusive on this point.[2] There is nothing in the Venetian stage records of the sixteenth century which cannot be understood without reference to the Byzantine mime, and it has been shown that Pulcinella comes from Naples at the beginning of the seventeenth century.

[1] Op. cit., p. 679.
[2] *Saggi sulla letteratura italiana del Seicento* (1911), vol. i, p. 261.

ATELLAN COMEDY

Theories of the connexion between the Commedia dell'arte and the Atellan Comedy are more popular and persistent. It was fashionable for literary critics in the sixteenth century to refer to farce and the comedy of the Zanni with contempt as no better than the farces of Atella.[1]

In 1634 Aldeano went further in fitting the popular comedy of his day with a classical terminology:[2] but it was left to Riccoboni to declare openly that there was no break between the popular comedy of Rome in the third and fourth centuries and that of Italy at the Renaissance. He insists that 'Zanni' is etymologically connected with 'Sannio', a clown, and visualizes the patched Arlequin as a survivor of the 'Mimus centunculus'.[3] Quadrio in 1744 echoes Riccoboni and leads off a second line of comparison by finding in Pappus, Maccus, Buccus, and Dossenus, the fixed characters of the Atellan farces, the prototypes of Pantalone, Arlecchino, Pulcinella, and the Doctor.[4]

The issue is further confused when classical scholars supplement the obscure and fragmentary records of Atellan comedy by introducing comparisons with the masks and methods of the Commedia dell'arte, giving to the obvious analogy the emphasis of fact. Thus Munck sanctions the

[1] Minturno, *Arte Poetica*, ed. 1563, lib. ii, p. 161: 'quelle comedie, le quali in questa città si chiamano Cavaiole: sono simili all'Atellane'. B. Varchi: *L'Ercolano* (1570), p. 259. 'Credo che i nostri Zanni facciano piu ridere che i loro Mimi non facevano, e che le comedie del Ruzante di Padova cose contadine avanzino quelle che dalla citta d'Atella si chiamavano Atellane'. N. Rossi, *Discorsi sulla Commedia*, Vicenza, 1584, p. 34: 'Ne commedie io numero quelle che da gente Sordida et mercenaria vengono qua e la portate, introducendovi Gianni Bergomasco, Francatrippa; Pantalone et simili buffoni se non volessimo assomigliarle ai mimi alle Atellane ed ai planipedi degli antiche'. B. Davanzati (1529–1606), *Opere de C. Tacito* (1637), Postilla, lib. iv, p. 450. 'Mattaccini o Zanni, o Ciccantoni, che come gl'antichi oschi, e Atellane ancora oggi ... fanno arte del far ridere, e corrompere la gioventù'. See also B. Zito, *Comento alla 'Vaiasseide' del Cortese* (1628), p. 221, describes the farces that were given at weddings as 'sciorta de composezione simmole a le commedie atellane, perché non hanno nesciuna forma de rapresentazioni drammateche; né tampoco se ponno assemmegliare co li poemma antiche: chiú priesto eie na certa spezie de satera: pe chesto creo che non s'ausano chiú'. Quoted by Croce in *Teatri di Napoli* (1916), p. 28.

[2] Aldeano, *Ragionamento sopra la Poesia Giocosa* (1634), pp. 67, 70.

[3] Riccoboni, *Histoire du Théâtre italien* (1728).

[4] Quadrio, *Della Storia e ragione d'ogni Poesia* (1744).

connexion,[1] and Michaut argues from his acquaintance with modern Italian comedy that the degree of improvisation which the Atellan farces seem to have entailed as they were popularized on the Roman stage makes it unlikely that they would continue to be played by amateurs.[2] These comparisons give support but no proof, and the actual evidence is scanty and subject to contradictory interpretation.

Among the extant fragments of the works of Pomponius of Bologna and his companion dramatist Novius are a few titles which are vouched for as belonging to Atellan farces: others contain traces of characters which on independent authority are known to be Oscan.[3] From these and other references it appears that towards the end of the third century B.C. farces presenting rustics of the village of Atella in the Oscan territory, were introduced on to the Roman stage as a rival attraction to the Greek comedy imported by L. Andronicus. For some time at least the *ludi Atellani* were played by amateurs who distinguished themselves from the professional slaves by wearing masks throughout the performance. The four masks commonly recognized were: Maccus, a yokel with a hump, a close-shaven head, a beaked nose and protruding ears, and Buccus his rustic companion; Pappus, or in the Oscan dialect, Casnar, the old man, bald, big-bellied, or decrepid; and Dossenus as the variant 'Dorsennus' hints another hunchback who shows some sparks of clownish cunning.

During the first century B.C. Pomponius and Novius gave this popular material some degree of form and permanence by adapting it for the 'exodiae' which followed serious plays. Only fragments and titles survive. Some of these suggest parody; others testify to the popularity of farcical disguise intrigues; *tricae Atellanae* became proverbial. Of these five are regarded as authentically Atellan,[4] others contain recognizably Oscan characters.[5] It is impossible to say how far

[1] *De Fabulis Atellanis* (1840), pp. 37, 131.
[2] G. Michaut, *Sur les Trétaux Latins* (1912), ch. 2.
[3] For a detailed bibliography see Schanz-Hosius, *Gesch. der röm. Lit.*, 1927, pp. 246 seq.

[4] Aedituus; Kalendae Martiae; Maevia; Porcetra; Galli Transalpini.
[5] Of *Pomponius*: Agricola sive Pappus Agricola; Bucco adoptatus; Bucco Auctoratus; Hirnea Pappi; Maccus; Macci gemini; Maccus miles; Maccus sequestor sive equester; Maccus Virgo.

Pomponius and Novius may have modified their popular material. Michaut insists on distinguishing between the primitive rustic farces developed by the people of Atella and the later literary Atellan which was written and produced by professionals, and refuses to believe that in Rome actors continued to use the full Oscan dialect, but supposes that they spoke some kind of *patois*.

The general idea which emerges, apart from the controversy as to the exact limits of the use of dialect, of improvisation and amateur performance, is of a comedy very comparable in function and appeal to the popular drama which was to appear in the sixteenth and seventeenth centuries. It is tempting to press the coincidence of the racial similarity between the Maccus of Atella and Pulcinella of Acerra, villages within the same territory, into a theory of direct historical descent between the two forms of popular comedy.

De Amicis draws attention to the parallel titles that indicate farces over the disguise of a popular character; thus the comedy derived from seeing Maccus as a maiden, as an exile or a soldier, corresponds to the various appearances of a recognizable Pulcinella as a damsel, a servant, an innkeeper, a soldier, and so forth. The range of subordinate characters in the Atellan repertory, its soothsayers, bakers, fullers, procurers, foreigners, misers, and backbiters compare with the tradesmen, rogues, strangers, Jews, and the caricatures of professional types in the Commedia dell'arte. To complete the comparison De Amicis borrows the description of the 'Sanniones' of the later Mimes who wear sandals and have bald heads and faces stained with soot, to account for the shaven heads, flat shoes, and black masks adopted by some of the Zanni. His belief in the identity of Maccus and Pulcinella was to be reinforced by the discovery of the Pompeian fresco of an actor who is also humped and hook-nosed. Dieterich's advocacy of this possible prototype has already been discussed.[1]

Pappus praeteritus; Sponsa Pappi. Of *Novius*: Bucculo: Duo Dossenni; Macci; Maccus Caupo; Maccus Exul; Pappus praeteritus, Sanniones. Extant farcical fragments also contain traces of Oscan characters: Aruspex sive Praeco rusticus: Campani: Philosophia: Pictores. See E. Munck, op. cit.

[1] See *supra*, ch. ii.

The weakness of the theory is disclosed as it is brought to bear on the individual masks. Not only does it entail the borrowing of features from several characters, or even from kindred types of drama to furnish an adequate comparison, but also it is apt to neglect the simple and practical reasons for parallel developments of dress and behaviour. A tumbler will adopt flat supple shoes without tradition to guide him. The comic possibilities of the caricature of a great nose, a bald head, a ragged garment, or a protruding stomach might occur to any buffoon though he never came into contact, consciously or unconsciously, with Maccus, Pappus, or the *mimus centunculus*. The sooty face of a collier is a better prototype for the black mask of Burattino than a Roman mimus 'cum viso fuligine tincto'.

The attempt to show the means of transmission is even more disappointing. The silence of the Middle Ages breaks down the best laid comparisons. The patristic indictments of the stage do not offer any satisfactory evidence as to the nature of the drama whose immorality they denounce. Records of jesters and mummers prove the continuity but leave us with no precise idea of the form assumed by the comic spirit. V. Rossi shows up the shaky evidence and topsy-turvy reasoning by which Lorenzo Stoppato tries to support the interesting theory that there existed an Italian popular comedy alongside the liturgical drama of the Middle Ages until the neo-classical revival of the Renaissance.[1] Italy is a country of survivals: on this account Stoppato's thesis deserves longer consideration than if it referred to the more lately civilized tracts of Europe. No one could deny that the talents of miming or improvisation are latent in the Italian people. 'Éloquence de corps' is always with them, and the spark of extempore wit is still alive: but how much is spontaneous and how much traditional remains an open question. After ten centuries circumstances favoured the resurrection of this talent, but how it persists meanwhile or when it will revive we cannot say. The connexion between Italy's two examples of popular comedy remains as one of the unlaid ghosts of literary history. It is more worth our

[1] In *Giorn. Stor.* ix, pp. 279–97, *Re* reviews *La Commedia popolare d'Italia*, of L. Stoppato (1887).

while to turn from hereditary to environment, and setting aside the pedigree to concern ourselves with the upbringing of the Zanni.

THE COMMEDIA DELL'ARTE IN RELATION TO THE DRAMATIC ACTIVITIES OF THE RENAISSANCE

The idea of the nature of the Commedia dell'arte that may be constructed from the miscellanies should help us to feel a way through the conflicting tendencies. Plainly the Commedia dell'arte presents a compromise between the two chief manifestations of the dramatic instinct during the Renaissance; that is, between the classical comedy as it was modified by the academicians into Commedia erudita, and the indigenous comic talent, which has no abiding form but flickers up from the spontaneous wit of an individual (the fool, both in the original and artificial sense of the word) in mimicry and parody often to be found organized into the rustic plays of a district. From the range of dramatic activity in the sixteenth century we are to seek the antecedents of the comedy which in 1568 was described to a Bavarian audience as 'all'Italiana' and later in Italy known variously as 'all'improviso, a soggetto, dell'arte', or 'de' zanni'. It was the nature of the Commedia dell'arte to wander. Spain, England, and Bavaria received it; it was naturalized in France, it went the round of the cities of Italy picking up fresh matter and new forms as soon as the old became threadbare. It had many lodgings but no home. Its chief characteristics, the use of local dialects, of improvisation, of tumbler's tricks, and of fixed characters or 'masks' appear in Troiano's account, while a study of the scenari confirms the impression that the setting, the intrigue and functionally the personages owe much, in turn, to Latin comedy, Italian pastoral, and Spanish tragedy, and helps to determine at what stage, in what degrees, and by what means the new blend was produced. Its strain, therefore, is so mixed that we would seem to be committed to a survey of dramatic enterprise in Italy for the first half of the sixteenth century, the period of its incubation, on a scale wholly disproportionate to this study and quite beyond the capacity of its author. The undertaking might be lightened by selecting one city from whose records the stage variety may be sampled, it would then seem difficult to choose between Ferrara, bright with Ariosto, Bibbiena, and Guarini, Rome attracting a more miscellaneous programme, and Mantua where the documents, thanks to D'Ancona, are best ordered and most accessible, were it not that the tradition which connects the names of Cherea, Ruzzante, and Calmo with the origins of the Commedia dell'arte points in the direction of Venice where the diaries of Marin Sanudo covering the critical period 1503 to 1533 best record the popular taste in theatrical entertainment. Following up this lead it is worth noticing that of the comedians mentioned in the Bavarian records by any more accurate epithet than 'Italian', the majority are Venetian, and that of all the masks the first and toughest are Pantalone the Magnifico, and Zanni the type of Bergomask porter as he was known in that city.

These head the list of 'Lasca's' buffoons: 'Messer Benedetto and Zanni, excellent comedians', come forward while the other chosen players, lovers, ladies, hermits, and soldiers, are left on guard in the hall. These characters caught Du Bellay's eye in 1558,

> Voici le carneval, menons chascun la sienne,
> Allons Baller au masque, allons nous pourmener,
> Allons voir Marc Antoine, ou Zany bouffoner,
> Avec son Magnifique a la Venetienne.[1]

By 1571 they were common carnival masks. 'Zanni' is soon adopted as a comprehensive term for all the professional actors of improvised comedy.

Calmo's old men caricature the Venetian for the Venetian; they were relished in their own city, no doubt, as it takes an Irishman to appreciate—though not necessarily to enjoy— the *Paycock*. Later for a Florentine audience Pantalone's eccentricities acquire a new satiric flavour, his appeal becomes as general as that of the stage 'Paddy'. To play Pantalone it was not necessary to be a Venetian, nor for Zanni in real life to come from Bergamo; as 'Lasca's' comedians have it: 'Here we are Tuscans, but on the stage

---

[1] *Regrets*, cxii.

Venetians and men of Bergamo.' But, however, the dialects might degenerate into a jargon by unskilled mimicry or for the benefit of a foreign audience, their origins were never forgotten. Pantalone and Zanni had the start of the other masks. Whether their survival was due to their functional importance, or to the talent of their earliest impersonators, or to the fickleness of popularity, it is now impossible to judge, but it is not unreasonable to suppose that something is due to the impetus of the Venetian acting tradition at the beginning of the sixteenth century.

DRAMA IN VENICE 1503–33

The programme of dramatic activities of Venetian society during the first thirty years of the sixteenth century which can be drawn up from the diaries of Sanudo[1] shows that alongside the splendid 'momarie', comedy was the staple entertainment. On 7 February 1526 in Casa Trevisan on the Giudecca, after a magnificent banquet, three comedies were presented, one by Cherea, another by Ruzzante and Menato in the rustic style, and a third by Cimador, son of Zan Polo the buffoon.[2] This was a representative programme, and is for us particularly interesting, since we have here two out of three of the principal actors who have been credited at one time or another with a share in the founding of the Commedia dell'arte. On examining their claims and assessing their contributions it will appear that Cimador is a not inappropriate substitute for the missing Calmo.

CHEREA.

From a petition to print four eclogues and a translation of Plautus presented in 1508 Cherea has been identified as

---

[1] Marin Sanudo, Secretary to the Republic, kept an official diary and letter-book from 1503–33, which has been published in fifty-two volumes. See Appendix D.

[2] 7 Feb. (1526): 'in chà Trivixan, fo fatto uno bellissimo banchetto et recitate tre commedie, una per Cherea, l'altra per Ruzzante e Menato a la vilanescha, l'altra per el Cimador et fiol di Zan Pollo, bufona; fato questa festa per il Patriarca di Aquileia, dove erano 16 done di le più belle di la terra, et questi oratori, il Legato, do di lo Imperator, do di Franza, quel dil re di Ingilterra, do di l'archiduca di Austria, non fu Milan, Ferara et Mantoa, vi era il primocierio di San Marco, il vescovo di Basso Pexaro, il vescovo di Concordia, il cavalier di Garzoni e alcuni altri'. Sanudo, *Diarii*, xl, p. 789.

Francesco de' Nobili di Lucca, chancellor to Fracasso di
Sanseverino. He was the delight of Venice between 1503
and 1513 and again from 1522–6.[1] Sansovino in 1581
laments the corruption of comedies in that city:[2]

In former times Francesco Cherea, the favourite of Leo X, was of
great renown, holding the foremost place among stage reciters (whence
he had the Terentian cognomen of Cherea); at the unhappy sack of
that city under Pope Clement VII he fled hither. He found great
favour among our people, and as the inventor of comedy in these parts,
gathered together several fine wits who recited well and honourably.
Among these was Antonio da Molino, known as Burchiella, a delightful
fellow who spoke Italian mingled with Greek and Slavonic with the
most ludicrous and fantastic invention and caprices in the world;
Brother Armonio of the Order of the Cross, the organist of San Marco,
Valerio Zuccato of the Mosaics, Lodovico Dolce and several others;
and the most notable performer was one Polonia, the wife of Valerio.

From a misquotation of Sansovino, Quadrio, and after
him Klein, argued that Cherea 'fu inventor in qualche parte
de recitar comedie a suggetto'. Bartoli and Rossi correct this
error. Everything that is known of Cherea is consonant with
the classical origin of his nickname and confines him to the
sphere of the Commedia erudita. One doubts if this cultured
stage enthusiast would appreciate the honour of fathering the
Commedia dell'arte. It is not directly as a player or as a
dramatist that Cherea is important, but rather as the leading
spirit of an interest in amateur theatricals, one of the pro-
pagators of the pleasures of stage recitation. Of his companions, 'Burchiella' was a merchant in the Levant, who
organized comedies in Corfu and Candy and on his return
promoted an academy of music, which was also to contribute
towards the production of comedies. He was said to be
among the first to use dialects on the stage and made a part
for himself as a bravo, Manoli Blessi, Stradiotto.[3] Burchiella

---

[1] For a list of performances see
Appendix D.

[2] *Venetia città nobilissima et singolare*
(1581), lib. x, pp. 168–9.

[3] L. Dolce, in his preface to *I Fatti
e le prodezze di Manoli Blessi Strathioto*
by A. Molino, detto Burchiella, 1561,
observes: 'E fu il primo che le mutò
in più lingue.' This edition is quoted by

A. Mortier, but I have not been able to
examine a copy. Among the miscellaneous Italian tracts in the British
Museum are two broadsheets which
have not, I think, been noticed hitherto.
Both were published in Venice in 1572
and are bound in the volume 1971. g. 7.
They are entitled: Il Vero / Successo /
della presa / di Nicosia / in Cipro /

reappears as a mutual friend connecting Cherea with Andrea Calmo, whose plays bring us a step nearer to the type of popular drama from which the Commedia dell'arte was begotten.

RUZZANTE.

The theory that the Commedia dell'arte was invented by Angelo Beolco seems to have originated with Riccoboni[1] and was popularized by Maurice Sand's study of Ruzzante in *Masques et Bouffons*. A superficial survey gives this theory every support. Dialect, the recurrence from play to play of fixed types, dramatic *motifs*, and a certain scope for improvisation, all belong to Ruzzante's method: but the closer the study the more untrustworthy these resemblances are seen to be. Early landmarks vanish and lines of comparison are swallowed up in the shadows of contrast. A dramatist who uses a stiff regional dialect must lose inestimably by translation, but thanks to M. Mortier's rendering and critical edition it is now possible to demonstrate the old fallacy by looking into Ruzzante's work more narrowly.[2]

Acting was Beolco's hobby, and from 1520 until his death in 1542, whenever he could leave the management of the family estates, he was to be found in Padua, Venice, Ferrara, or at the house of his friend and patron Alvise Cornaro, with some monologue, farce, or comedy to entertain the company after dinner or between the courses of a banquet. His dramatic work was interrupted and probably taken up year by year as Carnival came round. Of his companions we know that Marco-Aurelio Alvarotto played as *Menato*, Hieronimo Zanetti as *Vezzo*, and Categnola as *Bilora*. Six of his plays were published posthumously in 1551 under the care of Cornaro; one, *La Piovana*, had already appeared in 1548; another, *Il dialogo Facetissimo*, was to come in 1554; two, *La Rhodiana* and *Il Terzo Oratione*, were falsely attributed

Di Manoli Blessi Strathiotto and Barzeletta / de quattro com/pagni Strathioti de Albania, / Zuradi di An/dar per il Mondo / alla Ventura / Capo di loro Ma / noli Blessi da Napoli / di Romania.

[1] Riccoboni can hardly have known any of Ruzzante's comedies, in attributing the masks of the Commedia dell'arte to his invention he implies that Ruzzante introduced Pantalone and the Bolognese doctor, personages who never appear in his work.

[2] A. Mortier, *Ruzzante*, 1925-6.

to him, and a fragment known as *La Commedia senza titolo* remained in manuscript until 1894, when it was printed by Lovarini.

As we recognize in Beolco's work a blend of the two dramatic traditions of the Renaissance, the neo-classical comedy and rustic farce, we are bound to consider its connexion with the Commedia dell'arte which appears to be of the same mixed origin.

Ruzzante's application to the Doge and Senate in 1537 for ten years' copyright for the comedies entitled *Truffa* and *Garbinello*, translated into Paduan from Plautus, refers to *La Piovana* and *La Vaccaria* which are drawn from the *Rudens* and *Asinaria*. The names *Truffa* and *Garbinello* advertise the chief attraction of the rustic servant as he was played by Beolco. His appearance as Ruzzante in *L'Anconitana* is the only element by which that comedy, with its intrigues of three slaves seeking ransom for a girl disguised as a boy and an amorous old lover, could be distinguished from the more popular types of Commedie erudite.

La Pastorale represents Beolco's essay with the fashionable court eclogue. *La Commedia senza titolo* develops from the 'contrasti' and 'mariazzi', the disputes and wedding farces. The traditions of classical and rustic comedy which are distinct in these two groups are fused to make *La Moschetta* and *La Fiorina* where the values of intrigue and humorous character-drawing seek a compromise. Just such a compromise between popular and academic comedy was to be attempted in the Commedia dell'arte, but where character and realism were evolved as the highest values of Ruzzante's drama, caricature and intrigue dominated the popular stage. In each case old material is given new currency by the originality of Ruzzante's conception of rustic character.

The Middle Ages established the peasant as the butt of vicious satire,[1] so that in the Renaissance drama he might be exploited as brutally as the lunatic on the Elizabethan stage; but Ruzzante presents him not as a brute but as an animal, comic, pathetic, and dignified. His attitude is as untainted by satire as by sentimentality. Sympathy makes him sensitive to the tragedy of Bilora whose wife has run

---

[1] D. Merlini, *Saggio di ricerche sulla Satira contro il Villano* (1894).

away with the old usurer Andronico: he comes stumbling
in faint with hunger, hardly knowing why he should trouble
to seek her in this strange city.[1] A friend advises him how
best to approach Andronico and calls the wife to the balcony.
'Good evening. How have *you* got here? How are you? Are
you all right?' she asks him; and Bilora says weakly, 'I'm
very well. And you? You look well enough.' 'God knows
I'm none too grand,' says Dina peevishly, 'and to tell you the
truth I'm fairly sick of living with this old man.' 'I can
believe it,' says Bilora, 'he can hardly get about; young and
old never go well together. We were better suited, you and
I.' She promises to come back to him, and then, as Ruzzante
makes realism steady the balance as it tilts towards sentimentality, she rejects him again for Andronico. Bilora waits
in the dusk for his rival and throws him into the canal.

In the Commedia dell'arte the peasant's clumsy ways may
make him 'the ambassador of mirth', as Trojano has it, or he
may be harnessed to the plot as a servant and take on a new
nature as Arlecchino of Bergamo or Pulcinella of Acerra. He
appears as a grotesque and then as a caricature, but for
Ruzzante he is an individual with ideas crude enough to
make us laugh, and motives so sound that we must also feel.

Beolco's personality is the leaven of his drama. He created
for himself the character of a Paduan countryman, a subtle
mixture of shrewdness and simplicity, of humour, cowardice
and meanness, and called himself Ruzzante, 'the gossip', or,
as we understand from his practice, the man who talks to
himself. The friendly confidential attitude towards his
audience that makes the Orations delightful reading even
now, is assumed with this mask and carried over into the
soliloquy and dialogue of the plays where Ruzzante appears
as the servant (*L'Anconitana*), the husband (*Moschetta*), the
village lover (*La Fiorina*), or the cowardly recruit (*Primo
Dialogo*). It is not as a plot-agent to accelerate, or as a
buffoon to check the intrigue, like the astute and stupid
Zanni of the Commedia dell'arte, that Beolco uses the mask,
but for the joy of spinning comedy out of nothing. In
L'Anconitana M. Thomao, an amorous old man, waits for
his servant to bring a message from Doralice the courtesan.

[1] *Il Secondo Dialogo.*

Ruzzante comes in gloating over a kiss from Besa, the serving maid, which has reminded him of his old love affairs. 'She is promised to me,' he confides to Thomao, and sets out upon interminable reminiscences of the days when he used to go courting at the village fêtes. He and his dog would walk as many as eight leagues. 'Yes, indeed! and that reminds him how once they met a wolf with eyes like two candles.' . . . Thomao keeps interrupting, but nothing will prevent Ruzzante from demonstrating the howl with which he kept that wolf at bay. Then there is the fête to describe, the singing, the drinking, and the girl! After the fête there are meetings in church, love-messages whispered under the Paternoster, what she said to him and what he said to her under the hedge. Then there was the village dancing. . . . 'Well, well, you danced and you jumped,' says Thomao, trying to precipitate the end: 'No, I did not jump. I was never much of a jumper,' says Ruzzante demurely, and he takes breath for fresh circumstances. The reminiscences seem endless; Thomao almost suffocates with rage until by a prodigious détour Ruzzante winds round to the cakes that he has bought to bribe Doralice's maid to speak for his master. 'But you could have said all this in two words,' shouts Thomao, and Ruzzante agrees, 'Perhaps I have been rather a long way round.'

The comedy of the delayed message was to be exploited by professional comedians to pad out a thin scenario. But Ruzzante made an art of wasting time: Zanni and the Doctor only found it expedient.

Beolco's creation of the mask of Ruzzante is the most cogent reason for associating him with the Commedia dell'arte, but here again there is no direct connexion. No one inherited the mask, it superseded his own surname and at his death was put aside together with the rustic Paduan dialect that had been the vesture of his wit. The radical difference between the use of dialect by Ruzzante and the 'comici dell'arte' has a modern parallel in the contrast between the use of a brogue by the Irish Players which has an artistic value, and the pseudo-Irish of the music-hall anecdote which is a comic handicap. Beolco is the J. M. Synge of the early sixteenth century and his peasants the Playboys and tinkers of north-east Italy.

Again, deceived by distance, critics have seen in Ruzzante the prototype of the braggart soldier of the popular stage. Apart from the inevitable combination of cowardice and bravura, Ruzzante's conception of the part is as far removed from the Spanish Captain on the one side as it is from Falstaff on the other.[1] Ruzzante returns from the wars and meets Menato, he is convicted of running away, and makes no attempt to deny it but reiterates, 'If only you had been there . . . Gossip, if only you had been there.' His descriptions of the horrors of battles and camps is as realistic as it is comic. Beolco used this type again in the *Dialogo Facetissimo*.[2] Menego and Duozzo meet at the time of the great famine, and when they have exhausted the subject of food they discuss their womenfolk. Duozzo's warning that Menego has a rival for Gnua is turned aside with a brag. But Gnua has hardly appeared when Nall the rival rushes in: Duozzo escapes, Menego rolls with astonishment, and Gnua is snatched away. When Duozzo sneaks back Menego is groaning over his wounds and has ready a story of the numbers that assaulted him. Duozzo is not in a position to contradict his figures, and after some comic delay he borrows Menego's knife for fear of wolves and goes into the wood to fetch a necromancer. Menego is left to debate the advantages of suicide. In this speech it is restraint and not exaggeration that makes for comedy. All the desperations of the Spanish captain are weak and ineffectual beside Menego's deliberations:

. . . Good, it is agreed. I will kill myself. But how? Ah, Gossip, pest on you, you are the cause of my ruin. Just when my knife is wanted you have carried it off. Plague on me for having given it to you! Still, knife or no knife I will kill myself. At least I shall die well filled in spite of the famine. No one will suspect: they will say

---

[1] The claim has been made by P. Bettole, 'Il Padre di Falstaff' in *La Vita Italiana*, 10 Jan. 1895.

[2] 'You know no one; you don't know where to go; you see a mass of men who shout, "Kill, kill, strike!" Artillery, musketry, arrows . . . and look! there lies one of your comrades slain, killed, and some one else is running up to kill you. When you try to escape you may stumble into the midst of your enemies, not to mention the chance that the fugitive may get a bullet in his back. I tell you it takes some courage to run away. How many times do you think I pretended to be dead and even let a whole squadron of horse pass over me?' *Primo Dialogo*, translated from Mortier's version, p. 225.

that this traitor assaulted me and that the dogs eat me afterwards. He will be banished. Yes! you shall be banished, you great brute! Soft though, take care! Think about it if only for your Gossip's sake. Oh, Gossip, you are causing me a great anxiety now, because if I kill myself this brigand will pretend that you did it, Gossip, for no one will have seen the assault and what is more you have my knife. Bah! it is decided. It is you, Gossip, who will be banished unjustly. Forgive me, Gossip. Banished or not banished, I am going to kill myself. Patience good Gossip. The knife I bequeath to you. Oh, my shoes you are about to witness such a suicide as has never been known before, the death of a frantic man who is going to eat himself. Heavens! what a pity that I am going to die so young.

Just as he begins a Paternoster Menego returns and the resolution wanes.

It is a nice point what 'extempore acting' may imply when the player is his own dramatist. The question of the extent of Ruzzante's improvisation is insoluble. Were his speeches composed to his audience and for the occasion, or did he write his play before he attempted presentation? From the flow of his gossip it is easy to imagine improvisation, while the artistic economy of effect in his dialogue argues premeditation. Whether they were written up before or after the first performance, Ruzzante's comedies were evidently fixed. The publication of his compositions cuts them off from the Commedia dell'arte, not because improvised comedy which is expanded in print sounds like a contradiction in terms, for there exist many such contradictions, but because the plays themselves prove that Beolco's work was more literary than popular. Reduced to skeleton plots his plays might suggest a comparison with the scenari of the professional comedians, but put one of the plays that were written up and printed from such scenari beside one of Ruzzante's comedies and the measure of difference is at once apparent.[1] It is only in the least characteristic scenes, when Ruzzante himself is off the stage, that we are reminded of the Commedia dell'arte.

[1] In G. B. Andreini's *Prologo fra Momo e la Verità* (1612), there is an interesting remark: Scipio and Lelio, it is said, did not write comedies, but they suggested subjects to Terence, 'Come ancora a' nostri tempi al ridiculoso Ruzzante il groppo e suggetto delle sue favole e stato somministrato dal dottissimo Bembo.' Sig. B. 4!.

CALMO.

Signs of transition are felt in *La Rodiana*, a comedy which was printed in 1540 in Ruzzante's name, but claimed by Andrea Calmo in his preface to *La Travaglia* in 1556. The connexion between Ruzzante and Calmo is emphasized but not elucidated by comparing the two plays of *La Fiorina*. Calmo's was printed in 1552, Ruzzante's in 1551–2. Calmo uses Ruzzante's subject of the peasant lovers Bonelo and Fiore, and takes over the first scene almost word for word. The part of Sandrino, a Bergomask who corresponds to Ruzzante's Melchiore, the rival lover, is recast, and Calmo's Messer Coccolin is entirely new. There seem to be no means of determining the exact circumstances of this curious coincidence, but whichever way the debt should be read it is sufficient proof of the friendly rivalry between the dramatists. Calmo's work was not represented in the programme for the evening of 7 Feb. 1526, which we have taken to represent the mixed origin of the Commedia dell'arte, but it will be best to examine it here before considering the contribution of Cimador, son of Zan Polo, the last performer.

Calmo's reputation as the chief literary influence in the development of the Commedia dell'arte is now in the ascendant, but the recognition of his importance was delayed until Rossi edited the *Lettere facetie e chiribizzose* with an admirable introduction in 1888. Calmo, the son of a Venetian fisherman or a gondolier, was born in 1509 or 1510. How soon he took to the stage is not known, but it appears from a letter from his friend Parabosco, written from Piacenza, 14 February 1548, that his reputation was well established:

Have you not in hand as is your wont some pleasing and instructive comedy? Are you not at this moment giving all Venice the joyous and marvellous delight of your performance which she so greatly craves? Methinks I can see you on the stage enslaving all who see and hear you. Even at this distance I can hear the applause of the people who climb up the walls where you are, who break doors, cross canals, and jump down from the heights, and run the risk of a thousand deaths simply to be able to enjoy the sweetness of your words for a single hour.

Calmo's *Rodiana* was played in 1540; in 1547 he began to publish his letters, and two years later his comedies. In the prologue to *La Pace*, published in 1561, the ghost of Gigio

Asthemio, painter and playwright, congratulated Burchiella, Calmo, and d'Armano on being honourably quit of the decadent modern comedy.[1]

According to Zilioli, Calmo as a young man 'made his way among the famous companies of players who flourished at that time in Italy, and playing the parts of Pantalone and the Cantor, distinguished himself so rapidly that he was in demand above all others'. Zilioli has no reputation for accuracy and his statement is suspect on two counts.[2] So far we have recovered notice of only two companies of professional comedians, one in Apulia and one in Padua, for the first half of the sixteenth century. But as the distinction between amateurs who played by request on public occasions and professionals under special patronage is hardly felt until the rise of the companies in the second half of the century, it is possible, as Rossi suggests, that Zilioli is referring loosely to the groups of actors collected by Cherea and Ruzzante as 'Comici'.

The more questionable point is the reference to Calmo as a Pantalone: so far the earliest appearance of the name is in 1565[3] and it never occurs in Calmo's work. We can put no trust in the letter of Zilioli's statement, but its drift is sound. The type of Pantalone is there all but the name in Calmo's old men, Coccolin, Collophonio, Melindo, and Zurlotto. The pattern is cut from the 'senex' of Latin comedy but the stuff and the tailoring is Venetian. We do not want a better Magnifico. Collophonio in *La Travaglia* speaks Venetian seasoned with Latin at great length and to any or no purpose. It was Calmo's favourite jargon and he uses it throughout the *Lettere* facetie. The old man is represented as being in love, he is very nervous and comforts himself with the cases of some twenty-two heroes and seven immortals who have been through the same throes. Afraid of his son as a rival

---

[1] *La Pace*, M. Negri, ed. 1584, Venezia: 'Perche le comedie hoggidi sono venute in tal conditione che ogni vil scioccarello ardisse d'imbrattare carte, et alle sue goffarie dare titolo di comedie, et ogn'uno gli corre dietro, come vedetequi talche pienamente io lodo il piacevole, e pieno di soggetti Messer Antonio detto Burchiello, e il famoso Messer Andrea Calmo, e l'ingenioso, e gentil Messer Pietro d'Armano, se

hanno con honore di tal carico levati.'

[2] Rossi does not give any reference for the passage which he quotes. Presumably it is taken from the manuscript *Istoria delle vite dei poeti italiani*, compiled in the eighteenth century and preserved as MS. X no. I Bib. Marciana. It is used circumspectly by A. Mortier. *Ruzzante*, i. p. 17.

[3] See *infra*, ch. ii.

he trusts that the young man's poverty will keep his amours in check, and goes out to array himself in white and green like a lily and a laurel to symbolize his innocence and sprightliness. A little later, rejected by Leonora, he is left gasping and howling; and soliloquizing or quarrelling or bargaining over the price of eggs, he is just such a fussy amorous mean old man as the Pantalone of the Commedia dell'arte. Later in the play he meets the procuress Cortese, at whose little jokes he 'chuckles like a blunderbuss'; she advises him to come disguised to Leonora. When he reappears masked he is coached how to act, to whistle, and sing by the grinning servants, while the ladies enjoy the scene from the balcony. True to his nature, when he is dismissed without an interview he goes off arguing over the bill.

In Act III he changes clothes with Gianda the servant and is caught in Leonora's house by Proculo, her supposed father. A description of the beating gives him another monologue. He cannot learn and before the end of the act he has consented to be carried to his lady in a coffer, on the assurance that lovers dying unshriven go direct to Venus in Paradise. The Captain who is in the secret challenges the porters, and after a great expenditure of breath and bribery the miserable Collophonio is let out of the chest, only to find that his clothes have been stolen, and that there is nothing left for it but to accept the friar's frock offered by Cortese. It then takes some time to persuade Brocca that the creature shivering on the doorstep is his master. After this Collophonio decides to tackle Proculo directly and ask for Leonora. He is too late, his son has already eloped with the lady, and Collophonio's lamentations are lost in the rush of confessions, agnitions, and trumped-up marriages that wind up the comedy.

From this single strand it is evident what Calmo owes to the intrigues, themes, and methods of dénouement common to the Italian written comedy of the period. Again, it is the increase in the part of the old man that distinguishes *La Travaglia* from its counterparts in the Siennese *Gl'Ingannati*, and Parabosco's *Viluppo*, which are in their turn compounded from Bandello and the *Menaechmi*.[1]

---

[1] *Gl'Ingannati degl'Intronati* (1531). *Il Viluppo*, printed 1547. Rossi thinks that Calmo's play may have preceded Parabosco's on the stage. Op. cit., p. lv.

La Rodiana, *La Fiorina*, and *La Pozione*, which is a redaction of Machiavelli's *Mandragola*, may be grouped together as plays in which the commedia erudita is popularly rendered. By this we mean that the well-exercised motifs of love intrigues suggested by astute servants to thoughtless and unscrupulous young men and women, fables of conjugal squabbles from Boccaccio, and romantic tales of the young girl who follows a faithless lover disguised as a page, form the staple entertainment, but they are served up hot and hot. Calmo knew the value of picturesque diction and had seven dialects, Venetian, Bergomask, Paduan, Torcellan, Dalmatian, and Italian broken by German or Greek, at his command. With these he tried the old simple recipe for hashing up scenes of savoury comedy from the stalest material. The Latinism with which he inflates Collophonio's speech differentiates his dialect from the Venetian used by Ruzzante. Calmo uses dialect exactly in the manner to be adopted by the commedia dell'arte, each character is given a jargon as a comic handicap.

Where Ruzzante had penetrative insight and imagination, Calmo had abundant invention. In the prologue to *Il Saltuzza* he declares that he wishes 'to represent real life and to give his comedy the full naturalness of actuality', if there are no lost children to be identified in the last scene the omission is intentional, he is bent on flouting the fashion, and 'whoever does not wish to remain, pray let him leave by the exit which he will find open'.

In this comedy Saltuzza, who speaks Bergomask, promises to help Polidoro to woo Clinia, the wife of an advocate Melindo, who is himself entangled in 'lacci cupidineschi' for love of Pamphilia, the sister of Polidoro. Saltuzza is also in the pay of the old man.

It is arranged with Rosina the maid that Polidoro is to come by night wearing the clothes of Leccardo, the parasite. Melindo announces his intention of dining out, and all appears to be going well, but Rosina is nervous that the youth and inexperience of Polidoro may ruin him. She dresses up Saltuzza in her cap and petticoat and tells him to lie in wait lest Leccardo should return inopportunely. But Polidoro is up to time.

'Who would not kneel to enjoy so sweet a fruit?' he mur-
murs. 'Come up here and I'll give you fruit and branch too,'
grunts Saltuzza mistaking his man. The whacks resound.
Then Rosina realizes that she has been entertaining the real
Leccardo by mistake; she thrusts him out of the house into
the arms of Melindo, who is surprised to find lights and
noise in his house so late. The parasite narrowly escapes a
beating, but is consoled with the price of a couple of old hens,
a tip from Polidoro. Rosina apologizes for her blunder and
confides to Saltuzza that it is she and not her mistress who
is in love with Polidoro.

Saltuzza now gives his attention to the other love affair.
He waits until Melindo puffs in disguised 'alla cavalarescha',
and rousing Clinia asks what she would give for a sight of her
husband making love to Rosina. She catches the old repro-
bate and he grovels; they agree to let bygones be bygones
and Leccardo is given *carte blanche* with the menu for
supper.

There is much in this comedy to show that it was not so
easy as Calmo supposed to throw off old habits and conduct
a play on modern lines. The pieces and general conduct
of the game still belong to the Commedia antica. There is
even the distinctively Latin parasite whose part is to be
played by the hungry Zanni in the Commedia dell'arte. It
is the new proportions rather than new ingredients that distinguish *Il Saltuzza*. The intrigue is subordinate to the
characters in comic interest: there is scope for the development of incidental comedy with the stupid porter Baluardo
who knocks up the nurse, and finds he has forgotten his
errand, and from the urchin who tells Melindo that he has
seen Rosina treating Leccardo to sausages. Rosina's independence is new. In aspiring to Polidoro she seems to forestall the Franceschina of the Commedia dell'arte, the wife or
the sweetheart of Zanni, who, with her regular work of
carrying letters, providing disguises and accommodating
lovers, combines the intrigues of her own affairs of love and
jealousy and develops the part of the maid until it is far more
entertaining than that of the mistress.

Now that the persons are of more importance than the
plot it does not matter that the knot of the intrigue is cut

rather than untied by Rosina's apology and explanation at the end of the fourth act. Simplification of intrigue is the natural tendency of popular comedy, which when it is left entirely to the players becomes a series of practical jokes connected by a common object and by the renewed efforts of inventive Zanni.

Calmo experimented further with simple forms in *La Spagnolas*. Messer Zurlotto of Torcello finds himself in love, and at his age called on to endure the 'lightnings, fears, griefs, spasms, heart-tremors, and thousand unknown ills, for (as Tully once observed) "amor stringit suum funem ubi est debilitatis nervorum"'. He proceeds to a ludicrous diagnosis of his disease, the main theme of the soliloquy for all Calmo's old men. A peasant is persuaded to carry his love-letter, and the answer, delivered after much quibbling and banter, is that he is to be carried into the lady's house by a collier. The second lover Stradioto—whose name suggests that he was meant to be a caricature of the Greek soldiers of fortune who plagued Venetian society, as the Spaniards plagued Naples and Milan—has bribed a porter to do his errand, and is told to approach his lady on horseback. The part of Scarpela, the bergomask, was evidently played by Calmo himself, perhaps to show off his histrionic versatility. Scarpela is advised by the bravo Spezzaferro on no account to 'Spagniolize' in his wooing, the women are tired of that fashion; at length he decides to be drawn up to her window in a basket, and goes out to the barber to make ready. On his return he is strapped in by Spezzaferro and left suspended. Calmo now begins to plait his three strands. Scarpela implores the help of a passing peasant who bargains for his belt as the price of letting him down to earth. The peasant's disgust at finding no money in the wallets is only soothed by Messer Zurlotto who bribes him to fetch a collier for his adventure. Scarpela meanwhile has mistaken Senilia, a stranger, for his brother Spezzaferro, and takes his revenge. The officers who arrest them for carrying arms accept a bribe, and Scarpela relieves himself by making off with the bravo's mistress.

The collier, relieved of his burden by Stradioto, who frightens Zurlotto out of the basket, gets the price of a drink out of the soldier whom he hails as an old acquaintance.

Stradioto is attacked in his turn as he is on his way to visit his lady on horseback. Relations are by now sufficiently strained for any one to assault any one else, and this invigorating state of warfare prevails until Zurlotto negotiates a general amnesty.

By the crude motives, rapid action, and scope for horseplay, and the picturesqueness of the dialectal abuse, we are reminded again and again of the Commedia dell'arte. We are to laugh at every one, and with nobody: in this respect *La Spagnolas* differentiates itself both from the comedies of Ruzzante in which some feelings of justice and sympathy are aroused, and from the plays in which vice professes to be comically exposed as a wholesome example.

Calmo's dialect babel finds a way into the four eclogues which, to judge by their prologues and epilogues, were at least intended for stage representation. Alpheo the satyr talks Slavonic to the two old shepherds, a Bergomask and a Torcellan. The enchantress invokes her demons in the Greekish jargon used in comedy for the procuress.[1] A Ragusan doctor delivers the prologue.

How much of Calmo's dialect was due to the companions with whom he produced his plays some years before they were printed is now impossible to determine. We have noticed that Burchiella was famous for a jargon of Italian and Slavonic. Finally there is the question of improvisation. Rossi, in considering Calmo's connexion with the Commedia dell'arte, notes that the song for Bonelo in *La Fiorina* is left to the actor, and that Carina in *La Saltuzza* speaks of these affairs 'così all'improviso'; but the latter does not refer to the dialogue, and the former is quite unimportant. These do not help us one way or another to know whether Calmo wrote up his plays before or after their performance.

From Cherea and Ruzzante we may reckon on impetus and example: but in Calmo's work we have at last the very stuff of the Commedia dell'arte ready to be adapted by the travelling players who made improvisation their profession.

ZAN POLO AND CIMADOR.

The performance of Cimador, the fourth Venetian

[1] Egloga III.

comedian to whom a share in the making of the Commedia dell'arte may be ascribed, must be considered together with the career of his father Zan Polo. There is a racy account of Cimador's buffoonery in the *Ragionamenti* of Aretino.[1] Nanna corrupts Antonio with the story of her escapade on the night when she slipped out of the convent in her page's dress.

Ah, ha, ha! I laughed at the fellow called the son of Ciampolo, a Venetian, I believe, who withdrew himself behind a door and counterfeited a variety of voices. He mimicked a porter better than any man of Bergamo, and as the porter he enquired of an old woman for my lady, and then impersonating the old woman he asked, 'And what do you want with my lady?' Then he replied that he wanted to speak with her, and like a sly fellow said, 'Lady, Lady, I'm dying, I can feel my lungs thumping like a boiling of tripe.' Then, as the porter, he made the most tender lamentation imaginable and began to touch her and laughed and told her jests that were enough to make a man spoil Lent and break the fast. In the middle of this gossip up came the lady's old dotard of a husband and a fine row he made as he saw the porter like a peasant putting his cherries into a sack, and the porter said, 'Master, O Master, ha, ha, ha!' and grinned and made signs and gestures like a simpleton. 'Be off with you', said the old man, 'Drunkard! Ass!' When he had been untrussed by the maid, and had told his wife something or other about the Sophy and the Turk, fit to make everyone roar with laughter, he undressed, took an oath to eat no more windy food and lay down to sleep. As he snored the same fellow returned as the porter and entertained the lady so well that they let the cat out of the bag.

Cimador appears to have inherited his talent. Zan Polo, the father, had been employed by the chief academies of Venice between 1512 and 1529 as a professional entertainer. He would lead the Carnival procession through the piazza or come on for his turn after the dancing, tumbling, and rustic music to deliver a few witticisms or play with his hands upon a stool. By way of an interlude during a performance of the *Miles Gloriosus* he introduced a little comedy of his own invention, and pretended that he had just arrived from Hell where he had found his late companion Domenico Taiacalze herding goats, and as a necromancer he summoned up Taiacalze to execute a dance with his beasts.[2]

[1] *Ragionamenti*, pte. i, p. 58, ed. 1584.   [2] See Appendix D.

Domenico Taiacalze is mentioned by Sanudo as an excellent comedian and one of the first in Venice for facetious parts. On 15 Dec. 1504 he and Zuan Pollo set up their stage in the piazza and by disguising themselves gave as good entertainment as the spectacular performance which had just taken place. In 1508 their names were cried on the Rialto for the theft of two silver basins stolen in the raid made by the *Eterni* on the house of Grimani after a wedding feast.

E. Picot has drawn attention to a pamphlet in the Bibliothèque de Chantilly containing 'Una historia bellissima laquel narra come el spirto de Domenego taia calze aperse a Zuan Polo narrando tutte le pene de l'inferno, et come dice haver veduto in esse molti Capetanii de gente darme Francesi e Spagnoli, et altre sorte di gente, et insito de linfernal Stigio finge andar al paradiso con altre cose notabile'.

In this poem Domenego interviews the potentates of Hell. Lucifer who is delighted by his songs in the Greek, Bergomask, and Albanian dialects asks after the priest Perino and Zane Cimador.[1] In the familiar satirical style Taiacalze reports that Berto de la biava, Marco dal Spechio, and Zanpiero Verzo are safe below, and brings news of Francesco, Paulin, Luchetto, and 'nostro Tedesco'. Berto de la Biava is mentioned by Calmo, and Francesco is probably the Francesco Gata whose name occurs in the same connexion together with Zan Polo, Cimador, Taiacalze, and three otherwise unknown buffoons, Desena, Razzer, and Vistoso.[2]

In February 1516 Zan Polo was sent for daily to cheer the orator of Ali bei Dragomano with his buffoonery; he was arrested for manslaughter in March 1523, but by June he is found complimenting the Doge in verses of his own composition. There are several occasions on which father and son are to be found playing together.[3]

Zan Polo's importance as a type of the early professional

---

[1] Mortier suggests that the poem, which is quite undramatic in form, celebrates Zan Polo's performance and may have influenced Ruzzante when he wrote *Commedie sans Titre*, in which Nale appearing from Hell says that there was respite from torment only on the day when the buffoon Domenego Taiacalze arrived and sang a song in his great plaintive voice that made all its abysses tremble. Op. cit., ii, p. 109.

[2] Calmo, *Lettere*, ed. cit., ii, p. 139.

[3] See Appendix D.

comedian is self-evident. It is just possible that as an individual he is to be more closely associated with the Commedia dell'arte, as the first Magnifico the predecessor of Pantalone. The form of the name Zan Polo is apt to mislead one into imagining him as a Bergamask type. This was the dialect adopted by Cimador but not necessarily by his father. The name is given variously as Zan Polo, Zuan Polo, Zuan Pollo,[1] Ciampolo,[2] Paulovichio Juan,[3] but the two words are never separated and the first is no more than the regular Venetian form for 'Giovanni'.

The records of his performance suggest that he was celebrated as a general mimic, transformist, and acrobat; only twice do we get a hint of his particular impersonations. The first is in Sanudo's description of his performance on 11 February 1525:

> Zuan Polo was in excellent form, the intermedii were very fine with all kinds of vocal and instrumental music and costumes of Moors, Germans, Greeks, Hungarians, pilgrims and others, they wore no masks however, and Zuan Pollo's habit was first of them all and he called himself Messer Nicoleto Cantinella.

The second occasion was on 9 July 1533:

> Zuan polo that excellent buffoon performed before the Doge and the Council on a stage set up in front of the Clock tower. He was dressed as a poet with a laurel wreath, and his son and some one else in disguise were with him. He made a speech to them all and recited his own composition which has been printed as 'Rada Stizoso' and costs — soldi.

As this latter performance entails no controversial point it may be dealt with first. It appears from the *Libero del Rado Stizuxo* printed in Venice 'per Maistro Bernardino de Vitali Venetiano 1533', and from the undated *Libero de le Vendette che fese i fioli de Rada Stizoxo*, that on this occasion Zan Polo burlesqued the exploits of the heroes of the chivalric romances speaking a mixed dialect of Venetian and Dalmatian.[4] The performance in 1525 is more suggestive. Zan

[1] Sanudo, xvi, p. 187; xxxii, p. 445; xix, p. 443.   [2] Aretino, op. cit.
[3] Melzi-Tosi, *Bib. dei Romanzi di Cavalleria*.
[4] I have not been able to examine these pamphlets which are described by

Melzi-Tosi, *Bib. dei romanzi di Cavalleria* (1865), pp. 222–3. It is possible that the 'Strambotti de Misser Rado e de Madonna Margarita: cosa nova', preserved in a miscellany of Italian tracts in the British Museum (C. 57. l. 7. 46),

Polo's assumption of the name *Cantinella* tempts the theory that he is to be identified with the actor Benedetto Cantinella who appears as the Magnifico in the *Canti Carnascialeschi*. The earliest mention of Cantinella is in 1538. Annibale Caro, stranded at Velletri, wrote to Silvestro da Prato describing a scene which had just taken place between his travelling companion, a certain pretentious Capitano Colluzzo—a mutual acquaintance—and an old hag who accosted him as a former mistress. The scuffle and the baiting which had ensued was 'too good to be described, the very stuff of comedy, Cantinella himself could not have bettered the actuality'. All this was sent to Silvestro so that he may have something with which to amuse Monsignore at table, and, Caro continued, 'Hand it over to be expanded (*fatela distendere*) by our comedians to be ready against our return'.[1]

Cantinella was evidently a general mimic, who, like Cimador, would play first one part and then another. Eight years later he appears in Rome as *Mro Benedetto Cantinella* and is rewarded for a comedy given by himself and his companions before the Pope.[2]

It seems reasonable to suppose that it is to the same actor that Francesco Franchino refers when he writes to Duke Ottavio Farnese describing a performance on the Giudecca

may be another of Zan Polo's compositions. It consists of two quarto leaves. Below the title on the first recto is printed the verse:

Buttele tutti qua de uui cervello
Piancile quisto cor su rampigon
Che per dolur le faro ravanello.

The rest of the page is occupied by a rough woodcut of a bleeding heart pierced by an arrow, a sword, a dagger, a gridiron, a grater, and a fire-hook. Other instruments are grouped round a wooden tub from which the heart rises. On the verso is printed in double columns a 'Canzon alla Schiavonescha' in which Rado and Margarita lament over each other's cruelty for 16 verses in the Dalmatian-Venetian dialect. On recto 2 are 8 stanzas of 8 lines each with the refrain, 'Vaten via malinconia'. On 2 verso is a 'Barcelletta damore' in 7 stanzas of

6 lines, each using two lines of the initiatory and final verse as a refrain:

Ogni cosa vince amore
Non bisogna contra stare
Non si po con lui durare
che le troppo gran signore.

1 A. Caro, *Lettere familiari* (1572), Velletri, 30 April 1538.

2 '1546, marzo 10. A Mro Benedetto Cantinella quali N.S. gli dona per haver recitato con li suoi compagni una comedia in castello nanti a S. Sta., scudi 27, bol. 50.' Estratti dal Registro della Tesoreria Segreta dallo Gen. 1545 al 20 Maggio 1548 tenuto da Piero Gio. Aleotto. *A. Bertolotti*, 'Spesiere segrete e Pubbliche di Papa Paolo III Atti e memorie delle R. R. Deput: di Storia Patria per le Provincie dell'Emilia,' vol. iii, pte i.

on 19 February 1555 in which the comedians went to pieces and had to apologize: the letter continues:

tanto è che la cosa è risoluta che la persona per ridere et haver solazzo non può far meglio che andare ad ascoltare quelle che si fanno ogni dì in diversi luoghi ad imitation di Catinella.[1]

The disagreement of the Christian names Benedetto and Nicoleto presents a real but not insuperable difficulty. In the *Canti Carnascialeschi* Lasca plainly uses 'Benedetto' and 'Cantinella' synonymously:

Noi che oggi per Firenze attorno andiamo,
Come vedete, Messer Benedetti
e Zanni tutti siamo,
recitator eccellenti e perfetti.
Gli altri strioni eletti,
amanti, donne, romiti e soldati,
alla stanza per guardia son restati . . .

L. 46.

Alfin vogliamvi una benfatta e bella
prospettiva di nuovo far vedere,
la dove il Cantinella
e Zanni vi daran spasso e piacere.

But in the Madrigal XXXIII the representative couple are Zanni and Stefanello:

ma or piu lodati
Giovani d'oggi e piu lodato quello
che contrafa un Zanni o Stefanello.

It would not be inconsistent with the practice of the comici dell'arte if Cantinella varied his Christian name; similar slight modifications seem to have been adopted in the seventeenth century. If it is granted that by 1546 'Benedetto' may have ousted 'Nicoleto', Zan Polo may perhaps be considered as one of the earliest Magnifichi. His reputation with Sanudo as a general mimic, his impersonation of the bravo in 1533, and the non-committal references by Caro and Franchini do not injure his claim. Success in one mask did not keep the comedians from further experiment: for after playing a Sicilian Doctor, a Necromancer, and a Shepherd,

[1] Quoted by Molmenti, *Storia di Venezia nella Vita Privata*, ii, p. 325, from Farnese documents in the Archivio di Stato di Parma.

Francesco Andreini created the mask of Capitano Spavento; and Silvio Fiorillo as Pulcinella gave himself a rest from the vociferations of Capitano Mattamoros. I would suggest that towards the end of his career Zan Polo may have taken the lead from the old Venetians of Calmo's comedy, and after studying the part himself from real life, have evolved the mask of the Magnifico which was to make his name in Rome and Florence. The alternative supposition is that Cantinella was a surname, like 'de Bisognosi', adopted by more than one comedian.

COMEDIANS AS PRIVATE ENTERTAINERS

In their quality as hired buffoons Zan Polo and Cimador may be taken to represent the miscellaneous entertainers who in skill, status, and reputation fill in the gap between the jesters, charlatans, and groups of amateurs, and the professional players. For in the second half of the sixteenth century the buffoons who provide amusement between the courses of a banquet are the professional actors of the Commedia dell'arte. Giovan Batista Rossetti describes a German feast prepared for Gasparo di Monte by the Duke of Ferrara in 1582.[1]

In the middle of the first table where their Excellencies were sitting was a hole big enough for a man to come up, and over it was a huge empty pasty which was cut out to the size of the hole in the table and covered with a lid that could be raised. Unknown to all except the Duchess, Pedrolino the player was hidden under the table, and when they had been served with the dishes which I will presently describe, Pantalone came into the room pretending to look up and down where they were eating, for Pedrolino the greedy porter; and then this fellow poked his head out of the pasty, and as they laughed at him, he told them that his greed had taken him into the kitchen where by ill-luck the cooks had made him into a pie. Then he retired under the lid and all the time the gentlemen dined he went on talking inside the pasty and was quite audible through the many little holes which had been concealed under the leaves.

When the jester has a companion the transition from the related to the acted anecdote is inevitable, there is no hard

[1] *Scalco* (1584), p. 171; cf. p. 306. On another occasion Pedrolino, Pan- talone, and two other of their fellows amused the guests.

and fast line between the public entertainers and the comici.
Ruzzante with five companions and two women went to and
fro among the tables singing and disputing 'di cose conta-
dinesche, vestiti alla moderna' during the sixth course of a
banquet at Ferrara in 1529, and they were· followed by an
entertainment of 'Buffoni alla Venetiana et alla Bergomascha
et contadine alla Pavana'.[1] Rossetti's Pedrolino was probably
Giovanni Pelesini, one of the most travelled Zanni.[2]

At another Ferrarese banquet in 1570 Zanni Ganassa performed some very amusing antics tumbling with a Spaniard
Ernandico, during the sweetmeat course.[3] We meet Ganassa
two years later at the head of a troop of improvising comedians
in Paris. The Italians at the Bavarian Court had been required to serve in the same double capacity. In 1618
Jonassen Schiessel is described as Hof- und Tafel-Comedien
to the Emperor.[4]

When Orlando di Lasso travelled into Italy in the winter
of 1573–4 to find musicians and acrobats for William of
Bavaria he found the comedian Venturino a pleasant companion. A letter written from Rotten Holtzen on 12 February 1574 gives good news of their progress:
'Il Venturino ci racconta alcune volte comedie, et istorie,
fabule, mottj e strambottj con molte coionerie'. Again
four days later Venturino's solo performance of a comedy
between three persons, the Magnifico, the Zanni, and Franceschina conducted behind a door, a bed, or a curtain
described as a sight to make the spectators weep with
laughter, reminds us of the performance of Cimador.[5]

CORRESPONDING DRAMATIC ACTIVITIES IN OTHER ITALIAN CITIES

Much as we regret that Sanudo's diaries end in 1533, the
loss is probably less than we might anticipate because of the
subsequent prohibitions of dramatic performance in that

---

[1] Cristofero di Messisbugo, 'Libro novo nel qual s'insegna a far ogni sorte di vivandi . . . et il modo d'ordinar banchetti', quoted by D'Ancona, op. cit., ii, p. 121.

[2] See *infra*, ch. v.

[3] Solerti-Lanza, *Giorn. Stor.* xviii, p. 159.

[4] Schlager, 'Über das alte Wiener Hoftheater', in *Sitzungsberichte der Kais. Akad. der Wissenschaften, Phil. Classe*, Bd. VI, S. 147 ff.

[5] A. Sandberger, op. cit., pp. 253–4.

city. Venice is no longer the centre of attraction, and the rise of the regular companies draws our attention to the dramatic patronage and production in other Italian courts. Cherea's performance can only be taken as representative of the neo-classical revival that encouraged the presentation of the comedies of Plautus and Terence in the original, in translation and adaptation. Calmo's production should stand for the modification of the classical models into the Renaissance social drama. Ruzzante presents a fine example of the rustic drama that was taking shape in other districts and achieved some literary form in Lombardy, Naples, and Sienna.[1] Zan Polo is the type of the professional entertainer. His versatility marks him out as a fit representative for the jesters, tumblers, and mountebanks who swarmed in Garzoni's memory and fascinated English travellers in the Piazza S. Marco.

The cities were collective as well as dynamic centres of dramatic enterprise. In 1495 Serafino dell'Aquila, the court poet of the Duke of Calabria, was borrowed to devise entertainment for a Mantuan Carnival.[2] Ercole d'Este regrets that he cannot send Gonzaga the translations of Plautus lately prepared for the court of Ferrara, because the parts have been dispersed with the actors, but he will hasten a transcript.[3]

The work of Ariosto, Bibbiena, Macchiavelli, and Piccolomini soon spread and was regarded as Italian rather than as Ferrarese, Florentine, or Siennese. It is perhaps more surprising that dialect comedy should have travelled so well. Ruzzante and his Paduans are commanded to Venice and Ferrara. During the pontificate of Leo X (1513–21) Rome patronized the Siennese actors who had already formed the Congrega dei Rozzi. This academy of the illiterate was founded officially in 1531 with the object of enabling those who worked with their hands, spoke the vernacular, and had some accomplishment such as reading, writing, or dancing to spend their leisure to some honest profit or pleasure. The comedy and pastoral which they produced is strengthened by a course strain of realism: it is precisely comparable in kind, though hardly in quality, to the work of Ruzzante. The

---

[1] See F. Flamini, *Il Cinquecento*, p. 299, &c., for bibliography, p. 557.
[2] D'Ancona, op. cit., ii, p. 365.
[3] Ibid., ii, p. 369.

enthusiasm for the stage was not peculiar to any class of society. It seems that any one might act, from the Duke of Ferrara and his seven-year-old daughter, who took part in a private performance of the *Andria* in 1539, to the fishermen who presented a comedy in honour of Monsignore Gonzaga in Rome in 1513, and his shepherds who entertained the Venetian virtuosi in 1515. Frate Armonio, organist of S. Marco, played with Calmo and Burchiella. The performance of the Jews won them some concessions from the Duke of Mantua.

The Commedia dell'arte taps all these resources by drawing its actors from all regions and many ranks of society and by travelling from city to city making game of their local types. By the middle of the sixteenth century it appears as a fact in the history of the stage and is studied best by tracing the rise of the professional companies.

CHAPTER V
THE PROFESSIONAL COMPANIES
EARLY COMPANIES IN ITALY

PADUA.

THE status of Ruzzante and the Rozzi as amateurs who were not above taking rewards represents the transition from dilettante to organized professional acting which took place towards the middle of the sixteenth century.

The earliest notice of a regular company is, so far, that of eight actors who in 1545 bound themselves under the leadership of Maphio dei Re, *detto* 'Zanini', to travel for six months playing 'le sue comedie'. Sa. Esther Cocco, to whose article in the *Giornale Storico* we are indebted for the discovery of the documents,[1] is inclined to stress the pronoun 'sue' to the interpretation that Maphio was an actor-dramatist like Ruzzante: this, however, is not certain. It was reckoned in this agreement that from Ash Wednesday until the end of the octave of Easter no comedies would be allowed, in June the actors were to return to Padua, and at the beginning of September each was 'to go his own way'. Two treasurers were appointed to arrange for the weekly distribution of the money into equal shares. General expenses of travel and lodging and illness were to be met by the common fund, but any member who should leave the company to its disadvantage forfeited his share and was liable to a fine of 100 'lire di pizole', which was to be divided between the authorities of the town where they were lodged, the poor, and the company itself. Gambling with anything but food was prohibited.

Another notary's bond dated 22 June 1546 confirms a new agreement already of two months' standing between Maphio with two of his former companions, Francesco *detto* 'Moschino' and Vincenzo 'Scoffionari', and six others to act together for three years. In 1549 a quarrel (between Tagliapietra and Moschini abetted by Maphio and a certain Zuanne da Treviso) led to reformation of the company, and in August Maphio, Moschini, and Gio. Pietro Zambelloti,

1 *Giorn. Stor.* lxv.

together with Hieronymo di S. Luca and Zuanne da Treviso of the first troup, compacted for six years. Before setting out for Rome at the beginning of November they admitted Simone Spadacini, and for the woman's parts engaged Francesco, the son of a smith at Concarolo, who was to have only a half share with the promise of 6 ducats if he stayed with the company until the beginning of Lent. The takings were now to be divided immediately after each performance, and Maphio, Zuanne, and Moschinio were to receive each two ducats extra from every performance until moneys advanced to the present company and the fine still owing to their former companions should be paid. These three were to divide between them Spadacini's premium of 8 ducats and Checo's half share.

Sa. Cocco conjectured that these actors were the Venetians who played in Castello S. Angelo in December 1550 and the following February. In 1553 Maphio was killed in a brawl with a Bolognese horse-tamer: his daughter Angela, described as about twelve years of age and 'pauperrima', was left to the care of his fellow countryman Alessandro da Torreglia, and his place was taken temporarily by Paolo di Gerolamo of Brescia.

ROME.

From the accounts of the Pope's Privy Purse we have a fleeting glimpse of other actors in Rome at this time. On 23 January 1551 Matteo, Andrea, and Frosia were rewarded for a dialect performance—'recitato da Norcino'. There were also payments to a certain 'Marcantonio', described in 1550 as 'delle comedie' and the next year and in 1553 as 'buffone'.[1] In the *Regrets* (1559) Du Bellay recalls the Roman Carnival with its 'Marc Antoine', and possibly both are to be identified with *Marc Antonio de Gabiati*, one of the seven members of a company formed in October 1564 for the following Carnival. This company admitted Lucrezia of Sienna, one of the first professional actresses. Again the

---

[1] The agreement was made on 10 October 1564 between Joannes Carolus Guarnera, Alfonsus Castaldus, Michael Angelus Coletti, Marcus Antonius de Gabiati, Dominicus de Rossis da Forli, Claudius Ursinus, Da Lucretia Senensis. See *Giorn. Stor.* lxiii, p. 296.

name 'Marcantonio', this time specifically a Venetian, occurs in the bond between Guglielmo Perillo of Naples and Angelo Michele of Bologna, published by Belgrano from the Genoese Archives.[1]

NAPLES.

The usual conditions for equal shares, for provision for the sick, fines for absence and injunctions for the observance of church festivals, were proposed for the five players who compacted for two years in Naples in 1575.[2]

THE PROBLEMS OF IDENTIFICATION

The practice of adopting fanciful titles after the fashion of the Renaissance Academies distinguishes the professional companies of the second half of the sixteenth century, but the older habit of referring to the name of the patron, or the leader, or the most popular actor, crops up sometimes to clear, but more often to confuse, the task of identification. It is not always possible to decide whether the presence of a certain comedian at a particular festivity implies that he came alone by request or brought the whole company, and the problem is complicated by the use of a mask name by more than one actor and of more than one mask by each actor.

In attempting to follow the groups of players year by year and from place to place we must be prepared for the inconsistencies of expedience. Contrary tendencies govern the composition of the troop. On the one hand stood the players' recognition of the importance of the unity of the company: the success of improvised comedy depended almost entirely upon the relationship between the actors; a strange Zanni, whatever his quality, might wreck the play for a Pantalone with whose mannerisms he was not acquainted. Only the discomforts of persistent quarrels could make a change of *personnel* desirable by the company as a whole. But on the other hand the ambition of individuals exposed them to the danger of offers from royal and noble patrons who would

---

[1] *Arch. Stor. It.*, 1872, Series III, vol. xv, p. 422.

[2] Mario di Tommaso detto Lepido di Siena, Jacopo Antonio de Ferraris di Napoli, Alfonso Cortese, napoletano, Giulio Cesare Farina di Milano, Fr. Viziani di Lucca. See B. Croce, *I Teatri di Napoli*, p. 776.

plan special performances and 'star' companies. Such temptations, together with professional jealousy and a natural love of change, are sufficient to account for the continual shifting which actually took place. Therefore, while it is reasonable to assume that, roughly, within a decade, a company would remain substantially the same, it is not safe to presume too far upon the details of its *personnel*. The fragmentary character of the lists extracted from licences and letters justifies a moderate use of supposition. With a grasp of the controlling principles and the constant check of these lists some kind of a survey of the fortunes of the chief companies and dominant personalities between 1560 and 1630 may be attempted.

EARLY COMPANIES ABROAD

Some notice has already been taken of the stray actors who appear singly or in twos and threes in South Germany between 1549 and 1590.[1] The majority are described as jugglers, tumblers, or musicians, but there is evidence that they varied their acrobatic shows by presenting comedies. The German entries give little clue as to their identity. The early date 1569 makes it impossible to suppose that the 'Franncischo Ysabella' of Linz were the Andreini,[2] but 'Julio', who was in Vienna in 1570, is probably the Giulio Pasquati of the *Gelosi*, and there can be little doubt that the 'Antonio Soldino florentino' who appears alone in Munich in 1570 and at Rome together with Pantalone as witness in a lawsuit between two otherwise unknown comedians, Scevola and Tarasso, is the same as the 'Soldino' who entertained Charles IX while he was in retirement for his health at Blois in the spring of 1572. Four entries in the registers of the Compts de l'Espargne show that two companies indulged the king's tastes for 'comédies e plaisants jeux'. On 25 March Soldino and eleven companions are paid 250 livres, and two days later 'Anthoine Marie Vénetien' receives a like sum for himself and nine others. For an amalgamation on 11 April involving eighteen performers, in recompense for their good services and towards the expenses of the journey back to Paris, 'où ilz font leur residence', the reward is doubled.[3]

[1] See ch. i and Appendix D.   [2] Rasi, op. cit., i. 59.   [3] Baschet, op. cit., pp. 34–38.

ZAN GANASSA.

The Italian comedies followed by vaulting with 'notable supersaltes', and the 'Labores Herculis', with which the Earl of Lincoln and his companions were entertained in June, may have been provided by members of this joint company.[1] The chances of the honour must be shared, however, with Alberto Naseli,[2] who was also in Paris during the summer, and was rewarded for a performance in August and again for himself and six companions in October.[3] This actor, better known by his stage name of *Zan Ganassa*, appears twice in Italy—at Mantua in 1568, at Ferrara two years later—and again at Lyons in December 1571, on his return from an unsuccessful visit to Paris, but he found his best audience on the other side of the Pyrenees.[4] In 1574 he advanced '600' *reals* towards the erection of a covered theatre in the Corral de la Pacheca in Madrid, agreeing to reclaim the money at the rate of 10 *reals* for each play, and to give sixty performances. His prices were, an entrance fee of half a *real*—roughly threepence—with a further charge of one *real* for a chair, and a quarter *real* for a seat on the benches. His season in Seville in 1575 drew the common people in such crowds to the Corral de Don Juan that there were petitions for his prohibition, with what immediate result does not appear; at least he was back again in 1578.[5] *Ganassa* evidently liked a full house; on 27 August 1579 he refused to play to a poor audience in Madrid and returned the entrance money.[6] With the exception of a few days at Corpus Christi, when he was in attendance upon the King at Toledo, he played twice or three times a week in Madrid in the Corrals of the Puenta and the Pacheca from June 1579 until the middle of the following February. From 30 November 1581, with the exception of two private performances, one 'en casa del Comisario general' and the other

---

[1] See *infra*, p. 348.

[2] See Cotarelo, *Revista de Archivos Bibliotecas y Museos*, 1908, pp. 42 ff., quotes 'Alberto Anaseli' from the documents, but confirms 'Naseli' as the correct form by the signature.

[3] Baschet, op. cit., pp. 43–4.

[4] D'Ancona, op. cit., ii. 455.

[5] Sanchez-Arjona, *Anales del Teatro en Sevilla* (1898), pp. 48–9, and H. A. Rennert, *The Spanish Stage in the time of Lope de Vega* (1909).

[6] Ibid., Appendix A.

by command of D. Roderigo de Mendoza at Guadalajara, he acted almost daily in the Teatro de la Cruz until the end of February 1582. On the 27th of that month records are interrupted by the entry 'No represento Ganasa a causa de su prision'. What his offence may have been is not known, but although there is no record of his public performance until Corpus Christi 1583 in Seville, there are among the Carte Strozziane in the Archivio di Stato in Florence two slips, undated but placed between documents connected with a journey to Lisbon (1581–3), on which are entered notes of the debts amounting to over 3,200 scudi[1] of D. Pietro de' Medici to 'Ganassa comediante'.

Pellicer gives an undocumented reference to *Ganassa* in Spain in 1603, and Ottonelli has it from Barbieri, who had it from a friend in 1644, that *Ganassa* was touring there in 1610.[2] In France the performance of 'Zany dont Ganasse Nous a représenté la façon et la grâce' was recorded in *L'Art Poétique* of Du Fresnaye Vauquelin,[3] and in the satires he is coupled with Taborin. Lope de Vega, who enjoyed his acting[4] in Madrid, associates him with Trastulo in the *Filomena*, Epistola IV. Ricardo de Turia mentions 'el famoso Comico Ganaça, que en la primera entrada, que hizo en ella [España] robó igualmente el aplauso y dinero de todos'.[5] Pellicer quotes another mention from an anonymous poem 'La Asinaria', and Pineda in a dialogue licensed in 1581 gives interesting details of the kind of plot upon which the Italian actors based their improvisation.[6]

In 1572 *Ganassa* had six companions: for 1581 we have

[1] *Carte Strozziane*, LVIII. 19. cc. 167 and 168 v. The sums are 3278 and 3276.4 scudi. Reckoning the scudo at 4*s.* this amounts roughly to £460.

[2] Ottonelli, *Cristiana moderazione*, ii. 37.

[3] See Baschet, op. cit., p. 45, where a reference to the satires in which Ganassa is mentioned together with the Comédiens de Taborin is quoted.

[4] Processo de Lope de Vega. Ed. Perez Pastor, 1901, p. 42.

[5] C. Pellicer, *Tratado Historico sobre el origen y progresos de la comedia y del histrionismo en España* (1804), p. 72.

[6] 'Que no se os cubra la cara de vergüenza de que os vean autorizando y gozando de los cuentos de Medea y de Jasón, y de París y Elena, y Eneas y Dido, y de Piramo y Tisbe.' Juan de Pineda, 'Primera parte de los Treynta y cinco diálogos familiares de la Agricultura christiana'. Salamanca, 1589. Aprobación dated 1581, quoted by Cotarelo y Mori, *Bib. de las Controversias sobre la licitud del Teatro en España*, 1904, p. 505.

The story of Pyramus and Thisbe is the argument of the burlesque scenario in 'La Caduta del gran Capitan Belis-

the names of seven actors and two Spanish musicians who composed his troop: Vincenzio Botanelli, known as *Curzio Romano* on the stage, Cesar de Novile (or Nobile?), Juan Pietro Pasquarelo, Cipion Graselli, Julio Villante (Vigliante?), Iacomo Portalupi, Carlos de Masi.[1]

Ganassa's success seems to have attracted other companies to Madrid. From 29 June until 25 July (St. James's Day) an Italian tumbler performed in the Pacheca, and from the end of August a company described alternately as *Italianos Nuevos* and *Los Corteses*[2] acted there until the middle of November. A document published by Pérez Pastor[3] helps us to identify this troop with the comedians under the leadership of Massimiamo Milanino and Marc Antoine Scotivelli, who were paid for their attendance upon Henry of Navarre at Nerac in 1578, for it is Marc Antonio and his wife Maria Imperia who appear as executors for Maximiliano Milimino, who was killed in a brawl in Madrid on 19 October 1582. The records of the *Confidenti* in Madrid in 1587 are best taken later in connexion with that company.

THE *GELOSI*

The convenient information provided by Francesco Andreini as he allows Trappola to cross-question the Captain Spavento about his former companions in the fourteenth Ragionamento has given rise to some misleading generalizations over the composition of the *Gelosi*. The list is of the first importance in assuring us that before 1604 there belonged to that company: Ludovico of Bologna, *Dr. Gratiano*;

sario / Sotto la condanna Di Giustiniano Impre / Tragedia bellissima del Sig. Dr. Giacinto A. Cicognini.' Roma, 1663. Here Passarino—another Quince—gloats over his travesty: 'Prima l'ucciss Tisbe in colera, sentendo così al vien Piramo, e al pee corre all'amo, ò quest si è un bel success, un hà dolor, e l'altr piang, ma chi non haveria compassion di questi afflitti Amanti. Scena Terza, Tisbe in colera, Piramo piang, la serva vol al salari, Piram dis, che l'e fallido, ò bella comedia, e finisce l'atto primo. Atto Secondo. Scena desdott, Speranza,

e Desgratia, al servitor ò in gallia, ò alla forca, a no son pui Comediant, al vien nuova ch'è mort Piram, e Marfisa, che se ved in camisa, e la codognella, al pesce me pias fritt in la padella, e finisce l'opera; la non è miga brutta, no alla fè.' Atto II, sc. x, p. 55.

[1] Cotarelo, *Revista de Archivos*, 1908, pp. 52–3.

[2] Possibly connected with the Neapolitan company containing Alfonso Cortese; see *supra*, p. 257.

[3] *Nuevos Datos*, p. 335.

Giulio Pasquati of Padova, *Pantalone*; Simone of Bologna, *Zanne*; Gabrielle of Bologna, *Francatrippe*; Oratio, a Paduan, and Adriano Valerini of Verona, *Lovers*; Girolamo Salimbeni of Florence, who took the parts of *Piombino* and of an old Florentine called *Zanobio*; Isabella Andreini and Prudentia of Verona as first and second ladies; Silvia Roncagli of Bergamo for *Franceschina*; and Francesco Andreini, best known as *Capitano Spavento da Val Inferna*, an arrogant boasting soldier, but also apt for the parts of a ridiculous Sicilian Doctor, for *Falsirone*, a necromancer with an amazing command of five languages, and as a shepherd *Corinto*.[1]

Other documents remind us that this list will not cover the thirty-six years during which the *Gelosi* tour the cities of France and Italy. The company with its motto 'Virtù, fama ed Honor ne fer Gelosi' appears in Milan in 1568, but it is not until after their visit to France in 1571 and their performance of *Aminta* in Ferrara in 1573 that we have any notice of the individual members. On 12 February 1574 'Rinaldo [Petignoni] altrimenti *Fortunio*, . . . per nome suo e de la compagnia dei comedianti detti li Gelosi', sends from Venice an apology to the Duke of Mantua for not visiting him during Carnival.[2] In the following July the company, who were in Milan for the festivities for the victory of Lepanto, were summoned back to Venice at the special request of Henry III, who was passing through on his way from Polonia. 'La femme appelée *Vittoria*' is mentioned in his note,[3] and from Porcacchi, an eyewitness who immediately published a description of the festivities, the Zanni and the Magnifico can be identified as Simone da Bologna and Giulio (Pasquati) the Venetian.[4] Sir Philip Sidney, who was in Venice in 1574, may have seen something of their skill.

Vittoria, surnamed Piissimi, was still with the company in 1576. By 13 February Canigiani writes that the Duke had managed to detain a few of the *Gelosi* in Ferrara to grace the weddings of Laura Sanvitale to the Conte di Scandiano and Bradamante d'Este with Conte Bevilacqua, but that the women and the better actors had betaken themselves from

[1] *Le Bravure del Capitano Spavento* (1609), f. 35.

[2] D'Ancona, op. cit., ii, pp. 463–4.

[3] T. Porcacchi, 'Le Attioni d'Arrigo Terzo Re di Francia, et Quarto di Polonia descritte in dialogo.' Venetia, 1574, f. 27 v.

[4] Baschet, op. cit., pp. 57–8.

Florence to Venice, where they had prospects of an excellent season. But five days later these defaulters—'cioè la *Vittoria* ed *Ottavio*'—were lured back by the 'chink of scudi', and a stage was being prepared for them under the loggia of the Cortile.[1]

In June 1576 Pasquati was at the Emperor's Court, but presumably not with the full company. In answer to Henry's request for the *Gelosi*, M. du Ferrier, the French ambassador in Venice, replies that he will provide them with money for the journey as soon as the Magnifico, who is in special request, shall have returned.[2] By a letter addressed to the Grand Duke from 'Graciano delle Godige comico Geloso'[3] they may be traced in Florence at the beginning of November.

After being put to ransom by the Huguenots at Charité-sur-Loire on 25 January 1577, they reached Blois, where they played in the Salle des États until the spring, when they returned to Paris. On 19 May they made their first appearance in the Salle de Bourbon, hired from the Confrères de la Passion at an 'écu tournois' for each performance. Their popularity unfortunately provoked the disapproval of the Parlement, by whose order comedies were prohibited at the end of July. It was only by express royal command that they were resumed in September.[4] It is not known precisely when the *Gelosi* returned to Italy. Magnin gives no evidence for stating that they were in Florence in 1578,[5] but a discreditable episode betrays them in the following May. An order for the expulsion of the *Gelosi* from the territory of the Duke of Mantua, quoted by D'Ancona,[6] mentions Simone,

---

[1] *Giorn. Stor.*, xviii, p. 165. There is no other mention of Ottavio as a mask or a proper name among the *Gelosi* records. To identify him with Ottavio Onorati, the *Mezzettino* of the second *Confidenti* in 1614–20, or with the Ottavio Bernardini Romano, who played the serving-maid *Franceschina* for the *Uniti* in Genova 1614 (Rasi, ii. 359), is to give either of these actors a remarkably but not uniquely long career. Pellesini, for instance, was still playing *Pedrolino* at the age of 87 (Rasi, ii. 241).

[2] Baschet, op. cit., pp. 63–4.

[3] See ch. ii, pp. 37–9, for an attempt to identify this actor.

[4] Baschet, op. cit., pp. 73–6.

[5] C. Magnin, *Rev. des Deux Mondes*, 1847, vol. xx.

[6] 'D'ordine del Duca, che tosto abbiano ad essere cacciati dalla città e dallo stato di Mantova i Comici detti *Gelosi*, che allogiano all'insegna del Bissone, e similmente il sigᵣ. Simone, che recita la parte di Bergamasco, e il sigᵣ. Orazio e il sigᵣ. Adriano, che recitano la parte *amantiorum*, e Gabriele detto dalle Haste, loro amico.' D'Ancono, op. cit., vol. ii, p. 464.

who played the Bergomask part, and Orazio and Adriano the lovers. The Orazio of Andreini's list is described as a Paduan, and D. Bruni gives him the surname of Nobile. He cannot therefore be identified with, but he is probably related to, other actors of the same name.[1]

The Orazio of the *Gelosi* was commended for having wit enough to stand up to the formidable erudition of Adriano Valerini, while quite demurely Bruni suggests that this second lover, whose stage name was *Aurelio*, was somewhat too well read in Latin and Greek. A tragedy *Afrodite* in the classical style (1578), some allusions in the sequence of Madrigals (1592), the citations in the description of his native city of Verona (1586), and the funeral oration in 1569 for Vincenza Armani, for whose sake he appears to have left the other famous actress, Lidia da Bagnacavallo, are ample evidence of his acquaintance with and facility for polite literature, and support Barbieri's description of him as 'comico . . . gentilhomo Dottore et assai buon Poeta Latino e volgare'. After the expulsion from Mantua, Adriano seems to have left the *Gelosi* and associated himself with the *Uniti*.[2] In 1583 he is the hero of an encounter with Cardinale Borromeo whom he persuades into licensing his scenari. Presumably it is from his association with Braga and Pellesini on this occasion that Valerini has been regarded

[1] The first is Nobile de Nobile di Bologna, of whom we catch a glimpse in the census of the Mantuan population taken in 1590 (see Rasi, ii. 184): the second, Cesare di Nobili of Florence, was with Ganassa in 1581, and appears with Diana among the *Uniti* in 1586. Belgrano's suggestion that he may have been the father, seems preferable to Rasi's supposition that he was the husband, of Camilla Rocca-Nobile, the 'Delia' of the *Confidenti* who died in 1613, since the Oratio de Nobili Fiorentino, who belonged to the *Gelosi* in 1590, had a wife called Vittoria. A third—or possibly the fourth—is mentioned as the leader of a rival company in a letter from the Duke of Mantua to Don Antonio di Medici in Florence 29 May 1609: 'Questi miei Comici m'hanno fatto saper il desiderio loro di recitare in cotesta città al Santo Martino prossimo sino al Natale, ma che dubitano d'esseri stati prevenuti della licenza da un Nobile Comico d'altra Compagnia ch'a bello studio va preoccupando le stanze delle città principali.' Arch. Med. Filza 5130. c. 504. Another Nobile, who was certainly connected with the stage, but not necessarily himself an actor, is mentioned in a letter from Scala to Don Giovanni de' Medici on 10 July 1619. Arch. Med. Filza 5150. c. 484.

[2] D'Ancona, op. cit., p. 472 n., quoting from an article by Belgrano in the *Caffaro*, 1882, says that Valerini was in Genova in 1581, but as the month is not recorded we have no further information as to his company. From June to August the *Uniti*, and in November the *Gelosi*, were in that city.

as the founder of the *Uniti*. This may be so, but it will be noticed that he did not remain with them long; in the detailed list of 1584 there is no place for him. With the passage from the *Bravure* in mind it is probably safe to suppose that he returned to the *Gelosi*.

It is difficult to think of the *Gelosi* without the Andreini couple, but they cannot have joined the company before 1576, for according to the usual computation Francesco, born in 1548, was taken prisoner by the Turks at the age of twenty and remained a slave for eight years. Isabella gave birth to her eldest son in Florence on 9 February 1576, and it is known that the *Gelosi* did not leave this city for Venice until about the thirteenth of that month: the probability that Francesco remained behind with Isabella may account for the 'Ottavio', the puzzle of whose appearance with Vittoria in Ferrara has been remarked already.

The licence granted in July 1579 to ten members of the *Gelosi* to act in Genova[1] does not mention the Andreini. D'Ancona is wrong in suggesting that the birth of Giovan Battista may account for this omission, for the horoscope discovered by Rasi puts it beyond question that he was born in 1576;[2] but the birth of another of her seven children would be an equally good reason for her absence. Francesco was certainly with the *Gelosi* in 1583, when he refused a tempting invitation from the Duke of Mantua: but the appearance of an Isabella among the *Uniti* in Ferrara a year later (3 April 1584) suggests that in the end he may not have resisted the offer. There is no mention of Francesco himself among the *Uniti*, but they are not likely to have been parted, and the *Gelosi* were playing in Genova. It is not quite certain that this Isabella was the Andreini—Vittoria degl' Amorevoli played under this stage name at the beginning of the seventeenth century—but the *Uniti* in 1584 were admittedly a reorganized company and advertised themselves as 'reunited with *Pedrolino* and supplemented by experienced comedians —personaggi famosi nell'arte comica'.[3] A list of the *Gelosi*

---

[1] *Caffaro*, 22 Dec. 1882.

[2] It is remarkable that on the title-page of the *Florinda*, 1606, Giovan Battista gives his age as 28. Was this vanity, or an attempt to reconcile his age with the official date of his parents' marriage, always given as 1578?

[3] D'Ancona, op. cit., p. 486.

in Florence 1589 shows *Pedrolino* and *Capitano Cardone*, old *Uniti* men, once again as Andreini's companions, and in 1601 Isabella and *Pedrolino* appear together in a Milanese document. These notices probably refer to temporary amalgamations, such as that organized for a few days between the *Uniti* and the *Gelosi* in Bergamo celebrated in Corbelli's poem.[1]

After 1579 Vittoria Piissimi seems to have strayed in and out of the company. In this year and again in 1581 she was with the *Confidenti*, but in May 1589 she reappears among the *Gelosi*. The company was in attendance for the wedding of Ferdinando de' Medici and Cristina of Lorraine and was probably temporarily augmented. From an anecdote of the rivalry between Isabella and Vittoria we are not bound to conclude that there were two companies at that time in Florence. A similar episode among the *Confidenti* shows that the mad-scene was continually the cause of jealousy within the company.

Pavoni remembers how in the *Gelosi* play of *La Pazzia* Andreini distinguished himself by mimicking his companions one after the other, speaking now like *Pantalone*, now like *Gratiano*, like *Zanni*, *Pedrolino*, *Francatrippe*, *Burattino*, *Capitano Cardone*, or *Franceschina*.[2] This reassembles for us the chief masks of the *Gelosi*. With the exception of *Burattino* and *Cardone*, these can be identified as Pasquati, Ludovico and Gabrielle da Bologna, Pellesini, Simone da Bologna, and Silvia Roncaglia. Rasi reckons that counting in Vittoria and Isabella we have 'the usual ten' to correspond to the *Bravure* list, but the numerical correctness is misleading. Instead of the two lovers we have in the Florentine cas *Burattino* and *Capitano Cardone*. The latter, whose real name

[1] D'Ancona (ibid., p. 465) notes Quadrio's statement that this amalgamation took place in 1580, supposing, with Solerti, that Quadrio depends upon the Madrigal composed for the occasion when 'i comici Uniti, di cui era parte principale la s. Angelica . . . si unirono qui in Bergamo per alcuni giorni con i Comici Gelosi'. The poem was printed in G. Borgogni's collection of *Rime di diversi celebri poeti dell'età nostra*, Bergamo, 1587, p. 310. The implicit distinction seems to invalidate a suggestion of Prof. Nicoll's (*Masks, Mimes, and Miracles*, p. 314) that the *Uniti* and *Gelosi* were 'fundamentally the same company'; though occasionally amalgamating and interchanging their *personnel*, they were evidently regarded as distinct bodies.

[2] Quoted from the *Diarii del Pavoni*, 1589, by Rasi, op. cit., ii. 243.

we do not know, appears again among the *Uniti* in 1584 and 1593, his mask is used in Scala's scenario of *Li Due Capitani*; no doubt he was the predecessor of Captain Spavento before Andreini changed from the lover to the Spanish braggart. *Burattino* may have come along with Vittoria, but four Zanni offers an unusually large choice and it is possible that *Burattino* is an alternative name for *Zanni* or *Pedrolino*.[1]

After this temporary amalgamation, and perhaps as the result of the rivalry which it caused, there seems to have been a redistribution of the *Gelosi*. In 1589 the *Confidenti* petition in the name of Isabella for licence to act in Parma,[2] and the company proceeds to Milan in September and Mantua at Christmas. Meanwhile the company called the *Gelosi*, who acted in Milan in October 1590, consisted of Vittoria Piissimi, Nora, a Florentine; Aurelia, a Roman; Lutio Fedeli, a Paduan; Oratio de' Nobili, a Florentine; Giuseppe Scarpetta and Giovan Battista Trombetti, both Venetians; Carlo Vegi from Piacenza, Bernardino Lombardi Bolognese, Emilio Baldovini of Parma, Girolamo Salimbeni (Florentine), Giulio Vigiante Neapolitan with their children, attendants, and three general servants.[3] Of these only Girolamo Salimbeni belongs to Andreini's list, and in 1593 he is again associated with Vittoria among the *Uniti*.

Lombardi and Trombetta up to this time had been of some importance in the *Uniti* and *Confidenti*: Scarpetta reappears in 1596 with the *Desiosi*. The reappearance of Emilio Baldovino in Mantua 1592 tells us nothing further of his company. The Aurelia was probably the actress whom the Duke of Mantua wished admitted into the company of

---

[1] It is worth noticing that in Gattici's comedy Bettina comes in search of her son Burattino and describes him to Nespola: 'L'è vestid de canevaz, cai l'ho filad mi bianch, l'ha el mostaz un poch negher, ch'as dis che terra negra fà bon gran, à cà nostra al se nominava Pedrolin.' Gattici, *Le Disgratie di Burattino*, Act II. Licensed 25 May 1619. The edition in the Casanatense collection is for 1626 in Venice. Quadrio records one earlier issue for Ferrioli in Milan, 1623, and one later, for Marelli in Milan, 1671. The comedy reappears under the title *Le Disgratie di Trufaldino*, of which the only edition I have seen contains a dedicatory letter dated Venice, 4 Feb. 1690. Allacci, however, quotes four other issues: (1) Venice for G. B. Combi, 1614. (2) Rome for Grignani, 1628. (3) Venice, 1690. (4) Bologna for Sarti, undated.

[2] D'Ancona, op. cit., ii, p. 476.

[3] Paglicci-Brozzi, *Gaz. Mus. di Milano*, 1891, No. 34.

Vittoria in 1593. Possibly 'Carlo Vegi' is to be identified with the 'Carletto' described by Catranj as a *Franceschina* in 1598[1] and with the 'Carlo de' Vecchi' who was killed by Cecchini in Turin in 1600.[2]

Towards the end of the century the company was able to draw on the second generation of players. One January evening in 1594 a quaint figure in 'un pelliccetto, ed un paro di sottocalze per le saccoccie, delle quali spingevo fuori le braccia', set out from Bologna on the road to Florence in search of his father who was reported to have returned from Sicily and Naples and to be serving the *Gelosi*. This was Domenico Bruni, who tells the tale of how in the excitement of his arrival he embraced the innkeeper and embarrassed the good man with his wife by hailing him as his father. Francesco Andreini took the boy under his protection, fitted him out with a 'vestito di panno', set him to learn a Prologue, and fostered the talent which made Bruni famous on the stage as *Fulvio* the lover, and behind the scenes as the author of the Prologues, Dialogues, and *Le Fatiche Comiche*.

In the *supplica* of the *Gelosi* presented in Genova 1596, D'Ancona, quoting Belgrano, includes an actress Virginia, fabricating for her the surname of Maloni-Andreini. The double name is the result of a misleading supposition. Both Giovan Battista Andreini's wives, distinguishable on the stage as *Florinda* and *Lidia*, bore the Christian name Virginia, but neither was surnamed Maloni. There is, however, an undated letter from Virginia and Lucilla Maloni asking for the patronage of the Duke of Mantua, and it appears that the former was the mother of *Celia* Maloni of the second *Confidenti*.

Solerti's suggestion that the *Gelosi* were in France in 1599 is undocumented.[3] The years 1596–1603 are blank in the history of the company. Isabella appears with *Pedrolino* at the head of a troop calling themselves the *Uniti* in June and October 1601; it appears from her letter that it was a picked company summoned from Mantua to Milan and Milan to Pavia for the meeting of Cardinal Aldobrandini with the

[1] D'Ancona, op. cit., ii, p. 525.   p. 615.
[2] *Gaz. Mus. di Milano*, No. 38,   [3] *Giorn Stor.* xviii, p. 163.

Prince of Savoy.[1] She may have been accompanied by other members of the *Gelosi*: there is always some ambiguity about the title *Uniti* which might easily be applied to any amalgamation. Pedrolino and the Andreini were evidently a desirable combination, and in November 1602 Ferrugières, the agent of Henry III in Turin, went to some trouble to collect a company for the French Court which should include *Pedrolino*. The negotiations resulted in his visit in the company of the *Gelosi* for whom Giovan Paolo Fabbri now played the lover *Flaminio*.[2]

In August 1603 they acted first in Paris and then at Fontainebleau,[3] and again in the Hôtel de Bourgogne, and stayed at the French Court until the following April. The personal note supplied by Henry as a safe conduct for 'Isabella commediante' and her company, for the 'hardes, armes, bagages, bagues, joyaux', and the letter of recommendation from the Queen to the Duchess of Mantua, read sadly now, for on 11 June Francesco Andreini lost his wife in childbirth at Lyons, and the company was disbanded. He retired to Venice and occupied himself with the publication of Isabella's literary remains and his own *Bravure*, Pastorals, and *Ragionamenti*: he never acted again, but he appears from time to time as friend and adviser of Scala in his direction of the Confidenti of Don Giovanni de' Medici. His son Giovan Battista carried on the literary and dramatic traditions of the family under the patronage of the Duke of Mantua.

DIANA AND THE *DESIOSI*

From time to time between 1581 and 1599 occurs the name *Desiosi* for a company of which no complete list survives. Montaigne met them in Pisa in 1581 and records the fantastic Zanni name of *Fargnocola*.[4] Behind the scenes he visited the actresses and sent presents of fish.[5] These little attentions are interesting in view of the curious condition

[1] Paglicci-Brozzi, *Il Teatro a Milano nel sec. xvii. Gaz. Mus. di Milano*, 1891, No. 34.
[2] Baschet, op. cit., p. 126.
[3] Ibid., pp. 137-8.
[4] Giovanni Gabrielli, *Sivello*, used the name in his Bergomask poem 'Maridazzo di M. Zan Frognocola con Madonna Gnigniocola'. Venetia and Trevigi, 1618, quoted by Rasi, op. cit., i, pp. 954-5.
[5] *Voyage en Italie*, ed. D'Ancona, 1895, pp. 472, 484, 488.

delivered with the licence to this company to play in Rome in 1588. Their performances were to be without women, 'senza donne'. D'Ancona's inclination to apply this restriction to the cast rather than to the audience is supported by the record of at least two private performances of the *Desiosi* during this season witnessed by noble Roman ladies.[1] It is, however, in the name of a woman, *Diana Comica Desiosa*, that the company obtains a licence in May, 1595.[2]

Scanty notices of the *Desiosi* may be supplemented by putting alongside the references of the company of Diana. It is time that this actress, whose surname was Ponti of Ferrara[3] and stage name *Lavinia*, should appear with other companies. In 1582 the *Confidenti* could not start from Florence until she had arrived with *Graziano*,[4] in 1586 Cesare de Nobili is her companion in Genova in a company called *Uniti*,[5] in 1601 she was with Cecchini and Martinelli who travelled in France as the *Accesi*. But in the rhymes prefixed to *Il Postumio*, published in Lyons 1601, during this tour Diana continues to style herself *Desiosa* as in the Milanese licence of 1595. It seems fairly safe then to assume that the players, under her direction, called themselves *Desiosi* or *della Diana* indiscriminately. In July 1585 the Duke of Mantua tried to tempt Ludovico, the *Graziano* of the *Gelosi*, away from Milan to act with the company of Diana which was expected in Mantua; but Ludovico refused to be parted from Giulio his *Pantalone*.[6] At the beginning of 1590 there is a batch of correspondence to dispatch Andreazzo,[7] the *Graziano*, with the company of Diana to serve the Cardinal Montalto in Rome: exhausted by the negotiations the Conte Ulisse Bentivoglio comes to the conclusion that 'this is a brothel of love-affairs between wantons and knaves'.[8]

In December 1595 Tristano Martinelli was with this company in Cremona,[9] and the 'Giambattista Lazarone Comico', to whom letters were addressed, was probably

[1] D'Ancona, op. cit., pp. 500–1.
[2] G. Pagani, *Del Teatro in Milano avanti il 1598* (1884).
[3] *Riv. Teatrale It.* 1906, p. 13.
[4] D'Ancona, op. cit., p. 481.
[5] *Riv. Teatrale It.* 1906, p. 11.
[6] D'Ancona, op. cit., p. 489.

[7] Sanesi, *La Commedia*, vol. ii, cap. 6, p. 11, tries to identify this Andreazzo with the Andrea Zenari who played Graziano for the *Uniti* in 1593; but there is no proof.
[8] D'Ancona, op. cit., pp. 496–7.
[9] Ibid., p. 519.

another member of the company, and is possibly to be identified with the Battista Lazaro who was not too successful in Paris in 1584.[1]

In January 1596 a commendation of their performance preceded them to Mantua, where their reception was so cordial that on 15 February they write from Bologna begging the Duke to accept some little token of their gratitude, to be acknowledged by a word addressed to Giuseppe Scarpetta.[2] In May 1597 they acted in Genova, under the direction of Scala,[3] in July in Piacenza,[4] and two years later in Verona.[5] The last notice of Diana is her appearance in Modena and Genova in 1605, at the head of a company patronized by the Duke of Mirandola.[6]

COMPANIES OF THE *DUKES OF MANTUA*: CONSTITUTION OF THE *UNITI* AND *FIRST CONFIDENTI*

The politic rearrangements of the companies which from time to time claimed or were subject to the patronage of the Gonzaga family is extremely confusing. The chief companies during the sixteenth century, the *Uniti* and the *Confidenti*, were of changing composition, and each was ambiguously described as the company of the Duke of Mantua. With possible exception of two occasions the companies are nominally distinct throughout the period, but the change and interchange of membership makes it dangerous to co-ordinate the scanty references with the alternative description of the companies by the name of favourite players, such as the company of *Pedrolino*, of Vittoria, of Angelica, or to supplement the broken itineraries from hints of the whereabouts of individual actors who may or may not be travelling professionally. But the bare facts of names and dates set out under the headings of separate companies are hardly intelligible without some attempt to explain circumstances. To insist upon a rigid division between these companies would be to work against the grain; and with the safeguard of the lists for reference it will be better to trace their development

---

[1] See *supra*, ch. ii, p. 82.
[2] D'Ancona, op. cit., p. 520.
[3] Ibid., p. 520.
[4] Jarro, op. cit., p. 11, letter from

T. Martinelli, 28 July, Piacenza.
[5] D'Ancona, op. cit., p. 596.
[6] *Riv. Teatrale It.* 1906, p. 13.

alongside, showing how special festivities, and patrons' negotiations lead to amalgamation, and actors' quarrels to fresh divisions.

The *Confidenti* are first mentioned in a petition dated 8 June 1574, asking for a renewal of licence to play in Milan. From a letter of 25 June it appears that in the early summer they had been in Cremona and Pavia, where their Zanni, Battista Vannino da Rimino, had been arrested for helping a frightened child to escape from the officers. The next June they are found in Milan,[1] and in 1579 at Massa.[2]

Meanwhile in 1576 the company of *Pedrolino* was touring in Tuscany. A letter from Capponi informs the Grand Duke that the notable scandals of the love-affairs of the actresses had made it advisable to forbid their return to Pisa in July.[3] In April 1580 the comedies of *Pedrolino* were successful both in the private rooms of the Duchess of Ferrara and below 'in Banchi'.[4]

It will be remembered that between 1576 and 1589 there are no signs of any connexion between Vittoria Piissimi and the *Gelosi*. At the end of August 1580 a company appearing in her name was recommended by the Duke of Mantua for licence to play in Padua,[5] and in the autumn Vittoria and *Pedrolino* join forces and call themselves the *Confidenti*. A letter from Drusiano Martinelli to the Duke explains the new arrangement and clears up many obscurities. Martinelli understands that His Highness wishes him and his wife Angelica to join the company of *Pedrolino*, and he protests that he would have obeyed but 'the *Pedrolini* are agreed with the Sᵃ. Vittoria, and I shall have a good company because I shall be able to provide the better for it, and it shall be the third company'. If His Highness will have players in Mantua for Carnival, there is not a better company than this to be found, for the *Gelosi* and the *Confidenti* are going to Venice.[6] Abject letters of apology in the name of Vittoria and *Pedrolino* for playing in Venice instead of in Mantua on this occasion put it beyond doubt that they were the *Con-*

---

[1] Pagani, op. cit.

[2] Sanesi, op. cit., p. 12.

[3] D'Ancona, op. cit., 476 n.

[4] Solerti-Lanza, *Giorn. Stor.* xviii, p. 167.

[5] D'Ancona, op. cit., p. 475.

[6] From Florence, 17 Sept. 1586, quoted by D'Ancona, op. cit., pp. 478–9.

fidenti.[1] The usual assumption that before the amalgamation this name belonged to Vittoria's company and that the actors with *Pedrolino* were the *Uniti* is not borne out by such evidence as we have. On 30 May the Duke of Mantua recommended the *Confidenti* to the Podestà of Verona.[2] On 22 June Vittoria was in Mantua, complaining bitterly that the Duke was trying to dismember her company by insisting that they should join the company of some rival referred to cryptically as 'that woman'.[3] At the end of August it has been mentioned that Vittoria and her players received letters of commendation to Cardinal D'Este for permission to act in Padua. It is, of course, possible that the *Confidenti* did not leave for Verona at the beginning of June, or that after a brief visit they returned to Mantua, but on the whole it is more likely that the company of *Pedrolino* were the original *Confidenti* whose title Vittoria accepted for a time. In October they played at Ferrara,[4] in November at Bologna,[5] and spent Carnival at Venice.[6] They seem to have made up for the truancy from the Mantuan Carnival by attending the wedding of Vincenzo Gonzaga, who sped them to Bologna in May.[7] The next year we catch another glimpse of them at Bologna in July, waiting only for the arrival of Diana and *Gratiano* from Florence to obey a summons to Mantua.[8]

The discovery of a licence to Battista Trombetta in the name of the *Confidenti* to play 'their usual and respectable comedies' in Genova for three months from 6 August 1581[9] has led to the suggestion that there were two branches of the *Confidenti* in 1582:[10] it is a possible but not a necessary conclusion. Another Genoese document, however, shows that the next year some shifting took place. On 2 April the Duke of Mantua writes to inform a certain Giulia Bolico that the *Confidenti* who are with him in Mantua wish her to join their company.[11] On 25 April licence to act in Genova was granted to the *Uniti-Confidenti* in the name of Bernardino de' Lombardi.[12] It is not any difficulty over the dates that suggests

[1] Rasi, op. cit., ii, p. 289.
[2] D'Ancona, op. cit., p. 474.
[3] Ibid., p. 475.
[4] Rasi, op. cit., ii. 289.
[5] *Giorn. Stor.* xviii, p. 168.   [6] Ibid.
[7] D'Ancona, op. cit., p. 480.

[8] Ibid.
[9] Belgrano in *Caffaro*, 1886, No. 157.
[10] D'Ancona, op. cit., p. 481, and Sanesi, op. cit., p. 13.
[11] Ibid., p. 485.
[12] *Caffaro*, 1886, 157.

a redisposition of the players, but rather the new title, together with the appearance of *Pedrolino*, quondam member
of the *Confidenti*, in company with Valerini and Braga, who
are usually associated with the *Uniti*. If Rasi is right in
dating the letter which mentions *Pedrolino* and Iacomo
Braga as acting in Modena, Milan, and Bergamo, as sometime in 1583, the company certainly called themselves the
Uniti at this time.[1]

We must now return to trace the *Uniti*. The word is
always a little ambiguous, and it is probably wrong to conclude that it is invariably used as a proper title. The first
occurrence when in February 1578 Canigiani records a performance of the 'Uniti Comici' before the Duchess of Urbino is a doubtful case.[2] Three years later, however, we can
be certain of the company in Genova for July and August.[3]
It will be remembered that in 1580, after mentioning the
Gelosi and the *Confidenti*, Drusiano refers to his own company
as worth the consideration of the Duke for Carnival. At
first they seem to have been known as the '*Comici nuovi*'.
Lanfranco Turino inspected a company so called in Ferrara
in July 1580, and reports that except for the actress, who is
of good appearance and sings quite agreeably, and some
young acrobats, the troop is poor, but full of confidence that
when they have found a Pantalone and an Inamorato they
will be able to satisfy the Prince of Mantua who, he understands, is already financing the company for the sake of the
said actress.[4] The attraction was probably Drusiano's wife
Angelica, who was perhaps 'that woman' so dreaded by
Vittoria. The association of Angelica's name with the *Uniti*
in Corbelli's sonnet on the occasion of their joint performance
with the *Gelosi* at Bergamo at about this time, makes it almost
certain that this was the style assumed by Martinelli's troop.

Returning then to the re-grouping of 1583, it seems that
it was through the intermediary stage of a troop known as
the *Uniti-Confidenti*, and the branching off caused by its
formation, that *Pedrolino*, who belonged to the *Confidenti* in
1581, changed over and appeared in 1584 at the head of the

[1] Rasi, op. cit., ii. 243.   [3] A. Neri, *Rivista Teatrale It.* 1906,
[2] Solerti-Lanza, *Giorn. Stor.* xviii,   fascio 4, p. 98.
p. 166.   [4] *Giorn. Stor.* xviii, p. 169.

players who describe themselves as the 'Comici Uniti returned once more with the company of Pedrolino, as formerly,
and augmented by other well-known comedians'.[1] Besides
the masks of the *Magnifico*, *Gratiano*, *Cardone*, *Grillo*, *Franceschina*, *Flaminio*, and *Bertolino*, the only proper names given
are those of Lutio, Gio. Donato, Isabella, and Giulia
Brolo. In the 'Giulia Brolo' D'Ancona recognizes the 'Giulia
Bolico' commended to the *Confidenti* in 1583:[2] the most
likely *Magnifico* would be Braga, the *Gratiano*, Lombardi.
Cardone and Isabella would be the desirable additions from
the ranks of the *Gelosi*; for Lutio one might suggest Lucio
Fedele; for *Flaminio*, Giovan Battista Fabbri. For *Franceschina* there is too wide a choice to make supposititious identification worth while: for *Grillo*[3] and *Bertolino* there is no
choice at all. Notices of the *Uniti* in Reggio, Ferrara, and
Mantua during the summer of 1584[4] keep them quite
separate from the *Confidenti* who were patronized by the
Duc de Gioieuse in France. Something of the composition
of the latter troop can be gleaned from the publication of *La
Fiammella* of Bartolommeo Rossi and the *Angelica* of Fabritio
Fornaris, *Capitano Coccodrillo* in Paris 1584. The 'Battista
da Rimino', praised by Rossi as the Zanni of the *Confidenti*,
who spoke the true Bergomask dialect, is plainly the 'Battista Vannini' who belonged to the company ten years before.
The choice of the actors who may have played *Arlecchino* on
this occasion, and the possible membership of Battista Lazaro,
has been discussed in another connexion.[5]

The company allowed in Genova on 27 April 1586 is
described by Neri as the *Uniti*[6] and by Belgrano as the
Confidenti of a different composition;[7] the only names mentioned in the document are Diana Ponti and Cesare di
Nobile, but as these suggest the *Desiosi*, it is impossible to say
what rearrangements may have taken place.

Sometime before November 1587, a company, described

[1] See *supra*, p. 265.

[2] Op. cit., p. 485.

[3] D'Ancona, ii, p. 487, assumes that *Grillo* is the stage-name of Giovan Donato Lombardi da Bitonto whom he is inclined to identify with Giovan Donato. Since he does not comment upon *Grillo*, it is to be supposed that he regarded it as Donato's stage-name. Sanesi (op. cit., p. 17) depends upon the intervening comma and reckons for two actors.

[4] D'Ancona, op. cit., pp. 486, 488.

[5] *Supra*, p. 82.

[6] *Riv. Teatrale It.* 1906, p. 11.

[7] *Caffaro*, 1886, No. 157.

in the Spanish records as *Los Confidentes Italianos*, was obliged to ask for special licence for the actresses Angela Salomona, Angela Martinelli, as married women travelling with their husbands. *La Francesquina*, which Puertocamera supposes is a woman's part, is included in the permission granted.[1]

From a letter dispatched by Drusiano Martinelli in August we know that Tristano was with the *Confidenti* who intended to stay in Spain until the end of 1587.[2] On their return they appear in Tuscany with 'Isabella delli Anderini' [*sic*]. Probably the redivision which makes Isabella temporarily one of the *Confidenti* and gives to the curious list of performers in Milan in 1590 the name of the *Gelosi*, is the result of the temporary amalgamation in Florence 1589.

Three actors, *Panzanini*, *Cardone*, and Salimbeni, regularly associated with the *Gelosi*, sign a petition on 12 October 1593 for licence to act in Genova as the *Comici Uniti*,[3] but of these only the last reappears with the company a year later as it assembled for the festivities of Aro in Milan. On this occasion *Leandro* (Francesco Pilastri) superintended the performance of his twelve companions in the spectacular shows that were arranged as interludes for a five-act comedy. Vittoria appeared as a syren, *Pedrolino* and *Arlecchino*[4] in their own masks, *Piombo* (Salimbeni) as a rustic,

[1] 'Si la Françesquina es la que yo vi en la posada del Señor Cardenal, no la tengo por muchacho y ansí podra representar.' Pérez Pastor, *Nuevos Datos*, p. 21. Since the part of Franceschina was shared by actors and actresses until the beginning of the seventeenth century (see App. E, p. 80), the spectator may well have been uncertain of the sex of this player. Professor Atkinson, to whom I appealed in difficulty over this passage, reminds me of the prohibitions of 1614 and 1641 in which actresses were forbidden to play the parts of men and vice versa. On this earlier occasion 'Françesquina' was allowed the benefit of the doubt.

[2] Rasi, op. cit., ii, p. 104.

[3] Belgrano, *Caffaro*, 1886, No. 171, and A. Neri, *Fanfulla della Domenica*, 4 April 1886.

[4] The appearance of *Arlecchino* and *Pedrolino* among the *Uniti* in 1594, taken together with a letter of 4 December 1595, in which Tristano Martinelli announces that he has left the company of *Pedrolino* because they wanted to be masters and not companions, and remarks that he is not the first who has found their insolence intolerable, enables us to comment upon a curious direction in an earlier letter. On 10 April 1595 Cheppio in Mantua writes to Bellone in Milan that his messenger will be either 'Mess. Drusiano Martinelli, che nelle comedie recita la parte d'Arlecchino', or some other member of the 'Compagnia de' Comici Uniti', che per altro nome si chiama la Compagnia del S^{mo} Sig^{re}. Nostro'. This is the only evidence that we have for supposing that the Martinelli brothers shared the mask of

Ottavio (perhaps the actor associated with Vittoria among the *Gelosi* in 1576) played Phaeton, Lucilla and Virginia, who are surely the Maloni sisters, played Climene and the Sun, Emilia represented the Earth, *Fortunio* (Petignoni) Winter, Silvio (Gambi or Fiorillo?) Autumn, *Franceschina* doubled the parts of Epafo and Summer, Angelica of Aurora and Spring, *Leandro* himself took a lion's share as Time, the river Po, and Jove.

A letter referring to the Martinelli three years later confirms our impression of their continual association with the *Uniti* and *Confidenti*. In April 1598 Alessandro Catrani, a Mantuan soldier, set out in writing the complaint, which he had already made in person to the Duke, against Drusiano Martinelli, whose son he had adopted six years ago, whose wife he had saved from destitution, and who had been living on his bounty for the last five months, doing nothing the while but eat, sleep, and let the world go by.[1] *Pedrolino*, *Cardone*, and 'Carletto who plays the part of *Franceschina*', are named as witnesses of the disloyalty towards the house of Mantua shown by both the Martinelli in Parma and Turin. Presumably Drusiano's holiday at Catrani's expense accounts for the appearance of Flaminio Scala in his place as conductor of the *Uniti* in Genova that April.[2] Catrani's threatenings proved a sufficient excuse for Tristano, who in May did not wish to return to the Duke of Mantua's company, but preferred to keep faith with the Grand Duke of Tuscany for the following carnival.

EARLY *ACCESI*

Under whatever name *Arlecchino* and Diana may have acted at this time, it was again as the comedians of the

Arlecchino: on all other occasions Drusiano, when he is not merely 'the husband of Angelica', is 'the brother of Arlecchino'. D'Ancona takes it that Tristano was already with Diana when this letter was written (4 Dec. 1595), but if so it is odd that he should have waited for over seven months before informing the Duke of the change. I do not think it unjustifiable scepticism to suppose that Cheppio may have mistaken the Christian names. D'Ancona (ii. 518) notes the ambiguity of the record that in March 1593 'the brother of Arlecchino' presented himself to Pomponazzi the Mantuan ambassador in Venice with a letter from the Duke asking for a recommendation to the Emperor's ambassador in Constantinople which by 20 March has been procured.

[1] D'Ancona, op. cit., ii. 519.
[2] *Caffaro*, 1886, No. 171.

Duke of Mantua, but with the new name of *Accesi*, that they formed the nucleus of the company touring in France in 1600–1. A remark in one of *Arlecchino's* letters to the Grand Duke, written on 11 March 1597, hints of a prospect of an earlier visit to the French Court.[1] Martinelli wishes to draw 600 ducats at the Monte di Pietà as he passes through Milan on his way to France. Letters from Piacenza in July 1597,[2] and from Modena the following May,[3] make it unlikely that the plan was carried out. But in March 1600 he responds to a personal invitation from Henry III and assembles a company for France.[4] They travelled by way of Bologna, Milan, and Savoy, preceded by Drusiano to Lyons. When the King arrived in July the players were still detained at Turin, but Drusiano fetched them by the beginning of August. Wars with Savoy prevented the King from enjoying their performance during the autumn and delayed his marriage with Maria de' Medici.[5] Arlecchino seems to have occupied himself with the preparation of his *Compositions en Rhetorique*, in which he congratulates Henry both as conqueror and bridegroom by addressing him as 'Conte di Mommeillan ... Conseiller Souverain au Conseil de guerra contre les Plamantois... Terreur de Savoyard ... Secretaire Secret du plus Secret Cabinet de Madama MARIA DI MEDICI....'

The *Accesi* stayed in France until the autumn of 1601; in October Marie de Boussu still hoped to persuade them to visit Flanders on their return journey, but it appears that they reached Rome sometime before Christmas.

Echoes of friction between the Zanni before the company left Italy, and again in Paris, inform us that Cecchini, whose mask of *Fritellino* was soon to rival Arlecchino, was with the *Accesi* on this tour. From the publication of *Il Postumio, comedia del Signor I. S.*', in Lyons 1601 at the instance of Flaminio Scala, prefaced by verses by Diana Comica Desiosa, we are assured of two more members.

While the *Accesi* were in France a company of the *Uniti* toured in Italy, and are to be found in Genova in July 1600,[6] and the following summer in Mantua, Milan, and Pavia,[7]

1 'Jarro', op. cit., p. 43.
2 Ibid., p. 11.
3 D'Ancona, op. cit., ii. 526.
4 'Jarro', p. 48, and A. Bartoli, op.

cit., p. 134.
5 Baschet, op. cit., p. 108.
6 *Caffaro*, 1886, No. 171.
7 *Gaz. Mus. di Milano*, 1891, No. 34.

where their association with Isabella Andreini has already been mentioned. A performance of *La Pazzia di Lelio* in Florence, December 1604,[1] suggests that Giovan Battista Andreini, who published his *Florinda* in Florence the same year, and was known on the stage as *Lelio*, was acting with the *Uniti* for a time.

There is a gap of nine years before the next notice of the company who, according to Sanesi, were playing in Milan in 1613. A list of comedians in Genova the next year revives the name, but only three actors, Jacomo Braga the *Pantalone*, Ottavio Bernardino for *Franceschina*, and G. P. Fabbri for *Flaminio*, connect the troop with the earlier company. It will be best to postpone discussion of this list until the new generation of actors has been assembled.

After 1599 notices of the *Confidenti* are equally scarce. The company appears in Lucca and Genova in April 1606,[2] and possibly at Modena, Reggio, and Carpi in 1610.[3]

COMPANIES OF THE EARLY SEVENTEENTH CENTURY

The disbanding of the *Gelosi* in 1604, and the blank in the records of the *Desiosi*, *Uniti*, and *Confidenti*, gives to the first few years of the seventeenth century the appearance of a turning-point in the history of the companies. Drusiano Martinelli died before 1608, and no more is heard of Angelica; Tristano is left to carry on the family name; *Pedrolino* is still playing, but it is often said that he is too old; the second generation of the Maloni, the Gabrielli, and the Andreini, and Francesco's protégé, Domenico Bruni, take the stage; the Cecchini and the Fiorelli, the Antonazzoni, and the Onorati popularize the new masks of *Fritellino*, *Mattamoros*, *Pulcinella*, *Scapino* and *Mezzettino* respectively, and sort themselves in and out of the companies of the *Accesi*, the *Fedeli*, and the new *Confidenti* under the patronage chiefly of the Duke of Mantua and Don Giovanni de' Medici.

There is, of course, no actual break, and having once drawn attention to the general change, we may return to study the overlapping by tracing the development of the company

---

[1] Solerti, *Musica, Ballo e drammatica alla Corte de' Medici*, 1600–37 (1905).

[2] *Riv. Teatrale It.* 1906, p. 14.

[3] Rasi, op. cit., ii. 183.

of the *Accesi* in which Martinelli represents the older and Cecchini the younger generation.

ACCESI AND FEDELI

The name of the *Accesi*, assumed by the company of the Duke of Mantua in France in 1600, was used ten years earlier by the players recommended by him to Brescia in January 1590.[1] It is tempting to connect the new name with the first mention of *Fritellino* Cecchini as a professional Zanni when he appears among the company of the 'Duca di Sab-bioneda' the following June.[2] Cecchini's success as an amateur in 1583 decided his career, and by 1622 he reckons that he has served the Gonzaga family with hardly a break for thirty-five years. He may very well have invented the name *Accesi* at the beginning of his career about 1587; on his title-pages he uses no other style, and his association with that company is as close as that of G. B. Andreini with the *Fedeli*. The fortunes of these two companies must be told together for the reason that the apparent confusion of the lists and the contradictions of the itineraries are occasioned by the periodical amalgamations into a special company which is variously named after its patron the Duke of Mantua, or one of its chief personages *Lelio*, *Florinda*, *Fritellino*, *Flaminio*, or *Arlecchino*. It will be best to deal with them together along the lines already adopted to explain the shifting membership of the *Uniti* and *Confidenti*. For an elucidation of the bare notices of performances we depend upon the flare of correspondence struck out by the friction between Cecchini, Andreini, their wives, and admirers. When the flint and steel of these two families fail, the little world is set alight by the sly negotiations of Martinelli who continues to wander in and out of the two companies, making them indefatigably, and breaking them recklessly, a man spoiled by patrons and dreaded by his companions.

In spite of the disagreements in Paris in 1600, we have Zuccaro's authority that in the winter of 1605–6 *Arlecchino* was still in partnership with the Cecchini,[3] but not even the persuasiveness of Maria de' Medici and the Gonzaga could

---

[1] D'Ancona, op. cit., ii. 495.
[2] *Giorn. Stor.* xviii, p. 182.

[3] *Il Passaggio per Italia con la dimora di Parma* (1608), p. 28.

make him consent to travel with them in France in 1607.[1]
The Duke of Mantua tried to prepare the way for the substitute, *Cola*, by assuring His Majesty that this new personage with his satires and tricks ought to please as much as
Arlecchino, over whom he had the advantage of youth.[2] It
appears from the later list that this promising Zanni was
Aniello di Mauro, a Neapolitan. He had already made a
name for himself in Italy, for in 1605 Zuccaro described as
'the titbit of the feast' the performance of a child who danced
in imitation of *Cola*, the Neapolitan comedian.[3]

The success of the visit to France is memorable in occa-
sioning a tribute to *Fritellino's* skill in keeping the unity and
appropriateness of *soggetti*.[4]

The other members of the *Accesi* are known to us by the
stage-names that caught the attention of the little Dauphin:
child-like he continued the play in his own imagination, and
his tutor Heroard records that *Fritellino, Pantalone, Cola,
Piombino*, and *Stefanello* provided him with passwords for
the guard for several days.[5] Besides these masks under
which we recognize Cecchini, Federigo Ricci, Aniello di
Mauro, Girolamo Salimbeni, the company included a
Spanish Captain, probably Garavini, the *Capitano Rinoceronte* who was with Cecchini in 1606, and it employed
Battista Austoni as door-keeper.[6]

The connexion of G. B. Andreini and *Florinda* with the
company of the *Fedeli* dates with certainty from 1604[7] and
possibly goes back to the earlier appearances in Genova in
1601. In 1606 complaints in Cecchini's letters are heard as
mutterings of many stormy amalgamations with the *Fedeli*.
In September the persecutions of *Florinda* seemed intolerable, but it seems that he stood it until the next year.[8] But while

[1] Baschet, op. cit., p. 155 seq. Cp.
Arch. Mant., Serie Francia, E. xv. 666,
a letter from Trajano Guiscardi, Ambassador in Paris.

[2] Baschet, op. cit., p. 163; Rasi, op.
cit., i. 672, has already remarked that
this letter is no longer to be found in its
place in the Mantuan Archives.

[3] Op. cit., p. 20.

[4] Baschet, op. cit., p. 169.

[5] Ibid., p. 184.

[6] Ibid., p. 170. See Arch. Mant.,
Serie Francia, E. xv. 666. T. Guiscardi,
19 March, 1608.

[7] In *La Saggia Egiziana*, 'Dialogo
Spettante alla lode dell'arte Scenica',
published in Florence in 1604, p. 33,
Andreini refers to the *Gelosi* 'che
seguon lieti (Emuli professer) quei, che
FEDELI COMICI appella l'uno e l'altro
Polo'.

[8] Rasi, op. cit., i. 154.

the *Accesi* were in France, *Florinda* was distinguishing the *Fedeli* by her performance in the opera of *Arianna* at Mantua.[1] At a week's notice she took the place of Caterina Martinelli and later appeared with her husband in the 'balletto delle Ingrate'. We owe our knowledge of the membership of the *Uniti* to the disagreements over the next experimental merging with the *Accesi* who had returned from France in the winter of 1608. The first news comes from Florinda, who reports the scandal of *Flaminia*, Cecchini's passion for *Cintio* (Fidenzi?), and promises to procure the one hundred 'ottave' and the forty sonnets in which Marino is said to have written upon the subject to relieve the feelings of the gentlemen of Milan, among whom the company is already in disrepute. The Cecchini are not on speaking terms with the rest of the company and even insult them publicly on the stage. *Lelio*, writing on behalf of Hieronimo (Garavini) Federigo and Carlo Ricci, Aniello and Bartolomeo (Bon Giovani?), pours out the whole story to the Duke of Mantua and beseeches him as shepherd of the flock to cast out the infected sheep. They would rather be idle till Carnival than continue in the company of such odious people. On the other side, *Fritellino* relieved his feelings by planning to retire and set up a little academy in Rome where he might amuse himself now and then with private performances.[2]

The company divided up again; *Fritellino* produced his comedy of *Flaminia Schiava* in Milan at the end of the summer[3] of 1610, and a letter of thanks for clothes and medallions received from the Grand Duke shows that the *Accesi* were in Florence at the end of the year.[4]

The *Fedeli* are to be found in Venice in August 1610,[5] and from Mantua, where they had planned to spend Carnival, *Florinda* applies for a licence to play in Genoa, which, though it was granted on 4 November, may not have come into effect,[6] for in March 1611 she complains that *Fritellino* has managed to persuade the Duke of Mantua to forbid her performance in Genoa and Milan.[7]

[1] *Giorn. Stor.* xxiii, p. 119.
[2] Bevilacqua, *Giorn. Stor.* xxiii, p. 123, and A. Bartoli, op. cit., p. cxxxviii, and *Nuova Rassegna*, 1893, p. 798.
[3] *Gaz. Mus. di Milano*, 1891, No. 38.
[4] Rasi, op. cit., i. 637.
[5] *Giorn. Stor.* xxiii, p. 126.
[6] *Riv. Teatrale It.* 1906.
[7] *Giorn. Stor.* xxiii, p. 129.

The feud between *Flaminia* and *Florinda*, which had spoilt all the Duke of Mantua's efforts to provide for the King of Hungary in 1611,[1] made the choice of a company for the next French tour extremely difficult. The task was thrust upon *Arlecchino* by Maria de' Medici, who writes cunningly in September 1611 that she has arranged that the Signora Hippolita Fodra shall act as her proxy when the next little *Arlecchino* is baptized, but insists that her gift to her god-child must be received in person, charging Martinelli to bring a good company to the French court as soon as possible.[2] In December Martinelli suggests that the flattery of a personal invitation to the other comedians might be effective: *Florinda* is to be found in Bologna, but all letters should come through his hands, and in each he should be mentioned as the leader of the troop.[3] In the Duke of Mantua's opinion the company of *Florinda* and *Arlecchino*, as he had seen it in Ferrara at the end of 1611, was not fit to be sent into France.[4] The Queen was anxious that *Fritellino* should be one of the troop, and that the quarrels which had now arisen within the *Fedeli* between *Florinda* and *Flavia* (Garavini) might be settled. As Martinelli understood it, her ideal company would consist of the Andreini, the Cecchini, the Garavini, himself, and a good *Gratiano* and *Pantalone*,[5] but he knew that this was hardly practicable and went on with his own plans. In August 1612 he still lacked a Zanni; *Pedrolino* was considered too old, but 'Zan Farina, o verò Scapino', might well be enticed from *Fritellino*'s company, where he shared the 'parte moderna' with *Mezzettino* (Ottavio Onorati). If they could also get *Fulvio* (Bruni), who could play the Doctor as well as the Lover, they would be complete.[6] He does not attempt to incorporate the Cecchini, but does his best to bring back *Flavia*, entreating Cardinal Gonzaga to use his authority, and if sweet medicine will not cure her, let him try something bitter, for upon her acceptance the welfare of a whole company depends.[7] At the

[1] Baschet, op. cit., p. 208.
[2] Ibid., pp. 202–3.
[3] Ibid., pp. 204–5.
[4] Ibid., p. 208.
[5] T. Martinelli to Cardinal Ferdinando Gonzago, 26 Oct. 1612. See

'Jarro', p. 53, and F. Marriotti, MS. cit. doc. 29.   [6] 'Jarro', p. 30.
[7] See a letter from T. Martinelli, 6 Nov. 1612, Bologna, MS. Marriotti, Doc. 28, quoted also by A. Bartoli, p. cxli, and 'Jarro', p. 51. Compare a

end of November we see the results of his negotiations in the signatures to a letter from Florence.[1] Bartolomeo Bongiovanni was their *Gratiano*, Federigo Ricci their *Pantalone*, and his son the lover *Leandro*. *Pedrolino* had joined up once more with the two Andreini. The Duke's suggestion of Silvio Fiorillo as *Capitano Mattamoros* had been rejected in favour of their old companion *Rinoceronte* (Garavini), but there is no mention of *Flavia* his wife. The second woman's part was taken, presumably, by *Lidia* Rotari; her husband's role is not specified. We have no means of identifying *Nicolina*, who was probably a Franceschina type.

The Queen's hope that the Italians might be with the court to cheer the 'sad winter days' was not realized. The season in Florence was too remunerative to be curtailed. Until July 1613 Maria continues to extend her welcome to 'tutta l'Arlecchineria', even arranging for a deposit for travelling expenses in Lyons, but the company did not reach Paris until the late autumn.[2] They had earned 500 ducats in a fortnight in Turin; the Governor of Chambéry had paid all their expenses and rewarded them with 50 ducats for one performance, and in Lyons four comedies brought in another 220, apart from special rewards which were expected from the gentlemen.[3] At Fontainebleau the King was even more liberal. Delighted with the first performance, he gave the company 500 ducats and assigned them a salary of 200 ducats a month, paying their expenses and giving more privately to Martinelli for his wife and children.[4] In spite of these extraordinary favours, Martinelli was restless even before the year was out and wanted to return by the next June. He was concerned about his pension and property in Mantua, and tired of the company which, as he confides to the Duke, might please the French audiences but included some who repeated like parrots.[5] Seven years later[6] the Andreini accused him of having broken up the company by

---

letter for 12 Nov. 1612, quoted by Baschet, p. 220.

[1] T. Martinelli to the Duke of Mantua, 26 Nov. 1612, transcribed by Marriotti, II, i, p. 275.

[2] Baschet, op. cit., p. 232.

[3] 'Jarro', op. cit., pp. 54–6.

[4] D'Ancona, op. cit., ii, p. 530, and 'Jarro', op. cit., pp. 58–60.

[5] Letter of Martinelli to the Duke, 3 Feb. 1614, see 'Jarro', op. cit., p. 60.

[6] 2 July 1621. *Giorn. Stor.* xxiv, p. 90.

taking with him the Rotari and the Doctor. In July the Andreini received separate letters of recommendation to the Duchess of Lorraine and the Cardinal Gonzaga.[1]

A proposal that the Andreini, the Cecchini, the Rotari, *Cintio*, and a good Zanni should visit France as the company of 'Duca Nostrano et Moderno', made by *Arlecchino* in a jesting letter to Maria 'his most Christian gossip' in June 1615, does not seem to have materialized.[2]

In September 1612, while the Andreini were in France, *Fritellino* had a good company in Padua complete with three women, three lovers, two *Zanni*, a *Pantalone*, and a *Graziano*.[3] Later the *Accesi* went to Vienna where Cecchini received his patent of nobility from the Emperor Matthias.[4]

In 1615 and 1616 *Fritellino* managed to forestall the *Confidenti* and the *Uniti* in Florence, but according to Scala his company was poor.[5] There are signs of his luck changing during the next year. In March his licence for Florence is to be cancelled in favour of the *Confidenti*,[6] and in February Cecchini offered to give up his licence in Milan to prove that he is innocent of any malice towards the *Confidenti* of Don Giovanni di' Medici.[7] Perhaps the will served for the deed: the *Accesi* were certainly at Novara and Milan between Ascension and Michaelmas.[8]

There is a curious reference to *Fritellino*, *Flaminia*, and *Cintio* as Comici Fedeli in a petition for licence to act in Genoa, conceded on 12 April 1617,[9] but there are no other

[1] Baschet, op. cit., pp. 254–5. See also Mantua Arch., Serie Francia, E. xv. 670. Letter from L. Rotari, 22 Dec. 1613.

[2] Facsimile given by Rasi, op. cit., ii. 103.

[3] Francesco Hondedei to Camillo Oliveri, Padova, 21 Sept. 1612, published by Saviotti in *Giorn. Stor.* xli, p. 51.

[4] F. Barbieri, *Notizie delle Comiche*.

[5] Solerti, *Musica, Ballo e drammatica alla corte de' Medici, 1600–1637* (1905), quotes from the Diary of Tinghi, 1615. 'Nov. — . . . sendo venuto a Firenze Fritellino con una parte de' suoi comici . . .'. A letter from Scala, 5 Nov. 1616 (Arch. Med. Fa 5150. c. 452), refers to their arrival. Placed next to this letter (c. 453) is an undated unsigned note endorsed 'F. Scala', in which he remarks that the company is bad. The note is followed by a letter dated 4 April 1621, which makes the dating a little uncertain, the only other occasion to which it might refer is the season in October 1619, when Fritellino was certainly doing badly in Florence. See letters from Scala, 29 Oct. and 12 Nov. 1619. (Arch. Med. Fa. 5150. c. 619 and 591.)

[6] F. Collareto, 12 March 1617, Livorno. Arch. Med. Fa. 5176. c. 75.

[7] 7 Feb. 1617. Ferrara. Arch. Med. Fa. 5143. c. 247.

[8] *Gaz. Mus. di Milano*, 1891, No. 38.

[9] Belgrano in *Domenica Letteraria*, 1885, IV. i.

signs of an amalgamation in any of the appearances recorded for either troop until proposals for another visit to France brings the Cecchini and Andreini into collision once more.

Baschet draws attention to letters written in December 1618 inviting *Arlecchino* to collect a company for France, but Martinelli had been at work in the previous January trying to wreck the *Confidenti* by taking *Scapino* and *Fulvio*. By this means he hoped to compensate for a rupture between *Fritellino* and *Cintio* by persuading Cecchini to play Pantalone and take *Scapino* as his Zanni.[1] Warned by Scala, Don Giovanni refused to allow the *Confidenti* to be broken up in this way.[2] In January 1618 Martinelli tried again, confiding to Don Giovanni that in deference to the wishes of Louis he had approached *Fritellino*, but found him as untrustworthy as ever, and asking for permission to take *Scapino* from the *Confidenti* to join *Lelio*, *Florinda*, *Gratiano Campanaccio*, *Capitano Rinoceronte*, *Lidia*, with Gabrieli and his wife for *Franceschina*, and if possible Braga for *Pantalone*, and *Flaminio* for the second lover.[3] Unabashed by Don Giovanni's response, which he admits he quite expected, he wrote again at the end of January bargaining for *Mezzettino*, who was to take it in turn with him to play the principal Zanni.[4] The day before *Lelio* wrote to the same effect, reminding Don Giovanni that three Zanni in the company would be neither unusual nor superfluous.[5] The three Zanni who belonged to the *Fedeli* in May were *Arlecchino*, *Gallotta*, and *Cola*, but Andreini is still hoping for *Farina*, and perhaps for Fabrizio.

According to Martinelli, in January 1619 Cecchini's company was so wretched that even *Cintio* had left them.[6]

[1] F. Scala, Mantova, 10 Jan. 1618. Arch. Med. Fa. 5150. c. 581.

[2] Rasi, op. cit., i. 963.

[3] T. Martinelli, Ferrara, 22 Jan. 1619. Arch. Med. Fa. 5143. c. 487.

[4] Ibid., Fa. 5143. c. 488.

[5] Arch. Med. Fa. 5141. c. 763.

[6] Scala mentions a separation in January 1618, but since Martinelli refers to it as a recent occurrence, and according to Baschet both *Cintio* and *Leandro* were with Cecchini in Naples in December 1618, and the company was popular in Rome in the New Year, it is to be supposed there were two quarrels. Certainly by November 1619 the company was notoriously bad: Scala is surprised that Troni should attend to *Fritellino's* application for the rooms in Venice after their poor reception in Florence. By July 1620 he was driven to join up with the Andreini, and Milan is once more the scene of their vicious intrigues and insults. Arch. Med. Fa. 5150. c. 591.

Friction with the Andreini in the summer of 1620 paralysed the amalgamation of *Fedeli* and *Accesi*, who were waiting in Milan for the return of a messenger from France. Even *Lelio* admits that they had lost all public favour and were as needy as 'Pantaloni in gibbone'.[1] Cecchini keeps the Duke informed of all the scandals. In the middle of July he writes to the Duke ostentatiously suppressing many grievances in order to work his accusations to a climax. All the injustices in *Lelio's* casting of the parts, to gratify his favourite actresses and thwart his rivals; all his schemes to leave *Fritellino* high and dry without a company as soon as the French arrangements can be made; all these and more might be overlooked, but his flirtation with *Baldina* is insufferable. Baldo Rotari, the injured husband, seems careless of the insult and is engrossed in tyrannizing over his fellow actors, but *Florinda* is miserable, *Bernetta* often reduced to tears, and the reputation of the company jeopardized. The only remedy is to get rid of *Baldina*, and Cecchini remarks maliciously that she would be the life of 'that company now in Venice'.[2] By the beginning of August Andreini gets wind of the Duke's displeasure and writes facetiously and effusively to protest that his only offence consists in being foolishly long suffering. He regards the affair with *Baldina* as a woman's scandal, and not the first from which he has suffered, remarking that it would indeed be a punishment to be in love with such a creature. His account of the distribution of parts is quite different. As soon as *Fulvio* left, *Aurelio*—'istrice Napolitano' that he is—chased the poor stupid Florentine off the stage and took the lead 'ex improviso' without saying so much as a word to *Lelio*, who was left with a fencing scene, and that in an opera, or allotted the part of a musician who amuses a melancholy king, or allowed to serenade as Coccalino, or, ridiculously dressed, to make a proclamation.

At the end of August *Gallotta* reported that the French patrons were set upon having *Scapino*. Cecchini, therefore, urges the Duke to approach the *Confidenti* yet again, but hardly expecting him to succeed, suggests as an alternative that Pavolino Zanotti (who appears later as *Finocchio*, and is

---

[1] G. B. Andreini to the Duke of Mantua, 18 July, 1620. Arch. Mant.   E. XLIX. 1751.

[2] Arch. Mant. E. XLIX. 1751.

mentioned as a second *Scapino*) should be decoyed from Venice. Although a Spanish-speaking Captain is in request he hopes that the excellence of *Rinoceronte's* Italian may compensate for this deficiency. The present Pantalone is weak, but Cecchini offers to take that part himself. The sting of the letter is in the tail. The company will do no good in France or Italy until it is rid of *Baldina* whose evil influence is reducing *Florinda* to the wildest hysterics.[1]

But Cecchini did not get his own way. A month later Martinelli announces that they have sent for another Pantalone and are taking for the Zanni *Fichetto* (Lorenzo Nettuni?), who has actually been more popular than *Fritellino* in Milan.[2] *Baldina's* intrigues were evidently preferred to Cecchini's grasping conceit. Cecchini felt the insult deeply and once again talked of giving up the stage, but in six weeks' time he was deep in plans to provide a troop for the Mantuan Carnival at all costs. A letter written from Piacenza at the beginning of December lets us into many stage and domestic secrets, and introduces a new set of players whose status is described as something between the 'comico' and 'ciarlatano'. After acknowledging a grant of 50 ducats which is to be reserved for travelling expenses, Cecchini comments spitefully that Barilla and his wife, who have found an excuse for not responding to his invitation, should not have the gratification of thinking that they were indispensable. He hopes that their failure in this matter may be remembered, and particularly that the fat Signor *Fulvio* (Odoardo), who is at the back of it all, may be snubbed. As usual he has another plan red-hot. 'Subito, ma subito', His Highness must send for a company which is now somewhere in the region round Cento, Modena, Finale, or Carpi, with *Flaminio* (Fabri?) who had often served in Mantua with the late Braga. With them is an actress called Silvia who, he understands, is not bad as the second lady: she is the wife of Gio. Maria Bachino, who, as the lover *Fortunio* was the rival, though perhaps the inferior, of Sr. Adriano. *Fortunio* is a Mantuan, however, and therefore can hardly refuse a summons from the Duke. With them is a certain Bolognese who, according to *Matta-*

[1] 28 Aug. 1620. Quoted in part by Rasi, op. cit., i. 153.
[2] A. Bartoli, op. cit., cxlii.

moros, is a passable Magnifico, and, what is more important, his wife *Barzelletta* is excellent as the serving maid. If she can be procured *Olivetta* may go, for her misdemeanours cannot be denied, and she is not wanted in Mantua. These, together with a Neapolitan Gio. Serio Contrallo, should be summoned at once lest they are snapped up for Mirandola. The more economical plan would be for them to remain as they are until after Christmas, and then to proceed direct to Mantua, where Cecchini will meet them. If this chance is lost the Duke will be entertained by a company consisting of *Flaminia,* Aurelio, *Mattamoros, Policiniela, Trofaldino,* with Piermaria (that is Cecchini) left to sustain the parts of the Magnifico, the Doctor, Fritellino, and Pipe, a Florentine. If only Silvia and Fortunio can come, he could manage, but there must be no delay. The letter ends with a characteristic intimacy: 'My wife who is still in bed is shouting at the top of her voice, Kiss the hand of Signor Margliani'.[1]

The company evidently held their own at the Mantuan carnival; but in May Fiorillo received the Duke's permission to visit his family in Naples, and took with him Aurelio, here surnamed 'a Porto'. Their arrangement to join up with the company of *Celia* on their return was not mentioned to *Flaminia* lest her flattering tongue should persuade them to remain with *Fritellino* whose tyranny had become unbearable. Cecchini resented their departure and slandered them by saying that they were in his debt. Fiorillo does not appear again in connexion with the *Accesi,* but Aurelio still considered himself bound to *Fritellino,* and in June wrote quite sincerely to explain that his plan to go into Sicily with Signor Francesco Antonio, alias *Fabrizio,* was prevented by his wife's illness, and he had pledged himself to Sig^r. Andrea della Valle to act for three months in Naples for a salary of 102 scudi, but by September he hopes to be with Cecchini again in Venice in the service of Sig^r. Giustiniani.[2]

The *Fedeli* meanwhile travelled into France by the usual way of Savoy. In Turin there was an exchange of gifts and pleasantries, *Arlecchino* jests with the little Princesses and

[1] See D'Ancona, *Lettere di Comici Italiani,* published 'per nozze Martini-Benzoni', Pisa, 1893, p. 16 seq.

[2] Letters from Mantuan Archives published by W. Smith in *Giorn. Stor.,* 1928, xcii, p. 208.

replenishes his wardrobe and his purse.[1] At Chambéry the young Ricci died and they were short of an Inamorato. They performed regularly at court in January and February 1621 and at the King's special request remained until after Easter. Towards the end of April *Lelio* wished to remain yet another year, but Martinelli, making his age an excuse, begged leave privately to return home. *Lelio* was then persuaded against his better judgement to make this the occasion for inflicting the Duke of Mantua with a seven-page letter in which the company relieved themselves of the accumulated irritation that *Arlecchino's* vanity and imperious temper had caused throughout the tours: even grievances seven years old are revived. The Duke had the sense not to send back *Arlecchino* disgraced, fined, and reprimanded in order to gratify the company; whether he was able to provide a substitute or to send Aurelio, who was suggested to fill the gap left by *Leandro* Ricci's death, does not appear.[2] The Andreini stayed until the following February, and the publication of five comedies in Paris in 1622 shows that Giovan Battista at least had occupied himself profitably.[3] At the end of his campaigns in October 1622 Louis wrote for yet another troop.[4] In December he found players ready to entertain him in Lyons before continuing his journey to Paris. Baschet takes it for granted, but Bevilacqua thinks it unlikely that these were the *Fedeli*.[5] The Andreini were certainly in Turin at Easter:[6] but on the other hand when the King wrote in August asking the Duke of Mantua to send a company for the autumn he mentioned the Andreini, Federigo Ricci and Garavini, who had lately given him such pleasure.[7] The Andreini responded more promptly than usual, and were on their way by November,[8] and stayed in

[1] Baschet, op. cit., p. 277.

[2] Baschet, op. cit., pp. 280 and 298. With the exception of two letters from Louis XIII to the Duke of Mantua (8 Aug. 1621 and 3 Feb. 1622, Mantua Archivio, Serie Francia, E. XV. 628) I have not succeeded in finding the originals of the letters upon which Baschet bases his narrative.

[3] *La Sultana*; *La Ferinda*; *L'Amor nello Specchio*; *I due Lelii Simili*; *La Centaura*. See *Giorn. Stor.* xxiv, p. 114.

[4] Henri de Bourbon, 29 Oct. 1622. Arch. Mant. E. XV. 628. Cp. Baschet, op. cit., p. 314.

[5] *Giorn. Stor.* xxiv, pp. 116–17.

[6] F. Bartoli, *Notizie Storiche*, i. 18.

[7] Louis XIII, 6 Aug. 1623, and the Duke of Nevers, 14 Aug. 1623, Arch. Mant. E. XV. 628.

[8] G. B. Andreini writing from Turin, 12 Nov. 1623. Transcript in Marriotti, MS cit. pt. ii, vol. ii, p. 321.

France at least fifteen months.[1] They had at last succeeded
in attracting from the *Confidenti* Barbieri and *Scapino*.[2]

In a postscript to a letter dated from Turin 12 Nov. 1623
Andreini informs the Duke of Mantua that a certain *Cintia*
is shaping well. Bevilacqua, reading the name as *Cintio*,
laughs at Baschet for supposing that this is a new actress.
His correction would be plausible enough if it were not that
in November *Cintio* was with *Fritellino* in Florence.[3]

Notices of the *Accesi* for this period are scarce but clear:
they were in Piacenza in 1620,[4] in Venice[5] and possibly in
Mantua in 1621, in Venice in 1622,[6] and probably Florence
in 1623.[7] Quarrels in Cremona in 1626 indicate the last of
the *Fedeli* and *Accesi* amalgamations.[8] By September an
attempt to join forces produced the usual crop of angry
correspondence. The company was bound for Mantua when
Cecchini announced his intention of joining the company of
Cintio in Rome, and invited Andreini to accompany him if he
cared for the unity of the troop. For once Cecchini got the
best of it and Andreini was stranded. In a desperate attempt
to muster a company fit to accept an invitation for carnival in
Venice he suggested fetching Carpioni from Piacenza. For
the sake of keeping *Arlecchino*, who was acting again in
Cremona, Andreini was prepared to play the haunted lover
(*innamorato spiritato*) himself to give him a chance for his
famous tumble. He was anxious not to miss the opportunity,
for the other companies were promised at Naples, Rome,
and Modena, and in Venice there would be only that of
'*Moschetta*, *Cintio*, and *Scappino*', with whom he is afraid
Fritellino may also appear.[9] Andreini published *La Cam-
panaccia* in Venice during 1627, and at the end of the year
tried his fortunes at the Emperor's Court. The letter in
which he presents himself to the new Duke of Mantua as his
most devoted servant and minutest worm is dated from
Prague 29 January 1628.[10] The removal of the company to
Vienna is attested by a letter addressed to the Archduchess of

[1] *Giorn. Stor.* xxiv, p. 120.
[2] Baschet, op. cit., pp. 322–3.
[3] Solerti, op. cit., quoting Tinghi, 12 Dec. 1623.
[4] Sanesi, op. cit., p. 21.
[5] *Giorn. Stor.*, 1928, xcii, p. 208.
[6] Sanesi, op. cit., p. 21.
[7] Solerti, op. cit.
[8] Rasi, op. cit., i. 155.
[9] Letters published by Bevilacqua, *Giorn. Stor.* xxiv, pp. 125–6.
[10] *Giorn. Stor.* xxiii, pp. 130–1.

Tuscany in November 1629 from *Lidia* the widow of Rotari, who was shortly to become Andreini's second wife.[1]

There is a note of defiance in the letters of 1633 which are the last records of Andreini's leadership. Rumours of the boasting of Carpioni whose company after that of *Scapino* has been preferred in Mantua before the Duke's own comedians, provokes Andreini to inform His Highness that though he may favour the younger men, these 'our Sibyls' are still in request in Venice, Bologna, and Ferrara. In December, with an admirably sarcastic touch, he announces that 'this miserable remnant of ours' only waits for a second boat since one is not large enough for our belongings, ourselves, and our servants before embarking for Mantua.[2] There is a suggestion of coldness between the *Fedeli* and their patron, but the relationship seems never to have lapsed entirely. Among the last notices of Andreini is a letter dated 1652 applying for the arrears of his pension of 150 ducats and recapitulating the favours and privileges of a lifetime.[3]

SCALA'S *CONFIDENTI*

The history of the *Uniti* and the first *Confidenti* resolves itself into a study of the permutations and combinations of two groups of players: that of the *Accesi* and *Fedeli* presents a sequence of warnings of the wisdom of parting betimes: the fortunes of the *Confidenti* in the seventeenth century are an example of the value and difficulty of maintaining unity within a single company. In the letters of Scala we have an unusual opportunity of estimating by what means and at what cost this was achieved. Even when dissension was hottest the word 'Unione, Unione' was all that their patron could extract as a policy. The weight of responsibility fell upon Scala who acted as the go-between for the players and their patron. There is a characteristic flicker of humour through his despair as he ends his report of the usual disturbances by remarking that 'In short all these accidents are designed for the great tribulation of the poor *Flavio*, for I can think of nothing else but how to maintain a unity, and if you could see me it would remind you of Moses keeping

---

[1] *Giorn. Stor.* xxiii, p. 134. Bevilacqua conjectures that *Florinda* died *c.* 1630.
[2] Ibid., p. 141.
[3] Ibid., pp. 148, 150.

up the hopes of the Hebrew people'.[1] But he was experienced in the profession and took his trials philosophically.

SCALA'S CAREER.

It is presumably the testimony of affection shown in the preface which Francesco Andreini contributed to his friend's *Teatro delle favole rappresentative*, together with the names of the chief masks in those plays, that have misled so many critics into supposing that Scala was ever a member of *Gelosi*. There is no positive evidence for such an attractive theory. No doubt it is right to see in the *Capitano Spavento*, *Isabella*, *Aurelio*, *Oratio*, *Vittoria*, and *Pedrolino* of the scenari, the Andreini, Valerini, Nobile, the Piissimi and Pellesini of real life; the *Zanobio* of scenario 8 and *Piombino* of number 39 obviously owe something to Girolamo da Salimbeni, whose stage name was *Zanobio da Piombino*. *Pantalone*, *Gratiano*, and *Franceschina* are less distinctive, but they were famous masks among the *Gelosi*. But to be consistent we must continue the process and identify *Arlecchino* with Martinelli, *Flaminia* with Orsola Cecchini, *Flavia* with Margharita Garavini, *Cinthio* with Jacopo Fidenzi, *Cassandro* with G. B. Zecca, *Nespola* with the wife of Marcello de' Secchi, players who belonged variously to the *Accesi*, *Fedeli*, and *Confidenti*, but who never appear among the *Gelosi*. Other masks, although not yet to be identified with individuals, can be assigned to their companies: of these *Burattino* is known to have belonged to the *Gelosi*, but *Stefanello Bottarga* is connected with *Ganassa*, *Grillo* with the *Uniti* of 1584, *Ricciolino* with the *Accesi* (1605/6), *Claudio* and *Olivetta* with the second *Confidenti*. For a dozen names we have no clue, but as eight of them are used only once it is not unlikely that they were invented for artistic variety.[2] Obviously Scala has in mind the chief actors of his day without regard to the composition of a company at any particular period. He is working with such an all-star cast as the Duke of Mantua and the King of France had dreamed

[1] 10 Nov. 1618. Arch. Med. Fa. 5150. c. 606.

[2] Ortensia, Ardelia, Laura, Cornelio, Cavicchio, Nicoletto, Cataldo, Leone Adorne, Pasquella, Tofano (there was an actor Thofano early), Silvia (Silvia Bachino ?), *Fabritio* (Fornaris ? or the *Fabrizio* known to Aurelio? See *supra*, p. 289).

of but rarely achieved. His chances of obtaining information about the *Gelosi* through Francesco Andreini, whom he knew intimately during his retirement in Venice, are sufficient to reconcile us to the rejection of the old theory that he was with the company in France. All that we know for certain of his varied experience is that in Genoa in 1597[1] and 1598[2] he was licensee of a troop which Belgrano is probably right in describing as the *Uniti* of the Duke of Mantua; and from the publication of *Il Postumio* at his instance in 1601 we may assume that he was with the *Accesi* in Lyons. Under his stage name of *Flavio*, Scala gives himself a part in thirty-one of his scenari and appears in Andreini's *Due Commedie in Commedia*, but nowhere else is there any reference to his appearance on the stage. Like Drusiano Martinelli he was a director, producer, and agent of companies rather than an actor. As director of the *Confidenti* he lived in Venice carrying on his business, purveying delicacies for his patrons, occupying himself with the publication of his comedy and his tragedy, keeping in close touch with the troop and ready in any emergency to descend upon them with advice, or consolation, or threat, but not making it his business to accompany them on all their tours. Andreini's description of him as of gentle birth (*nobile*) is in keeping with the tone of the letters to Don Giovanni. He was successful with the company because the players respected him, one and all depending upon the tact and good sense of Signor *Flavio*.

In spite of the old name, the *Confidenti* under Scala and Don Giovanni is so entirely different in its composition from that of the former *Confidenti* protected by the Duke of Mantua that it would be misleading not to make a sharp distinction between them. The latest notice that certainly refers to the first *Confidenti* is of their performance in Lucca and Genoa in April 1606.[3] On the authority of Rasi, who does not state his evidence, Lorenzo Nettuni (*Fichetto*) belonged to a company of this name which was touring in the territory of Modena in 1610.[4] It is possible that this was the company of Scala which just then gave such offence to the Cardinal,

[1] D'Ancona, op. cit., ii, p. 520, quotes a number of the *Caffaro* (1882), which I have not been able to check. In this Belgrano refers to Scala in May 1597.

[2] *Caffaro*, 1886, No. 171.
[3] *Riv. Teatrale It.*, 1906.
[4] Op. cit., ii. 183.

that he advised that it should be prohibited.[1] This identification is very insecure, and we know nothing of the *personnel* of the *Confidenti* until 1613, when in the *Rime Funebre*, published in her honour, Camilla Rocca-Nobile is described as *Delia Comica Confidenti*, and her admirer Francesco Antonazzoni assumes the same style. Domenico Bruni, another contributor, does not mention his company, but reappears with Antonazzoni as a loyal member of the troop that came under the patronage of Don Giovanni de' Medici some time during this year or the next.[2]

A letter from G. Z. Hondedei gives an admirable description of the *Confidenti* as he saw them in Bologna at the beginning of November 1615.[3]

This is perhaps the best company that is now on tour, they are always engaged from one carnival to the next, and from here they go to Venice, where they earn what they please. Now as for the personages, first there are two Zanni, the sly one who does the plotting (*che intriga*) is called *Scappino*, and the other who is so witty (*grazioso*) that you could never hear his like, is *Mezzettino*. There are four women, first *Lavinia*, who is the prettiest, the youngest and acts the best, the second *Valeria*, and the other two who take the part of the maid-servants are *Nespola*, and *Spinetta* the wife of *Scappino*. There are two lovers, *Fulvio*, the first, speaks the better, and as I am told once acted at Pesaro in the house of Sig.ʳ Federigo, and this one is the brother of *Valeria* who is no chicken (*la quale è assai di tempo*). The second is *Ortenzio*, husband of *Lavinia*: a *Pantalone*, a Bergomask *Beltrammo*, a *Spanish Captain*, an Italianate Frenchman called *Claudione* complete the troop. *Fulvio*, however, also takes the part of a *Romagnuolo* and of a *Graziano*, and so all play two parts when occasion demands.

Three days later the company is mentioned by name as the *Confidenti*. Hondedei's letter provides an excellent basis for reconstruction. *Scapino* was Francesco, the son of Giovanni Gabrieli, better known in his mask as *Sivello*, a favourite comedian of the Cardinal Caetani, who recommended the son to the Duke of Mantua in 1611. By the spring of 1614 he had proved himself the most attractive member of the *Confidenti* for whom Innocenzo Giustiniani was reserving his theatre in Venice. The quaint rhymes of the *Infirmità*,

[1] Ibid., ii. 513.   5135. c. 12.
[2] I. Giustiniani to Cosimo Baron-   [3] Saviotti, *Giorn. Stor.* xli.
celli, 22 March 1614, Arch. Med. Fa.

Testamento e Morte di Francesco Gabrielli detto Scappino, printed in 1638, give some idea of his famous performance on all kinds of instruments.[1] *Mezzettino* was Ottavio Onorati, a brilliant and versatile actor, but excitable and *spaventoso* and difficult to control.[2] In *Fulvio* we recognize Domenico Bruni trained among the *Gelosi*: Hondedei is mistaken in supposing that he was the brother of *Valeria,* who was by birth an Antonazzoni, the sister of Francesco, the second lover of the troop and husband of the attractive *Lavinia. Valeria's* husband is not mentioned among the comedians, but he was certainly with the company the previous August, acting as their door-keeper and factor, a capacity in which he had served the *Accesi* in 1608. Another member whose presence may be argued from that of his wife was Marcello de' Secchi, the husband of *Nespola*: his stage name was *Aurelio,* but it is possible that in the plays seen by Hondedei he was playing an alternative part such as that of *Claudione.* The *Pantalone* was a Ferrarese Marcantonio Romagnesi, and *Beltrame* was Nicolo Barbieri, author of *La Supplica* and *Oratio Inavvertito.* The Captain is less easy to identify: in 1615 he is called *D. Lopez,* but his real name does not appear.[3] In 1619 Scala is searching for some one to take this part; *Mattamoros* (Fiorillo) is mentioned, but he evidently refused.[4] According to Bruni the new member was not a success, but Scala considers that he will improve.[5] It was probably in some such emergency that Antonazzoni took to playing the Captain,[6] though according to *Scapino* it was because he was too lazy to study for his original role of the lover.[7]

This interpretation of Hondedei's list depends upon the correspondence occasioned by the quarrel between Romagnesi and the Austoni which upset the company in Genoa in the summer of 1616. Battista Austoni took advantage of an insult offered to *Valeria* to bring up an old grievance, and complained that as *portinaro* he was not given a fair share in the company's consultations. The dismissal of Battista,

---

[1] *Propugnatore,* Bologna, 1880, anno XIII, Disp. 1, 2, p. 446.

[2] Scala to Giovanni de' Medici, 2 July 1619. Arch. Med. Fa. 5150. c. 459.

[3] 8 July 1615. Arch. Med. Fa. 5143. c. 65.

[4] Fa. 5150. c. 537.

[5] Arch. Med. Fa. 5150. c. 622.

[6] D. Bruni, Milan, 24 April 1619. Arch. Med. Fa. 5143. c. 529.

[7] Rasi, op. cit., i, 964–5.

advised by Don Giovanni, entailed the loss of an actress. *Ortensio* (Antonazzoni) promises that *Spinetta* will do as much as she can, but she is not strong. The company are against the wife of *Leandro*, who is untrained and has ties of relations and companions, against Isabella because she is married and cannot read, against the daughter of Virginia for fear of her mother, her brother, and their presumption, and decide to invite a certain Violina who is experienced in comedy, learns verses, and sings, provided that she will leave the good-for-nothing husband behind.[1]

The discussion is interesting although it had no practical issue. By September *Valeria* was received back into the company, but Battista's interest in their affairs was strictly limited along lines proposed by Scala.[2] At first *Valeria* was remarkably meek and willing to give up her *Pazzia*, but Scala suspects that *Lavinia's* remarkable success during the season in Florence may be the cause of the returning ill-humour of the Austoni.[3] A year later they were as dangerous as ever and had won *Fulvio* over to their side. They will scarcely return Scala's greeting, and *Fulvio* talks of deserting to the company of *Fritellino*.[4] In the end it was the Austoni who left the *Confidenti*. In March the Antonazzoni were drawn into the quarrel. *Ortensio* suspects that it is *Valeria* who is making *Fulvio* unwilling to act with *Lavinia*: his letter may be reduced to the simple petition that his wife should at least have her share of the lead, but should not be made to act with his sister, nor, if possible, with *Fulvio*.[5] By April Battista has taken leave of the company, but wishing to remain in the favour of Don Giovanni, asks his permission to join *Fritellino* or some other company.[6] The last that we hear of him is sad news; in June 1619 Scala tells Don Giovanni that Battista Austoni has gone blind and mad.[7]

Some time before the departure of the Austoni the *Confidenti* had summoned *Leandro* from Naples, probably to take

---

[1] Letters from Bruni, Pantaleo Balbi, Barbieri, and Romagnesi. Arch. Med. 5143. cc. 191–3, 195, 6.

[2] Lucca, 8 September. Rasi, op. cit., pp. 962–3.

[3] Scala, 23 Oct. 1616. Arch. Med. Fa. 5150. c. 483.

[4] Ibid., c. 476. 10 Oct. 1617.

[5] Maria Antonazzoni to Don Giovanni, 3 March 1618. Arch. Med. 5143. c. 315. See also *Gazz. Lett.*, 11 May 1889.

[6] Arch. Med. Fa. 5143. c. 334.

[7] Ibid., 5150. c. 536.

the place of Marcello de' Secchi, who died in 1617. The new lover is referred to as a young actor,[1] and is probably to be identified with Benedetto, the son of Federigo Ricci, who had already been in France with Andreini and Martinelli. In 1616 his wife was considered hardly experienced enough to take *Valeria's* place,[2] and this presumably is the reason why in April 1618 *Celia* joined the *Confidenti*, accompanied by her mother Virginia and her brother Andrea Maloni. Earlier suspicions of the difficulties that might arise from the admission of this trio were amply realized before the end of the year. The dispute, as usual, is occasioned by the rivalry between the actresses over the mad scene (*la Pazzia*). The company objected to *Celia's* recitation, as far as she can judge, merely because they had heard it before, and tried to change the date of her performance, and in revenge some hasty young gentlemen of Lucca, the admirers of the Maloni, interrupted *Lavinia's* mad scene in *Arianna* with hisses and jeers. The play broke up in confusion, and a day or two later Andrea was assaulted in the street, the company's licence was withdrawn, and everything was referred to Scala, who at once besought Don Giovanni to fulminate against 'this wretched triangle' in a letter that might be read to them publicly as soon as the company should arrive in Florence.[3] The matter was patched up, and by 20 October Scala reports that they are giving complete satisfaction in Florence except for the scandal caused by that 'cursed old woman' who always wants to be on the stage by her daughter's side, teaching her to ogle the Cardinal and the gentlemen who are quite aware of her arts. Behind the scenes they are still in confusion: the 'triumvirate' is generally hated, but *Lavinia* is loved, for although she has her own devil and pride, at least she is not ill-bred and vituperative.[4] By the beginning of November *Celia* has 'sufficiently' recovered from the shock of her reprimand to persuade her brother and the Cardinal de' Medici to write to Don Giovanni on her behalf.[5] The

[1] F. Antonazzoni, 4 March 1618. *Gazz. Lett.*, art. cit.

[2] Arch. Med. Fa. 5143. c. 196.

[3] Scala, 17 Oct. 1618. Arch. Med. Fa. 5150. c. 519. The letters dealing with this scandal have also been published by A. Neri in *La Scena Illustrata* (1887).

[4] Arch. Med. Fa. 5150. c. 545 and 517.

[5] *Scena Illustrata* (1887), and Arch. Med. Fa. 5141. cc. 216, 225–7.

Cardinal's remarks were guarded and her own weak excuses end with the naïve admission of her financial reasons for holding *riffe* in her rooms.[1] Scala finds this practice is damaging the company's interests in Florence, for the young gentlemen who gamble with *Celia* at home object to paying at the door when they come to the play.[2] Peace was at length restored by Don Giovanni, who 'acted like an angel from heaven'. Scala hopes he may be pardoned for stealing a copy of his letter.[3] *Celia* admitted that she had been foolish and misled by her family, and Scala regained her confidence by befriending her when she was humiliated by some young men in the audience during her performance in December.[4] After this satisfactory mortification her behaviour was exemplary, and it is only the 'old woman' who makes difficulties in 1619 when *Celia* wishes to marry *Cintio*, who had just joined the company.[5] Later groupings of the *Confidenti* indicate that she managed to prevent the match.

As soon as Scala had settled the domestic affairs of the company he was aware of enemies without. There was never any difficulty in finding work: they were successful in Florence, they were always welcomed in Genoa and Bologna, and often in request at Mantua and Modena. When there seemed to be some doubt of getting good terms from Ettor Troni, Bruni was able to show letters from Parma proving that it was not for lack of other invitations that they wished to appear in Venice.[6] They agreed to give ten or twelve comedies in Mirandola in 1619,[7] and could only accept the repeated invitation to Ferrara by promising to attend on the

---

[1] The conduct of this fashionable gambling game is explained by Ottinelli. 'The lady puts on the table some trinket, as for example a ring, to serve as a prize for the winner in the subsequent lottery; before the draw each player makes a deposit of the sum, or customarily something over the sum, at which he values the prize, and this money is handed over to the lady who in the end usually recovers the ring in addition, for the winner would hardly be considered well-bred who did not reward the actress very gallantly.' (*Christ. Moderatione* (1655), pte. i, p. 157; quoted by D'Ancona in his translation of Montaigne's *Voyage en Italie* (1895).)

[2] Arch. Med. Fa. 5150. c. 608.

[3] Ibid., Fa. 5150. cc. 613, 614.

[4] Scala, 25 Nov. 1618. Fa. 5150. c. 549. *Celia*, 30 Nov. Fa. 5141. cc. 269, 270, and Scala, 15 Dec. Fa. 5150. c. 617.

[5] Arch. Med. 5150. c. 546, 29 Nov. 1619.

[6] Arch. Med. Fa. 5143. c. 668, 12 Nov. 1619.

[7] Romagnesi, 14 Nov. 1620. Arch. Med. Fa. 5143. c. 898.

Cardinal there if the season in Venice would permit.[1] Other companies occasionally forestalled them, but only once, when the *Confidenti* are upset by the quarrels of the Austoni, does Scala admit any anxiety that a rival performance might lessen their reputation. The danger lay from the opposite direction and was the result of their success.

At the beginning of 1618 *Arlecchino* was collecting a company for France, and to Scala's annoyance begins to hover round the *Confidenti*, approaching Scala, Bruni, and Gabrielli personally, and putting pressure to bear on Don Giovanni by letters from the Duke of Mantua. The *Confidenti* were willing to go into France as Don Giovanni's company, but refused to be broken up.[2] But Martinelli persisted and set Andreini to work.[3] The Duke sent *Lucchesino*, a favourite comedian, to Milan to entice the Antonazzoni and *Scapino*. *Lucchesino* pretended that his business was only to deliver to *Lavinia* the 500 lines which she was to memorize for the comedy that the Duke of Mantua was preparing for the Grand Duke, but Scala had wind of his plots through *Mezzettino*, who was in the confidence of the Duke of Feria and admitted that he could do nothing but shrug his shoulders and say it is the Duke; meanwhile he said nothing to *Scapino* because of his pride and ambition, but bided his time.[4] His policy succeeded, and in July he reported that, thanks to the Duke of Feria, *Lucchesino* had been discovered as a fraud and his talk of 1,030 scudi had gone up in smoke.[5] The suggestion that the whole company should go into France was Scala's next problem. The invitation came through the son of Giovanpavolo Pij, who had been commissioned to choose players for Louis, and preferred the *Confidenti* before the company with *Fritellino*. All except *Scapino* favoured the plan.[6] For the sake of the company Scala was willing to accept the offer, though for himself he dreaded the fatigue of the journey.[7] But as soon as the matter came into the hands

[1] Scala, 3 Dec. 1619. Arch. Med. Fa. 5150. c. 620, 451, 695.

[2] Scala, 10 Jan. 1618. Arch. Med. Fa. 5150. c. 581, 583, and Rasi, op. cit., i. 963.

[3] Martinelli, 22 Jan. 1619. Fa. 5143. c. 487; Andreini, 29 Jan. Fa. 5141. c. 763.

[4] 2 and 10 July 1619. Arch. Med. Fa. 5150. c. 459 and 484.

[5] 24 and 31 July. Fa. 5150. c. 569 and 536.

[6] Fa. 5150. c. 619.

[7] Ibid., c. 486.

of the Duke of Mantua the prospect clouded.[1] He wished the company to travel in his name, to include *Arlecchino* and other players in his patronage. Scala appealed to Don Giovanni who was embarrassed to know what to advise. Separately each of the *Confidenti* refuses to leave his patronage: collectively, in spite of all their quarrels, they have but one cry 'Unione, Unione'. He sees that division would be their ruin, but as a poor gentleman he cannot pretend to support them in such luxury as the takings of their last year have provided. He has no right, therefore, to order them to go or to stay, but speaking from long experience of the ways of comedians, he informs the Duke that if any of the *Confidenti* are sent as the subordinates of *Arlecchino*, *Lelio*, *Fritellino*, and *Flaminia*, not a company but a tower of Babel will be sent into France.[2] The Duke had pledged himself to the Grand Duke and the Grand Duke had already sent the list to the King.[3] They expostulate, but Don Giovanni and Scala evidently stood firm, for the *Confidenti* remained intact and were much in demand in Italy until the end of 1621.

There is a note from Scala, written from his house in Venice on 2 April 1621, admitting that he is weary of the squabbles of the company; quite suitably this is his last appearance in connexion with the players,[4] but until May 1626 there was still a company in the patronage of Don Giovanni.[5] In 1621, however, there seems to have been a division of the *Confidenti* into two groups. Fiorillo refers specifically to the company of *Celia*,[6] who in September asks the Duke of Mantua to recommend her company to Carlo de' Medici.[7] When *Scapino* and Beltrame returned from France in 1626 they parted, the one to the Maloni and the other to the Antonazzoni faction. At the beginning of 1627 Gabrielli writes to A. Constantini 'da *Scapino*', and not 'da Franchesco', as he observes, giving him his private opinion of all his old companions, discouraging the suggestion made

[1] Arch. Med. Fa. 5150. cc. 588 and 620.

[2] Rasi, op. cit., ii. 517–19.

[3] H. Marliani, 25 March 1620. Arch. Med. 5143. cc. 752, 753.

[4] Arch. Med. Fa. 5150. c. 457. The latest letter extant seems to be the note

written on 24 April. Ibid., c. 454.

[5] P. Balbi, 20 May 1626. Fa. 5143. c. 1054.

[6] 11 May 1621. *Giorn. Stor.* xcii, p. 209.

[7] V. Gonzaga to Cardinal de' Medici, 23 Sept. 1622. Fa. 5187. c. 160.

by the Duke of Mantua that his group should join up with
the Antonazzoni and other old members of the *Confidenti*
who were now associated with the Cecchini. His remarks are
most illuminating. We learn that not only would it be difficult to get *Lavinia* without taking Beltrame, who was his
creditor for 500 scudi, but also that she is useless in improvisation and can only be used in premeditated comedy.
Ortensio is a failure both as a lover and a captain. *Cintio*
will not leave *Franceschina* and her husband, and to have
all three would destroy the balance of parts. *Mezzettino*
does not tumble, and in any case will not come without *Olivetta*, whose mask only duplicates that of *Spinetta*
Gabrielli. *Fritellino* is universally disliked and had better
find some more princes to finance him: his wife is old but
still wants to play the simple maiden. The gouty *Pantalone*
(*Pantalone della Podagra*) is well named, for he is so stiff that
he cannot even unlace his mask and stands on the stage like
a block. *Scapino* goes on to insist that there is no need to
augment his own company. *Flavia* is beyond praise both in
prepared and improvised comedy. *Pantalone* is experienced
in old and new *soggetti* in his mother tongue: *Bagattino* is
a second *Arlecchino*. *Scapino* himself and his wife, the
Doctor, the *Captain* and *Citrullo* (i.e. *Policinella*, possibly
Fiorillo) need no commendation. The *Inamorato* is their
only weakness, but they hope to find some studious youth in
Florence, that school of Tuscan speech.[1]

From Gabrielli's description we recognize the other branch
of the *Confidenti* when it appears in distress six months later
in Genoa. There had been trouble with *Mezzettino*, who had
decided that *Olivetta* would be the ruin of his fortune, his
body, and his soul. But when a good *Graziano* had been
found to take the place of *Olivetta*, *Mezzettino* immediately
announced that he could not do without her. He was told
that he should keep her, but at his own expense and without
saying a word, while the company were performing *Filli di
Scio*, he ran away still owing them 100 scudi. He was over-
taken near Piacenza but refused to yield, and the company
sent for *Bagolino* or *Gonella* to fill the gap. The letter
was signed by five members of the old *Confidenti*, Fidenzi

[1] Rasi, op. cit., i, pp. 964-5.

(*Cinthio*), Barbieri, Romagnese, Francesco Antonazzoni, and his wife together with Paolo Zanotti for *Finocchio*, Fulvio and Leonora Castiglioni for the lovers, Hercole Nelli as the *Doctor*, G. B. Zecca as *Cassandro*, and his wife *Franceschina*.[1] *Scapino* continued in the patronage of the Duke of Mantua until 1636, when his troupe was disbanded out of disgust for the mistress whom he wished to introduce into their company.[2] *Cinthio* and *Beltrame* appear with Castiglioni in 1638.[3]

The extant correspondence of the members of the *Accesi*, *Fedeli*, and second *Confidenti* tends to bring these companies to the fore. Undoubtedly they led the profession for the first thirty-five years of the seventeenth century, but the chance survival of other letters and pamphlets show that they were not quite alone in the field. *Florinda's* petition for licence to act in Genoa refers to five companies in 1610.[4] Notices of a troop calling themselves the *Avventurosi*,[5] who were engaged to play in Florence in that year, and of the *Comici Costanti*, who, after some delay, had succeeded in obtaining a licence for Genoa the preceding summer,[6] help to make up her total. From the single mention of the *Avventurosi* it is impossible to say whether they were a regular or a dilettante group. For the *Costanti* we have a list. Among them was Gabrielle detto *Francatrippe*, styled *Comico Geloso*, together with Hippolito Montini, who was certainly, and Vittoria Amorevoli (*Isabella*) who was probably, formerly of the *Uniti*. It is unfortunate that the letter quoted by Rasi in which seven members of the company apply to the Duke of Modena for aid in recovering a debt from Pantalone Scarpetta should be undated. A limit is set, however, by the occurrence of the name of *Aurelio* de Secchi, who died in 1617.[7]

The pamphlet of *La Scena Illustrata*, published by Bartolomeo Cavalieri in 1634, quoted by Francesco Bartoli in his *Fatiche Comiche*, which is the original source of information

---

[1] Arch. Med. Fa. 5176. c. 464. See also *Riv. Teatrale It.*, 1906.

[2] Hondedei, May, 1636. See Saviotti, *Giorn. Stor.* xli.

[3] Rasi, op. cit., i. 880.

[4] *Riv. Teatrale It.*, 1906, fascio 4.

[5] Card. Bonifacio-Caetani to Antonio de' Medici. Rome, 22 Sept. 1610. Arch. Med. Fa. 5131. c. 61.

[6] See *Riv. Teatrale It.*, 1906, fascio 4; B. Brunelli, *Teatri di Padova*, p. 64; Rasi, op. cit., i. 743.

[7] F. Scala, 22 June 1617. Arch. Med. Fa. 5150. c. 480.

on the *Affezionati*, suggests that this company was of later composition. From an oblique reference in Sir Aston Cokaine's expanded scenario of *Trappolino suppos'd a Prince* it may be assumed that Silvio Fiorillo, as well as his son Giovan Battista, belonged to the *Affezionati* in 1632.[1]

According to A. Bartoli, Silvio Fiorillo once belonged to a company called the *Risoluti*, and Maria Malloni to another known as the *Spensierati*.[2] Of these there is no corroborative evidence.

ECONOMY OF THE COMPANIES

It is not merely for lack of information that the history of the companies must be told largely in terms of the inter-action of individual actors and their patrons. Personality still counted for most. There is no need to amass examples of the way in which the system of patronage explains the apparent contradictions between the accepted custom and the official pronouncements. From 1560 to roughly 1620 is a period of adjustment. The profession had not yet achieved complete independence. It was still more advantageous to please the influential few than to attract plebian crowds for whom they could not always be sure of adequate accommodation in the hired rooms.[3] The players, however, did not make the mistake of confining themselves to one or other audience, but attempted a precarious existence serving both. Their status was determined by their charm: as favourites they might rise to a patent of nobility, like Cecchini and Costantini to privileged offices, or to the licence of familiarity: they took care to grapple their admirers with the hoops of god-parentage. Meanwhile their finance and scenic resources were determined by their status.

FINANCE: REWARDS, TAXES, AND CHARGES FOR ACCOM-MODATION

As a general financial policy the scheme of profit-sharing on the basis of the proportion originally contributed to the company's capital, with deductions for the common expenses of travel and accommodation, which is laid down in the agree-

---

[1] See *Mod. Lang. Rev.*, xxiii.

[2] Op. cit., p. cl.

[3] D'Ancona, op. cit., p. 499. In 1572 the *Gelosi* complain that the 'stanze' in Genova only take about 150 gentlemen.

ments of the early Paduan, Roman, and Neapolitan troupes, seems to have worked satisfactorily. The practice no doubt kept the players aware of their mutual dependence and so made for unity. The system was not quite rigid: youths such as Checo the smith were hired for a part share or a fixed salary, and older players made terms for a season.[1] Favourites like *Arlecchino* received extra rewards over and above the sums paid them on behalf of the company. In 1621 the King gave him a chain of 200 *écus*, 'comme à mon compère mais non pour les comédies'.[2] Some members of the *Gelosi* travelled with their private servants who were to be distinguished from the general servitors. The 'ragazzo' of Orazio de Nobile was presumably an attendant, and perhaps an apprentice.[3] It is impossible to make any estimate of the average income of the company or the individual in terms of modern monetary values. For the purposes of precise reckoning the fragmentary details that remain are probably more misleading than instructive. We have notices of rewards given to itinerant Italian entertainers at the Imperial and Papal Courts, but we do not know the number of actors or performances that they were to cover. The French records are a little more circumstantial but not always consistent. In 1572 the sum of 'six vingt quinze livres turnois' (approx. £5, Elizabethan) was disbursed three times, once to Soldino for his expenses from Paris to Blois,[4] a second time for himself and eleven companions, and again to Anton Maria. The amalgamated troop of Soldino and Anton Maria, amounting to 18 persons, received 250 *livres turnois* (£9 7s. 6d.). In the autumn of that year *Ganassa* and 6 companions received 75 *livres turnois* (£1 16s. 3d.), and later as a gift '500 livres turnoys et XVII testons à 12 sols six deniers turnoys pièce' (approximately £18 16s.). In 1578 Massimiano was paid 35 *écus sol* (£17 10s.), and Paolo di Padova and his companions '30 *escuz* sol vallant 90 livres tournoy'.[5] According to the official entry the *Gelosi* received 600 *écus* for five months, but Isabella writes that the company was granted 200 *écus* a month.[6] Possibly there was some intermediate or

---

[1] See *supra*, p. 256.

[2] Quoted by Baschet, op. cit., p. 290.

[3] *Gazz. Mus. di Milano*, 1891, No. 34.

[4] Baschet, op. cit., p. 35.

[5] Ibid., pp. 42, 44, 87.

[6] Ibid., p. 137.

supplementary payment. Martinelli's company received 600 *livres* a month for entertaining Louis in 1614.[1] The Duke of Mantua advanced 1,000 *scudi* to *Fritellino's* company for their journey into France in 1607.[2] It was the Queen's custom to allow Martinelli to claim his travelling expenses from her treasurer in Lyons; in 1612 they amounted to 1,200 *ducats d'or*; on the arrival of the troop in Paris they received another 500 with a promise of 200 a month. Martinelli as usual had private presents in return for pledging his future children to royal god-parentage.[3]

The visit to the Duke of Savoy before crossing the Alps was always worth the delay. Martinelli is exuberant over their entertainment in Turin in 1620. In seventeen performances they had made 250 *ducatons*.[4] Every one had received gifts: *Lelio* 200 *dobblone* (about £100) and a fine scarlet coat, *Florinda* a jewel, *Lidia* 'une belle toilette', *Arlecchino* a magnificent garment from the Ducal wardrobe, a medallion, a jewelled hat band, and a chain of 100 *dobblone*; a fine horse was to be at the disposal of the company at their departure and there was talk of 'un millier de ducatons' (*c.* £300).[5] At Lyons in 1613 four public performances brought in about 220 *ducats* at a charge of 10 *soldi* a head with free accommodation. At Chambéry M. de Lanoze lodged and fed them and gave a reward of 50 *ducats*.[6]

Martinelli, Cecchini, and Andreini and other favourites may have lived sumptuously, but special rewards cannot be taken as a basis of income, and Ottonelli remarks that the poor prospects of the acting profession in Italy at the middle of this century made it impossible for players to live decently without the help of their patrons. Barbieri was said to have left a fair fortune, but many went hungry.[7] In 1618 the *Confidenti* were in debt for 350 *scudi*, and Scala writes that

[1] Baschet, op. cit., p. 249. Reckoning that these were as usual 'livres tournois', the salary was approximately £22 10s., or in modern values £170.

[2] T. Guiscardi hoped to be able to recover the sum from His Majesty's Treasury, but Cecchini made difficulties and was obviously penniless. 13 Feb. 1608. Arch. Mantua. E. XV. 666.

[3] D'Ancona, op. cit., ii, p. 530; and Baschet, op. cit., p. 234.

[4] At Coryat's reckoning a 'ducaton' was worth six shillings.

[5] Baschet, op. cit., p. 234.

[6] T. Martinelli, 26 Aug. 1613. 'Jarro', op. cit., p. 37.

[7] Ottonelli, op. cit., p. 127.

a gift from the Duke of Mantua, who was expected to be in Florence for Carnival, was their only hope.[1]

Of the takings and expenses of public performances we have only the scantiest notices and it is impossible to co-ordinate them with any scale of charges. *Ganassa* proposed to recover the 600 *reals* (£15) advanced towards the im-provement of the theatre in Madrid at the rate of 10 *reals* for each play. Beyond the entrance fee of half a *real* he charged a *real* for a chair and a quarter of a *real* for a seat on the benches.[2] In Paris his list of prices varying from 3 to 6 *sous* was considered excessive.[3] The *Gelosi* were allowed to take a *demi-teston* from each spectator admitted to their comedies in the Salle des États at Blois: in Paris they charged 4 *sous* and compounded with the Confrères de la Passion at the price of one *écu turnois* for each performance.[4] In Lyons the price rose to 10 *sous* for the special performances of Martinelli's company in 1613.

In Rome the *Desiosi* are said to have demanded one *giulio* for a comedy, two for a tragedy, and 10 *scudi* for a private performance.[5] In 1619 Cecchini was asking 25 *scudi* to-gether with provisions (*cose mangiative*) for each comedy and was prepared to play twice daily.[6] Obviously the charges vary according to the standard of accommodation, the class of the audience, and the popularity of the players: no doubt they got always as much as they could and less than they would.

Receipts from public performances were diminished by the cost of hired accommodation. Of the arrangements be-tween the players and the owners of suitable rooms we have very little information. In 1567 the Duke of Mantua ap-proved the request of Leone De Somi for a ten years' monopoly of a room furnished for professional players,[7] but we do not know what conditions De Somi proposed to the companies. In view of a poor season in 1590 the *Gelosi*, who were delayed for some months in Milan, petitioned to be excused payment for the reserved Salone in Florence.[8]

[1] Arch. Med. Fa. 5150. c. 608.
[2] See *supra*, p. 259.
[3] Baschet, op. cit., p. 20.
[4] Ibid., pp. 73–4.
[5] E. Calvi, 'Teatro popolare Roma-nesco nel cinquecento' in *Italia Mo-derna*, 1908.
[6] Rasi, op. cit., i. 637.
[7] D'Ancona, op. cit., ii. 106 and 404–5.
[8] Arch. Med. Fa. 823. c. 497.

Francesco Andreini made his contract with Alvise Michiele, owner of the 'Stantia' in Venice, an excuse for refusing an invitation from the Duke of Mantua in 1583.[1]

In 1619 Scala found it hard to choose between Lorenzo Giustiniani, who offered half the receipts from the boxes (*palchetti*), and the Troni, whose rooms the *Confidenti* had usually hired. According to the usual arrangement, the Troni gave a quarter of the takings from the boxes, nothing from the stanza, and left the hiring of the seats to the company.[2] But a letter from Ettor Troni cancelling the offer of the box-receipts upset Scala's calculations. He admits that for other than festival seasons it was usual to pay 2 *zecchini* a day and to expect nothing from the boxes, but insists that at Christmas and Carnival the players depended on the use of the boxes free of charge. During the negotiations for a recovery of the original terms Scala discusses invitations from four other cities. The prospect of Modena does not please because it is reported that the room is poor, but Ferrara could give free accommodation and 100 *scudi*, and this year they would give 500 *scudi* with the certainty of an unbroken season. At Mirandola they could earn 100 *scudi* for ten or twelve comedies. The details of the offer from Parma are not given.[3] In 1614 the Andreini paid 400 *livres turnois* for the rent of the premises of the Hôtel de Bourgogne with its 'grand (*sic*) salle, loges, théâtre et galleries' for two months.[4] In 1621 the rent of a 'stanza' in Naples advanced by Andrea de della Valle was 102 *scudi*.[5]

There were also taxes imposed by the civic authorities. The Sala del Pallone in Bologna was rented to players for 100 *lire* paid in alms to the 'suore della santa'.[6] A propor-

---

[1] D'Ancona, op. cit., ii. 484–5.

[2] 'Vogliano li signori Troni dare alli comici che recitano nelle loro stanza, il 4 di quello si cava delli palchetti, e stanza per nulla affitando noi per noi le seggie.' The matter is discussed in six letters from Scala, written in October and November 1619. See Arch. Med. Fa. 5150. cc. 592, 619, 591, 588, 590, 589. According to Ottonelli (quoted by D'Ancona, op. cit., ii. 405), the four grades of accommodation in the *stanzone* were, the *stanzino*, the *palchetto*, *scabello*, and *sedia*.

[3] Arch. Med. Fa. 5150. c. 592.

[4] Baschet, op. cit., p. 251.

[5] *Giorn. Stor.* xcii., p. 209.

[6] C. Ricci, *Teatri di Bologna nei secoli xvii, xviii* (1888), quotes from Giudicini, 'Cose notabili della città di Bologna' 1868, 'nel 1581 vi si recitarano comedie da istrioni venali i quali durante le recite pagarono lire cento la settimana in elemosina alle suore della santa'.

tion of the receipts was demanded for like charities in Naples[1] and Lyons.[2] In 1601 the Governor of Milan ordained that the Collegio delle Vergini Spagnole should be partially supported by dues from 'Comici, Ciarlatani, Montaimbanci, and Erborari' and other merchants and entertainers of the market-place with the exception of vendors of medicine. In 1611 by special concession persons appointed by the administrators of the college might demand not more than 5 soldi for a 'cadrega' and half the price for a 'scabello', and were authorized to collect the money themselves and to sell fruit, wine, and other refreshments. According to the same ruling the players might charge up to 5 soldi for an ordinary, and 10 for a special comedy, with the provision that in certain cases when the cost of production was very heavy the prices might be raised by special concession.[3] From this it appears that it was the custom in Italy as in England for the players to charge a uniform entrance fee and for the owners of the house to collect what they could for the seating accommodation which they provided. The Milanese arrangement throws some light on the negotiations between the Scala and the Troni. Disturbances such as those experienced by Battista Austoni, whose duties as door-keeper in 1608 involved him in a brawl with the Parisian who had refused him the entrance money, and the trouble with the youths of Florence and Lucca who claimed free admittance as the friends of *Celia*, prove the wisdom of the Milanese precaution that the owners of the rooms should also appoint responsible people to help at the door so that no one might slip in free. Possibly the abuse of loiterers was the reason why the players wished that the door opening on to the street from the Duke's *stanzino* in Florence might be built up. As Salimbeni explained in his letter, Padre Barbarino might reach his box by another entrance and the inconvenience formerly suffered by the actors would be avoided.[4]

THE ECCLESIASTICAL OPPOSITION

The ecclesiastical disapproval of the stage manifested

[1] Croce, *I Teatri di Napoli.*
[2] Baschet, op. cit., p. 25 n. 1.
[3] *Gaz. Mus. di Milano*, 1891, No. 36.
[4] G. Salimbeni, detto *Piombino,*

to the Secretary of the Grand Duke. 3 Dec. 1594. Arch. Med. Fa. 853, c. 636.

itself in the compilations of bulky tracts of quotations from the Fathers, corroborated by instances deduced from the natural disasters and social corruptions which might be regarded as signs of Divine retribution for the indulgence of this form of amusement.

The patristic denunciation of representation or disguising as reminiscent of the abuses of the later Roman stage and the itinerant *mimi* was an old-fashioned weapon dragged into position in each treatise and left as an imposing rather than an effective emblem of defence. The most valuable contribution made in these treatises is the contemporary testimony of the reputation and character of the chief actors of the period. It is needless to remark that while he is addressing the general public all Cecchini's geese are swans, but allowing for this bias the facts which he provides are valuable in reminding us of the status of the best actors and support the reputation of the professional against the generalized accusations better than the well-worn arguments and questionable incidents of conversion. Even Ottonelli is bound to admit the virtuous character of Garavini and Chiesa. The controversy over the morality of the acting profession was apt to turn on the interpretation of the word 'istrione'. Locatelli makes it synonymous with the mercenary players from whom he dissociates himself entirely, and addresses his observations to the 'virtuoso accademico'. For professionals such as Barbieri, Andreini, Cecchini, and Giovan Paolo Fabri, who were concerned to justify their position, there were other means of evasion. Andreini distinguishes between charlatans and stage players,[1] Barbieri protests against the injustice of condemning modern comedians for the misdemeanours of bygone generations.[2] The discussion is apt to resolve itself into the bandying of quotations and examples, and Cecchini supplies anecdotes illustrating the salutary effects of comedy by way of a counterblast to the classical instances of corruption, ingeniously making use of the testimony of courtesans and makers of playing-cards who were obliging enough to complain that the superior attraction of the comedians had ruined their trades.[3] The old argument that vice is cured by

[1] *Saggia Egiziana* (1604). *Prologo in dialogo fra Momo e la Verità* (1612).
[2] *La Supplica.*
[3] *Discorsi intorno alle Comedie* (1614).

the spectacle of vice overthrown is worn as shabby as the Ciceronian definition of comedy as 'imitatio vitae, speculum consuetudinis, imago veritatis'.

Ottonelli distinguishes *comedianti* who act in private houses or in appointed rooms from *ciarlatani* who act in the piazza. On the whole he disapproves more of the open-air performances and considers that it is a graver sin to encourage the 'ciarlatani del banco' than to frequent the 'stanzone'.[1] He is not quite consistent on this point, for on another occasion he remarks that the Comedia of the 'stanzone' is the more dangerous and expensive practice,[2] and admits further that he could not resist the attraction of that mountebank in Palermo, whose tales were so wholesome and laughable that the people would leave the Zanni troop and flock to him.[3] Even his preliminary distinction is blurred by his own description of the intermediate type of players here called 'Comici ciarlatani'. A company of these fine fellows come to a city with their womenkind, without whom they are of little account, and advertise a free entertainment. They choose a central position for their stage, and at a popular hour a Zanni begins strumming or singing to collect an audience, he is joined by other actors, and often the woman shares in their preliminary variety show until the head arch-charlatan arrives to cry his remedies. When he has secured the collection the comedy begins: the boxes and trunks are packed away, the benches changed into a scene, each charlatan into a comedian, and there begins a dramatic performance which delights the people for about two hours.[4]

The set of practical reasons used for the attack on the players are fairly represented in the letter of Cardinal Paleotti of Bologna. This shrewd observer declared that experience no longer served the ancient purpose of correcting vice. Apart from the fact that those who act for a livelihood have no legal status, he insisted that the majority of the players were notorious vagabonds accompanied by women of a like reputation. He regarded the playhouses as the haunts of women of doubtful character, and comedies as an excuse for the youths to play truant and to steal from their parents and

[1] Op. cit., p. 489.   [3] Ibid., p. 446.
[2] Ibid., p. 457.   [4] Ibid., p. 455.

employers, and a temptation to the nobility to squander their estates upon the actresses. In times of heresy and pestilence the crowding at the comedies was particularly undesirable.[1] From unbiased evidence outside the clerical connexion incidents might be produced in support of each of these objections, but throughout the period of the Renaissance the Church was on the losing side. The theory of the educational value of the comedy of Plautus and Terence and the tragedy of Seneca made a fatal breach in their defensive attitude. The humanistic revival of classical drama awoke a natural aptitude for plays and made it increasingly difficult to maintain a standard. Popular comedies found a way into the private rooms of Cardinals. Even within the ranks of the clergy there were those who dared to publish their reasons in favour of the art. Reports of Cardinal Delfino's defence of comedy —classical comedy though it was—agitated Carlo Borromeo in 1566; and the case of the Friar of Brescia who, after housing the players and writing a pamphlet in praise of their art, was received back as Prior of his convent, so scandalized the Council of Milan that they forbade the offer of hospitality to players of any sort within the diocese.[2]

The reiteration of the rule that members of religious orders should not attend plays hints at the frequency with which this counsel of perfection was evaded. Up till the time of a special prohibition in 1567 Rogna notes that in Mantua as many as twenty-five clergy might be seen together at the comedies.[3] In Lucca the deterrent was a fine of 2 gold *scudi* and fifteen days imprisonment.[4]

It is particularly ironical that it should have been in Milan that the English observer remarked the Jesuits' enjoyment of the performance of the *Gelosi*.[5] They laughed under the very nose of S. Carlo Borromeo whose efforts to control theatrical activities may be taken as representative of the sixteenth century. The documents are collected in the *Sentimenti di S. Carlo Borromeo intorno agli spettacoli* (1759)

[1] *Sentimenti di San Carlo Borromeo intorno agli Spettacoli* (1759), p. 88 n.

[2] M. Scherillo, *La Commedia dell'arte*, ch. VI, 'San Carlo Borromeo e la Commedia dell'arte'.

[3] 31 July 1567. D'Ancona, op. cit., ii. 454.

[4] Sanesi, op. cit., p. 51.

[5] State Papers, Foreign, 1585. Newsletter LXXII, 23.

and commented upon and partly supplemented by Scherillo in his study of the Commedia dell'arte.

In a letter to Paleotti in 1578 Borromeo admits that practical difficulties have now and then reduced his ideal of the abolition of 'histriones et mimos caeterosque circulatores' to expedients of temporary or partial restrictions.[1] In sermons and proclamations in Milan he denounced the stage and all its works incessantly, and during the election of Gregory III did his utmost by propaganda among the Spanish Cardinals. The authorities were not wholeheartedly or consistently on his side. Rome was a broken reed. Borromeo was alternately alarmed, reassured, and alarmed again by news of its prohibitions and patronage of comedies. A remark in the letter of Cardinal Carniglia in January 1574 typifies the uncertainty of the situation:

'At the occurrence of a representation in Rome of a decidedly immoral comedy (*assai dishonesta*) attended, it is said, by several Cardinals, His Holiness has issued a proclamation forbidding the comedians even in private houses, and I hope it may be observed.' In 1570 the prohibition of stage plays in Rome during the wars between Turkey and Cyprus was extended to Milan: when Borromeo visited Ferrara, Verona, Venice, and Vicenza comedies were suspended in deference to his views. But as soon as the war crisis was over, or the Bishop had gone elsewhere, the comedians returned. Letters from the Bishop of Cremona and from a gentleman of Piacenza begging Borromeo to use his influence to check the comedians who were pandering to social vices refreshed his zeal, but the taste for theatrical entertainments shared by the majority of the Spanish Governors of Milan was stronger than their regard for public rebukes and excommunications, and with the exception of the revocation of a licence in 1578 and temporary prohibitions in 1580 and 1582, the most that he could obtain was the repetition of the orders of 1566 against playing in Lent, on Church festivals, or during the hours of Divine Service, and the recommendation of the plan for censorship laid down in 1569. This last was only a nominal check, even Barbieri admits its impracticability: the censors were too busy with

[1] *Sentimenti*, p. 90.

other affairs and were content to take the word of the actors that the rest of their plays were no less decent than the specimens already submitted.[1] The story told by Barbieri and Riccoboni of how in 1583 Adriano Valerini appealed directly to Borromeo and succeeded in persuading him to endorse the company's scenari suggests that the Saint was less shrewd than his fellow Cardinal Paleotti, who realized that Censorship for improvised comedy was a farce, for, as he observes,

they always add words or remarks that are not set down, for they write out nothing beyond the summary or argument, and the rest is all done extempore, and the difficulty is to condemn them for this. Moreover they use the most lascivious and indecent gestures that are not indicated, they introduce women of the town and quite shamelessly they will suddenly devise such things as it would never occur to one to forbid. In short, to keep a check on their behaviour is like authenticating their ravings which are things better avoided.

The popularity of the Comici outstripped the prejudice of the moralists. Borromeo died in 1584 and his successors were content to recommend the Governor to enforce the reasonable restrictions which had existed substantially since 1566. By these, players were forbidden to wear clerical clothes, to discuss Scriptural or doctrinal matters, to name God or the saints, to rent rooms from the Jews, or to act during Lent or the appointed festivals of the Church. They were bound to observe decency and propriety in their love scenes and conversations, and were cautioned against libel and required to submit their plays to the censors.[2] The regulations are substantially the same in the three proclamations which have survived for the years 1566, 1573, and 1614. From time to time they were revived, stressed, or supplemented. In Milan in 1575 it was forbidden to any one not actually needed for the performance to go or remain under the stage or behind the curtains.[3]

In Bologna Paleotti's restrictions were more severe. Comedies were not allowed for more than three days a week, nor might they be held in the Sala del Podestà, in the piazza,

[1] *Supplica*, XXXVI.

[2] F. Barbieri, 'Per la storia del Teatro Lombardo nel seconda metà del secolo xvi', *Athenaeum*, Pavia. April 1914,

p. 387.

[3] G. Pagani, *Del Teatro in Milano avanti il 1598* (1884), p. 36.

near churches or monasteries, or after the Ave Maria.[1] No women, youths, children, priests, or friars were to be admitted. There was to be no advertisement by a parade of actors through the streets with their drums or playgear. The prices were to be fixed and no one in the audience might carry arms.[2]

In Mantua the Duke required that spectators of the comedies in his palace should wear masks.[3] In Pisa it was necessary to forbid the flinging of lemons, oranges, apples, turnips, and other disagreeable substances.[4]

Secretary Vinta took the precaution of making a special prohibition of all comedies and piazza entertainments throughout the dominions of the Duke of Tuscany during the octave of Easter 1602.[5]

In 1599 Tristano Martinelli appealed to the Duke against some extra prohibitions in Mantua. The office of overseer over comedians and mountebanks of all kinds of which Martinelli had the reversion at the death of Filippo Angeloni brought with it certain emoluments. Martinelli insists that he never claimed more than a third of what was due to him from the travelling entertainers, and objects that his enemies should represent him as a tyrant and cut him off from this source of income by coaxing a limited prohibition from S. Cotti and proceeding to apply it beyond the appointed period. According to the account given to the Duke by Martinelli himself, all players and charlatans had been turned out of Mantua at an hour's notice, and Gasparo, a tumbler who arrived in the city a few days later, was racked, and the Duke's own comedians had only escaped imprisonment by Diana's personal appeal to the Duchess.[6]

[1] In the *Stanzone* in Florence evening performance was possible. Tinghi mentions the second hour of the day or the first of the night as the usual hours, which, according to the Italian system of reckoning from sunset to sunset, are approximately 6 and 9 p.m. respectively. The average comedy lasted two hours, but special performances such as that arranged for the Duke and ladies of his court in the Pitti in 1618 might be restricted to one hour.

Spectacular plays Barbieri could recollect protracted to five hours. See Mic., op. cit., p. 205.

[2] A. Solerti, 'Rassegna Bibliografica della litteratura Italiana', Anno 2. 1894, p. 195.

[3] D'Ancona, op. cit., p. 473.

[4] Ibid., p. 478.

[5] Florence Arch. di Stato, Fa. 908. c. 103.

[6] D'Ancona, op. cit., ii. 527.

SYSTEM OF LICENSING

It was left to the civic authorities to make out the precise terms of the licences. In 1596 the *Uniti* were permitted to act in public or private anywhere within the city or territory of Milan.[1] In Genoa the usual period was for three months.

From the collective signatures on the applications (*suppliche*) we have some valuable lists, more often, however, the request is made by one member in the name of the whole company. The formula is sometimes amplified by the mention of the reputation or favours or promises: often it is accompanied by the personal recommendation of a patron to some gentleman whose name would carry weight. Pietro Balbi in Genoa[2] and F. Colloreto in Florence[3] seem to have acted as intermediaries between the civic authorities, the *Confidenti*, and Don Giovanni de' Medici their patron. Probably some financial interest in the accommodation made it worth their while to prevent delays and misunderstandings.

The licensing system seems to have been a tolerably efficient means of regulating the rotation as well as the behaviour of the companies. There was mention of cancelling the licence of Cecchini for Florence in favour of the *Confidenti*. In Venice *Florinda* forestalls Scala. In Lucca the licence is withdrawn after the commotion over *Celia's* scandal in 1617. The *Gelosi* were turned out of Mantua in 1579 by the Duke's express order because they dared to interpret his permission for private performance as licence to act publicly in the city.[4] On the other hand not even royal patronage was always effective against the interference of the civic authorities. Twice in Paris it happened that the royal patents were not sufficient to save the players from arrest and delay.[5]

Civic, aristocratic, and ecclesiastical authorities are a roughly matched three-in-hand. At a general reckoning the ecclesiastical attitude was determined by moral, the civic by practical, and the aristocratic by personal reasons. Now and then the players found themselves kicked by a sudden access of zeal and efficiency on the part of one authority, or

[1] G. Pagani, *Del Teatro in Milano avanti il 1598* (1884), p. 41.

[2] Arch. Med. Fa. 5143. c. 325.

[3] Ibid., Fa. 5139. c. 31 and Fa. 5176.

c. 75.

[4] D'Ancona, op. cit., ii, p. 488.

[5] Baschet, op. cit., pp. 19–26, 74–6.

crushed by converging prejudices, but more often they managed to play off one against the other.

PRODUCTION

In whatever concerns the art of stage-production the patron is the most important influence. Until at least the middle of the seventeenth century the players made or professed to make his taste their first concern. The relations were intimate: many of the negotiations were conducted by personal notes; it was the custom of the Duke of Mantua to come on to the stage after the comedy and associate freely with the players.[1] The more intelligent actors knew how to benefit by the social experience. It was obviously as much to their artistic as to their economic interests that they should seize every opportunity of taking part in the special festival performances which brought them into contact with the best appointed stages and gave them the experience of erudite tragedy and comedy, of academic pastorals, of masques, and later of opera which excited their artistic ambitions.

CO-OPERATION BETWEEN 'COMICI' AND 'VIRTUOSI'.

More important than the chances of witnessing academic theatricals was the co-operation between professionals and dilettanti. On such occasions the Comici adapted themselves to the conditions of premeditated drama. In 1619 *Lucchesino* was sent to the *Confidenti* in Milan, ostensibly to convey to *Lavinia* her part in a special comedy prepared for the Duke of Mantua for which she was to memorize at least 500 verses.[2] *Florinda* brought lasting credit to the *Fedeli* by her performance as Arianna at short notice in the absence of the original *prima donna*. The complimentary sonnets to Orsola Cecchini celebrate her appearance in formal tragedy.[3] The *Gelosi* were used in Frangipane's dithyrambic tragedy in Venice in 1574. Scala's *Confidenti* played Tasso's *Aminta*.[4] The performance of Salvadori's *Medoro* with the intermedii, setting and battle scene prepared for Sacrepante was given

---

[1] F. Scala, 22 Jan. 1618. Arch. Med. Fa. 5150. c. 515.

[2] F. Scala, 2 July 1619. Arch. Med. Fa. 5150. c. 459.

[3] Rasi, op. cit.

[4] F. Scala, 27 Oct. 1618. Fa. 5150. c. 517.

by *Comici di Zanni* in 1626.[1] In 1567 the rivalry between Flaminia and Vincenza was as much a matter of staging as of the attraction of the actresses. In Vincenza's tragedy Cupid liberated the nymph Clori who had been metamorphosed into a tree, Jove cast his bolt at the tower of a giant who had imprisoned certain shepherds, a sacrifice was offered, Cadmus sowed the teeth from which armed men sprang up to do battle, the replies of Phoebus and of Pallas were presented visually before the foundations of Athens were laid. Flaminia's stage was excellently appointed with gilt leather, her nymphs most beautifully habited, and the woods, hills, meadows, streams, and springs of Arcadia were transported to Mantua, satyrs and magicians were introduced into the *intermedi*, and 'of the morris dancing they are talking still', says Rogna who describes the contest.[2] When a few days later Cesare Gonzago chose to honour the company of Flaminia again, he was entertained with yet another elaborate production devised upon the story of Io.[3] Zuccaro reports that the comedies presented at the court of the Duke of Savoy during the Carnival of 1606 were 'gratiose, sententiose ed honeste', and compares the scene painted for the pescatory and pastoral performances with that used in Florence for the wedding of the Grand Duke Francesco. The *Accesi* were in Turin during this season and would be able to observe, even if they did not actually share in, the sumptuous shows.[4]

Tinghi records a performance of the ordinary comedians in 1608 augmented by the *intermedi* which had been used at Court.[5] Leonora Castiglione informed the Duke of Modena in 1634 that instead of the *machine* of Aurora, which she had intended to use for the prologue to her performance of *Li sette Infanti del'Ara*, she had been persuaded, by the verses provided by the courtiers, to adopt two other devices, one of the Sun concealing himself for shame at the treachery imminent, and the other of Nemesis herself revealing the punishment of the traitors.[6]

To linger over the possibilities of the interaction between

[1] Solerti, *Musica, Ballo e drammatica alla Corte de' Medici 1600-37*, p. 186.
[2] D'Ancona, op. cit., ii, p. 451.
[3] Ibid., ii. 453.
[4] Op. cit., p. 27.
[5] C. Mic, op. cit., p. 202.
[6] Rasi, op. cit., i. 606.

the professional and academic stages on such occasions would involve an investigation into the art of theatrical production during the Renaissance which would lay quite a disproportionate stress on the scenic element in the Commedia dell'arte. There is good evidence that the Comici knew what it was to have everything handsome about them, but they knew also that the secret of their strength lay in the co-operation of the actors, not in the craft of the producer. Their art consisted in physical and verbal wit, and to this all else was to be subordinated, as desirable but not essential. Their livelihood depended upon their adaptability. They were, in a sense, still jesters studying either the taste of one head with many whims, the patron, or the inarticulate confused desires of that monster with many heads, the public. If the audience is constant, the play, the company, or the theatre must vary. It was remarked when they repeated themselves. After about a month in Mantua the audience of the company of Flaminia dwindled.[1] On another occasion Leopoldo de' Medici observed that with no more than a change of names and the addition of a single episode the players gave exactly the same comedy, even to the details of the repartee.[2]

Theirs was an impromptu comedy, not because the play was new, but because it was renewable. Everything we know of their methods and materials shows that their art consisted in artistic opportunism. Nothing was stable: nothing was final. They had no décors. Their only tangible and distinctive contributions to the scenic side of theatrical art was the costume of the masques; it might be reduced to the outlines of Pantalone, Gratiano, the Captain, and the Zanni in the engravings of Callot or the portfolio of M. Fossard. The difficulty of isolating the Commedia dell'arte element has been experienced already in dealing with the commonplace books; as the professionals draw upon classical and neoclassical drama for their scenari, so on the stage they move

[1] D'Ancona, op. cit., ii. 453.
[2] 22 Oct. 1640. 'Ieri sera fui alla commedia per la prima volta e fecero i commedianti la medesima commedia per l'appunto che fanno costà, anzi in molte risposte con le medesime parole solo con i nomi diversi, et in una altra cosa ancora, facendo il Padre d'Adolfo che sconsiglia il figliolo dalle nozze della Contessa, che viene ancora in questa parte ad osservarsi meglio il costume.' Marriotti MS. cit., pt. ii, vol. i, p. 26.

to and fro against the conventionalized scenes of streets, palace-courts, sea-shores, and forests.

STAGING.

Garzoni's description of the procession of the comedians attracting attention by their drums and playgear, which culminated in a rude stage in the piazza with the scene drawn out in charcoal, represents the extreme of simplicity: the description of the décors required and evidently realized by Giovan Battista Andreini, the extreme of elaboration. The actual style of production for any given play would be determined by the conditions of each particular performance. We have property lists and a few illustrations and descriptions to help us to locate it more precisely in certain cases. The details are invaluable as suggestions but insecure as a basis for generalization. It hardly concerns us to know the precise dates of the erection of permanent theatres in the several Italian cities. Players who were not averse to acting on benches in the piazza made good with the accommodation of halls and apartments provided in palaces or hired in the city. The difference between academic and popular staging is a matter not of kind but of the degree of adequacy and makeshift demanded, and since the professionals owed everything to the private enterprise of courts and academies, it is better to work from elaboration to simplicity, from the maximum of Andreini's sumptuous directions to the bare minimum of the property lists.

Stage directions in the dramas of G. B. Andreini.

The reputation of Giovan Battista Andreini as a dramatist is parasitic upon *Paradise Lost*. Synopses and accounts of his *Adamo* are so accessible that little notice is taken of the exquisitely illustrated edition of 1613 in which Milton might have delighted, supposing that he never-saw the famous play upon the stage. Meanwhile the real significance of Andreini's work as an example of the interaction between the popular and erudite drama has fallen between two stools.[1] The literary critic finds the popular element nauseous and the

[1] See, however, W. Smith, 'G. B. Andreini as a Theatrical Innovator'. *Mod. Lang. Rev.*, 1922, vol. xvii.

dramatic allows the veneer of pedantry to excuse his neglect. Riccoboni refused to include his plays in his select list of good Italian drama: Bevilacqua, his latest critic, finds them tedious reading. But once we have learnt to allow for the academic contamination they are valuable as documents of the Commedia dell'arte. Andreini cultivated the society of wits and inherited a taste for polite literature along with the proud memory of the honours done to his mother by poets and scholars. His reiterated defence of the art of comedy, his persistence in moralizing his plays and pointing out in the preface what is to be learned from each character, the flourish of his dedicatory epistles, and complimentary addresses, and the cold bulk of his verse tragedy, *La Florinda*, remind us continually of his parentage and his upbringing in Bologna. His religious poems keep his respectable piety up to date and explain his choice of the stories of the creation and the conversion of Mary Magdalen for dramatic treatment. But mingled with these refinements is a love of theatrical experiment all the more effective for its coarseness. Everything points to the fact that as the leader of the *Fedeli* he catered admirably for the taste of the wealthier audiences of the seventeenth century. Readers of *Lo Schiavetto* are invited to observe that 'the actors, who composed such fictions, were the most valiant foes to harmful idleness': Andreini's energy as an actor-dramatist was inexhaustible. The publication of sixteen secular and three sacred plays, six volumes of devotional verse, and one immense romance in twenty-five cantos is spread over some twenty-seven years of an active stage career. There are extant besides half a dozen pieces of occasional verse, funeral laments, welcoming prologues, and five separate publications in defence of the art of comedy, which is ever the topic of his prefaces. He was prudent enough to distribute his dedications over a wide range of patrons, addressing himself more than once only to the Queen of France and the Duke of Nemours. The standard of production in *L'Adamo* and *La Florinda* and the multiplication of editions of his other plays testify to his popularity and prosperity.

The habit of trying out plays in extempore recitation and expanding the most successful in the intervals of his stage activities accounts for the curious mixture of popular and academic elements in Andreini's drama. The Prologue to *La Turca* explains that this comedy and its companion *Lo Schiavetto* were written up from 'soggetti' that he composed as a player,—'ch'io composi recitando'. The plot of *Li due Leli Simili* was inherited from his father. The lists of dramatis personae are indexes of the degree of change which has taken place in the process of expansion for the reader. *Lelio* and *Florinda* are regularly the chief lovers, and though in most cases they appear for the first four acts under some pastoral or slave pseudonym as the disguise intrigue dictates, they are recognizable as the stage names of Andreini and his wife. Giovan Paolo Fabri, called *Flaminio*, contributes prologues to three plays; *Lidia* as the second lady, the *Rinoceronte* among the braggart captains, *Pedrolino* and *Tartaglia* among the Zanni, are familiar mask names. Lovers are no more disguised by the fancy names of Lisandro, Filmenia, Ermellinda,[1] Rovenio, Zelandro, Solinga, Arminia,[2] Ferinda, Ardenio,[3] than are the Zanni who are called Scarnuccio, Tarquillo, Bighetto, Ghimberto,[4] Trinchetto,[5] Zolfanello,[6] Fringnello,[7] Calandra or Rondello,[8] or simply distinguished by their local dialects as Tedesco, or Ferrarese in *Lelio Bandito* and *La Ferinda*.

PLAYS WITHIN PLAYS.

Often the attempt at some individual characterization suggested by the use of proper names hardly goes beyond the exploitation of a mannerism—a variation which might well have been due to the bent of the comedian with whom the part originated—but on two occasions it is used for an effective contrast. Andreini is fond of commenting upon his art by the device of a play within a play. No doubt the piazza comedy in *Lo Schiavetto* and the two performances in *Le Due Commedie in Commedia* are as intentionally old fashioned as the plays of *Pyramus and Thisbe* and the *Murder of Gonzago*, but allowing for some such distortion they are valuable evidence, the one as a sample of a primitive

1 *La Rosella.*
2 *Le Due Commedie in Commedia.*
3 *La Florinda.*
4 *La Centaura,* Act I.
5 *I Due Leli Simili.*
6 *Lo Schiavetto.*
7 *La Turca.*
8 *Le Due Commedie in Commedia.*

exhibition of the Commedia dell'arte, the other of the close relationship between professionals and amateurs over the conventions of performance.

In *Lo Schiavetto* Faceto and Zolfanello disguise themselves as players and lodge at the inn, exciting the curiosity of the audience assembled in the square below by promising a comedy containing ten characters. After a few words of Prologue the couple impersonate the Magnifico and his Zanni, the Doctor and Nespola, skipping from one dialect to another and no doubt making full use of the curtains, as Cimador and Venturino had done before them. A taste of this comedy is enough, and the audience demand a pastoral instead. Over the curtain for comedy (*tela di comedia*), another cloth painted to represent a wood and a flowery field is lowered; the change does not please, one spectator is scared by the barking of dogs and wolves and calls for a tragedy, but the black scene and the braying of trumpets and drums, the noise of water and false fire and the apparition of the Ghost is even more disastrous. The audience is left unsatisfied until Orazio the lover in the main plot rises to propose his own story as the theme (*soggetto*) for a comedy and so leads back to the principal intrigue.

In *Le Due Commedie in Commedia* professional and amateur companies present rival shows. Rovenio persuades his friends the academicians to help him entertain Solinga, a poor proud lady with whom he is in love. They are to act a comedy 'all'improviso', for Lelio their leader is said to have them so well trained that they need only see the scenario of any comedy before they are ready to present it. According to Andreini's directions the Academician's parts are made out on rolls, presumably they contain instructions and not lines to be memorized. Fileno watches them wander about, each with his part in his hand, ruminating. Lidia, who is to be the first lady, leans out of the window and gives Rovenio and his friends a taste of her quality: 'O Ciceronessa!', they exclaim, while her father informs them that she is so fluent that she can discourse in this fashion extempore without any special study. Rovenio erects a stage in his 'Cortile' which, as he points out, like many others in Venice is conveniently private, for the owner can lock all doors and provide for himself and his tenants a theatre at home by the mere dropping of a curtain. Stools are set out for the guests who wear masks: they chatter through the overture of violin music.

The Academician's play, which is appropriately entitled the *Commedia dell'Incerto Fine*, is introduced by a short verse prologue by Lidia wearing the conventional costume of Peace. When she has spoken her lines she places her spear and olive branch where they may stand 'in trofeo' and leaves the stage for the Magnifico and Gratiano whose dispute over a dowry is prolonged by the roars of laughter and applause. Then Lidia, 'richly dressed, not quite in the style of a royal comedy, but still very fine', reappears as the lady who plays off Medoro the Spanish Captain against Narcisso, the son of Pantalone, her rival wooer. At the crisis of the comedy she forsakes the plot and breaks out with her own story horrifying the guests and Rovenio into the admission that he is the murderer of her old lover Mirando: the situation is saved by the discovery that Mirando is actually alive and present in the person of Alidoro, alias Zelandro. The mutual recriminations between the lovers and their families are checked by Lidia's resumption of the role of Peace. They consent to her marriage. Meanwhile Alfesimoro, the third lover of the main plot, has returned to Venice with the professional *Comici detti Appasionati* who have taken him into their company because of his experience as an actor in academic circles. The comedians are to be quietly dressed with no gold or feathers the better to contrast with their playing apparel, but they are well armed, and the Innkeeper, mistaking them for soldiers, drives them away. As soon as he discovers that they are players he implores them to return and patronize his establishment.

Thwarted by the *Commedia dell'Incerto Fine*, Rovenio, who has read of the talent of the players on the 'Cartelli di Commedia' which they have posted up in the city, commands a second play for Solinga. The device of sorting out the misunderstandings between lovers by fictitious representation is repeated. As the professionals have only a boy to play the woman's part they take advantage of the offer of Arminia who also has the reputation for extempore recitation. There is no essential difference between the performances of the professional and the dilettanti in the details of presentation. The second comedy is preluded by vocal music: the subject of the Prologue is Matrimony impersonated by a youth symbolically dressed, fettered, and bearing a yoke on his neck, in his right hand he bears a ring, in his left a quince (*pomo cotogno*), and under his foot there is a snake.

The Academicians had had first choice of the popular masks, the professionals introduce the remainder, the Pedant, Ceccobimbi the old Florentine, a stuttering Tartaglia and a crowd of tradespeople, a sweep, a miller from Bologna, a Neapolitan gardener, a Milanese cook. An interesting touch is given to the Gascon confectioner: when the play is finally interrupted by a dispute between the lovers in the audience this actor discovers himself as Flaminio Scala who offers to turn this remarkable intrigue into a comedy that will make the world envious. Whether this is merely compliment or a trace of Scala's actual performance with the *Fedeli* it is impossible to say.[1]

Andreini's description of the plays inset provides us with the simple conventions of presentation; the advertisement by bill and procession, the use of a prologue, of incidental music, and a drop curtain.

THEATRICAL TRICK-WORK.

Andreini himself was seldom content with comedy that required no more than the street scene and properties for the old-fashioned *lazzi* of beating, flouring, and covering with soot. His *Amor nello Specchio*, which is hardly more than a series of practical jokes arranged by the magician to confound

[1] In the list of the players those who are to act in the second comedy have each three names: the first is the stage name of a well-known contemporary actor; the second, a proper name belonging to their part in the intrigue of the play; and last the mask assumed for the inner comedy: the others have double parts assigned. *Leandro* Giovane farà il Prologo del Matrimonio. *Fabio* per vero nome, Partenio; in commedia farà Alfesimoro. *Orazio*; poi Oliviero huomo attempato; farà nella Commedia Ceccobimbi.' *Fabricio* in Commedia farà il Tartaglia.

Flaminio farà il Pedante.
Flavio il Pasticcier Francese.
Adriano farà il Servo.
Cintio il Cuoco Milanese.
Aurelio l'Hortolano Napoletano.
Silvio il Fornaro.
Fulgentio lo Spazzacamino.
Fortunio ⎫
Artizio ⎬ Usciranno per separar una questione.
Luccio ⎭
For identification see lists of masks in Appendix E: it is doubtful whether Andreini's choice was determined by the *personnel* of his own company at any particular period.

the lovers and buffoons, may have been redeemed by the ingenuity of the device by which *Florinda*, already divested of her petticoats for safety's sake, slips out through the false side of the chest to make way for the demon who is to spring from it in a few moments later scattering flames all over the stage. *I due Leli Simili* and *La Venetiana* are perhaps his most modest productions, though the illustrations for the Venetian scene and the introduction of Pantalones and masquers in gondolas show that the latter comedy was designed to attract by its spectacle as well as by its dialects.

La Sultana calls for battle scenes and makes use of two camels in a procession. In response to a demand from Federigo Gonzaga for a comedy which might be sumptuously staged at Casale to celebrate his wedding with the Princess of Savoy, Andreini turned again to an Oriental scene and composed *La Turca*. The elaborate procession in which the Captain is to be drawn by the Turks in a car adorned with banners and trophies is perhaps a luxury, but there seems no suggestion that the rest of the play might not be produced on other occasions, and Andreini implies that it was part of the ordinary repertory of the *Fedeli*. The scene is laid in the island of Tabarca. The perspective shows three houses adorned but not concealed by arbors and flowers. In one there should be a large window through which a woman may escape. The plainest (the least *frascata*) should represent an Inn. Behind the houses are seen the tops of six turrets and in the distance is a view of sea and mountains. The stage carpenter is to construct a castle and little huts of painted board, and is warned to contrive his hills so that the actors may seem to walk among them and come down to the stage as from the mountains. The silvan tragicomedy of *Lelio Bandito* was played against a scene of woods and mountain caverns, high on the right in the distance was a castle from which it was possible to descend into the forum of the theatre, on the left was a hut to be approached from the stage by a ladder painted to represent a rock. In the middle of the great cave which occupied the centre of the scene stood a large chest painted to resemble a rock covered with a fine carpet to serve as a bed for Lelio the outlaw chief.

Andreini admits that the sumptuous operatic performances

witnessed in Florence and Mantua had inspired him with the idea of the setting for *La Ferinda*. Limiting himself to a single scene he required that it should be a fine perspective of the city of Venice with a contrivance by which many gondolas and one pinnace in full sail might appear. The play opens with a ballet, instead of operatic music he depends upon an attractive mixture of dialects, upon the devices of mysterious voices and echoes, and provides Spanish songs for special performances.

The spectacular element can go no farther than in the *Adamo*, the *Maddalena*, and *Tecla*, but Andreini's religious dramas have little to do with his interests in the Commedia dell'arte though the apparatus was used for the appearance of angels, devils, and saints in glory required for some of the scenari drawn from Spanish plays. The illustration for *La Florinda* shows the multiple scene, but the tragedy is exclusively literary. Andreini's pride that it should have been read by the *Spensierati* is the excuse for publication, and there are no directions for production. The third act of the composite play *La Centaura* is the only example of pure tragedy for which he has left instructions.

In the pastorals the scene is taken for granted and Andreini is chiefly concerned with the behaviour of the wild beasts. The lion's part should be taken by an unusually large man who is to be warned before he goes on to the stage not to be a lion in name and an ox in behaviour. When the tiger has had his raging fit he is to be carried out on two stout poles. If the actors are well trained the hunting scene may be admirable, but it is rarely that it is worthily enacted and it is apt to foul the theatre.

SCENES AND PROPERTIES REQUIRED IN THE MISCELLANIES OF SCENARI.

Andreini's directions help with the elucidation of the property lists provided for the scenari and the illustrated title-pages of the Corsini miscellany. The tidy arrangement of Scala's lists contrasts with the entertaining confusion of babies, basins, bladders, and blunderbusses, of monsters and maccaroni that is to be found in the manuscript collections. When there is no room for the supers among the dramatis personae, Turks and Christians, children, bears, lions, and bulls are relegated to the property lists.[1]

Comedy.

The frontispieces for comedies in the Corsini manuscript offer some variations in the architectural details of the conventional street or piazza, but show no signs of an attempt to represent the topography of the particular city in which the play is located, which was a realistic effect sometimes advocated by more ambitious producers.[2]

Signs marked out inns and lodgings,[3] gratings distinguished the prison, and it seems from the illustration of the *Arme Mutate* that private houses were sometimes distinguished by heraldic medallions in order to help the audience to appreciate the confusion caused by the misdirection of foreigners by a stupid or knavish Zanni.

When painted hangings were used instead of scaffolding the actors unashamedly disturbed walls by holding back the curtains to eavesdrop: of this an engraving in the *Balli di Sfessania* and the woodcut from Bricci's *Pantalone Imbertonao* are good evidence.[4] But the use of balconies and window-sills, and the appearance of Burattino from between the houses on the right-hand side of the stage in the illustrated

[1] See *Elisa Alii Bassa. Proteo. La Bellissima* and *Il Cavaliero Perseguitato.*

[2] The woodcut for *La Veneziana* represents the Piazza S. Marco. In academic plays it is not unusual for the speaker of the Prologue to introduce the comedy by pointing out the principal buildings in the imagined locality: presumably they would appear on the 'prospettiva'.

F. Zuccaro (*Passaggio per Italia*, 1608, p. 27) describes the production of Guerino's *Idropica* for the marriage of Francesco Gonzago. By way of a prologue a great curtain displaying the city of Mantua was raised to the sound of music. A nymph appearing slowly from a cloud descended to a little island among the reeds and in song welcomed the Deities who blessed the scene from their cloudy stations. The island parted, the clouds sank, and the scene changed to the city of Padua where the

comedy proper was to take place. A. Ingegneri (*Della Poesia Rappresentativa et del Modo di Rappresentare le favole sceniche*, 1598, p. 62) observes that 'The stage should resemble as closely as possible the place in which the story of the play is laid. For example if the tragedy takes place in Rome, the Campidoglio should be shown with the great Palace, and the temples and other important buildings. If the play is a comedy, the Pantheon should appear with the column of Antony or of Trajan, and the Tiber and some other recognizable features.'

[3] *Li dui Scolari*, Cors. ii. 7 and *Li Stroppiati*, Cors. i. 27. *Est Locanda. Li dui finti Pazzi*, Cors. ii. 42 has 'Insegna d'allogiamento'.

[4] For Callot's sketch see Rasi, op. cit., i. 462, and compare a sketch reproduced from a Russian collection by Mic, op. cit., 15.

frontispiece to *L'Amor Costante* point to solid constructions. The title-page for *La Sepoltura* shows that the tomb from which Pantalone rises is little more than a large chest painted to represent stone-carving. For *L'Abbattimento d'Isabella* and *Il Pozzo* there was to be a well; in *La Mula Grande* the Doctor is to ride his beast on to the stage.

The commonest properties for comedy are the disguises and devil-masks, the bladders and stage cudgels for the beatings, kitchen-ware for the mock battle, chests, sacks, flasks, flour, plates of food, and purses for the practical jokes, ladders and blunderbusses charged with blank shot for Zanni's antics, the false arm for the 'lazzo' of the 'braccia finto', lanterns for the night-scenes which were indicated by the convention of bringing lights on to the stage, and acqua vita and pitch for the conflagrations. Costumes were comparatively easy to provide and transport. Pantalone, Gratiano, the Captain, and the Zanni had their conventional garments. The lovers' clothes were as rich and fashionable as they could afford: Andreini only distinguishes broadly between the degree of handsomeness suitable to ordinary and to royal scenes. Among the properties there are provided for the disguisings, extra Zanni clothes, garments for the false Captains, Doctors, and Pantalones, skirts and veils or towels for the supposed brides, cloaks and travelling boots for pilgrims and strangers, robes, a wand and a beard for the Magician, turbans, caps, and badges for Turks and Jews, rags for beggars, arms for the officers, baskets for pedlars, and tools for the butchers, sweeps, woodcutters, and other tradespeople. From the rapidity of some of the changes it is to be supposed that often the mere symbol of a disguise sufficed. Zanni's garments were notoriously adaptable, he turned down the brim of his hat and hid his face in a fold of his rough cape and the lover was not to recognize him: Arlecchino bound slippers to his head for ears and went on all fours as Pantalone's donkey; he seized a basket and some brushes and, still palpably Arlecchino to the chuckling audience, passed into his enemy's house as a sweep. The very incompleteness of the disguise was its point: the audience appreciated the transparency of the make-believe and delighted in an effect of dramatic irony visually presented.

Tragedy and Tragicomedy.

Considering the comparative trouble and expense of production it is easy to understand why the miscellanies should contain about five comedies for every tragedy or tragicomedy and twenty-four for every pastoral. Preparations for the tragedy planned by Scala for the *Confidenti* in August 1618 kept *Mezzettino*, who fancied himself as a scenic expert, busy for some weeks.[1] In Milan the players were allowed to double their charges in consideration of the cost of production.[2]

Tragicomedy often made use of a mixed scene part city and part wood; the directions and illustration suggest that some convention not unlike that of the multiple décors of the medieval stage was adopted. For the *Teste Incantate* Locatelli required a prison with two gratings, and a tomb which might be opened; to these the Corsini list adds a part of a wood and a palace and illustrates accordingly. In the *Giusto Principe* a prison gateway is to be shown in perspective. The title-page of the *Principe d'Altavilla* explains the demand for a 'ponte su il steccato' for the jousting takes place on a bridge set up between the palaces. The same erection is needed for *La Giostra*, a play in which provision is made for the Captain's horse. *La Battagliola* shows Bologna stormed by the Turks, scaling ladders are needed for the assault of the fortress which in the illustration appears as a somewhat ludicrous encampment fenced off in one corner of the scene. In the list for the *Forsennata Principessa* Scala includes a fine ship, two battles, and a pavilion; the gates of the fortress of Fessa are in the middle of the scene which is to be arranged so that it is possible for the action to take place on the sea or on dry land.

In the later miscellanies the increasingly elaborate discoveries and changes of scene seem to have been effected by the use of alternative perspectives. *La Vendetta del Marito*[3] allows for several complete changes. The first scene presents a mansion standing in its own garden with a distant view of the country; the next the bedchamber of Leonora, the third a wood, the fourth a hall, and the last the bedchamber scene

---

[1] Arch. Med. Fa. 5150. cc. 485, 582.   36. Ordinance for 1611.
[2] *Gaz. Mus. di Milano,* 1891, No.   [3] MS. Corsini 976.

again. The *Cavalier Discreto* is the only scenario in the Venetian miscellany in which any attention is given to the setting, but here a 'prospettiva che si leva' is needed. The second Casanatense collection[1] makes full use of the new methods. The double setting of city and wood, with special arrangements for palaces, temples, tombs, and fountains is quite common. Sometimes the sea, sometimes a mountain, once a serraglio for the lions is to be seen. Erections for towers and galleries are used. An important innovation is that of the Great Chamber variously furnished with a throne or a bed; for the drama of *Capa y Spada* an interior is essential, and the 'Camerone' is opened and shut continually. The marginal directions 'Day, night, dawn and evening' presumably to guide the actors to mention the time of day in accordance with Perrucci's instructions.

The properties for the Casanatense scenari are particularly sumptuous. They are lavish with costumes for Turks, Amazons, and guards, with their provision of furniture for the palace and mourning for the court, their devices for the representation of ships, battles, conflagrations, for the spectacles of heaven and hell, for executions by impaling and beheading. In *La Rosa* Andreini confides an ingenious economy. The basin provided should have a hole in the bottom covered with flowers; when it is placed on the ground at Florinda's feet Lelio, who is standing under the trapdoor, is to put up his head, and as the flowers are dropped in horror and the basin taken up he is to withdraw rapidly.[2] Possibly Loccatelli had some such contraption in mind when for the *Giusto Principe* with the usual basin he required a table with a hole in it—'una tavola segata con il bacile'. A similar trick for the decollation of John the Baptist, is illustrated at the end of the Thirteenth book of Reginald Scot's *Discoverie of Witchcraft*. The togas, fancy tunics, and antique armour illustrated on the frontispiece for *L'Adrasto*, and the demand for enough Persian garments to clothe the whole caste in Scala's *L'Innocente Persiana* indicate a feeling for costume which should be picturesque, if not for historically

---

[1] Codex 4186.
[2] I have not been able to examine a copy of this play; the direction is

quoted by W. Smith, *Mod. Lang. Rev.*, xvii, 1922.

correct. Discussing the problem of equipment, De Somi remarks that there are but few tragedies for which a tactful producer will not be able to borrow from a patron's wardrobe enough rich stuffs for cloaks, gowns, with their knots and girdles after the fashion of the ancients, provided that the material is not cut or spoilt in the adaptation.[1]

Pastorals.

For Pastorals a woodland scene, for Piscatorials a prospect of the sea was provided together with the suitable tackle for hunting or fishing. A mountain enclosing the temple of Cupid is needed for *Li Ritratti*, the grotto of *La Maga* must fly open at her touch. In *Il Gran Mago* besides a grotto and a fountain it was necessary to construct a temple for Bacchus and a fiery abyss which could be opened and shut. The preparations for *Pantaloncino* are even more elaborate. Merlin's tomb and the grotto arched by the rainbow of desire must open. Jove is to appear on his eagle amid clouds, lightning and thunder: Pluto rises from hell with a rattle of chains, with fire and an earthquake. Besides the tree in which Olivetta is hidden, and the ass-head for Pantalone the Corsini list has lions and muskets, and Locatelli refers the producer to the thirty-third canto of *Orlando Furioso* for further information about Merlin. For the *Arcadia Incantata* the 'apparenze' of 'Mare tempestoso, con Nave naufragandosi. Tempio—Selve.' are distinguished from the general properties. After a short scene in the woods there appears the stormy sea with the shipwreck, the dripping buffoons have their scene of recognition on the shore and then return to the woods. It is possible that the marginal direction of 'Tempio' which precedes the entry of the priest who is about to sacrifice Pollicinella merely indicates the opening of the temple which is so often placed at the end of a glade in the Arcadian forests. This would involve a solid structure but would reduce the changes of scene. From the directions for *La Nave*, however, it seems that before 1620 Locatelli had allowed for the coming and going of the sea. Here the buffoons meet by the fountain in the woods in front of the temple of Bacchus, but towards the end of the first act

[1] *Dialoghi* quoted by Rasi, op. cit., i. 113.

the Captain appears swimming on a Dolphin and invokes Mars and Jupiter from their clouds. The deities promise their assistance, and as they retire the Captain leaves the stage and the sea disappears (Capitano parte, e mare sparisce via). At his second entry he announces that he has disembarked at the lost island to rescue the Queen of Thessaly from Falsicon the magician. His servant beats a drum and there issue from the tower first a lion, then spirits scattering flames, and at last the magician himself. The Captain bargains with him and departs to his ship. In the third act the magician enters from the grotto, and after invoking a storm takes refuge in his tower while the Captain and the Queen appear in distress on the labouring ship. By magic they sink and once again the sea disappears: the enchanter retires into his tower where later he is disposed of by a shaft of lightning and during the tumult made by bellows and blunderbusses is converted into a stone.

In the title-page for *Li Tre Satiri* the artist has contrived to show Burattino emerging from the mouth of the whale, Zanni breaking out of his rock, and the satyrs cudgelling Pantalone in the grove as though they were simultaneous occurrences, but other stage directions show that this is not to be taken as an exact representation of the scene. The illustration does not include the grotto from which the magician appears, the temple which the buffoons mistake for a cavern, or the tree from which the nymph is to be released. Only the head of the whale is shown at one corner of the stage whereas, according to the direction, when the sea appears there are to be seen vessels and boats which then give place to the whale.

Locatelli's heaviest property list is for *Orlando Furioso* with its wood, river, bridge, tower, sepulchre, and cave, its contrivance for beheading Isabella, its false heads and arms and faked wounds, Astolfo's hippogrif, armour for the particular knights, for the pirates and outlaws, kitchen weapons for the buffoons, and dummies, tree-trunks, and scrolls ready for Orlando's destructive frenzy. With the exception of this paladin the Magician was the most extravagant personage, but no doubt the attraction of his shows made the expense worth while. The metamorphosis of nymphs into bushes and

of Zanni into stones called for solid properties. Scala's
Albero Incantato required a sea-cliff, and a tree bearing apples
which should rise by magic, as well as a painted tree for
the transformation. They were lavish with fireworks and
ominous signs in the sky. Serlio explains how these might
be presented:[1] the Comici no doubt had similar if cruder
methods.

The curt directions of 'Pelli da Pastori' in the miscellanies,
and the coronets, lambskins, arrows, staves, and hoops for
garlands of the English Revels Accounts[2] are inadequate in
themselves but valuable as hints to send us back to the
picturesque detail of Leone De Somi's discussion of the
clothes suitable for pastoral plays. The individual dramatist
is to be free to dictate in the case of the enchantress and of
any special deity which he may introduce, but for the fanciful
costume required for the nymphs and shepherds De Somi
claims the authority of the ancient poets. The men should
wear sleeveless shirts of taffeta or stuff of a pleasing colour
with skins slung from the shoulder to thigh. Young actors
may appear with bare legs and arms, otherwise flesh-coloured
tights are recommended. All must be shod with some kind
of handsome boot or sock. One might carry at his belt a
little flask or a wooden box, another a knapsack swinging
from his shoulder. Each should have a staff, plain or fantastically wreathed. The hair may be natural or artificial,
curled or smooth, garlanded with laurel or ivy for variety.
The nymphs are to have rich cloaks draped to show their
embroidered bodices which may be caught in by necklaces
and sashes of coloured silk and gold, the sleeves should be
full, and even puffed to give a graceful effect. Their coloured
skirts are to be caught in to show the instep and the orna-
mented buskins. Some wear their hair loose, others use
golden snoods, wreaths, silk ribbons, and even those fine
veils which float across the shoulders with such grace. They
carry arrows or darts, and should they bring their hounds with
them on to the stage they should be well-trained beasts and
fitted with pretty collars and coverings. De Somi gives most
attention to the attractively sophisticated Arcadians, simpler
folk follow the fashion of their masters in rougher plainer

---

[1] *Architettura* (1551), see Chambers, op. cit., iv. 363–4.   [2] *Infra*, p. 353.

FRONTISPIECE IN THE CORSINI MS.

Setting for 'La Tartarea'. G. Bricci

Antismodeo   Mago

Demonio   Ombra

Figures from 'La Rosmira' (1676)

gear. It is not to be supposed that the travelling professionals could keep up the standard of elegance proposed by fastidious and wealthy dilettanti, but it is evident from the allusions and from the cuts illustrating Giovanni Bricci's pastoral *La Rosmira* that in this, as in other questions of production, they accepted the conventions and followed the lead of the Commedia erudita as best they could.

CONCLUSION

Longer seasons and the establishment of permanent theatres so increased the resources of the professionals during the second half of the seventeenth century that apologies for crude and simple décors are no longer necessary. But prosperity was not altogether wholesome. Scenic luxury sapped the old vigour of improvisation and the Commedia dell'arte lost character under French patronage. The importance of the second period is rather for the critics of Molière, for the admirers of dramatic burlesque, and for all who are interested in the changes which an artistic form undergoes in the acclimatizing process. As far as the Italian drama in general, and the improvised comedy in particular, are concerned the seventeenth century is mainly a period of deterioration. Many a contingent but no final reason can be produced to account for the florescence of the Commedia dell'arte at the end of the sixteenth, and its disappearance during the eighteenth, century. On a general estimate there appear to have been as many obstacles as there were opportunities at its rising. This suggests that the element of opposition was healthy. Its development coincides with the rise of the companies who learned by hard experience that neither individual talents, nor the material advantages of patronage were to be preferred before the unity of the troop. Freedom was based upon independence: they were only safe when they moved together: the difficulty and complexity of such co-operation is surely a sufficient explanation of their qualified success.